D0265236

SCOUTING FOR BOYS

ROBERT BADEN-POWELL

SCOUTING FOR BOYS

A HANDBOOK FOR INSTRUCTION IN GOOD CITIZENSHIP

Edited with an Introduction and Notes by

ELLEKE BOEHMER

OXFORD
UNIVERSITY PRESS

Great Clarendon Street, Oxford OX2 6DP

Oxford University Press is a department of the University of Oxford.
It furthers the University's objective of excellence in research, scholarship
and education by publishing worldwide in

Oxford New York

Auckland Bangkok Buenos Aires Cape Town Chennai
Dar es Salaam Delhi Hong Kong Istanbul Karachi Kolkata
Kuala Lumpur Madrid Melbourne Mexico City Mumbai Nairobi
São Paulo Shanghai Taipei Tokyo Toronto

Published in the United States
By Oxford University Press Inc., New York

First published 2004

British Library Cataloguing in Publication Data
Data available

ISBN 0–19–280547–9

3

Typeset in Ehrhardt
by RefineCatch Ltd., Bungay, Suffolk
Printed in Great Britain by
Clays Ltd., St Ives plc

For Sam M.B.

CONTENTS

ACKNOWLEDGEMENTS

WHEN in early 2001, not long before the birth of our youngest son, I first took on the project of editing Baden-Powell's *Scouting for Boys*, Scouting was to me (forgive the metaphor) largely untracked ground. The staccato 'dyb, dyb, dyb' which friends, usually male, began rapping out in conversation on the subject, sounded exactly as it should to a non-initiate: mystifying mumbo-jumbo.

From that time a number of people have generously assisted and supported me in my efforts to explore and map my square inch of Scouting terrain, and provide keys to some of its codes. First and foremost, I should like to thank Paul Moynihan, Archivist at the Scout Association Headquarters Archive at Gilwell Park. Paul, who is every researcher's ideal archivist, gave unstintingly of his time, loaned books and videos, and open-handedly shared his vast knowledge of, and love for, Scouting history. Chris James, the Association's Book Editor, I thank for setting up the link with Oxford University Press, and for introducing me to Gilwell Park. I am grateful to Judith Luna, Oxford World's Classics Editor, for firing my interest in this 'empire' project in the first place, and for her enthusiasm, understanding, and keen commitment throughout the somewhat protracted editing process. Jeff Guy and John Phipson have given indispensable clarifications as regards aspects of Zulu language and history: thanks to both of you, as well as to Carol Phipson, ever a decoder. To two historians of Scouting, Nelson R. Block, untiring Scout biographer, and Mario Sica, Italian Ambassador to Egypt, with whom the work put me in touch, I am grateful for various pointers, and for copies of their work. Richard Phillips, Ross Forman, Alan 'Jumbo' Steel, and John Whale gave useful help in pursuing various obscure and not so obscure lines of interest. Many thanks to Andy Todd for unearthing his old Scout handbooks and other memorabilia, and to Gail Marshall for her quizzical no-comment. I am grateful to Roberta Davari-Zanjani at NTU and to Catherine Morley for stalwart help and support. Thanks to Danielle Battigelli, Alison Donnell, Susie Irvine, Astrid James, Nic James-Moore, Marianne Thrower, Jon Wood, and Robert Young for indulging me when Scouting and B.-P. became an ineradicable part of my conversation. I am grateful to the Conference on Cecil John Rhodes, held at St Antony's College, Oxford, on 30 November 2002, organized by William Beinart, and the Interdisciplinary Seminar in the French Department at Royal Holloway on 4 December 2002, piloted by Terence Cave, for hosting papers based on aspects of this editorial work.

Finally, and most importantly, the 'boys' with whom I live have been more than wonderful: Sam, for his jokes, Thomas, for turning B.-P. into a subject of *his* conversation, and Steven, always, for continuing to make everything not only bearable, but OK.

INTRODUCTION

WHO could have thought that when Robert Baden-Powell's *Scouting for Boys: A Handbook for Instruction in Good Citizenship* first appeared in a somewhat ramshackle six-part edition in early 1908, it would enjoy almost immediate success amongst young audiences, male and female alike? Could it have been predicted that it would within only a few decades of first publication already have earned a place as one of the most widely published, popular books of the twentieth century?[1] For, as the handbook's multi-part, rag-bag structure suggests, Baden-Powell composed it at speed—patched it together might be the more accurate phrase, in an experimental and even pell-mell way. At his elbow as he worked stood an old military dispatch box full of scraps: newspaper cuttings, extracts torn from adventure novels and travel writing, other magpie bits and pieces of information. From this miscellany he drew a text which, unsurprisingly, was itself very much a hodge-podge, almost literally a collage, comprising seemingly unrelated materials, including quotations from his own previously published books.[2] Amongst its many borrowings, his handbook, the foundational text of one of the world's largest international movements,[3] embraced within its encyclopedic scope 'true crime' anecdotes, stock adventure tales, campfire hints, potted history natural and imperial, first-aid tips, and recycled advice on the definitive scouting activities of observation and tracking.

[1] The book ranks as one of the best-selling Anglophone works of the 20th cent.: its publishing figures until after the Second World War were exceeded only by those of the Bible in the English-speaking world. See Tim Jeal, *Baden-Powell: Founder of the Boy Scouts* (New Haven and London: Yale UP, 2001), 396; John Springhall, *Youth, Empire and Society: British Youth Movements, 1883–1940* (London: Croom Helm, 1977), 68.

[2] If B.-P. casually cannibalized the texts of many other writers, he did not scruple to recycle his own work also, in particular, *Aids to Scouting* (London: Gale and Polden, 1899; of which pp. 51–9 appear as *Scouting for Boys* pp. 89–98), *The Matabele Campaign 1896* (London: Methuen and Co., 1897), and *Reconnaissance and Scouting* (London: William Clowes and Son, 1884). See also Jeal, *Baden-Powell*, 114; and Baden-Powell's memoirs *Lessons from the 'Varsity of Life* (London: C. Arthur Pearson, 1933), 143.

[3] The global reach of the Scout movement has probably been the most extensive of any worldwide movement. Since its inception Scouting has involved close on 350 million people across the globe and today exists in nearly all of the world's countries, bar about 5 or 6.

The appearance of *Scouting for Boys* coincided with a period of wavering imperial self-confidence in Britain following the pyrrhic victory of the Anglo-Boer War (1899–1902), a war marked by setbacks, stalemates, and stasis.[4] The book did therefore, it is true, respond powerfully to British national anxieties: in this must lie at least one substantial reason for its success. Where the failing strength of the nation was mirrored in the alleged deterioration of the male physique at the time, a practical handbook that proposed physical training as well as lessons in strategy derived from the writer's own military experiences, could not but be a winner. From the start, too, *Scouting for Boys* was cleverly marketed to sell. Published every other Wednesday from 15 January 1908 by Horace Cox, the printer owned by the *Daily Express* magnate C. Arthur Pearson, the 'self-instructor' was 'full of yarns and pictures' in the tried-and-tested formula of the *Boy's Own Paper* or of Pearson's own entertainment magazine *Tit-Bits*. (It is on this fortnightly parts edition that the present edition is based.) It sold at an affordable 4*d*. a copy, and the cloth-bound complete edition, published on 1 May, was also attractively cheap, at 2*s*. Throughout, the style was conversational and accessible: Part V advertised Baden-Powell's 'method' as 'pleasant, easy, anecdotal'. The cover of each part edition featured an eye-catching illustration by either John Hassall or Baden-Powell himself, of a Boy Scout absorbed in the fascinating activities of spying and spooring (or tracking), activities which to date had been confined to the pages of adventure romance.[5] Now, boys were being encouraged to go out and do these things themselves, and to do them in emulation of Baden-Powell or B.-P. (the initials serendipitously stood also for 'British Pluck', 'British Public', and, of course, 'Be Prepared'), the empire hero and leader during the siege of Mafeking, one of the few proud episodes, as will be seen, in the unedifying history of the Boer War. Already within a few weeks of first publication it seemed that *Scouting for Boys* was bearing out B.-P.'s own 1907 prediction: 'I am convinced that "Scouting" has an immense attraction for lads and could be used as a medium on a very wide scale for their moral improvement in a practical way.'

As the *Spectator* recognized in 1909, the nearly 107,000-strong

[4] It notoriously took 450,000 British troops three years to defeat 40,000 Boers.

[5] The cover illustration for Part II, probably by Baden-Powell, is reproduced on the cover of the present edition.

Boy Scout Movement to which *Scouting for Boys* had so spectacularly given birth, 'interwove' 'all strands of wholesome romance' and boyish ambition. Yet relatively little planning had in fact gone into the apparently far-sighted foundation of the new Movement. Scouting activities, B.-P. maintained at first, were designed to co-operate with and enhance existing organizations for boys, to supply 'novelty', not to supplant them. The popularity of Scouting caught even the 'hustler' publisher Pearson relatively unprepared. As early as the summer of 1908 rapid plans had to be made to establish some sort of organizational control over the hundreds of self-constituted patrols of boys—and some girls—who, book in hand, had already set out camping. Even as he experimentally composed his citizenship '*vade mecum*' (p. 334), therefore, Baden-Powell was involved in improvising—virtually in making up overnight, 'by ear'—the rules, rituals, ethos and organization, in short, the 'invented tradition' of the Scout Movement.[6] (The Girl Guides were founded, with his sister Agnes and later his wife Olave Baden-Powell at the head, in 1910.) Despite Arthur Pearson's well-oiled publicity plans, the two processes, the formation of the text and the foundation of the Movement, were effectively constituted through one another in remarkably instinctive ways—almost, one might say, in a fit of absence of mind, as, allegedly, was the empire itself.[7]

Yet it is probable that it was the handbook's essential casualness which so powerfully caught youthful imaginations (as of course did its encouragement of fun, make-believe, and of friendship between boys regardless of their class—'A SCOUT IS A FRIEND TO ALL', read the fourth Scout Law). Not to put too fine a point on it, the Scouting handbook as it first appeared *is* in every part a fragmentary, porous, non-cohesive mishmash of other texts. It is made up, as will be seen, of a multi-voiced mix of different prominent Edwardian discourses. It was therefore not only the imperative of fine-tuning the new Movement, but also the roughness of the 1908 parts edition which prompted B.-P. repeatedly to rework the book until the early 1920s.

[6] Eric Hobsbawm and Terence Ranger (eds.), *The Invention of Tradition* (Cambridge: Cambridge UP, 1983). Hobsbawm refers to Scouting as an exemplary invented tradition, authored and authorized by a single initiator, and set up virtually at a stroke (p. 4).

[7] The phrase derives from John Seeley's history, *The Expansion of England* (London: Macmillan, 1883): 'We seem, as it were, to have conquered and peopled half the world in a fit of absence of mind.' See Elleke Boehmer (ed.) *Empire Writing* (Oxford: Oxford UP, 1998), 74.

(Even in the Preface to the 10th edition published in July 1922, often agreed to be definitive, he invites his readers to get in touch with any suggestions which might arise following from their perusal of the book on the recommended, ritually inscribed St George's Day.) Yet this gunny-sack of a book, even so, spoke compellingly to the boys cooped up in the suburbs of the mushrooming new twentieth-century town and city (and not only in Britain), inviting them to get on with things, find a 'backwoods' for themselves, and go adventuring. Like Samuel Smiles's Victorian textbook of bourgeois self-improvement *Self-Help* (1859), which B.-P. frequently cites, it excitingly advises that as long as an individual is equipped with this 'self-educator' they can do all the rest for themselves. The reading of the bite-sized sections, it assures them, will not take long, no longer than a boy's attention span (p. 308), and the boy will very soon find himself, once he starts Scouting, feeling something like a colonial adventurer, useful, important and heroic rolled into one. Above all, therefore, *Scouting for Boys* succeeded because it appeared to place the ordinary, individual boy at the very centre of the imperial world. Throughout, B.-P. appeals to him in person: 'But you need not wait for war to be useful as a scout. As a peace scout there is lots for you to do any day, wherever you may be' (p. 13).

When viewed with the benefit of hindsight, Robert Baden-Powell's career prior to 1908 bears a made-to-measure legendary aspect: it is as if his time in the British Army was both an anticipation of and a preparation for his second 'life' as much beloved father and chief author of Scouting.[8] This quality is particularly offset by the fact that little about his biography up to that point was especially orthodox or predictable—regardless of what his mythmaking memoirs, much recycled for the benefit of providing object-lessons in Scouting, might claim. Born on 22 February 1857, the year of the Indian Mutiny, Robert Stephenson Smyth Powell was the eighth child (the fifth son to live past infancy) of the Revd Baden Powell, Savilian Professor of Geometry at Oxford and an evolutionist, and his strong-willed third wife, Henrietta Grace. Following Professor Powell's death, when young Robert, the family's 'prime comedian', was only

[8] The metaphor of having lived out two separate lives, or a 'double life', which has informed several readings of Baden-Powell's biography, first occurs in his own autobiography, *Lessons from the 'Varsity of Life*, 13–15.

three, Henrietta Powell proceeded to bend her considerable faculties towards consolidating her unsteady upper-middle-class social pretensions and to establishing successful careers for her sons. This project of 'getting on', epitomized in the embellishment of the family name to Baden-Powell in 1869, involved her ever afterwards in acts of theatrical pretence and energetic networking that were to have a profound effect on the outlook of her second youngest son. The rental of grand houses during the London season was made possible by cheap lodgings in seaside resorts in the winter. All possible strings were pulled to open the doors of the right colleges and schools to her children, in Robert's case Charterhouse. Henceforward, at school and later in the army, the boy Robert, or Stephe, would repeatedly rely on his aptitude for merry antics and for making the right contacts to gain favour and ensure self-advancement.

'No genius in school subjects' (as confirmed by his resistance to book-learning in *Scouting for Boys*), Robert Baden-Powell did, however, thrive at Charterhouse. As histories of Scouting like to recount, the woods neighbouring the school conveniently offered a prime site for 'out-of-bounds' amateur tracking and nature study. The public school ethos of cheerful courage under pressure, loyalty to the team, and 'playing the game', which was already powering the armies of the empire, suited the energetic sportsman, artist, and actor, and was later processed into his basic precepts for Scouts. 'The whole secret of success in life [is] to play the game of life in the same spirit as that . . . played on the football field,' he once told an audience of boys.[9] Nothing daunted after having failed to make it into Oxford (unlike two of his brothers), Baden-Powell in 1876 secured a commission straight into the 13th Hussars, stationed at Lucknow in India, his unexpected success in the army examinations having allowed him to sidestep conventional Staff College training.

It was to Lieutenant Robert Baden-Powell's disadvantage (however he later, characteristically, manipulated it to his benefit) that the early decades of his army career coincided with a long period of 'small' imperial wars, fought in order to secure colonial frontiers or guarantee the claims of chartered companies. As he knew well, active service alone, preferably in some important military action, secured promotion and a pay-rise. So it was that in 1878 in Afghanistan and

[9] Jeal, *Baden-Powell*, 41.

1888 in Zululand, in Ashantiland in 1895 and Matabeleland in 1896, he restlessly and mostly fruitlessly sought out intrigue, gore, and some form of decisive combat, often to his 'enemy's' bewilderment. After his not uncontroversial Matabele Campaign he was, however, finally promoted to command the 5th Dragoon Guards, again stationed in India.[10] As for the rest, the all too many longueurs between high points of military activity were devoted, pleasantly enough, to various kinds of diversion, sports of many kinds, especially hog-hunting and polo, amateur dramatics and impersonation (what was at the time also called 'skirt-dancing'). In the early days in India all these activities were carried out in the company of his close friend Kenneth ('Boy') McLaren. With the publication of his first instructional handbook, *Reconnaissance and Scouting* (1884), Baden-Powell also began in India a lifetime's exercise of turning his skills in the still informal military exercise of scouting—that is, tracking and reading enemy 'sign'[11]—into organized training schemes for men and boys. He had, he discovered, a flair for processing his experiences into fast-moving, accessible prose—a flair which bore the added advantage of attracting official praise. During these years he also wrote up, for the benefit of audiences in Britain, accounts of his sporting expertise and military campaigns, as in *Pig-sticking or Hog-hunting* (1889)—pigsticking success, he opined, proves 'our claim to superiority as a dominant race'—or *The Downfall of Prempeh* (1896).

If, by the time of the outbreak of the Anglo-Boer War in October 1899, it appeared that Baden-Powell's career progress around the British Empire had been dictated mostly by luck, as he himself claimed, sharpened by a tactician's eye for the main chance, then new developments would prove entirely in character. When hostilities began he found himself in inadvertent command of the small South African town of Mafeking just before its investment by the

[10] Baden-Powell courted controversy in Matabeleland due to his court-martialling of the non-Ndebele Chief Uwini. As will be seen, official and unofficial concern about his treatment of local people resurfaced during the Mafeking siege, due to the high differential between the food rations meted out to the white and black inhabitants of the town. Recent discussions of the siege propose that Baden-Powell acted strictly in accordance with the racialized definitions of his time and can therefore not be held individually accountable for the injustice.

[11] In *Reconnaissance and Scounting: A Practical Course of Instruction, in Twenty Plain Lessons, for Officers, Non-commissioned Officers, and Men* (London: William Clowes and Son, 1884), 1, Baden-Powell defines reconnaissance and scouting as 'the acquisition of knowledge of the country over which military operations are likely to be carried on'.

Boers. The town's success at surviving the longest siege of that inglorious conflict (October 1899–May 1900) without serious loss of life (though with some questions asked about the treatment of black Africans) would willy-nilly have elevated Baden-Powell to the status of imperial symbol, hero of an empire under threat. But it was his ability not only to succeed, but to do so with nonchalance and a taste for fun—with a combination of fake barbed-wire defences and Sunday baby competitions—that turned him in the eyes of the British public into the very epitome of pluck and team-spirit. It was this same mix of imperial fortification with fun, or of service and smiles, which would prove the winning formula of Baden-Powell's so-called 'boyology', his understanding of boys, in *Scouting for Boys*.

In the aftermath of the war, occupying a new post as Inspector-General of Cavalry (a sideways promotion, as some pointed out, for a military man who had become too much of a celebrity), Baden-Powell would not cease to capitalize on his most outstanding talent, of making things up as he went along—and enjoying himself as he did so. The lessons of his military handbook, *Aids to Scouting* (1899), the proofs of which had left for England on one of the last trains out of Mafeking, were being adopted by a number of boys' organizations as a way of inculcating military exercises in an entertaining manner. Prompted by post-Boer War fears of imperial decline and fall, Baden-Powell now began to contrive ways of developing his own programme for the training and recreation of young boys. The product of this exercise was *Scouting for Boys*, in which his delight in play-acting crosses with the two other keynotes of his first career or 'life', his belief in the games ethic of the Victorian public school and the bourgeois principle of individual self-advancement. The year 1908 therefore saw the birth not only of Scouting as such but of Baden-Powell in the new, avuncular role of Founder of the soon-to-be worldwide Scout Movement, one which was to win him myriad accolades. In 1920, at the First World Scout Jamboree at Olympia in London, he was proclaimed Chief Scout of the World before a vast crowd of boys; in 1929 he was created a peer; in 1937 he received the Order of Merit. He continued virtually until the time of his death in 1941 to travel the world promoting international brotherhood in the form of a scout organization that had already by 1918 become global in its reach.

Scouting for Boys energetically appeals to boys' powers of make-believe, yet it is also, at the same time, an imperial self-improvement text par excellence. It resonates profoundly with the preoccupations and paranoias of an especially fraught and defensive colonial period, one which coincided, paradoxically, with the high point of formal British imperialism. Built out of the bricks of Baden-Powell's unconventional military experience as a scout, converted into yarns and precepts, the text urges British boys to become 'real *men*' by going out adventuring to help expand the colonies (pp. 13, 300). In this duality of service mixed with the encouragement to fantasize, lies one illustrative aspect of the book's multi-voicedness, of the complicated textures of its many intertwined discourses: Tory imperialist, military, social Darwinist, educational, theatrical, environmental, and, above all perhaps, 'self-help'. Indeed it could be said that in crossing a variety of different narratives and influences, *Scouting for Boys* encapsulates in microcosm the multilayered, globalized, and commercial world of the British Empire that it itself so fervently supports. Its fragmentariness and multi-cultural examples, its different modes of address, nuggets of prepackaged advice, piled-up sayings, songs, and quoted voices drawn from various parts of the globe, give it the atmosphere of a kind of trading centre, a market or entrepôt of miscellaneous messages. It is a site where heterogeneous cultural forces and images briefly intersect, in order to be disseminated once again across its wide international audience. The sheer variousness if not contradictoriness of the text—offering a plenitude of knowledge parcels from multiple sources for its reader's edification, yet never ceasing to proclaim the 'one flag', the 'one throne' (pp. 282–3, 290–2), invites us to examine more closely its rough, uneven textures. To pick apart the nubs and warp of some of its different ideological claims will give a clearer picture of its appeal to its diverse implied audiences, and not only in 1908, but subsequently too.

'The touch of British Brotherhood': the imperialist handbook

It was from the pages of Rudyard Kipling's *Kim* (1901) and *The Jungle Books* (1894–5) that Baden-Powell derived the idea that empire, like life (and subsequently Scouting like empire) should be conducted by way of obedience to certain unchanging Laws—of duty, of obedience to authority, of loyalty to the group (pp. 44–6).

Despite its apparent class blindness, the Scout Law as expounded from the first edition of *Scouting for Boys* takes on the ideological burdens of imperial expansion, inculcating the values of service and discipline—and of racial self-defensiveness and self-promotion—that will consolidate the white Greater Britain beyond the seas. In its most exaggerated form, as in the bizarre cultural mix of the 'Pocahontas' 'Scouts' Play' which ends Part I, the Scout Law merges indistinguishably with the creed of empire. In the play, John Smith, having overcome some four 'Red Indians' single-handedly, cries out in defiance of King Powhattan's threats that Britain's mission is 'to *clean* the world' by spreading trade, loyalty, justice and the Puritan work ethic beneath the 'friendly wing of . . . world-wide power' (pp. 58, 61). Modelled on the hardy colonial frontiersman, the ideal Scout, disciplined and self-sacrificing, is also set up as the culmination point of a mythical lineage of British national history: he embodies the *virtu* and honour of the medieval knight, the stout-hearted courage of the Elizabethan explorer. As is clearly spelt out in the heavily rewritten Part VI addressed to instructors (once intended as the introduction to the book), Scouting will be to imperial Britain the training in discipline and patriotism that latter-day imperial Rome so woefully lacked (pp. 295–6).

The amount of nervous energy Baden-Powell expends in *Scouting for Boys* encouraging boys and men to 'hold' the empire and help it 'get on', gives an idea of the level of British anxiety at this time concerning not only the Empire but the state of the nation at its heart. In the aftermath of the 1899–1902 Boer War how secure were Britain's defences, how stable its society, how strong its men? The handbook appeared towards the end of a decade that saw the formation of the National Service League in 1901, the 1904 establishment of the Interdepartmental Committee on Physical Deterioration, and the anonymous publication in 1905 of Elliot Mills's influential *The Decline and Fall of the British Empire*. A mood of national crisis was pervasive. By 1900 Germany, the United States, and Japan had started to outstrip Britain's levels of industrial production. But from within the nation, too, the established order was under pressure from, amongst other forces, the newly organized labour movement and the rise of the New Woman and women's demands for self-representation. Already in 1893 Max Nordau's messianic *Degeneration* had given a doom-laden prognosis of the dangerous 'vast fatigue' which Europe's hectic urbanized life-styles were producing. Tories, Liberals, and Fabians alike blamed the perceived national decline on such factors as excessive taxation, bad parenting, a falling birth rate, and spectator sports. Like a sponge, Baden-Powell's handbook soaks up and renders back the sense of immanent collapse that these developments register or expose.[12]

In particular, Parts V and VI betray a social Darwinist logic of national growth, widespread at the time, whereby it was held that countries and empires that cease to grow and struggle to expand, will inevitably cease to thrive. Page after page is imbued with a sense of ever-present danger and threat: the need to be on constant lookout, to guard against weakness both social and physical, always to 'be prepared'. Scouts must learn to read signs of difference and possible degeneration—that is, class and racial features—off faces in a crowd, to pick out the foreigner and the deviant. A Scout, by definition, is never to be taken by surprise, certainly not by bad surprises of any kind, whether military ambushes or natural disasters. (As in Conan Doyle's Sherlock Holmes stories, a dead body must be treated with the greatest of caution: it is more likely than not to be a murdered one (pp. 70–1, 80).)

For Baden-Powell, as for the many military men and politicians preoccupied with the defence of the realm and problems of recruitment in this decade, the key index of the state of the nation's health and well-being—or lack thereof—was the body of the young male (pp. 184–5, 197, 297–8). The closing chapters of *Scouting for Boys* do not cease to press home that the 'deterioration of [the] race' is reflected in the physical breakdown of the 'rising generation', and, by implication, the reduction in their masculinity. The working-class 'loafer', weak-chested, slack-bodied, given to the excesses of smoking, drinking, and self-abuse, is, as Baden-Powell makes explicit in his stereotyped illustrations, a serious breach in the nation's defence system (pp. 68–9). Wishy-washy slackers without any 'go', patriotism, or manliness will lose the Empire for Britain. With its exercise

[12] For social histories of the rise of Scouting, see: Robert H. Macdonald, *Sons of the Empire: The Frontier and the Boy Scout Movement, 1890–1918* (Toronto: University of Toronto Press, 1993); Michael Rosenthal, *The Character Factory: Baden-Powell and the Origins of the Boy Scout Movement* (London: Collins, 1986); Springhall, *Youth, Empire and Society*, 53–70. On degeneration in imperialist and modernist discourse, see Rod Edmond, 'Home and Away', in Howard J. Booth and Nigel Rigby (eds.), *Modernism and Empire* (Manchester: Manchester UP, 2000), 39–63.

routines and advice on hygiene placed alongside its tips on spotting the loafer, *Scouting for Boys* takes keen steps to remedy the situation. It shows an avid—some might say invasive—interest in every aspect and angle of the boy-body—its fitness and muscular strength, its uprightness and cleanliness, the proper functioning of its orifices of nose, mouth, and anus (and, as the Appendix on 'Continence' shows, its urethra). The moral imperative of true manliness is physical restraint: the Scout must learn self-discipline, to control all attacks of 'incontinence', to regulate his bowel movements, breathe only through his nose. As is not difficult to see, 'health' rules such as these lock neatly together with the late-nineteenth-century middle-class virtues of will-power, thrift, and self-help: 'money-making goes with manliness, hard work, and sobriety' (p. 232)—and with national resilience. The syllogisms of Scouting thus all lead back to the question of the condition of Britain: 'getting ahead' combined with self-restraint equates also with doing 'really valuable work for the nation' (p. 229).

Yet there was a prime site on which valuable work for Britain and the Empire was already being carried out, and had been in good spirit for some generations, namely, the public school playing field. In the multi-faceted metaphor of 'playing the game' and 'keeping up the side'—prevalent throughout *Scouting for Boys*—the games ethic perfected by Victorian public school boys and their masters meshes efficiently with the ideals of imperial service.[13] As such, the public school ethos became one of the Empire's—and eventually one of the Scout Movement's—most influential cultural exports. To show loyalty to the group, to sacrifice oneself to its success, to practise honour, smile in the face of defeat: the games ethic was the guarantor of success in the colonies as well as of true masculinity. The enthusiastic former public school boy Baden-Powell does not mince his words on the matter. If the colony is the training ground of true masculine 'character'—brawny colonists are among the first of their 'race' and the mainstay of the Empire—then its cradle is the playing field. The ultimate fulfilment of the games ethic, furthermore, is to do one's best for one's country and demonstrate one's honour to the extent of risking one's life—or in early Scouting, one's Scout badge (p. 35).

Essentially, therefore, the mission of *Scouting for Boys* is to

[13] See J. A. Mangan, *The Games Ethic and Imperialism: Aspects of the Diffusion of an Ideal* (1986; London: Frank Cass, 1998).

distribute public school values to a wider social pool—of lower-middle-class and even working-class boys—than the public school itself was able to reach, while simultaneously, by emphasizing obedience to authority, keeping the class structure intact. 'Get the lads away from [spectator sports]', B.-P. instructs, 'teach them to be manly, to play the game whatever it may be, and not be merely onlookers and loafers' (p. 298). To emphasize the point he adapts Henry Newbolt's resonant poem 'Vitaï Lampada' (The Lamp of Life, 1897) into a 'Scout Recitation' renamed 'Play the Game!' for its epigrammatic refrain. Especially for those not yet exposed to it, this recitation, positioned towards the very end of *Scouting for Boys*, offers a rousing not to say suitably alarming performance of the derring-do spirit of manly self-sacrifice (pp. 336–7). Even as it supported social hierarchy, therefore, Scouting sought to enlist all boy Britons, as long as they held the correct values, into the ranks, or brotherhood, of the Empire. Imperial service was in effect a British birthright.

It was in this respect that the handbook made common cause with the popular imperialism of the time—the beliefs in the rights of whiteness, the superiority of Britain, which had already been widely disseminated via the adventure fiction of Ballantyne, Kingsley, or Henty and in the jingoist press. Its tough but populist message coincided, too, with the no-nonsense discipline of earlier, more militaristic youth movements. The 'muscular Christianity' of the Boys' Brigades, Church Lads' Brigades, and Boys' Empire League sought, like Scouting, to offer lessons in character-training to working-class boys 'independent' of 'good influence' (pp. 299, 301–2). In practice, however, Scouting even in the first flush of its popularity mainly attracted boys from the middle and lower-middle classes. They simply had greater access to the start-up resources, even if rudimentary, that were required. Besides which, the text was deeply scored through with a contemporary class prejudice which would have been off-putting to non-middle-class readers, as captured in the sharp aphorism that bees form a 'model community, for they respect their Queen, and kill their unemployed' (p. 117). Character observation in many ways meant reading for the signs of working-class poverty.

Popular fears and aversions of the day date fast. It is an irony of *Scouting for Boys* that several of its most potent popularizing features—its prejudices against social others, its pressures to conform, obey and practise self-restraint—were those that most rapidly became controversial and ultimately undesirable and unusable. The stern, uniquely explicit warnings against masturbation or 'self-abuse' that existed in the typescript did not even make it into the first edition, at the publisher C. Arthur Pearson's insistence, despite Baden-Powell's reluctance to remove them. (In this edition B.-P.'s plain-speaking passage on incontinence addressed to boys, which would have appeared as part of Yarn 18 (p. 200), has been partially restored in the form of the Appendix.) Most of the direct copies from the pages of adventure fiction, too, were cut from the final text to avoid charges of overabundant borrowing (as the Explanatory Notes point out in detail). But the first *Scouting for Boys* remains riddled with verbal excesses of a racist and class-based nature. These are particularly manifest in the playlets where, as in 'Pocahontas; or, The Capture of Captain John Smith', Scouts are asked to perform their racial superiority vis-à-vis cringing and defeated natives, to give them their civilizational come-uppance, as it were. The most rabid of these is undoubtedly the 'Display' towards the end of Part V in which the ferocious Indian Mutiny hero John Nicholson orders a local leader Mehtab Singh to demonstrate his deference by removing his shoes (pp. 279–81). Britain, 'all powerful for good of the world', requires those who fail to show due respect to learn their lesson by social humiliation. With the internationalization of the Scout Movement scenes such as these were removed from later editions of the text (the Nicholson display disappeared as soon as the second edition), although its class prejudices interestingly demonstrated a greater resilience than its racial feelings. A foremost area of interest in publishing the first edition as we do here, therefore, is that it reveals the handbook to readers in its raw or unadulterated imperialist state.

Weighing against its paranoid nationalism, however, the emphasis in *Scouting for Boys* on woodcraft and the outdoors, along with its live-and-let-live ethics (such as they are), participate in a different form of conservatism, or anti-industrial resistance, entirely. The book is not only shaped by, but itself contributed to shaping a radical new pastoralism, another powerful historical impulse of the time, though one whose tendencies were exactly contrary to the respect for authority generated by patriotic fears. Typically, colonial frontiersmen in *Scouting for Boys* are said to 'become "gentle men" by their contact with nature' (p. 153). Viewed in this light, Baden-Powell's handbook is the direct product of a turn-of-the-century social imagination moulded by the Victorian thinker John Ruskin's premodern nostalgia and the Arts and Crafts Movement's respect for manual skills and vernacular forms. Aversions to urbanized society found expression in the back-to-nature movements, outdoors clubs, and enthusiasms for the open air that proliferated both in Britain and on the Continent in this period, across a broad political spectrum, as in the German *Leibeskultur*. The educational theorist Charlotte Mason, for instance, whom Baden-Powell cites, and who in turn recommended his *Aids to Scouting*, encouraged lessons in 'the school of nature'. A pastoral escapism is openly celebrated in the less conventional work of the sexual theorist Edward Carpenter, and in the 'Neo-pagan' circle that in Cambridge gathered around the poet Rupert Brooke (who was influenced by Carpenter) in the same year that Baden-Powell's manual was published.[14] Such movements, too, celebrated the fit, healthy, and sometimes naked human form. To this extent it was almost inevitable that a preoccupation with the body, doubly reinforced, would predominate in *Scouting for Boys* (pp. 142, 144).

Avant-garde writers and artists of the new century also shared a curiosity about the revivifying powers of the so-called primitive arts and 'savage' rituals—a curiosity which Pablo Picasso and André Derain, D. H. Lawrence and T. S. Eliot, were shortly to embody in their work. In North America, emerging out of Ralph Waldo Emerson's transcendentalism, the prevailing romantic naturalism was distilled into the work of Stewart Edward White and Ernest Thompson Seton, amongst others. Seton, for example, whose books had a profound effect on Baden-Powell, found in the 'Outdoor Life' and the structures of 'Indian' tribal government the source of 'the physical regeneration so needful for continued national existence'.[15] B.-P.'s early mentor the professional scout Frederick Burnham, too, learned life-preserving tracking skills or woodcraft in North America, specifically the United States frontier, later transferring them to the 'last' colonial frontier of Rhodesia, where he taught Baden-Powell. (Note once again how *Scouting for Boys* becomes a temporary depot for insights and practices emerging from different geographic spaces,

[14] Paul Delaney, *The Neo-Pagans: Friendship and Love in the Rupert Brooke Circle* (London: Macmillan, 1987).

[15] Ernest Thompson Seton, *The Birch-Bark Roll of the Woodcraft Indians* (1902; New York: Curtis Publishing Company, 1903), 1.

which in some cases reach Europe only after several transcontinental journeys.)

Fully supporting such naturalist sentiments and interests, Baden-Powell's handbook inveighs against the passive diversions of the city and urges upon Scouts the improving influence of the open air, and activity based on native 'tribal' practices. In particular, the imprints of Seton's *The Birch-Bark Roll of the Woodcraft Indians* (1903) are everywhere to be discerned—in the text's games, lessons in wood-craft, ranks and honours—though the influence is, notoriously, not always fully acknowledged. Against the confinements and constraints of modernity, the book offers the romance of tracking in the wild as the means, in Max Weber's word, of re-enchanting the world.

Yet, if imperialist ideology lies scattered across the surface of *Scouting for Boys* in unmistakable and no doubt reassuring chunks, the appeal of the text was always greater than the sum of these somewhat obvious, unprocessed parts. As already suggested, it may be in fact that young male audiences worldwide were compelled precisely by the looseness of, and even lack of fit between, the text's hybrid pieces.[16] Baden-Powell, it is worth remembering, was a popularizer of disparate ideas, not a consistent thinker; he was also a master of knots and guises, dodges and decoys. As nicely suited its emphasis on individualist initiative, his handbook was what the reader made of it: it was that pick-and-mix quality again. In recent years critics such as Homi Bhabha and Gyan Prakash have offered incisive analyses of the colonial text as inherently unstable, fissured with contradictions (most typically, denying the humanity of the colonized, yet betraying a neurotic awareness of their presence).[17] *Scouting for Boys*, riddled with inconsistencies, is, according to this perspective, an intensely representative, or iconic, text of empire. Yet it is possible to take this reading one stage further, to make the observation that the book is in a very real sense nearly *all* contradiction. In other words, the 'scrambled-together apparatus of parts, chapter, yarns',[18] with its various modes of address (now to boys, now to instructors, sometimes, where italics have been mistakenly

[16] Notice in this regard how awkwardly the 10 chapters, comprising 28 yarns, map onto the first edition's 6-part structure.

[17] See, in particular, Homi Bhabha, *The Location of Culture* (London: Routledge, 1995); and Gyan Prakash, *After Colonialism: Imperial Histories and Postcolonial Displacements* (Princeton: Princeton UP, 1995).

[18] Macdonald, *Sons of the Empire*, 128.

omitted, as on p. 73, to an indeterminate in-between), is not only slippery as regards its ideological standpoint, or the precepts it teaches. In fact it is excessively, even *entirely* slippery (while also, paradoxically, remaining entirely imperialist).

Although they are multiple and interlocking, it is possible to unpick some of the more symptomatic of the book's contradictions. *Scouting for Boys* invites boys to learn toughness by playing at being men, yet, as will be seen in more detail, such play also aims to forestall for ever the process of growing up, of actually becoming a man. Similarly, the Scouting that it teaches is intoxicated with the flannel-shirted freedom of the frontier life, the independence of camping, yet it also inculcates respect for 'well-ordered rule' on which good citizenship depends. Western civilization, threatened with degeneration, is to be preserved by way of the reclamation of 'uncivilized', native ('Indian' and Zulu) practices and scouting skills. As will be outlined towards the end of this Introduction, primitive cultures are to revivify advanced societies. And again, the text casts doubt upon book learning in favour of the lore of the bush, and is in many respects anti-academic, as its cavalier unconcern about the accuracy of quotation and textual borrowing confirms. (It also attempts through its yarning to reinvent the oral tradition of story-telling at the fireside.)[19] Yet perhaps one of the more prominent of its many startling contradictions is that it is, even so, surprisingly literary. For the foundational text of a Movement that prized practice over theory, *Scouting for Boys* is extraordinarily devoted to verbal illustrations from the canon of romance and adventure fiction, as its first reading list neatly encapsulates (pp. 18–19). Tracking itself is represented as a decoding of nature or a reading for clues (pp. 89–90), detective work in the school of Sherlock Holmes (Part II). Most eccentrically, perhaps, *The Jungle Book* and *Jock of the Bushveld* are recommended as books to consult on animal behaviour and observation.

By granting literature the same status of veracity as history or zoology, Baden-Powell appears unknowingly to exploit another post-

[19] Macdonald, *Sons of the Empire*, 130–1; Macdonald notes that at a stylistic level, too, there is a contradiction between 'the dramatic and the educative'. Interestingly, the text is also wedged between two mutually reinforcing tautologies: to be a Scout (in the absence of more precise definition) is to be nothing other than a Scout, to perform 'Scoutness'; and, a Scout must continually prepare himself to Be Prepared.

colonial concept, concerning the imaginary dimensions of empire—the notion, as formulated by the cultural critic Edward Said, that the lived experience of colonialism was indistinguishable from the myth, story, and make-believe through which it was understood.[20] What is central to the clutch of contradictions through which *Scouting for Boys* turns is that these instabilities in effect undermine all its strenuous urgings, and give impetus to fantasy. Scouts, Part IV hilariously advises, should bestir themselves to show robust perseverance just as a 'manly frog' caught in a bowl of milk saves himself from drowning, unlike his spineless companion, by churning the liquid into butter with the force of his efforts to escape (pp. 241–2). The rub between the text's polarities creates what Ross Chambers has called 'the possibility of disturbance in the system', 'the space of play'.[21] It is fitting, then, within the terms of Chambers's reading, that such disturbance is in the handbook predominantly conceptualized as *play*, in two separate, but related, meanings of the word: as drama, and as game (including of course the sense of 'playing the game'). Scouts are to learn through acting out; by way of plays, pageants, and entertaining competitions. Moreover, Scouting with its sub-Masonic ritualized systems (embodied in its special names, coded signs, chants, and songs), is to be styled as a game for insiders, appealing to boys' imaginations and delight in secret codes. 'Boys', Baden-Powell writes, 'are full of romance, and they love "make-believe" ' (p. 312).

Getting a laugh on: Scouting as play

In his 'hotch-potch or plum pudding' of an autobiography, *Lessons from the 'Varsity of Life* (1933), Baden-Powell recommends acting as excellent training for a Scout: it teaches self-confidence, focuses the mind, and gives lessons in Kim-like impersonation; it may also, as in *Scouting for Boys*, teach wit, character, and history.[22] A note edited from the published text of the handbook (as the manuscript shows) expresses this 'man of the theatre's' own personal fascination for the

[20] Edward Said, *Culture and Imperialism* (London: Chatto and Windus, 1993).

[21] Ross Chambers, *Reading the Oppositional in Narrative* (Chicago: Chicago UP, 1991), p. xi.

[22] *Lessons from the 'Varsity of Life*, 32–56. See also Ian Buruma, *The Missionary and the Libertine: Love and War in East and West* (London: Faber, 1996), 54.

actor's demeanour: his 'peculiar hat and the longish hair and pallid shaven face'. Not only at school, but also during his time in the army and the colonial service in India and elsewhere, the waggish Baden-Powell, member of a 'charming circle' of actor friends, became well-known for his remarkable talents as a mimic and creator of stage-sets and costumes. As he moved through the ranks his conduct continued to be unorthodox in the sense that at every stage he encouraged play, and the putting on of plays. It was important, he felt, to allow his men to show initiative, in particular by learning to scout (as demonstrated, for example, in *Aids to Scouting*), but also, as at Mafeking, by inventing schemes and ruses of all kinds. He himself spent an inordinate amount of time, while ostensibly on official duty, engaged in games of strategy and camouflage, unofficial spying, horse-play, dressing-up, 'ragging' and 'gagging'—in short, staging 'plays' of one sort or another.

The success of withstanding the Boers at Mafeking itself could be attributed, as Baden-Powell later claimed, to diversionary bravado, 'joyous little dodge[s] of my own'. Where guns and ammunition were in short supply, and armed forces thinly spread, the town's defences depended on imaginative improvisation—dummy mine-fields, bogus orders shouted through a makeshift megaphone, make-believe barbed wire (which men mimed stepping through), and the kind of 'merry' morale these stratagems were able to sustain. The extent to which the whole of army life was to him essentially a game is captured in his famous retort to General Snyman, commander of the Boer forces at Mafeking. Before he could consider playing at cricket with the Afrikaners, Baden-Powell told Snyman, who had extended an invitation, he had first to finish the present game, the protracted siege, which so far had lasted '200 days, not out'. Life bore the aspects of fiction and, wherever it fell short, he was not above embellishing the quasi-mythical dimensions of his biography for the benefit of composing a memorable moral tale for Scouts. His weakness for liberal self-invention is typified in his rendition of his so-called African name, 'Impeesa' or *impisi* (which the Ndebele were said to have given him during the 1896 campaign), as the noble-sounding 'the Wolf that never sleeps'. The literal meaning of the Ndebele word is closer to 'creature that skulks by night', spy, or, in other words, the scavenging hyena.

Scouting, too, Baden-Powell on several levels represents primarily as a game that creates happiness, which, the autobiography also emphasizes, is success in life (along with health and helpfulness). Not only are Scouts encouraged to participate in the game of empire, they are also told to 'get a good laugh on' whatever the circumstances (p. 200). It is indicative therefore that the text of *Scouting for Boys* is studded with 'displays', and repeatedly advises boys to act out scenes from adventure and detective fiction. They are to perform 'songs, recitations, small plays, etc. . . . round the camp fire, and every scout should be made to contribute something to the programme, whether he thinks he is a performer or not' (p. 151). The Great Game of imperial strategy and defence, as in Rudyard Kipling's *Kim*, is, after all, to be accomplished by learning how to impersonate as well as perform tricks of memory, in the manner of 'Kim's game'. From this point of view, the hybrid mishmash of the 'Pocahontas' play, which appears to us now as absurdly arch and ironic if not as high camp, could be offered to boys, readers of the *Boy's Own Paper*, *Chums*, or *Tit-Bits*, simply as good, clean entertainment. In so far as Baden-Powell viewed all social roles and responsibilities as manifesting at the level of performance, it is the case that game and play, at the same time as they were fun, were also to his mind fundamentally in earnest. However, to approach the whole business of empire by way of dodges was efficient: a sure-fire means of avoiding adult charges of complicity in non-innocent activity, like killing your native enemy.[23] And there were spin-off benefits. Real life-saving skills, after all, could be acquired through improvisation. Saving up for theatre-going might well teach thrift (p. 312), and putting on plays could raise money (p. 234).

With its delight in games and fantasy, *Scouting for Boys* wholeheartedly indulges an Edwardian nostalgia for the nursery. Indeed, aspects of its hybrid imaginary world can be said to be every bit as bizarre as Alice's looking-glass adventures in Lewis Carroll. Even if exaggerated, this analogy draws attention to yet another contradiction in the make-up of the text: namely, that the colonies, which were founded on war, are predominantly represented as the territory of boys' make-believe. The ease-making 'hundred little dodges' of

[23] Significantly, in both Zululand and Asante, Baden-Powell's desire for bloody confrontation—the means to obtain promotion—was thwarted by the natives' refusal to behave as the enemy and take him on. This was one important reason for embellishing the historical record as he did.

camp-life, which Baden-Powell recommends to Scouts and imaginatively stages in the ideal camping ground of the veld or bush, at once romanticize and displace the violence of the colonial encounter (p. 136). In other words, in order to ring-fence the colonies as the perfect space for the training of Scouts, Baden-Powell must erase the actual conflicts of empire from the scene via the dodge, for such it is, of representing imperial activity in the main as a game. The wild is thereby transformed into the domain of the child.

The apparent contradiction whereby war converts into game is weirdly captured in Baden-Powell's favourite play, J. M. Barrie's *Peter Pan* (1904), which he saw many times in the years he was gestating *Scouting for Boys*. In the Neverland of the play, Peter's boys, the pirates, and the Indians relentlessly track after one another in a literal vicious circle that, though it is on one level all burlesque, an excessive late imperial pastiche of the commonplaces of children's fiction, is also deadly serious—as the final carnage on Captain Hook's ship vividly dramatizes. For Baden-Powell, the boy learns to rule both himself and the Empire not only by deciphering, but by participating in such irrationality and unruliness. This conjunction in *Scouting for Boys* of colonial disorder and play, so characteristic of late-Victorian children's literature, invites a further reading of the book *as* children's literature, which also sheds interesting light on the implied 'boy man' reader that such texts invoke.

Speaking for boys: the Boy Scout's appeal to children and to men

Writing for children, as critics of children's literature have observed, is as much a creation of adult ideals and desires as it is the imaginative property of children.[24] *Peter Pan*, the children's classic starring the eternal boy, the playful Peter flashing his milk teeth, offers us an apparently quintessential child figure. Yet the appeal of that figure lies first and foremost in the adult longing to stay young for ever, to fix the image of youth in an unchanging dimension of its own. At this level the story speaks most powerfully to the adult reader, or audience, not to children, who cannot participate in a nostalgia for something they have not yet lost.

[24] See Jacqueline Rose, *The Case of Peter Pan, or the Impossibility of Children's Literature*, rev. edn. (1984; London: Macmillan, 1992), p. xii. Note that Barrie's *Peter and Wendy* (1911), the story for children, appeared several years after the eponymous play.

The Boy Scout who, even as the generations pass, remains eternally young, was in this sense Baden-Powell's Peter Pan (after whom he named his son). It seems likely that he found in the figure of the Scout and of Peter, as well as in Kim, another boy-hero, a focus for his unformed and inarticulate—indeed, almost inadmissible—longings for boyhood, for being a boy, and being in the company of boys. The disciplined, resourceful boy of *Scouting for Boys*, the linchpin of imperial success, the stay against imperial decline, is an idealized figure, a projection of adult needs. Although dutiful, he is at the same time self-contained and self-directed. He is fit and disciplined, yet playful, a free agent. In particular, he is pictured as attractively independent of family ties and responsibilities, again like the orphan Kim or the adult-averse Peter. The ideological project of drawing lower-middle-class boys away from the bad influence of their families had to entail, of course, that they were members, primarily, of the society of themselves. Although Baden-Powell foresightedly recommends training for girls, if in passing (p. 305), many of the skills of camping even so involve finding at times farcical substitutes for domestic chores and utensils, to replace mothers and sisters at every possible level. The ideal scouting life of the frontiersman and the tracker meant enjoying the company of men only, as at public school, or in a gang of boys. It was this woman-free condition, too, which added to the appeal, to Baden-Powell, of the figure of the evergreen boy.

As in the half-playful advice to knead bread in one's coat (pp. 147–8), or to eat iguana (that looks and tastes like 'headless baby', p. 115), *Scouting for Boys* explicitly addresses itself *to* a boy's sense of humour. Yet it looks through a double lens, in that it at the same time knowledgeably represents boys *for* adults who yearn to be carefree boys again—boys amongst other boys. If anything, the text is more shrewd in relation to its boy audience than *Peter Pan*, more conscious of having to construct a child readership, and avoid talking down, yet simultaneously to maintain the interest of grown men 'who are interested in boys'. Slapstick, jokes, yarns, and anecdotes are used extravagantly as different ways of appealing to boys, yet all such attempts are objectified and transformed into a spectacle of boyhood in the inserted 'hints to instructors'. If anything, Baden-Powell skirts—but cannot solve—the puzzle of speaking at once for and to boys by casting his persona not as an eternal boy but as a 'boy man', the knowing faux-innocent (the term, B.-P.'s own, is one which his biographer Tim Jeal amongst others has used to describe him). The gap in the phrase 'boy man' can perhaps be seen as corresponding to the split between his two readerships, of boys playing at men, of men playing at being boys: it is a link, yet a self-conscious separation.

The interest in the young male body, and in brotherly friendship between boys and men in *Scouting for Boys*, has inevitably raised questions over the years as to whether one of its buried discourses is homosexual or homophilic (implying eroticized love between men).[25] Can it be read as a male-loving text? With the possible double entendre shadowing its title (in which we are invited to 'scout' for boys), does it permit a 'queer', sexually aslant interpretation? From the biographical details we have it does seem undeniable that Baden-Powell generally 'preferred men', in the broadest sense of the phrase. In India, Northern Ireland, and South Africa, he repeatedly and usually successfully contrived to be institutionally linked with his close friend the boyish 'Boy' McLaren—essentially his Kim.[26] Across his entire life, too, like many men of his generation, he sought out safe, male-only havens away from the woman-dominated space of the family, such as he had experienced at Charterhouse and in the military 'among good comrades and friends' (p. 237). As regards his handbook, the fit male form is certainly the focal point of its aesthetic, as of its politics and its emotional economy (consider the value it places on male company and brotherhood). Moreover, this bodily aesthetic is achieved, the text recommends, by means of practical activity in the company of other men, in the push–pull exercises which it pictures, in the give-and-take co-operation of scouts in the bush. Such descriptions are occasionally reminiscent of Kipling's image of 'two strong men', of whatever race, being able to meet face to face as equals in the Empire.[27] With an eye to this image, could we then say that for Baden-Powell the colonial context did not so much

[25] Questions have surfaced in particular following Piers Brendon's popular study (London: Secker and Warburg, 1979) and Tim Jeal's psychosexual reconsideration (1989), to the extent of becoming virtually a cliché of the history of Scouting. In the 1995 Channel 4 documentary on Baden-Powell, 'The Boy Man', directed by Dai Richards, which generated a media hubbub on the subject, the 'repressed homosexuality' of the Chief Scout was taken more or less as a given. Charges of homosexuality, repressed or not, should of course be carefully distinguished from those of paedophilia, for which there appears no evidence in Baden-Powell's make-up.

[26] Jeal, *Baden-Powell*, 74–109.

[27] See Rudyard Kipling, 'The Ballad of East and West' (1889).

sexualize such interrelations as make them more possible, more legitimate to express than at home? In other words, are audiences now asking the wrong questions of his apparent sexuality?

Scouting for Boys is, when all is said and done, remarkably uninhibited about its appreciation for relationships between men: it shares to some extent in the nineteenth-century's acceptance (at least before the Oscar Wilde trials) of male–male love or liking of different kinds.[28] The rights and freedoms of empire enjoyed by white men (and to a limited degree by native elites) did much to encourage such apparently fluid interaction. In colonial spaces remote from 'civilization', where divisions between the domestic and the exotic, the familiar and the foreign, were eroded, a wider variety of social relations—between men and women in certain milieux, as well as amongst men—was made available.[29] In *Scouting for Boys* it is noticeable, for example, that Scouting in several of its dimensions involves an open traffic in female signs—how to make a home and prepare a meal, how to acquire the feminine skill of social observation. Yet, developed out on the veld, this was a traffic still entirely alien to the separate spheres of the early twentieth-century British home. Perhaps the most that can finally be said on the subject of sexuality and *Scouting for Boys* is that the text's orientation, though provoking, must remain undecidable or indeterminate. The sexual energies of Baden-Powell's prose, such as they are—by analogy, so to speak, with the latent stage in childhood described by Freud—are dispersed, random, and above all displaced away from the conventionally eroticized body zones. For one as concerned about bodily control as Baden-Powell, it seems the case that male–male desire, or indeed any desire at all, lay in a place unamenable to conscious symbolization, although, as in his obsessive worries about opening and closing orifices, occasionally disruptive of it.

Whereas a homosexual reading lies at an oblique or inaccessible angle to *Scouting for Boys*, the text is, by contrast, entirely open about its preoccupation with a related issue, that of masculinity—

[28] Jeffrey Richards, 'Passing the Love of Women: Manly Love and Victorian Society', in J. A. Mangan and James Walvin (eds.), *Manliness and Morality: Middle-Class Masculinity in Britain and America, 1800–1940* (Manchester: Manchester UP, 1987), 92–122.

[29] See Christopher Lane, *The Ruling Passion: British Colonial Allegory and the Paradox of Homosexual Desire* (Durham, NC, and London: Duke UP, 1995). See also Eve Sedgwick, *Between Men: English Literature and Male Homosocial Desire* (New York: Columbia UP, 1985).

ideally clean and hard, yet in doubt. (This from a man who used scented soap in the bush.) The argument might in fact be made that *Scouting for Boys* protests too much, too excessively, about masculinity: the need to train it up, the need to preserve it. The frequency and urgency with which 'manliness' is pressed upon British boys, as has been seen, let slip that the masculinity, or strength, of the nation is far from settled or certain. The defensiveness is captured in the brusque (and discriminatory) plain-speaking of the maxim for instructors: 'Manliness can only be taught by men, and not by those who are half men, half old women' (p. 301). Baden-Powell's views on this score bear signs of the influence of, and were certainly retrospectively justified by, not fears of degeneration alone, but more particularly the late-Victorian 'race life' theory of human development whereby the growth of the child was seen as recapitulating the stages of human evolution.[30] One of the problems of modern society was that it was deemed to have neglected, or suppressed entirely, the primitive stage in young boys of learning to survive in the wild and roam in gangs. This neglect, however, Scouting would undertake to reclaim.

In recommending so-called primitive behaviours and rituals as well as heroic stories for the training of young boys as men (such as 'Zulu' and 'Swazi' initiation practices), *Scouting for Boys* takes an approach to identity-formation that seems from our point of view uncannily contemporary. Via narrative, or, more precisely, the performance of narratives of bush-survival and derring-do, male (and thereby national) selfhood is to be fashioned. Masculine identities are moulded and charged with legitimacy by means of story-telling, by recounting and performing John Smith's encounter with the Algonquin, or the bravery of the crew of the Birkenhead.[31] Dispatch running practice is carried out using disguises, except, self-evidently, 'dressing up as a woman' (p. 180). In these ways national courage and preparedness, even if they did not yet exist in fact, could be seen to take shape in performance, in the wishful, virtual space of Scouting imagination. The Scout's commitment to the 'British' virtues of

[30] Similar ideas are discernible in present-day popular theories of the need to retrieve a primitive masculinity, as in the writing of Robert Bly.

[31] See Graham Dawson, *Soldier Heroes: British Empire, Adventure, and the Imagining of Masculinities* (London: Routledge, 1994); Ben Knights, *Writing Masculinities: Male Narratives in Twentieth-Century Fiction* (London: Macmillan, 1999).

duty and loyalty to the Imperial Crown was itself enacted in the speaking of the Scout Law. With its devotion to maleness thus founded on word and in (performed) deed, it was small wonder that within a few years of the first publication of *Scouting for Boys*, the Scout would be hailed in the pages of *Punch* (1909) as an established symbol of national resilience.

A modernist Edwardian text

If the emphasis on performance in *Scouting for Boys* bears a present-day aspect, we could go so far as to say that features of its style might be called positively and hence presciently 'postmodern'. There is the text's delight in mini-narratives and citation, a lot of it cursory and inaccurate;[32] there is its non-progressive structure textured with pictures and subheadings in irregular font sizes.[33] Most obviously, perhaps, the handbook's collage format invites a pick-and-mix reading, in a hopscotch pattern, or through correspondences between one section and another. The text is, after all, intended as a 'palm guide', to be carried in a pocket and consulted at a glance, in 'short, pleasing sip[s] of one kind and then off to another' (p. 308).[34]

Yet, as the reader of twentieth-century writing will know, *Scouting for Boys* at the same time bears the traces of an earlier era of textual production, not only Edwardian—and it is in many ways, as was seen, characteristically Edwardian and late imperialist—but also

[32] A tracking of the text's sources and references reveals that a significant proportion of B.-P.'s quotations are from the opening pages of books or of chapters to books. He was a careless speed-reader with an attention span apparently not much longer than that of the boys he sought to address. Most prominent amongst his many misquotations and misreadings is his account of the Sherlock Holmes story, 'The Greek Interpreter' (p. 70), from Arthur Conan Doyle's *The Memoirs of Sherlock Holmes* (1894). The encounter in question is narrated in a conversation between Holmes and his brother Mycroft in which they *together* identify the circumstances of a passing NCO in *full* mourning dress from the *Royal Artillery* not the Royal Marines.

[33] As Brian McHale, *Constructing Postmodernism* (London: Routledge, 1992), suggests, the postmodern text or artefact gestures at its own constructedness by using effects such as these.

[34] It is noteworthy in this regard that Scouting—to which the book intends to introduce the reader—is at no point actually defined as such. In the first Camp Fire Yarn an account of the 'boy scouts' of Mafeking is followed by an idealized lineage of Scouting under 'Scout's Work', a précis of Kipling's *Kim*, and a short, somewhat literary reading list. Scouting itself is to be demonstrated, even in the book, strictly in the form of practices.

modernist, or at least protomodernist. With Baden-Powell's agreement it was brought out as a potential money-spinner using the scrapbook, hodge-podge template of the Pearson's entertainment magazine *Tit-Bits*. In the manner of a newspaper page, the text was therefore produced as a mosaic that yet aspired to the status of an encyclopedia, a compendium of bite-sized bits of useful knowledge. To divert the reader it carried mottoes, manifesto-style rules, and catchy headings; to instruct it used stories, albeit in snippets, enlivened with snatches of direct speech. Yet as such, even in its very use of the popular entertainment format, *Scouting for Boys* also dramatically pre-empted, respectively, the bold, sloganeering approach of the avant-grade magazine *Blast* (1914)[35] and T. S. Eliot's quintessentially modernist creation of bits and patches *The Waste Land* (1922).[36] It is, in its own sphere, as was the so-called Vorticist writing of Wyndham Lewis and Ezra Pound in the 1910s, a piece of textual and cultural 'blasting and bombadiering'.

Should the comparison, especially with Eliot's work, seem implausible, the Scouting handbook can be seen to resemble that iconic modernist poem in several striking respects. *Scouting for Boys*, whose author sought to grab the imagination of a young audience, attempts throughout to create effects of the now, touching on many subjects of contemporary importance: national 'degeneration', colonial brotherhood, the new science of microbes. It also demonstrates a liking for slogans and catchphrases, something that B.-P. shared with Pearson's Managing Director, Peter Keary, himself an author of self-improvement books. Yet the same attention to immediacy and the present-day, in effect to capturing the concentration of journalism, can be said to inform *The Waste Land*'s multi-story, 'many voices' fabric.[37] In *Scouting for Boys*, as in *The Waste Land*, reported speech and dramatic interludes convey psychological tension and social disorder. Moreover, in both texts quotation from authoritative sources is used both to shore up, and to interrogate, a civilization believed to be in decline. Finally, as this suggests, both *Scouting for Boys* and *The Waste Land* can be read as anxious meditations on and reactions

[35] Wyndham Lewis (ed.), *Blast 1*, foreword by Bradford Morrow (Santa Rosa, Calif.: Black Sparrow Press, 1987).

[36] T. S. Eliot, *The Complete Poems and Plays* (London: Faber, 1978), 59–80.

[37] See e.g. Tom Paulin, 'Many Cunning Passages: How Maynard Keynes Made his Mark on *The Waste Land*', *TLS* (29 Nov. 2002), 14–15.

against an empire perceived to be fragmenting, if not already to some extent in psychological pieces.[38]

The colonial book, as postcolonial or contemporary readers know, betrays, in spite of itself, traces of the influence of native or colonized cultures. Whether postmodern or protomodernist, *Scouting for Boys* is first and foremost, from this perspective, an extravagantly colonial, if not *hyper-colonial* text, in so far as it not only recommends but revels in a mixed array of native influences. Britain is, Dracula-like, to draw life force from subordinated cultures whose own vitality, arguably, has been forcibly repressed. Native American and Aboriginal tracking skills are used to help safeguard the British national defence-system.[39] Zulu war-songs are to empower white boys. So it is appropriate that on a 1920 poster advertising the Great Jamboree Pageant, held at Olympia, entitled 'The Genesis of Scouting', Aborigines, Sikhs, Zulu warriors straight out of the pages of H. Rider Haggard, and European-looking Boy Scouts, circle a maypole in a camp-fire war-dance. At the foot of the maypole sit John Smith and a 'Red Indian', and from it flies the Union Jack. The poster provides an emblem for what is the book's area of most flagrant if not outrageous borrowing, as well as for its multi-voiced extravaganza— that mingling or *hybridizing* of cultural discourses and sources which empire made possible. Baden-Powell is usually relaxed about acknowledging citations, yet when it comes to native people, whom colonization culturally dispossessed, and who are elsewhere in the 1908 text disparaged, plunderings such as these, especially of a covert nature, are the more ethically difficult, as well as, therefore, the more scandalous and unsettling.

This quality of the outrageous is fully epitomized, for example, in the cultural mix-and-match of the early Scout uniform which sports an Asante staff, colonial-style shorts (showing bare knees), and a Canadian 'Mountie' (or South African Constabulary) hat bearing a 'Mafeking native' bootlace for good luck (pp. 38–9, 220). It is also symptomatically captured in the history of the Scout leader's wood badge. The shape of the wood badges was imitated from the *iziqu* or wooden beads of the Zulu king Dinuzulu's ceremonial necklace.

[38] On the saturation of the modern, and the modernist, by colonialism, see Booth and Rigby, *Modernism and Empire*.

[39] See *Lessons from the 'Varsity of Life*, 129–31.

Baden-Powell is believed to have acquired a copy or version of the necklace (though not the necklace itself) while on campaign against the king in Natal in 1888.[40]

However, if from the point of view of its borrowings *Scouting for Boys* can seem a rather overtypical (indeed gamey) late-imperial book, it has also demonstrated a certain staying power, and not only in so far as it can now be read as an archive of its period. The multipart structure and miscellaneous content of the 1908 text has kept it open to twenty-first-century audiences, on several levels. Just as features of its style invite the label 'postmodern', so its topics and preoccupations reveal a capacity to readdress or recycle social concerns and political interests. For one, its anxieties concerning masculinity or the lack of it (the genetic and social retreat of maleness, its impact on the education of boys), resonate remarkably closely with our own. For another, regarding questions of bodily health and eco-friendliness, the book seems prophetic and relevant: take responsibility for your health, don't smoke, don't indulge in too much meat, exercise mind over matter. Most of all, avoid harming the environment. Then again, as demonstrated in the present-day popularity of travel books, our society entertains a B.-P.-like belief that the unfamiliar outdoors weathers and toughens the urbanized West. Finally, there is our time's continuing, if revamped, recognition of the enduring power of story-telling: how identity may be fashioned and refashioned in narrative, and not only through the narratives of one place, but, in a globalized world, via cultural mishmash, according to inclination. Therefore, although the Scout remains in present-day culture a primary symbol of social diligence and initiative, s/he will also retain compelling significations of make-believe, of the enduring appeal of self-invention and the far frontier.[41]

It was part of Robert Baden-Powell's talent as the founder of a worldwide youth movement, the most successful in terms of

[40] Baden-Powell owned a second Zulu necklace, which he had, by his own admission, removed from the body of a dead Zulu woman after a skirmish in northern Natal in 1888. Compare Baden-Powell, *Lessons from the 'Varsity of Life*, 152; Jeff Guy, 'Imperial Appropriations: The Dynamic History of *iziqu*', *Natal Museum Journal of Humanities*, 11 (December 1999), 23–42; and Jeal, *Baden-Powell*, 134.

[41] As pictured by the Kenyan writer Ngugi wa Thiong'o, 'Ambivalent Feelings About Biggles', *Guardian 2* (13 August 1992), the 'Boy Scout' is someone 'daring to try, never giving up, stretching the boundaries of what [is] credible'. Scouting became officially co-educational in 1991: a girl can, therefore, choose to become a Scout rather than a Guide.

numbers and sheer spread that has ever been seen, to hold contradictions in balance, and to contain multitudes. He espoused cultural stereotypes yet embedded diverse cultural influences in the structures of Scouting. He performed colonial appropriations, while at the same time, arguably, Africanizing his own everyday habits and lifestyle. He was an avid hunter, yet advised scouts against killing animals. He could entice boys, yet reassure their parents. He was hardly a deliberate writer, yet he has become perhaps one of the most widely read British authors of all time. He was a soldier and an artist; not only the hypercolonial, but the *Über*-youth. Within years of its invention his Scout Movement appeared age-old, an obvious inspiration, as natural as the day. Had he not existed—and before 1908 he perhaps did not in fact exist as such—the popular impact of *Scouting for Boys*, in Britain, and globally, would have invented his legend.

NOTE ON THE TEXT

PLANNED from at least 1904, and largely written in 1907, Robert Baden-Powell's *Scouting for Boys*, the world-renowned 'self-instructor' for boys, and all-time bestseller—possibly in fact the most influential youth manual ever published—first appeared in six fortnightly parts (every other Wednesday), at 4*d.* a copy, from 15 January 1908. (Part I, for example, advertised the publication of Part II on '30 [or 29] January'.) It was published by Horace Cox, a printer owned by the newspaper magnate, C. Arthur Pearson, proprietor of the *Daily Express* and *Pearson's Weekly*, who had, amongst others, personally encouraged Baden-Powell in 1906 to adapt his advice on Scouting for the training of urban boys.

The cloth-bound complete edition, distinguished by the incorporation of the handful more illustrations and observations which now appeared at the very end of the text as supplementary material (pp. 348–50), was published soon after, on 1 May 1908, also by Pearson. The fortnightly parts went through four reprints during 1908, the complete volume was reprinted five times in the same year. Once Pearson brought out a cheap edition, priced at one shilling, it began to sell five thousand copies a month. Fifty years later, in 1948, the book was still doing well: that year 50,000 copies were sold in Britain alone. It was only in 1967 that Pearson's first noted sales were declining. By the later decades of the twentieth century the original handbook had become even in the view of the Scout Movement something of a period curiosity. Its new, modernized handbooks gave priority to activities, skills, and awards, and minimized the overt ideological content of the original. The twenty-first-century equivalent to *Scouting for Boys* is *The Scout Matrix*, a glossy, state-of-the-art production resembling a filofax in which the Founder B.-P. is directly mentioned only in the opening historical introduction to Scouting.

In the fifteen years following the first publication of *Scouting for Boys*, up to 1922, Baden-Powell would repeatedly modify and remould the text to reflect the changing emphases of the Scout Movement: in particular, towards a greater pacificism after 1914–18, and away from an overt British imperialism. It was also necessary to keep pace with the increasing elaboration of the Scout Movement's organization and system of badges. Even pre-1950, therefore, it is the case that different editions of the text can differ markedly one from the other. However, it is the first, almost instantly popular 1908 parts edition (PE)—apparently rough and ready, yet carefully masterminded, in part newly generated, in part assembled out of already plotted precepts and plans—on which the present text is based. It was in this form that the blueprint of Scouting was first devoured by its hungry, ever-expanding boy readership. The differences between this and the complete edition, moreover, are essentially insubstantial.

The manuscript of *Scouting for Boys* had different points of genesis: several sections are cannibalized from other books by Baden-Powell, in particular, *Reconnaissance and Scouting* (1884) and *Aids to Scouting* (1899), as well as many books by other authors. He may have begun to draft a part of the book as early as November 1906. He was certainly working hard at it in the first half of 1907. As the incomplete manuscript or the Part MS[1] shows (it is held, along with the typescript—also incomplete—in the Scout Association Headquarters Archive at Gilwell Park, Essex), the book was written on different kinds of paper (hotel letterhead, funerary, notepaper lined and unlined), and now in pencil, now in ink. (Red ink, as opposed to black, is dedicated to the Notes to Instructors.) Baden-Powell was ambidextrous, so it may be that the book was also written in two hands (the handwriting at various points gives some grounds for suggesting this). Percy Everett, Pearson's Literary Editor, certainly records B.-P. making the sketches for the book using both hands.

It is possible to reconstruct to some extent the chronology of Baden-Powell's writing process from occasional notes in his diary, and marginal instructions to his typist Mr Cavan in the Part MS. He was writing the Observation group of yarns in June 1907, mainly in the Izaak Walton Hotel, Dovedale, Derbyshire. (The Deakin anecdote (Part MS 66; PE 94–5), however, is written on Savoy Hotel notepaper, turned upside-down.) Just before Part MS 70 (PE 98) there is a note to Mr Cavan on the back of a blue postcard with the printed address, 'Harwood, Bonchester Bridge, Hawick N.B.', dated 18 June 1907. In it B.-P. instructs Cavan to type up the MS so far,

[1] See list of abbreviations at the start of the Explanatory Notes (p. 353).

and order *Aids to Scouting*, from which on the next page he asks him to quote. It is thereafter, on Part MS 83, which concerns an example of deduction taken from *The Adventures of Sherlock Holmes*, that 'up to 27/6/07' appears in pencil in the margin.

Baden-Powell spent July 1907, a formative month for Scouting, writing at the Mill House, Wimbledon Common. The Brownsea Camp, the trial run for scouting and woodcraft as a practice, took place between 31 July and 9 August 1907. He was back writing in Wimbledon later in the year and in early January 1908, but spent part of the pre-Christmas period in Teesdale, again working on the text. The anxious, Tory imperialist 'Introduction' to the book, which went through several drafts, and eventually appeared as the truncated, deeply panicked 'Notes for Instructors' of Part VI, is dated 6 October. B.-P. intended this as a 'self-educator' for men. By late December he had mailed the material for the first two parts to the printer. Pearson was pressing for early publication, so Baden-Powell obliged with a quick turnaround of all proofs and correspondence. On 24 February 1908, his diary records, he sent off Part V of 'S for B', which was published on 11 March.

Scouting for Boys was planned as the core of a strenuous publicity campaign, directed by the media-savvy Pearson, strongly reminiscent of the hyping of big-name novels in the late twentieth century and subsequently. Between October 1907 and February 1908 Baden-Powell gave fifty promotional lectures on the 'Boy Scout Scheme' at various YMCA venues, based on the circulars he had sent out to selected influential people in 1907. These lectures were designed to create an audience for his Scouting ideas, and Pearson urged publication soon thereafter to capitalize on the interest generated. The fortnightly publication of the six parts was intended 'to catch the public when they are still hot and keen from my lectures', as Baden-Powell himself wrote to Pearson's Managing Director Peter Keary in 1908. He also received advice from Pearson throughout the writing process as regarded the composition of the text, its division into six parts, ten chapters, and twenty-eight yarns according to the entertainment formula of *Pearson's Weekly*, and its marketing. It was Pearson, through Everett the Literary Editor (who attended the Brownsea Camp), for instance, who dissuaded B.-P. from publishing the complete 'Notes for Instructors' with its patriotic vehemence about imperial decline and fall: it is in any case a kind of adumbration of

Chapter XI on 'Patriotism', addressed to boys. Pearson also joined with Horace Cox in insisting that Baden-Powell remove his forthright man-to-boy advice against 'incontinence' (Part TS 246–8; originally a section in Yarn 18, PE 226). (Given Baden-Powell's reluctance to edit out these plain-speaking passages, they have been restored to the present edition as the Appendix.) Pearson or Everett's red pencil, too, cut down several of the references to having a 'daily rear'. Moreover it was Pearson's idea, possibly influenced by Peter Keary, to tantalize public interest and appeal to the primary audience, boys, with the parts format, its bite-sized sections, pithy mottoes and sayings, attractively archaic or homespun yarns, and promise of more of the same at the end of the fortnight.

The attention to buzz and spin instantly paid off. With the household name of the hero of Mafeking, the single British success of the first year of the Anglo-Boer War, on its covers, the text seized imaginations long before Part VI appeared. In May, when the complete edition was published, boys across Britain were already organizing themselves into patrols. By September Baden-Powell had become aware that the still unofficial movement had grown far beyond the scope of his alleged initial idea—to set up a training scheme that might piggyback onto existing boys' organizations like the Boys' Brigade. The structures of an organization—advisory committees and travelling inspectors to accompany the already launched magazine, the *Scout* (14 April 1908)—were now expeditiously set up.

Scouting for Boys was written at considerable speed, with less than meticulous care for factual accuracy, the attribution of its many magpie borrowings, and grammatical correctness. Its several textual inconsistencies, too, betray its pell-mell composition. The reference to the Musketeer D'Artagnan's tracking as the basis for a Scouting game (p. 96), for example, alludes to an extended quotation from *The Three Musketeers* which was cut from the final text. Contrary to Baden-Powell's own signposting, the warning against having flies in camp appears after and not before his advice on keeping camp grounds tidy (pp. 142, 150). At times it is as if he were making mental notes for future conversations with boys and their instructors (see pp. 37, 60, 136–7, 295). Virtually throughout, the syntax unrolls in a relentlessly linear, add-on, or paratactic, fashion: many paragraphs tag on to the last with the opening word 'Also ...'

or 'Then . . .' (pp. 41, 74, 135); and comparison with the Part MS shows frequent modification from the third to the second person. In this edition the many dropped articles, misplaced apostrophes, reversed letters, and so on, have in most cases been quietly corrected (and Baden-Powell's own corrections to the PE incorporated), although not universally so, as on p. 88, where the notational quality as of working in haste has been preserved. Many of the recommended reading lists, too, are sketchy and incomplete (for example, pp. 89 and 123). Important missing details and acknowledgements are supplied in the Explanatory Notes.

Until 1922, the year the tenth edition was published, Baden-Powell modified *Scouting for Boys* between each and every edition. To enumerate these changes in full would be a fascinating task for the researcher interested in the shifts in belief and ideology which have marked the Scout Movement. In sum, Baden-Powell worked hard between editions to widen and globalize the text's cultural and social references, in order that Britain no longer be placed so firmly at the centre of the Scouting world. (As part of a related widening, between the Part MS and the PE, too, references to England are replaced with Britain, and the word 'Englishmen' with 'Britons'.) He also tried to reduce the text's claims of racial superiority in order to situate Scouting not so much within an imperial metropolis, as, in his view, an emerging commonwealth of nations. The grotesque imperialistic display involving John Nicholson and Mehtab Singh (pp. 279–81), for example, lasted but one edition: in the second it had been dropped. By 1922 the 'Pocahontas' playlet featuring an idealized John Smith had been removed too (from Part I). The mnemonic for the Scouting motto 'Be Prepared', 'B. P., my initials' (pp. 35, 44), which was given in the PE, was suppressed in the complete edition, no doubt for its egotism. So, too, the second edition offered a more careful acknowledgement of the woodcraft work of Ernest Thompson Seton from which B.-P. had so heavily borrowed. In the 1911 fourth edition the Scout Law is filled out with a tenth law, to make a decalogue, and to give expression to Baden-Powell's principle of chasteness: 'A scout is pure in thought, word, and deed'. Finally, there were, year on year, the many details of changes in badge rules and first-aid practices, which it was the job of each edition of *Scouting for Boys* faithfully to record and to recommend.

SELECT BIBLIOGRAPHY

Primary Texts

Bt.-Colonel R. S. S. Baden-Powell, *Aids to Scouting for N.-C.Os. and Men* (London: Gale and Polden, 1899).

Major R. S. S. Baden-Powell, *The Downfall of Prempeh: A Diary of Life with the Native Levy in Ashanti 1895–6* (London: Methuen, 1896).

Sir Robert Baden-Powell, *Indian Memories: Recollections of Soldiering, Sport, etc.* (London: Herbert Jenkins, 1915).

Lord Baden-Powell, *Lessons from the 'Varsity of Life* (London: C. Arthur Pearson, 1933).

Col. R. S. S. Baden-Powell, *The Matabele Campaign, 1896: Being a Narrative of the Campaign in Suppressing the Native Rising in Matabeleland and Mashonaland* (London: Methuen and Co., 1897).

Lieut.-Gen. Sir Robert Baden-Powell KCB, *My Adventures as a Spy* (London: C. Arthur Pearson, 1915).

Lord Baden-Powell, *Paddle your Own Canoe, or Tips for Boys from the Jungle and Elsewhere* (London: Macmillan, 1939).

Captain R. S. S. Baden-Powell, *Reconnaissance and Scouting: A Practical Course of Instruction, in Twenty Plain Lessons, for Officers, Noncommissioned Officers, and Men* (London: William Clowes and Son, 1884).

Lieut.-Gen. Sir Robert Baden-Powell, *Scouting Games* (London: C. Arthur Pearson, 1910).

Lieut.-General Baden-Powell, *Sketches in Mafeking and East Africa* (London: Smith and Elder, 1907).

Biographies and Historical Background

Frederick Russell Burnham, *Scouting on Two Continents*, first published 1926 (Prescott, Ark.: Wolf Publishing Co., 1994).

Hugh and Mirabel Cecil, *Imperial Marriage: An Edwardian War and Peace* (London: John Murray, 2002).

F. Davies, *A Cry from the Streets: The Boys' Clubs in Britain from the 1850s* (Hove: Wayland Publishers, 1975).

General Robert Irvine Dodge, *Our Wild Indians: Thirty-Three Years Personal Experience*, first published 1882 (Williamstown, Mass.: Corner House, 1978).

Malcolm Flower-Smith and Edmund Yorke, *Mafeking! The Story of a Siege* (Johannesburg: Covos-Day Books, 2000).

Stephen Gray (ed.), *Charles Rawden Maclean: The Natal Papers of 'John Ross'* (Pietermaritzburg: University of Natal Press, 1992).

Jeff Guy, *The View Across the River: Harriette Colenso and the Zulu Struggle against Imperialism* (Oxford: James Currey, 2002).

William Hillcourt (with Olave, Lady Baden-Powell), *Baden-Powell: The Two Lives of a Hero*, foreword by Nelson R. Block, first published 1964 (New York: The Gilwellian Press, 1992).

Tim Jeal, *Baden-Powell: Founder of the Boy Scouts*, first published 1989 (New Haven and London: Yale University Press, 2001).

Max Nordau, *Degeneration*, 2nd edn., first published 1893 (London: William Heinemann, 1895).

Thomas Pakenham, *The Boer War* (London: Weidenfeld and Nicolson, 1979).

Sol T. Plaatje, *Mafeking Diary: A Black Man's View of a White Man's War*, ed. John Comaroff (London: James Currey, 1990).

E. E. Reynolds, *Baden-Powell: A Biography of Lord Baden-Powell of Gilwell* (Oxford: Oxford University Press, 1942).

Frederick Courteney Selous, *Travel and Adventure in South-East Africa* (London: Rowland Ward and Co., 1893).

Ernest Thompson Seton, *The Birch-Bark Roll of the Woodcraft Indians*, first published 1902 (New York: Curtis Publishing Company, 1903).

—— *Two Little Savages: A Book of American Woodcraft for Boys. Being the Adventures of Two Boys who Lived as Indians and what they learned* (New York: Doubleday, Page and Co., 1903).

Iain Smith (ed.), *The Siege of Mafeking* (Johannesburg: Brenthurst Press, 2002).

Eileen K. Wade, *Olave Baden-Powell: The Authorised Biography of the World Chief Guide* (London: Hodder and Stoughton, 1971).

—— *The Piper of Pax: The Life Story of Lord Baden-Powell* (London: C. A. Pearson, 1931)

Secondary Texts

Robert Aldrich, *Colonialism and Homosexuality* (London: Routledge, 2003).

Robert Bly, *Iron John: A Book About Men* (Shaftesbury: Element, 1991).

Howard J. Booth and Nigel Rigby (eds.), *Modernism and Empire* (Manchester: Manchester University Press, 2000).

Piers Brendon, *Eminent Edwardians* (London: Secker and Warburg, 1979).

Joseph Bristow, *Empire Boys: Adventures in a Man's World* (London: HarperCollins, 1991).

Hugh Brogan, *Mowgli's Sons: Kipling and Baden-Powell's Scouts* (London: Cape, 1987).

Ian Buruma, *The Missionary and the Libertine: Love and War in East and West* (London: Faber, 1996).

Jonathan David Caverley, *The Development of Character: The Gentleman Spies of Erskine Childers and John Buchan* (Cambridge, Mass.: Harvard University Press, 1995).

Linda Colley, *Captives: Britain, Empire and the World, 1600–1850* (London: Cape, 2002).

R. W. Connell, *Masculinities* (Cambridge: Polity, 1995).

Graham Dawson, *Soldier Heroes: British Empire, Adventure, and the Imagining of Masculinities* (London: Routledge, 1994).

Patrick Dunae, 'Boys' Literature and the Idea of Empire, 1870–1914', *Victorian Studies*, 24 (1980), 105–58.

Brian Gardner, *Mafeking: A Victorian Legend* (London: Cassell and Co., 1966).

Mark Girouard, *The Return to Camelot: Chivalry and the English Gentleman* (London and New Haven: Yale University Press, 1981).

Martin Green, *Dreams of Adventure, Deeds of Empire* (London: Routledge and Kegan Paul, 1979).

Eric Hobsbawm and Terence Ranger (eds.), *The Invention of Tradition* (Cambridge: Cambridge University Press, 1983).

Paul Hoch, *White Hero, Black Beast: Racism, Sexism, and the Mask of Masculinity* (London: Pluto, 1979).

Richard Holt, *Sport and the British: A Modern History* (Oxford: Clarendon Press, 1989).

Peter Hulme, *Colonial Encounters: Europe and the Native Caribbean 1492–1797*, first published 1986 (London: Routledge, 1992).

Ronald Hyam, *Empire and Sexuality: The British Experience* (Manchester: Manchester University Press, 1991).

Sidney Hynes, *The Edwardian Turn of Mind* (Princeton: Princeton University Press, 1968).

Shamsul Islam, *Kipling's 'Law': A Study of his Philosophy of Life* (London: Macmillan, 1975).

Elwyn Jenkins, 'Names in the Symbolic Discourse of the Scout Movement', *Nomina Africana* 14.1 (2000), 19–28.

—— *South Africa in English-Language Children's Literature, 1814–1912* (Jefferson, NC: McFarland, 2002).

V. G. Kiernan, *From Conquest to Collapse* (New York: Pantheon, 1982).

Ben Knights, *Writing Masculinities: Male Narratives in Twentieth-Century Fiction* (London: Macmillan, 1999).

Christopher Lane, *The Ruling Passion: British Colonial Allegory and the Paradox of Homosexual Desire* (Durham, NC, and London: Duke University Press, 1995).

Robert H. Macdonald, *Sons of the Empire: The Frontier and the Boy Scout Movement, 1890–1918* (Toronto: University of Toronto Press, 1993).

John M. Mackenzie (ed.), *Imperialism and Popular Culture* (Manchester: Manchester University Press, 1986).

J. A. Mangan, *The Games Ethic and Imperialism: Aspects of the Diffusion of an Ideal*, first published 1986 (London: Frank Cass, 1998).

—— and James Walvin (eds.), *Manliness and Morality: Middle-Class Masculinity in Britain and America, 1800–1940* (Manchester: Manchester University Press, 1987).

Rosalind Miles, *Love, Sex and Death in the Making of the Male* (London: Paladin, 1992).

Thomas Pakenham, *The Scramble for Africa* (London: Weidenfeld and Nicolson, 1991).

Geoffrey Pears, *Hooligan: A History of Respectable Fears* (London: Macmillan, 1983).

Richard S. Phillips, *Mapping Men and Empire: A Geography of Adventure* (London: Routledge, 1996).

—— *et al.* (eds.), *De-centring Sexualities: Politics and Representation beyond the Metropolis* (London: Routledge, 2000).

Don Randall, *Kipling's Imperial Boy: Adolescence and Cultural Hybridity* (Basingstoke: Palgrave, 2000).

Jacqueline Rose, *The Case of Peter Pan, or the Impossibility of Children's Literature*, rev. edn., first published 1984 (London: Macmillan, 1992).

Michael Rosenthal, *The Character Factory: Baden-Powell and the Origins of the Boy Scout Movement* (London: Collins, 1986).

Raphael Samuel (ed.), *Patriotism: The Making and Unmaking of British National Identity*, vol. iii: *National Fictions* (London: Routledge, 1989).

Peter J. Schmitt, *Back to Nature: The Arcadian Myth in Urban America* (Oxford: Oxford University Press, 1969).

Eve Sedgwick, *Between Men: English Literature and Male Homosexual Desire* (New York: Columbia University Press, 1985).

Martin Short, *Inside the Brotherhood* (London: Grafton, 1990).

Elaine Showalter, *Sexual Anarchy: Gender and Culture at the fin de siècle* (London: Bloomsbury, 1991).

John Springhall, *Youth, Empire and Society: British Youth Movements, 1883–1940* (London: Croom Helm, 1977).

—— *Coming of Age: Adolescence in Britain, 1860–1960* (London: Macmillan, 1986).

Allen Warren, 'Sir Robert Baden-Powell, the Scout Movement and Citizen Training in Great Britain, 1900–1920', *English Historical Review*, 101 (1986), 376–98.

Further Reading in Oxford World's Classics

J. M. Barrie, *Peter Pan and Other Plays*, ed. Peter Hollindale.
Mrs Beeton's Book of Household Management, ed. Nicola Humble.
Empire Writing, ed. Elleke Boehmer.
H. Rider Haggard, *King Solomon's Mines*, ed. Dennis Butts.
Rudyard Kipling, *Kim*, ed. Alan Sandison.
—— *The Jungle Books*, ed. W. W. Robson.
Samuel Smiles, *Self-Help*, ed. Peter W. Sinnema.
Robert Louis Stevenson, *Treasure Island*, ed. Emma Letley.

A CHRONOLOGY OF ROBERT BADEN-POWELL

	Life	*Historical and cultural background*
1857	Born at 6 Stanhope Street, Paddington, London, on 22 February, the twelfth child of the Revd Baden Powell, Savilian Professor of Geometry at Oxford, and eighth child of his third wife, Henrietta Grace Smyth.	Indian Revolt or Mutiny.
1858		Indian Empire created. R. M. Ballantyne, *The Coral Island*
1859		Charles Darwin, *The Origin of Species* Isabella Beeton, *Household Management*
1860	Professor Powell dies months after the publication of *Essays and Reviews* to which he has contributed an essay developing his controversial work questioning the historical accuracy of the Bible.	
1865		Lewis Carroll, *Alice's Adventures in Wonderland*
1869	Baden-Powell's mother, in quest of social status, officially alters the family name to Baden-Powell.	
1870	Nominated for a scholarship at Charterhouse, and takes up his place at the school in November.	John Ruskin gives inaugural lecture at Oxford.
1871		Lewis Carroll, *Through the Looking-Glass*
1872		H. M. Stanley, *How I Found Livingstone*
1876	Unlike two of his elder brothers, Baden-Powell fails to gain entrance to Oxford, but wins second place for cavalry in the open army examination. Gazetted as	Victoria proclaimed Empress of India.

	Life	*Historical and cultural background*
	Sub-Lieutenant into the 13th Hussars, stationed at Lucknow in India. Quickly builds a reputation for having a merry, playful disposition combined with a steely will to 'get on'.	
1878		Second Afghan War breaks out.
1879	Spends an extended period of leave in England, mainly involved in amateur theatricals.	*Boy's Own Paper* first published
1880	At the end of the year, towards the close of the conflict in Afghanistan, Baden-Powell rejoins the 13th Hussars, now located near to Kandahar (and thereafter Quetta). Develops an interest in tracking when examining the battlefield of Maiwand. Meets Kenneth ('Boy') McLaren, who will be his best friend for nearly thirty years.	
1881	Stationed at Muttra, where he sets up with McLaren a bachelors' household teeming with exotic pets.	
1882	Promoted to the rank of Adjutant.	
1883	Sells sketches of Indian life to the *Graphic*.	R. L. Stevenson, *Treasure Island*
1884	*Reconnaissance and Scouting* published, his first book of advice for scouts, defined as men of intelligence and pluck. The book is based on his cavalry lectures to men on basic army tracking. 13th Hussars ordered for a time to Natal, South Africa.	G. A. Henty, *By Sheer Pluck: A Tale of the Ashanti*
1885	His *Cavalry Instruction* manual published. Returns to England in search of active service in order to achieve better pay and promotion.	Indian National Congress founded. General Gordon falls to the Mahdi. H. Rider Haggard, *King Solomon's Mines*

	Life	*Historical and cultural background*
1886	Sets out on an unofficial spying mission to Germany with his brother Baden.	
1887	Takes the opportunity to demonstrate 'machine-gun driving', Buffalo-Bill style, before General Wolseley.	H. Rider Haggard, *She: A History of Adventure*
1888	Works as ADC (and later Military Secretary) to his uncle General Sir Henry Smyth, Commander-in-Chief of the Cape Colony, and forms part of the army Smyth leads against a 'native rebellion' in Zululand. Dinuzulu, the dispossessed Zulu king, escapes his stronghold before a disappointed B.-P. is able to reach it. B.-P. controversially involved in the killing of local people.	
1889	*Pig-sticking or Hog-hunting* published. Visits Swaziland as secretary to the Special Commissioner.	Promulgation of first Japanese constitution.
1891		Arthur Conan Doyle, *The Adventures of Sherlock Holmes*
1890	Acts as Military Secretary and ADC to his uncle Henry Smyth, now Governor of Malta, and excels at amateur theatricals and 'skirt-dancing' (to 1893). Visits Italy and North Africa, allegedly on spying missions.	
1893	Misses the opportunity to go out with Sir Frederick Carrington to quell the first Ndebele or Matabele Resistance, led by Lobengula. Returns to his regiment, now stationed in Northern Ireland.	

	Life	Historical and cultural background
1894		Arthur Conan Doyle, *The Memoirs of Sherlock Holmes* Rudyard Kipling, *The Jungle Book*
1895		Rudyard Kipling, *The Second Jungle Book*
1896	Sent to Asante (or Ashantiland, in what is now Ghana) by Lord Wolseley, and leads a native levy in the British campaign against the Asantehene Prempeh, aimed at securing the annexation of his territory. Gravely disappointed at Prempeh's unwillingness to fight back. Publishes the rapidly prepared *The Downfall of Prempeh*.	
1897	As Chief Staff Officer to Sir Frederick Carrington, B.-P. assists in putting down the Matabele Rebellion or *chimurenga* in the British South Africa Company's territory, soon to be called Rhodesia (1898). Takes part in the only cavalry charge of the conflict and also, controversially, executes Chief Uwini of the Makalakas. Learns woodcraft from the American scout Frederick Burnham, and the 'Cape Boy' Jan Grootboom. *The Matabele Campaign* published.	Jameson Raid into the Transvaal defeated.
1898	Promoted to command the 5th Dragoon Guards, stationed in India (to 1899).	Fashoda Incident between Britain and France. Spanish-American War.
1899	Sent out to southern Africa by Lord Wolseley as Commander-in-Chief of the North-West Frontier Forces. Raises two volunteer regiments, with Lieutenant-Colonel Plumer, to defend Rhodesia and the Bechuanaland Protectorate	11 October: Anglo-Boer War breaks out.

	Life	*Historical and cultural background*
	and 'menace the back door of the Transvaal'. Moves his Protectorate Regiment to Mafeking in the Northern Cape, which is attacked and invested by the Boers on 14 October, to remain besieged for 217 days. *Aids to Scouting for N.-C.O.s and Men*, the proofs of which leave on one of the last trains out of Mafeking, published later in the year.	
1900	17 May: Siege of Mafeking lifted to widespread jubilation in South Africa and London, with B.-P. hailed hero of the war. Serves as Commander in the Western Transvaal (June–August).	
1901	June: Appointed Inspector-General of the new South African Constabulary. Employs McLaren as his London-based recruiting officer. Publishes *Notes and Instructions for the South African Constabulary*.	Rudyard Kipling, *Kim*
1903	Returns to England as Inspector-General of Cavalry. Appointed Honorary Vice-President of the Boys' Brigade.	G. A. Henty, *With Kitchener in the Soudan*
1904	William Smith of the Boys' Brigade invites B.-P. to adapt *Aids to Scouting* 'to suit boys'.	Russo-Japanese War (to 1905). J. M. Barrie's *Peter Pan* first performed
1906	Meets the newspaper proprietor C. Arthur Pearson and 'draws up a scheme with a handbook to it for the education of Boys as Scouts'.	
1907	Placed on half-pay with the rank of Lieutenant-General, and takes command of the Northumbria Division of the	Percy Fitzpatrick, *Jock of the Bushveld*

	Life	*Historical and cultural background*
	Territorials. Holds the first experimental Scouting camp at Brownsea Island, Poole Harbour, and writes the bulk of *Scouting for Boys. Sketches in Mafeking and East Africa* published.	
1908	*Scouting for Boys* published in six parts (January–April). The book enjoys unprecedented sales, and fires boys across Britain to form patrols on their own initiative. September: B.-P. sets up an office to manage and organize the burgeoning new movement. By the end of the year Scouting has spread to New Zealand and Canada.	
1909	B.-P. knighted. *Yarns for Boy Scouts* published. Scouting spreads to India.	
1910	Retires from army (reputedly at the advice of Edward VII) in order to devote all his time to leading the Scout Movement. Scouts in Britain number 107,000. The Girl Guides founded. Boy Scouts of America founded.	John Buchan, *Prester John*
1911	Mass Boy Scout rally held at Windsor Great Park.	
1912	Marries Olave Soames. *Handbook for Girl Guides, or How Girls can help build the Empire* published (written with Agnes Baden-Powell), as well as *Boy Scouts Beyond the Seas*.	
1913	Son Peter born.	
1914	*Quick Training for War* published.	First World War breaks out (to 1918).
1915	Whilst preserving the Scout Movement's independence from the War Office, B.-P. visits the front and is appalled	

	Life	*Historical and cultural background*
	at the carnage he witnesses. *Indian Memories*, and the controversial *My Adventures as a Spy* published. Daughter Heather born.	
1916	The Wolf Cubs, for younger boys, set up.	
1917	Daughter Betty born.	
1918	Acquires his family home, naming it Pax Hill. Olave Baden-Powell elected Chief Guide, having succeeded Agnes Baden-Powell, B.-P.'s sister. B.-P. shifts the emphasis of Scouting in the direction of internationalism and a greater pacifism.	
1920	First International Scout Jamboree is held at Olympia, London. B.-P. is proclaimed Chief Scout of the World. Scouts in Britain number 325,000. Gilwell Park is established as a woodcraft centre for Scouts.	Noncooperation led by Gandhi in India (to 1922).
1922	*Rovering to Success* published, as well as the tenth edition of *Scouting for Boys*. The first world census puts the number of Scouts across the globe at 1,019,205.	
1923		Rudyard Kipling, *Land and Sea Tales for Scouts and Guides*
1926		Balfour clarifies Dominion Status for colonies.
1927	*Life's Snags and How to Meet Them* published.	
1929	Created a peer and takes the title, Lord Baden-Powell of Gilwell.	Civil disobedience in India.
1930	Scouts in Britain number 438,000.	
1933	B.-P.'s autobiography, *Lessons from the 'Varsity of Life*, published. The Scout	

	Life	*Historical and cultural background*
	Movement worldwide comprises nearly 3 million Scouts.	
1935	*Scouting Round the World* published.	
1936	*Adventuring to Manhood* published.	Spanish Civil War breaks out.
1937	Receives the Order of Merit.	
1938	Retires from his work for Scouting, to live in Nyeri, Kenya. Netherlands World Jamboree held as a 'Crusade of Peace'.	
1939	*Paddle Your Own Canoe* published. Scouts worldwide number 3,305,149.	September: Outbreak of Second World War (to 1945).
1941	Dies at the age of 83, on 8 January. Buried at Nyeri.	
1977	Olave Baden-Powell dies.	

The Boy Scout in Action

Scouting for Boys.

A HANDBOOK FOR INSTRUCTION IN GOOD CITIZENSHIP.

BY

Lieut.-General R. S. S. BADEN-POWELL, C.B., F.R.G.S.

ILLUSTRATED.

London:

HORACE COX,

WINDSOR HOUSE, BREAM'S BUILDINGS, E.C.

SCOUTING FOR BOYS

CONTENTS OF THE PARTS

FOREWORD FOR INSTRUCTOR

[N.B.—Remarks printed in italics are, throughout the book, addressed to the Instructor.]

By the term 'Instructor' I mean any man or lad who takes up the training of either a Patrol (i.e., six to eight boys), or a Troop i.e., (several Patrols joined together).

By means of this book I hope that anyone, even without previous knowledge of scouting, may be able to teach it to boys—in town just as well as in the country.

The system is applicable to existing organisations such as schools, boys' brigades, cadet corps, etc., or can supply a simple organisation of its own where these do not exist. But in all cases I would strongly commend the 'Patrol' system: that is, small permanent groups, each under responsible charge of a leading boy, as the great step to success.*

The reasons for this, the objects of the training and full hints to Instructors I have already published in a pamphlet called 'The Boy Scouts Scheme'. Price Twopence. Published by Bradbury, Agnew, Bouverie Street, London, E.C. They will be further set forth in Part VI of the present book.*

I recommend the Instructor to begin with a Patrol of eight boys if possible, and when these have qualified as 'First-class Scouts' to select the best five or six to raise each a patrol of his own and instruct it under his (the Instructor's) supervision.

A great step is to obtain, if possible, a room, barn, or school to serve as a Club, especially for work on long winter evenings. It must be well-lit and warmed. And to have a camp-out in the summer.

There need be no great expense in working a troop of Boy Scouts.

*Finance must largely depend on the efforts of the Scouts themselves. Methods for making money will be indicated in Part IV. I do not hold with begging for funds if it can possibly be avoided.**

Any further information or advice will readily be given on application, and I shall be glad to have any suggestions or informal reports of progress and numbers trained. But I have no desire to trouble Instructors with red-tape returns, and so on.

Scouts' Badges, Medals, Patrol Flags, and Crests, Tracking Irons, and such articles of scouts' equipment, can be obtained at low rates on application here.

All communications should be addressed, not to me by name, but to:

THE MANAGER,
Boy Scouts,
Goschen Buildings,
Henrietta Street,
London, E.C.

R. S. S. B.-P.
January, 1908.

PART I

CONTENTS: CHAPTER I

SCOUTCRAFT

CHAPTER I

SCOUTCRAFT

NOTES FOR INSTRUCTOR

The following is a suggestion for the distribution of the work for the first week. It is merely a suggestion and in no sense binding.

FIRST EVENING:

INDOORS

Address the boys on 'Scoutcraft', giving a summary of the whole scheme, as in this chapter, with demonstrations or lantern slides, etc.

Swear in the Scouts, form Patrols, and give shoulder knots.

FOLLOWING DAY:

MORNING AND AFTERNOON

Practical work, outdoors if possible, as follows:—

Alternatives according to whether in town or country, indoors or out.

MORNING

Parade, hoist Union Jack and salute it.

Scouting game: e.g., 'Scout Meets Scout', (See page 47.)

Practise salutes, secret signs, patrol calls, scouts' chorus, etc.

Practise drawing scout-signs on ground or walls with stick or chalk.

Tie knots.

Make ration bags, leather buttons, etc.

MORNING

Parade. Prayers or Church Parade (if Sunday).

Physical Exercises.

Drill.

Self-measurement by each scout of span, cubit, finger joint, stride, etc.

Send out scouts independently or in pairs to do a 'good turn', to return and report how they have done it.

March out the Patrol to see the neighbourhood.

Make them note direction of starting by compass, wind, and sun.

Notice and question them on details seen, explain 'land marks', etc.

Make Scout's Marks on ground or chalk them on pavement or walls.

Practise Scout's pace.

Judge distances.

AFTERNOON

Play an extended Scouting Game. (See 'Games', p. 46.)

Or indoors if wet—'Ju-Jitsu', 'Scout's War Dance', Boxing, Scout's Chorus and Rally, etc.

EVENING

Camp Fire Yarns from this book or from books recommended (see p. 19).

Or rehearse a Scout play, or hold Debate, Kim's Game, etc.

Patrols to continue practice in these throughout the week in their own time or under the scout master, with final games or exercise on the following Saturday afternoon.

*If more evenings than one are available in the week one of the subjects might be taken in turn more fully each evening, and rehearsals carried out of a display such as 'Pocahontas'.**

CAMP FIRE YARN.—No. 1

MAFEKING BOY SCOUTS

WE had an example of how useful Boy Scouts can be on active service,* when a corps of boys was formed in the defence of Mafeking, 1899–1900.*

Mafeking, you may remember, was quite a small ordinary country town out on the open plains of South Africa.

Nobody ever thought of its being attacked by an enemy any more than you would expect this town (or village) to be attacked—the thing was so improbable.

But it just shows you how you must be prepared for what is *possible*, not only what is *probable* in war; and so, too, we ought to be prepared in Britain against being attacked by enemies; for though it may not be probable, it is quite as possible as it was at Mafeking; and every boy in Britain should be just as ready as those boys were in Mafeking to take their share in its defence.

Well, when we found we were to be attacked at Mafeking, we told off our garrison to the points that they were to protect—some 700 trained men, police, and volunteers. And then we armed the townsmen, of whom there were some 300. Some of them were old frontiersmen, and quite equal to the occasion; but many of them, young shopmen, clerks, and others, had never seen a rifle before, and had never tried to learn to drill or to shoot, and so they were hopelessly at sea at first. It is not much fun to have to face an enemy who means to kill you, when you have never learned to shoot.

Every boy ought to learn how to shoot and to obey orders, else he is no more good when war breaks out than an old woman, and merely gets killed like a squealing rabbit, being unable to defend himself.

Altogether, then, we only had about a thousand men all told to defend the place which contained 600 white women and children, and about 7,000 natives, and was about five miles round.

Every man was of value, and as their numbers gradually got less, owing to men getting killed and wounded, the duties of fighting and keeping watch at night got harder for the rest. It was then that Lord Edward Cecil, the chief staff officer,* got together the boys in the place and made them into a cadet corps, put them in uniform and

Lord Edward Cecil and Boy Scouts in Mafeking

drilled them; and a jolly smart and useful lot they were. We had till then used a large number of men for carrying orders and messages and keeping look-out, and acting as orderlies and so on. These duties were now handed over to the boy cadets, and the men were released to go and strengthen the firing line.

And the cadets, under their serjeant-major, a boy named Goodyear, did right good work, and well deserved the medals which they got at the end of the war. Many of them rode bicycles, and we were thus able to establish a post by which people could send letters to their friends in the different forts, or about the town, without going out under fire themselves; and we made postage stamps for these letters which had on them a picture of a cadet bicycle orderly.*

I said to one of these boys on one occasion, when he came in through rather a heavy fire: 'You will get hit one of these days riding about like that when shells are flying.' And he replied: 'I pedal so quick, sir, they'd never catch me.' These boys didn't seem to mind the bullets one bit; they were always ready to carry out orders, though it meant risk to their life every time.

Would any of you do that? If an enemy were firing down this street, and I were to tell one of you to take a message across to a house on the other side, would you do it? I am sure you would. But probably you wouldn't much like doing it.

But you want to prepare yourself for it beforehand. It's just like taking a header into cold water; a fellow who is accustomed to bathing thinks nothing of it; he has practised it over and over again. But ask a fellow to do it who has never practised it and he will funk it.

So, too, with a boy who has been accustomed to obey orders at once, whether there is risk about it or not; the moment you order him to do a thing on active service, no matter how great the danger is to him he does it, while another chap who has never cared to obey would object, and would then be despised as a coward even by his former friends.

But you need not wait for war in order to be useful as a scout. As a peace scout there is lots for you to do any day, wherever you may be.*

SCOUT'S WORK

I SUPPOSE every British boy wants to help his country in some way or other.

There is a way, by which he can do so easily, and that is by becoming a scout.

A scout, as you know, is generally a soldier who is chosen for his cleverness and pluck to go out in front of an army in war to find out where the enemy are, and report to the commander all about them.

But, besides war scouts, there are also peace scouts, *i.e.*, men who in peace time carry out work which requires the same kind of abilities.* These are the frontiersmen of all parts of our Empire. The 'trappers' of North America, hunters of Central Africa, the British pioneers, explorers, and missionaries over Asia and all the wild parts of the world, the bushmen and drovers of Australia, the constabulary of North-West Canada and of South Africa—all are peace scouts, real *men* in every sense of the word, and thoroughly up in scout craft, *i.e.*, they understand living out in the jungles, and they can find their way anywhere, are able to read meaning from the smallest signs and foot-tracks; they know how to look after their health when far away from any doctors, are strong and plucky, and ready to face any danger, and always keen to help each other. They are accustomed to take their lives in their hands, and to fling them down without hesitation if they can help their country by doing so.

They give up everything, their personal comforts and desires, in order to get their work done. They do not do all this for their own amusement, but because it is their duty to their King, fellow-countrymen, or employers.

The History of the Empire has been made by British adventurers and explorers, the scouts of the nation, for hundreds of years past up to the present time.

The Knights of King Arthur, Richard Cœur de Lion, and the Crusaders, carried British chivalry into distant parts of the earth.

Raleigh, Drake, and Capt. John Smith, soldiers and sailors of Queen Elizabeth's time, faced unknown dangers of strange seas, as well as the known dangers of powerful enemies, to take and hold new lands for the expansion of our small kingdom.

Capt. Cook in Australia, Lord Clive in India, opened up new countries. Speke, Baker, and Livingstone pushed their way through the savage deserts and forests of Africa; Franklin and Ross braved the ice and snows of the Arctic regions.

In the present time Selous, the great hunter, and Lieut. Boyd Alexander, who last year crossed Africa, are peace scouts.*

These are just a few names out of many hundreds of the scouts of the nation who have from all times down to the present spread the good name and power of our country in all parts of the world.

And there have been women scouts of the nation, too: such as Grace Darling, who risked her life to save a shipwrecked crew; Florence Nightingale, who nursed sick soldiers in the Crimean War; Miss Kingsley, the African explorer; Lady Lugard, in Africa and Alaska; and many devoted lady missionaries and nurses in all parts of our Empire.* These have shown that girls as well as boys may well learn scouting while they are young, and so be able to do useful work in the world as they grow older.

It is a grand life, but it cannot suddenly be taken up by any man who thinks he would like it, unless he has prepared himself for it beforehand.

Those who succeed best are those who learnt scouting while they were still boys.

Scouting also comes in very useful in any kind of life you like to take up, whether it is soldiering or even business life in a city. Sir William Crookes* says it is even valuable for a man who goes in for science, and finding out little things about air, and light, and so on.

So I am going to show you how you can learn scout-craft for yourself and can put it into practice at home.

It is very easy to learn and very interesting when you get into it. You can best learn by joining the 'Boy Scouts'.

'KIM'

A GOOD example of what a Boy Scout can do is to be found in Rudyard Kipling's story of 'Kim'.*

'Kim', or, to give him his full name, Kimball O'Hara, was the son of a sergeant of an Irish regiment in India. His father and mother died while he was a child, and he had been left to the care of an aunt who lived in an humble way in India.

His playmates were all natives, so he got to talk their language and to know their ways better than any European. He became great friends with an old wandering priest who was tramping about India, and with whom he travelled all over the north part of that country. At last, one day he chanced to meet his father's old regiment on the line of march, and in visiting the camp he was arrested on suspicion of being a thief. His birth certificate and other papers were found on him, and the regiment, seeing that he had belonged to them, took charge of him, and started to educate him. But whenever he could get away for holidays he dressed himself in Indian clothes, and went again among the natives as one of them.

After a time he became acquainted with a Mr Lurgan, a dealer in old jewellery and curiosities, who, owing to his knowledge from dealing with natives, was also a member of the Government Intelligence Department.

[*Explain this.*]

This man, finding that Kim had such special knowledge of native habits and customs, saw that he would make a useful agent for Government Intelligence work, that is, a kind of detective among the natives. But, first of all, before employing him, he put him to one or two tests to see whether he was sufficiently brave and strong-minded.

As a trial of his strong-mindedness he attempted to mesmerise him, that is to say, he tried to make Kim's thoughts obey what was in his own mind. It is possible for strong-minded men to do this with those of weaker mind. The way he attempted it was by throwing down a jug of water so that it smashed to pieces; he then laid his fingers on the boy's neck, and wished him to imagine the jug mended itself again. But, do what he would to make his thought reach the boy's brain, he failed; Kim saw the jug was broken, and would not believe it was mended, although at one time he nearly obeyed him, for he saw a kind of vision of the jug being mended, but it faded away again.

Most boys would have let their mind and eyes wander, and would not have been able to keep them on the one subject, and would so have easily become mesmerised by the man.

Lurgan, finding him strong-minded and quick at learning, then gave him lessons at noticing small details and remembering them, which is a most important point in the training of a scout—it is a thing that he should learn and be practising every hour of the day wherever he may be. Lurgan began it with Kim by showing him a tray full of precious stones of different kinds—he let him look at it for a minute, and then covered it with a cloth, and asked him to state how many stones and what sort were there. At first he found he could only remember a few, and could not describe them very accurately, but with a little practice he soon got to remember them all quite well. And so, also, with many other kinds of articles which were shown to him in the same way.

Then Kim travelled about the country a great deal with a fine old Afghan horse-dealer to whom he was much attached, who was also an agent of the Intelligence Department. On one occasion Kim was able to do him a good turn by carrying an important message for him, secretly; and another time he saved his life by overhearing some natives planning to murder him when he came along. By pretending to be asleep and then having a nightmare which caused him to move from his position, Kim got away from the neighbourhood of the would-be murderers, and was able to give warning to his friend in good time.

At last he was made a member of the Secret Service, and was given a secret sign—namely, a badge to wear round his neck and a certain sentence to say, which, if said in a peculiar way, meant he was one of the service. Scouts generally have secret signs by which they can communicate with each other.

The members of the Intelligence Service are very numerous in India, and do not know each other by sight, so they have to have a secret sign by which they will recognise each other among other people who may be their enemies.

Once when travelling in the train Kim met another member whom he did not know. This was a native, who when he got into the carriage was evidently in a great state of alarm, and was rather badly cut about the head and arms. He explained to the other passengers that he had met with an accident from a cart whilst he was driving to the station, but Kim, like a good scout, noticed the cuts were sharp and not grazes such as you would get by falling from a cart, and so did not believe him. While the man was tying up a bandage over his head, Kim noticed he was wearing a locket like his own; so Kim let his own be seen. Directly the man saw it he brought into conversation some of the secret words, and Kim answered with the proper ones in reply. So then the stranger got into a corner with Kim and explained to him that he was carrying out some secret service work, and had been found out and hunted by some of the enemies of the Government who had nearly killed him. They probably knew he was in the train and would therefore telegraph down the line to their friends that he was coming. He wanted to get his message to a certain police officer without being caught by the enemy, but he could not tell how to do it if they were already warned of his coming. Kim thereupon hit upon the idea of disguising him.

Kim disguising the native spy

In India there are a number of holy beggars who go about the country. They wear next to no clothing and smear themselves with ashes, and paint certain marks on their faces; they are considered very holy, and people always help them with food and money. So Kim made a mixture of flour and wood ashes, which he took from the bowl of a native pipe, and he undressed his friend and smeared these all over him, and finally, with the aid of a little paint-box which he carried, he painted the proper marks on the man's forehead. He smeared the man's wounds with flour and ashes, partly so as to heal them, and also so that they did not show; and he brushed his hair down to look wild and shaggy like that of a beggar, and covered it with dust so that the man's own mother would not have known him. Soon afterwards they got to a big station where on the platform they found the police officer to whom the report was to be made. The imitation beggar pushed up against him and got abused by the officer in English; the beggar replied with a string of native abuse into which he introduced the secret words. The police officer, although he had pretended not to know Hindustani, understood it quite well, and at once recognised from the secret words that this beggar was an agent; and so he pretended to arrest him and marched him off to the police-station where he could talk to him quietly. It was thus done without anyone on the platform knowing that they were in league with each other, or that this native beggar was the escaped Intelligence agent.

Finally, Kim became acquainted with another agent of the department—an educated native or Babu as they are called in India—and was able to give him great assistance in capturing two Russian officers who were acting as spies against the British on the north-west frontier of India.

[*Note.—Point out on map respective positions of British and Russians.*]

The Babu pretended to the Russians that he was the manager for a local native prince who did not like the English, and travelled with them for some time as representative of this prince. In this way he got to know where they kept their secret papers in their baggage. At last he got up trouble between them and a holy priest, whom they struck; this caused great excitement among the natives, who rushed off with the baggage and got lost in the darkness. Kim, who was among the natives, opened the luggage and found the secret papers which he took out and carried to headquarters.

These and other adventures of Kim are well worth reading, because they show what valuable work a boy scout could do for his country if he were sufficiently trained and sufficiently intelligent.

BOOKS

THE following books,* which may be got from a Lending Library or from friends, may be found useful in connection with Chapter I:—

'Rob the Ranger', by Herbert Strang, price 6s. (Published by Hodder & Stoughton), describes the exciting adventures of boy scouts in Canada in the early days, including tracking and backwoods life.

Also,

'Kidnapped', by R. L. Stevenson.

'Kim', by Rudyard Kipling.

'Siege of Mafeking', by Major F. Baillie.

'Two Little Savages', by E. Thompson Seton.

'Parents and Children', by Miss Charlotte Mason.

'The Romance of Every Day', by L. Quiller Couch, gives inspiring instances of heroism in everyday life. 5s.

'Heroes of Pioneering', by Edgar Sanderson. 5s. (Published by Seeley & Co.)

CAMP FIRE YARN.—No. 2

SUMMARY OF SCOUT'S COURSE OF INSTRUCTION*

To become a Boy Scout you join a patrol belonging to your Cadet Corps, or Boys' Brigade or club.

If you are not a member of one of these, or if it does not as yet possess a patrol of scouts, you can raise a patrol yourself by getting five other boys to join. They should, if possible, be all about the same age. One boy is then chosen as Patrol Leader to command the patrol, and he selects another boy to be the Corporal or second in command. Several patrols together can form a 'Troop' under an officer called a 'Scoutmaster'.

You all take the scout's oath, that is you promise, *on your honour*,* three things, namely:

1. To be loyal to God and the King.
2. To help other people at all times.
3. To obey the scout law.

You learn the scout sign of the scouts (see page 37), and also the call of your patrol (see page 42).

Every patrol is named after some animal, and each scout in it has to be able to make the cry of that animal in order to communicate with his pals, especially at night. Thus you may be 'the Wolves', 'the Curlews', 'the Eagles', or 'the Rats' if you like. No scout may ever use the call of another patrol. The second law binds you to be loyal, kind, obedient, and cheerful. Most of your work then consists in playing scouting games and practices by which you gain experience as scouts. When you have learned sufficient to pass the test you can win the badge of either a first class or second class scout.

That of the first class scout consists of a brass arrow head with the motto on it 'BE PREPARED'.*

That of the second class scout is merely the motto without the arrow head.

The meaning of the motto is that a scout must prepare himself by previous thinking out and practising how to act on any accident or emergency so that he is never taken by surprise; he knows exactly what to do when anything unexpected happens.

The following subjects are what you have to know about to pass the test as a scout:—

WOODCRAFT means knowing all about animals, which is gained by following up their foot-tracks and creeping up to them so that you can watch them in their natural state, and learn the different kinds of animals and their various habits. You only shoot them if in want of food; but no scout wilfully kills an animal for the mere sake of killing, unless it is a harmful creature.

A good story is told of a soldier in the South African War who killed a harmless animal, namely a sheep, when the order had been given out that nobody was to kill any animal except a 'savage wild beast'.

But the soldier wanted some mutton, and he found a sheep round at the back of a house; so he started to make it into mutton with his bayonet. Just as he was doing so an officer happened to come round the corner. The soldier saw the danger that he was in for disobeying the order, but he did not lose his head. Pretending not to see the officer, he again plunged his bayonet into the wretched sheep, shouting at the same time, 'Ah, you would bite me, would you? You "savage wild beast"!'*

By continually watching animals in their natural state one gets to like them too well to shoot them.

The whole sport of hunting animals lies in the woodcraft of stalking them, not in the killing.

Woodcraft includes, besides being able to see the tracks and other small signs, the power to read their meaning, such as at what pace the animal was going, whether he was frightened or unsuspicious, and so on. It enables the hunter also to find his way in the jungle or desert; it teaches him which are the best wild fruits, roots, etc., for his own food, or which are favourite food for animals, and, therefore, likely to attract them.

In the same way in scouting in civilised countries you read the tracks of men, horses, bicycles, etc., and find out from these what has been going on; noticing by small signs, such as birds suddenly starting up, that someone is moving near, though you cannot see them.

By noticing little things on the ground you will often find lost articles, which you can then restore to their owners.

By noticing details of harness, and so on, you can often save a horse from the pain of an ill-fitting strap or bit.

By noticing the behaviour or dress of people, and putting this and that together, you can sometimes see that they are up to no good, and can thus prevent a crime, or you can often tell when they are in distress and need help or sympathy—and you can then do what is one of the chief duties of a scout, namely, help those in distress in any possible way that you can.

Remember that it is a disgrace to a scout if, when he is with other people, they see anything big or little, near or far, high or low, that he has not already seen for himself.

Kim, when learning to be scout, was taught to notice small things quickly and to remember them, by being shown a tray full of small articles for a few moments and then having to state what he had seen.

[*Play Kim's game.* *See pages 48–9.*]

CAMPAIGNING.—Scouts must, of course, be accustomed to living in the open; they have to know how to put up tents or huts for themselves; how to lay and light a fire; how to kill, cut up, and cook their food; how to tie logs together to make bridges and rafts; how to find their way by night, as well as by day, in a strange country, and so on.

But very few fellows learn or practise these things when they are living in civilised places because they get comfortable houses and beds to sleep in, their food is prepared and cooked for them, and when they want to know the way 'they ask a policeman'.

Well, when those fellows go out to a colony, or try to go scouting, they find themselves helpless duffers.

Take even the captain of your cricket eleven and put him down on the South African veldt alongside the young Colonial,* and see which can look after himself. High averages and clean flannels are not much good to him there. He is only a 'tenderfoot',* and would be the object of continual chaff until he got some scoutcraft into him.

And scoutcraft, mind you, comes in useful in any line of life that you like to take up. Cricket doesn't matter a hang—though it is a jolly good game to play, and comes in useful to a certain extent in training a fellow's eye, nerve, and temper. But, as the American would say, 'it isn't a circumstance' to scouting which teaches a fellow to be a man.*

[*Make each boy lay a fire in his own way and light it. After failures, show them the right way (i.e., delicate use of dry chips and shavings, and sticks in a pyramid), and make them do it again. Also teach them how to tie knots. See Part III.*]

Chivalry.—In the old days the knights were the scouts of Britain,* and their rules were very much the same as the scout law which we have now. And very much like what the Japs* have, too. We are their descendants, and we ought to keep up their good name and follow in their steps.

They considered that their honour was the most sacred thing to uphold; they would not do a dishonourable thing, such as telling a lie or stealing: they would really rather die than do it. They were always ready to fight and to be killed in upholding their king, or their religion, or their honour. Thousands of them went out to Palestine (the Holy Land) to maintain the Christian religion against the Mahommedan Turks.

Each knight had a small following of a squire and some men-at-arms, just as our patrol leader has his corporal and four or five scouts.

The knight's patrol used to stick to him through thick and thin, and all carried out the same idea as their leader —namely:

Their honour was sacred.
They were loyal to God, and their king, and to their country.
They were particularly courteous and polite to all women and children and infirm people.
They were helpful to everybody.
They gave money and food where it was wanted and saved up their money in order to do so.
They taught themselves the use of arms in order to protect their religion and their country against enemies.
They kept themselves strong and healthy and active in order to be able to do these things well.

You scouts cannot do better than follow the example of your forefathers, the knights, who made the tiny British nation* into one of the best and greatest that the world has ever known:

One great point about them was that every day they had to do a good turn to somebody, and that is one of our rules. When you get up in the morning remember that you have got to do a good turn to someone during the day; tie a knot in your handkerchief or necktie, and leave the tail of your necktie outside your waistcoat to remind yourself of it; and when you go to bed at night think who you did the good turn to.

If you should ever find that you had forgotten to do it, you must do two good turns the next day instead. Remember that by your scout's oath you are on your honour to do it.

A good turn need only be a very small one; if it is only to put a halfpenny into a poor box, or to help an old woman to cross the street, or to make room on a seat for someone, or to give water to a thirsty horse, or to remove a bit of banana skin off the pavement where it is likely to throw people down, it is a good turn. But one must be done every day, and it only counts as a good when you do not accept any reward in return.

[*Make each scout tie a knot in his necktie to remind him to do a good turn next day.*]

SAVING LIFE.—You have all heard of the Victoria Cross—the little bronze cross given by Queen Victoria to soldiers who specially distinguish themselves in action under the fire of the enemy.

But there is the companion medal to it, and that is the Albert

A Boy Scout's necktie

Medal for those who are not soldiers, and who distinguish themselves in saving life in peace time.

And I think the man who wins this medal, as he does in the sudden appalling accidents which occur in big cities, mines, and factories, in everyday life, is no less a hero than the soldier who rushes into the thick of the fight to rescue a comrade amid all the excitement and glamour of the battle.

My great hope is that many of you scouts will in time to come win for yourselves the high honour of receiving the Albert Medal.

It is certain that very many of you will at one time or another get the chance of it if you are prepared to seize the opportunity. That is, you must *be prepared* for it; you should know what to do the moment an accident occurs—and do it then and there.

It is not enough to read about it in a book and think that you know how to do it—but you must actually practise, and practise pretty often, the actual things to be done; such as how to cover your mouth and nose with a wet handkerchief to enable you to breath in smoke, how to tear a sheet into strips and make a rope for escaping from fire,* how to open a manhole to let air into a gassy sewer, how to lift and carry an insensible person, how to collar, save, and revive apparently drowned people, and so on.

When you have learnt all these things you will have confidence in yourself, so that when an accident happens and everybody is in a state of fluster, not knowing what to do, you will quietly step out and do the right thing.

Remember the case at the Hampstead Ponds last year when a woman drowned herself in shallow water before a whole lot of men, who were too frightened to do anything but shout to her. It was a disgrace to our nation that there was not a real man amongst them. It would have been a grand opportunity for a Boy Scout, had there been one there, to go in and fetch her out. As it was, these cowards stood there clamouring and chattering on the bank—not one of them daring to go in because the others did not. And she was drowned before their eyes.

[*Teach the scouts how to lift and carry an insensible man. Also how to drag an insensible man through smoke, gas, etc. Also how to cover nose and mouth with wet handkerchief. Divide them off into pairs, and let each in turn act as insensible patient to be rescued by his comrade.*]

ENDURANCE.—To carry out all the duties and work of a scout properly a fellow has to be strong, healthy, and active. And he can make himself so if he takes a little care about it.

It means a lot of exercise, like playing games, running, walking, cycling, and so on.

A scout has to sleep very much in the open, and a boy who is accustomed to sleep with his window shut will probably suffer, like many a tenderfoot has done, by catching cold and rheumatism when he first tries sleeping out. The thing is always to sleep with your windows open, summer and winter, and you will never catch cold. Personally I cannot sleep with my window shut or with blinds down, and when living in the country I always sleep outside the house, summer and winter alike. A soft bed and too many blankets make a boy dream bad dreams, which weaken him.*

A short go of Swedish or ju-jitsu exercises* every morning and evening is a grand thing for keeping you fit—not so much for making showy muscle as to work all your internal organs [*Explain*], and to work up the circulation of the blood in every part of you.

A good rub-down* daily with a wet rough towel, even if you cannot get a bath, which of course is preferable, is of the utmost importance.

Scouts breathe through the nose,* not through the mouth; in this way they don't get thirsty; they don't get out of breath so quickly; they don't suck into their insides all sorts of microbes or seeds of disease that are in the air; and they don't snore at night, and so give themselves away to an enemy.

'Deep breathing' exercises are of great value for developing the lungs, and for putting fresh air (oxygen) into the blood, provided that they are carried out in the open air, and are not overdone so as to injure the heart, etc. For deep breathing the breath must be taken in slowly and deeply through the nose, not through the mouth, till it opens out the ribs to the greatest extent, especially at the back; then, after a time it should be slowly and steadily breathed out again without strain. But the best deep breathing after all is that which comes naturally from plenty of running exercise.

Alcohol is now shown to be quite useless as a health-giving drink, and it is mere poison when a man takes much of it. A man who is in the habit of drinking wine or spirits in strong doses every day is not the slightest use for scouting, and very little use for anything else.

Similarly a man who smokes much. The best war scouts don't smoke because it weakens their eyesight; it sometimes makes them shaky and nervous; it spoils their noses for smelling (which is of great importance at night), and the glow of their pipe, or even the scent of tobacco carried on them at night gives them away to watchful enemies. They are not such fools as to smoke. No boy ever began smoking because he liked it, but because he thought it made him look like a grown-up man. As a matter of fact it generally makes him look a little ass.

[*Show ju-jitsu or Swedish extension motions—one or two exercises only to begin with. Also deep breathing.*]

PATRIOTISM.—You belong to the Great British Empire, one of the greatest empires that has ever existed in the world.

[*Show on the map.*]

From this little island of Great Britain have sprung colonies all over the world, Australia, New Zealand, South Africa, India, Canada.

Almost every race, every kind of man, black, white, or yellow, in the world furnishes subjects of King Edward VII.*

This vast empire did not grow of itself out of nothing; it was made by your forefathers by dint of hard work and hard fighting, at the sacrifice of their lives—that is, by their hearty patriotism.

People say that we have no patriotism nowadays, and that

HOW TO FLY BRITAIN'S FLAG

Right way up

Upside down

HOW NOT TO FLY BRITAIN'S FLAG

therefore our empire will fall to pieces like the great Roman empire* did, because its citizens became selfish and lazy, and only cared for amusements. I am not so sure about that. I am sure that if you boys will keep the good of your country in your eyes *above everything else* she will go on all right. But if you don't do this there is very great danger, because we have many enemies abroad, and they are growing daily stronger and stronger.

Therefore, in all that you do, remember to think of your country first; don't spend the whole of your time and money on games and tuck shops merely to amuse *yourself*, but think first how you can be of use in helping your empire, and when you have done that you can justly and honestly sit down and enjoy yourself in your own way.

'Country first, self second', should be your motto. Probably, if you ask yourself truly, you will find you have at present got them just the other way about.

I hope if it is so that you will from this moment put yourself right and remain so always. Patriot first, player second. Don't be content, like the Romans were, and some people now are, to pay other people to play your football or to fight your battles for you. Do something yourself to help in keeping the flag flying.

If you take up scouting in that spirit you will be doing something; take it up, not merely beause it amuses you, but because by doing so you will be fitting yourself to help your country. Then you will have in you the true spirit of patriotism, which every British boy ought to have if he is worth his salt.

[*Show the Union Jack. Explain its history and composition, and which is the right way for flying it. (See Part V.)*]

WINTER'S STOB; OR, THE ELSDON MURDER

[*Note: The following story, which in the main is true, is a sample of a story that should be given by the Instructor illustrating generally the duties of a Boy Scout.*]

A BRUTAL murder* took place many years ago in the North of England; and the murderer was caught, convicted, and hanged chiefly through the scoutcraft of a shepherd boy.

WOODCRAFT.—The boy, Robert Hindmarsh, had been up on the moor tending his sheep, and was finding his way home over a wild, out-of-the-way part of the hills, when he passed a tramp sitting on

Observing the murderer's boots

the ground with his legs stretched out in front of him eating some food.

Observation.—The boy in passing noticed his appearance, and especially the peculiar nails in the soles of his boots.

Concealment.—He did not stop and stare, but just took these things in at a glance as he went by without attracting much attention from the man, who merely regarded him as an ordinary boy not worth his notice.

Deduction.—When he got near home, some five or six miles away, he came to a crowd round a cottage, where they had found the old woman (Margaret Crozier) who had inhabited it lying murdered. All sorts of guesses were being hazarded as to who had done the deed, and suspicion seemed to centre on a small gang of three or four gipsies who were going about the country robbing and threatening death to anyone who made any report of their misdeeds.

The boy heard all these things, but presently he saw some

peculiar footprints in the little garden of the cottage; the nailmarks agreed with those he had seen in the boots of the man on the moor, and he naturally deduced from these that the man might have something to do with the murder.

Chivalry.—The fact that it was a helpless old woman who had been murdered made the boy's chivalrous feelings rise against the murderer, whoever it might be.

Pluck and Self-discipline, Alacrity.—So, although he knew that the friends of the murderer might kill him for giving information, he cast his fears on one side and went at once and told the constable of the footmarks in the garden, and where he could find the man who had made them—if he went immediately.

Health and Strength.—The man up on the moor had got so far from the scene of the murder, unseen (except by this one small boy), that he thought himself safe, and never thought of the boy being able to walk all the way to the scene of the murder and then to come back, as he did, with the police. So he took no precautions.

But the boy was a strong, healthy hill-boy, and did the journey rapidly and well, so that they found the man and captured him without difficulty.

The man was Willie Winter, a gipsy.

He was tried, found guilty, and hanged at Newcastle. His body was then brought and hung on a gibbet near the scene of the murder, as was the custom in those days, and the gibbet still stands to this day. Two of the gipsies who were his accomplices were caught with some of the stolen property, and were also executed at Newcastle.

Kind-heartedness.—But when the boy saw the murderer's body hanging there on the gibbet he was overcome with misery at having caused the death of a fellow-creature.

Saving Life.—However, the magistrate sent for him and complimented him on the great good he had done to his fellow-countrymen—probably saving some of their lives—by ridding the world of such a dangerous criminal.

Duty.—He said: 'You have done your duty although it caused

The gibbet at Stang's Cross

you personally some danger and much distress. Still you must not mind that—it was your duty to the King to help the police in getting justice done, and duty must always be carried out regardless of how much it costs you, even if you had to give up your life.'

EXAMPLE.—Thus the boy did every part of the duty of a boy scout without ever having been taught.

He exercised—

Woodcraft.
Observation without being noticed.
Deduction.
Chivalry.
Sense of duty.
Endurance.
Kind-heartedness.

He little thought that the act which he did entirely of his own accord would years afterwards be held up as an example to you other boys in teaching you to do your duty. In the same way you should remember your acts may be watched by others after you, and taken as an example too. So try to do your duty the right way on all occasions.

Since writing down the above story I have visited the place, Stang's Cross, where the gibbet, with a wooden head hanging from it, still stands as a warning to evildoers. Some foolish people used to believe that toothache could be cured by rubbing the teeth with chips of wood cut from this gibbet, and used to come from miles round to get them. Mrs Haldane, the mother of our present Secretary of State for War,* remembers seeing the effigy of Winter hanging on the gibbet, and recalls with horror the doleful rattling of the chains on which it swung in the night wind on the lonely moor. The gibbet is known as 'Winter's Stob'.

Winter belonged to a notable family. He was not the only one who distinguished himself, for his father and his brother were also hanged for different offences. Another brother, feeling the disgrace of belonging to such a family, changed his name from Winter to Spring, and became—a prize-fighter.

CAMP FIRE YARN.—No. 3

BOY SCOUTS' ORGANISATION

It is not intended that boy scouts should necessarily form a new corps separate from all others, but the boys who belong to any kind of existing organisation, such as schools, football clubs, Boys' or Church Lads' Brigades, factories, district messengers, Telegraph Service, Cadet Corps, etc., etc., can *also* take up scouting in addition to their other work or play*—especially on Saturdays and Sundays.

But where there are any boys who do not belong to any kind of organisation—and there is a very large number of such boys about the United Kingdom—they can form themselves into Patrols and become Boy Scouts.

For this purpose officers are necessary.

Officers: The head officer of all the boy scouts in the world is called the *Chief Scout*.

A Scout Master is an officer who has charge of a troop. A troop consists of not less than three patrols. Scouts address the scout master as 'Sir'.

A Patrol Leader is a scout appointed to command a patrol. A patrol consists of six scouts. Any lad or young man who learns scouting from this book can make himself a patrol leader and collect and train five or seven boys to be scouts.

A Corporal is a scout selected by the patrol leader to be his assistant, and to take command of the patrol when he himself is away.

A Scout is of two kinds—first-class and second-class. First-class scout is one who has passed certain tests to show that he is able to scout.

Second-class scout is one who has passed certain easy tests in scouting.

A Tenderfoot is a boy who is not yet a scout.

A Court of Honour is formed of the scout master and two patrol leaders, or in the case of a single patrol by the patrol leader and the corporal. It decides rewards, punishments, and other questions.

Tests: To become a second-class scout and gain the motto badge, a boy must satisfy his scout master in the following details:

1. Tie four of the following knots in less than thirty seconds each knot: Bowline, fisherman's bend, reef knot, clove hitch, sheet bend.
2. Track a deer's 'spoor' (made with tracking irons) or a horse's track for a quarter of a mile in not more than fifteen minutes; or, in a town, to describe satisfactorily the contents of one shop window out of four observed for one minute each.
3. Go at scout's pace for one mile in not more than thirteen minutes.
4. Know the scout's laws and signs.
5. Know the composition of the Union Jack, and the right way to fly it.

To become a first-class scout and gain the whole scout's badge, a boy must pass the following test—in addition to those for second-class scout (above)—before a Court of Honour. (*N.B.*—In the case of a new troop the Scout Master can act as the Court of Honour.)

6. Point out the direction of different points of the compass where he stands.
7. Make a journey alone of not less than fifteen miles from point to point by walking, riding, boat, or bicycle.
8. Describe or show the proper means for saving life in case of one (selected by the Court) of the following accidents: fire, drowning, runaway carriage, sewer gas, ice-breaking; or bandage an injured patient, or revive apparently drowned persons.
9. Be able to read and write.
10. Have at least sixpence in the savings bank.
11. Show that he has brought a recruit to the Boy Scouts, and has taught him to tie the six principal knots.
12. To lay and light a fire, using not more than two matches, and cook a quarter of a pound of flour and two potatoes without cooking utensils.

Badges and Medals: The scout's badge is this:

Scout's badge

The scout's badge is the arrow head, which shows the north on a map or on the compass. It is the badge of the scout in the Army, because he shows the way: so, too, a peace scout shows the way in doing his duty and helping others.*

The motto on it is the scout's motto of

BE PREPARED

(B. P., my initials*), which means that a scout must always be prepared at any moment to do his duty, and to face danger in order to help his fellow-men. Its scroll is turned up at the ends like a scout's mouth, because he does his duty with a smile and willingly.

The knot is to remind the scout to do a good turn to some one daily.

A scout's badge represents and is called his 'life'. It is given him when he passes the tests in scout-craft necessary to make him a scout.

He will be called on at some time or the other to risk his life, that is to perform some difficult task, and if he fails in it he loses his life—that is his badge. In such case a Court of Honour may allow him to remain in the patrol, but he cannot have his badge again, unless he performs some very specially good work.

If he breaks his word of honour, or otherwise disgraces himself, his life is taken (that is his badge), and he is expelled from the patrol.

The badge is worn by scout masters on the left side of the hat or cap.

The badge is worn by patrol leaders on front of the hat or cap.

The badge is worn by corporal on the left arm above elbow with a strip of white braid below it.

The badge worn by scouts on the left arm above the elbow.

The badge worn by first-class scouts is the whole badge.

Only the motto part of the badge is worn by second-class scouts.

Badges of Honour are also given for certain tests. These are worn on the right arm below the elbow.

Signalling: ability to read and send Morse or semaphore message, twenty letters a minute.
First Aid: for passing the St John Ambulance tests in First Aid.
Stalking: series of twelve photos of wild animals taken from life by the scout and developed and printed by himself.
Merit: for twenty good marks for various good deeds.

Medals are worn on the right breast, and are as follows:

Bronze medal with red ribbon: For gallantry in saving life, or attempting to save life at risk of own life.

Silver medal with red ribbon: For saving and helping to save life without risk of own life, but where life might have been lost.

Silver medal with blue ribbon: Meritorious service, or assisting police at personal risk.

These are only granted by the chief scout on special recommendation from the patrol leader or scout master, who should send in a full account of the case when applying.

Marks are awarded by scout masters, from their own knowledge or on recommendation of patrol leaders, or as marks for competition.

Two marks are given to any scout who brings a recruit whom he has already taught to tie the regulation knots. Such recruit must be in addition to the one who enabled him to qualify for his scout's badge.

'*The Wolf*'.—The Red Indians of North America call their best scout 'Grey Wolf', because the grey wolf is a beast that sees everything and yet is never seen.

And the fighting tribes in South Africa* in the same way speak of a scout as a wolf.

In the Matabele War, 1896–1897, the enemy called me 'The Wolf'* for that reason.

Mr Thompson Seton,* the head of the 'Red Indian' Boy Scouts in America, is called 'Grey Wolf'.

So in the Boy Scouts a special badge and title of 'Wolf' will be given as a reward for very special distinction in scouting; not more than one will be granted in a year.

All medals and badges are only worn as above when scouts are on duty or in camp. At other times they should be worn on the right breast of the waistcoat, underneath the jacket.

A small arrow-head badge may be worn at all times in the buttonhole.

THE SCOUT'S OATH

Before he becomes a scout a boy must take the scout's oath, thus:

'On my honour I promise that—

1. I will do my duty to God and the King.
2. I will do my best to help others, whatever it costs me.
3. I know the scout law, and will obey it.'

(For Scout Law, see page 44.)

While taking this oath the scout will stand, holding his right hand raised level with his shoulder, palm to the front, thumb resting on the nail of the little finger, and the other three fingers upright, pointing upwards:—

Scout's salute and secret sign

This is the scout's salute and secret sign.

When the hand is raised shoulder high it is called the 'Half Salute.'

When raised to the forehead it is the 'Full Salute'.

SCOUT'S SALUTE AND SECRET SIGN

The three fingers held up (like the three points of the scout's badge) remind him of his three promises in the scout's oath.

1. Honour God and the King.
2. Help others.
3. Obey the Scout Law.

When a scout meets another for the first time in the day, whether he is a comrade or a stranger, he salutes with the secret sign in the half salute.

He always salutes an officer—that is, a patrol leader, or a scout master, or any officer of His Majesty's forces, army, navy, or police in uniform—with the full salute.

Also the hoisting of the Union Jack, the colours of a regiment, the playing of 'God Save the King', and any funeral.

A scout who has the 'Wolf' honour is entitled to make the sign with the first finger and thumb opened out, the remaining fingers clenched, thumb upwards.

A man told me the other day that 'he was an Englishman, and just as good as anybody else, and he was blowed if ever he would raise a finger to salute his so-called "betters": he wasn't going to be a slave and kow-tow to them, not he!' and so on. That is a churlish spirit, which is very common among fellows who have not been brought up as scouts.

I didn't argue with him, but I might have told him that he had got hold of the wrong idea about saluting.

A salute is merely a sign between men of standing. It is a privilege to be able to salute anyone.

In the old days the free men of England all were allowed to carry weapons, and when they met each other each would hold up his right hand to show that he had no weapon in it, and that they met as friends. So also when an armed man met a defenceless person or a lady.

Slaves or serfs were not allowed to carry weapons, and so had to slink past the freemen without making any sign.

Nowadays people do not carry weapons; but those who would have been entitled to do so, such as knights, esquires, and men-at-arms, that is anyone living on their own property or earning their own living, still go through the form of saluting each other by holding up their hand to their cap, or even taking it off.

'Wasters' are not entitled to salute, and so should slink by, as they generally do, without taking notice of the free men or wage-earners.

To salute merely shows that you are a right sort of fellow and mean well to the other; there is nothing slavish about it.*

If a stranger makes the scout's sign to you, you should acknowledge it at once by making the sign back to him, and then shake hands with the LEFT HAND. If he then shows his scout's badge, or proves that he is a scout, you must treat him as a brother-scout, and help him in any way you can.

SCOUT'S UNIFORM

If you already belong to a corps which has a uniform, you dress in that uniform; but on passing the tests for a scout given here you wear the scout badge, if your commanding officer allows it, in addition to any of your corps' badges that you may have won.

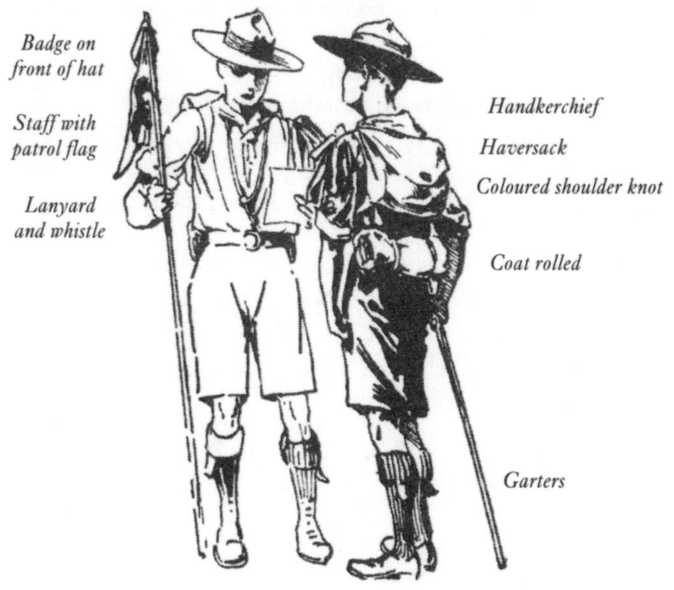

SCOUT'S UNIFORM
Patrol leader with scout

A scout does not use a showy uniform, because it would attract attention; but scouts in a patrol should, as far as possible, dress alike, especially as regards hats, or caps, and neckerchief.

If your patrol does not belong to any uniformed corps, it should dress as nearly as possible thus:

Flat brimmed hat if possible, or wide-awake hat.
Coloured handkerchief tied loosely round neck.
Shirt: Flannel.
Colours: A bunch of ribbons of patrol colour on left shoulder.
Belt, with coat rolled tight and strapped or tied on to it behind.
Haversack: To carry food, etc., slung on back across the shoulders.
Shorts: Trousers cut short at knee. A kilt if you are a Scotsman.
Stockings, with garters made of green braid, with one end hanging down one inch.
Boots or shoes.

Staff as high as scout's shoulder. Not shod, as it is for feeling the way at night quietly.

Badge on left arm above elbow.

Whistle, with cord round neck for patrol leader.

N.B.—The colour of the neckerchief, or necktie and shoulder knot, should be the colour of the patrol.

Corporal has a white stripe of braid three inches long stitched across his sleeve below the badge.

SCOUT'S WAR SONGS

1. *The Scout's Chorus.**

To be shouted on the march, or as applause at games, meetings, etc. Must be sung exactly in time.

Leader: Een gonyâma—gonyâma.
Chorus: Invooboo.
Yah bôbô! Yah bô!
Invooboo.

The meaning is—

Leader: 'He is a lion!'
Chorus: 'Yes! he is better than that; he is a hippopotamus!'

THE SCOUT'S CHORUS

2. *The Scout's Rally.*

To be shouted as a salute, or in a game, or at any time.

Leader: Be Prepared!
Chorus: Zing-a-Zing!
Bom! Bom!

(Stamp or bang something at the 'Bom! Bom!')

THE SCOUT'S RALLY

THE SCOUT'S CALL

For scout master to call together his troop by bugle; or for scout to whistle to attract attention of another scout.

PATROL SIGNS*

Each troop is named after the place to which it belongs. Each patrol in that troop is named after an animal or bird. Thus the 33rd London Troop may have five patrols which are respectively the Wolves, the Ravens, the Curlews, the Bulls, the Owls.

Each scout in a patrol has his regular number, the patrol leader being No. 1, the corporal No. 2, and the scouts have the consecutive numbers after these. Scouts usually work in pairs as comrades, Nos. 3 and 4 together, Nos. 5 and 6 together, and Nos. 7 and 8.

A white shoulder knot is worn by Officers and Umpires at games.

Each scout in the patrol has to be able to make the call of his patrol-animal—thus every scout in the 'Ravens' must be able to imitate the croak of the raven. This is the sign by which scouts of a patrol can communicate with each other when hiding or at night. No scout is allowed to imitate the call of any patrol except his own. The patrol leader calls up the patrol at any time by sounding his whistle and uttering the call of the patrol.

Also when a scout makes signs on the ground for others to read he also draws the head of the patrol animal. Thus if he wants to show that a certain road should not be followed he draws the sign across it 'Not to be followed', and adds the head of his patrol animal to show which patrol discovered that the road was no good, and his own

SIGNS AND CALLS OF DIFFERENT PATROLS

SIGN	NAME	CALL	COLOURS
	Curlew	*Whistle—* *'Curley'*	Green
	Owl	*Whistle—* *'Koot-koot-koot'*	Blue
	Wolf	*Howl—* *'How-oooo'*	Yellow and black
	Bull	*Lowing—* *'Um-maouw'*	Red
	Raven	*Cry—* *'Kar-kaw'*	Black
	Hound	*Bark—* *'Ba-wow-wow'*	Orange
	Ram	*Bleat—* *'Ba-a-a'*	Brown

number to the left of the head to show which scout discovered it, thus:

Each patrol leader has a small white flag on his staff with the head of his patrol animal shown in green cloth stitched on to it on both sides. Thus the 'Wolves'* of the 1st London Troop would have the flag shown below.

[*Patrol flags can be got on payment of fourpence each by applying to: The Manager, Boy Scouts, Goschen Buildings, Henrietta Street, London, W.C.*]

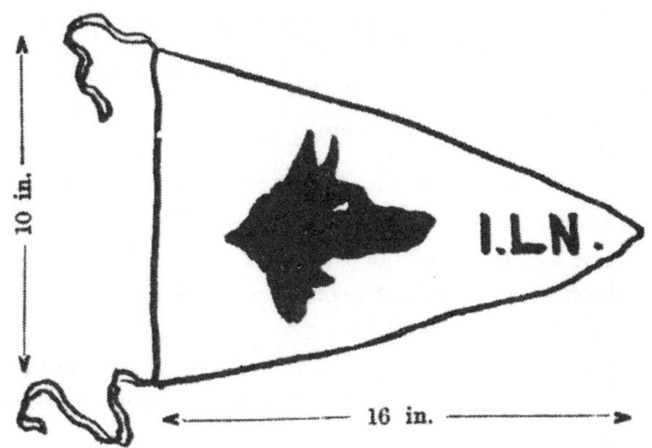

Patrol leader's flag of 'The Wolves Patrol' of the 1st London Troop

All these signs scouts must be able to draw according to the patrol to which they belong.

[*Practise with chalk on floor or walls, or with a stick on the sand or mud.*]

Scout signs on the ground or wall, etc.:

Road to be followed.
Letter hidden three paces from here in the direction of the arrow.
This path not to be followed.
'I have gone home.'
(Signed) Patrol Leader of the Ravens Fifteenth London Troop.

At night sticks with a wisp of grass round them should be laid on the road in similar forms so that they can be felt with the hand.

[*Practise this.*]

CAMP FIRE YARN.—No. 4

SCOUT LAW

SCOUTS, all the world over, have unwritten laws which bind them just as much as if they had been printed in black and white.

They come down to us from old times.

The Japanese have their Bushido, or laws of the old Samurai warriors, just as we have chivalry or rules of the knights of the Middle Ages. The Red Indians in America have their laws of honour, the Zulus, the natives of India, the European nations—all have their ancient codes.*

The following are the rules which apply to Boy Scouts, and which you swear to obey when you take your oath as a scout, so it is as well that you should know all about them.

The scouts' motto is founded on my initials, it is:

BE PREPARED,

which means, you are always to be in a state of readiness in mind and body to do your DUTY;

Be Prepared in Mind by having disciplined yourself to be obedient to every order, and also by having thought out beforehand any accident or situation that might occur, so that you *know* the right thing to do at the right moment, and are willing to do it.

Be Prepared in Body by making yourself strong and active and *able* to do the right thing at the right moment, and do it.

THE SCOUT LAW*

1. A SCOUT'S HONOUR IS TO BE TRUSTED.

If a scout says 'On my honour it is so,' that means that it *is* so, just as if he had taken a most solemn oath.

Similarly, if a scout officer says to a scout, 'I trust you on your honour to do this,' the scout is bound to carry out the order to the very best of his ability, and to let nothing interfere with his doing so.

If a scout were to break his honour by telling a lie, or by not carrying out an order exactly when trusted on his honour to do so, he would cease to be a scout, and must hand over his scout badge, and never be allowed to wear it again—he loses his life.

2. A Scout is Loyal to the King, and to his officers, and to his country, and to his employers. He must stick to them through thick and thin against anyone who is their enemy, or who even talks badly of them.

3. A Scout's Duty is to be Useful and to Help Others.

And he is to do his duty before anything else, even though he gives up his own pleasure, or comfort, or safety to do it. When in difficulty to know which of two things to do, he must ask himself, 'Which is my duty?' that is, 'Which is best for other people?'—and do that one. He must Be Prepared at any time to save life, or to help injured persons. And *he must do a good turn* to somebody every day.

4. A Scout is a Friend to All, and a Brother to Every Other Scout, no matter to what Social Class the Other belongs.

Thus if a scout meets another scout, even though a stranger to him, he must speak to him, and help him in any way that he can, either to carry out the duty he is then doing, or by giving him food, or, as far as possible, anything that he may be in want of. A scout must never be a snob. A snob is one who looks down upon another because he is poorer, or who is poor and resents another because he is rich. A scout accepts the other man as he finds him, and makes the best of him.

'Kim', the boy scout, was called by the Indians 'Little friend of all the world,'* and that is the name that every scout should earn for himself.

5. A Scout is Courteous: That is, he is polite to all—but especially to women and children and old people and invalids, cripples, etc. And he must not take any reward for being helpful or courteous.

6. A Scout is a Friend to Animals. He should save them as far as possible from pain, and should not kill any animal unnecessarily, even if it is only a fly—for it is one of God's creatures.

7. A Scout Obeys Orders of his patrol leader or scout master without question.

Even if he gets an order he does not like he must do as soldiers and sailors do, he must carry it out all the same *because it is his duty;*

and after he has done it he can come and state any reasons against it: but he must must carry out the order at once. That is discipline.

8. A Scout Smiles and Whistles under all circumstances. When he gets an order he should obey it cheerily and readily, not in a slow, hang-dog sort of way.

Scouts never* grouse at hardships, nor whine at each other, nor swear when put out.

When you just miss a train, or some one treads on your favourite corn—not that a scout ought to have such things as corns—or under any annoying circumstances, you should force yourself to smile at once, and then whistle a tune, and you will be all right.

A scout goes about with a smile on and whistling. It cheers him and cheers other people, especially in time of danger, for he keeps it up then all the same.

The punishment for swearing or using bad language is for each offence a mug of cold water to be poured down the offender's sleeve by the other scouts.

9. A Scout is Thrifty, that is, he saves every penny he can, and puts it into the bank, so that he may have money to keep himself when out of work, and thus not make himself a burden to others; or that he may have money to give away to others when they need it.

SCOUTING GAMES

For Winter in the Country

ARCTIC EXPEDITION

Each patrol makes a bob sleigh with ropes, harness, for two of their number to pull (or for dogs if they have them, and can train them to the work). Two scouts go a mile or so ahead, the remainder with the sleigh follow, finding the way by means of the spoor, and by such signs as the leading scouts may draw in the snow. All other drawings seen on the way are to be examined, noted, and their meaning read. The sleigh carries rations and cooking-pots, etc.

Build snow huts. These must be made narrow, according to the length of sticks available for forming the roof, which can be made with brushwood, and covered with snow.

SNOW FORT

The snow fort may be built by one patrol according to their own ideas of fortification, with loop holes, etc., for looking out. When finished it will be attacked by hostile patrols, using snowballs as ammunition. Every scout struck by a snowball is counted dead. The attackers should, as a rule, number at least twice the strength of the defenders.

SIBERIAN MAN HUNT

One scout as fugitive runs away across the snow in any direction he may please until he finds a good hiding place, and there conceals himself. The remainder, after giving him twenty minutes' start or more, proceed to follow him by his tracks. As they approach his hiding-place, he shoots at them with snowballs, and everyone that is struck must fall out dead. The fugitive must be struck three times before he is counted dead.

In Towns

Scouts can be very useful in snowy weather by working as a patrol under their leader in clearing away the snow from pavements, houses, etc. This they may either do as a 'good turn', or accept money to be devoted to their funds.

SCOUT MEETS SCOUT

In Town or Country

Single scouts, or complete patrols or pairs of scouts, to be taken out about two miles apart, and made to work towards each other, either alongside a road, or by giving each side a landmark to work to, such as a steep hill or big tree, which is directly behind the other party, and will thus ensure their coming together. The patrol which first sees the other wins. This is signified by the patrol leader holding up his patrol flag for the umpire to see, and sounding his whistle. A patrol need not keep together, but that patrol wins which first holds out its flag, so it is well for the scouts to be in touch with their patrol leaders by signal, voice, or message.

Scouts may employ any ruse they like, such as climbing into trees, hiding in carts, etc., but they must not dress up in disguise.

This may also be practised at night.

DISPATCH RUNNERS

A SCOUT is sent out to take note of some well-known spot, say, the post office in a neighbouring town or district. He will there get the note stamped with the post mark of the office and return. The rest of the scouts are posted by their leader to prevent him getting there by watching all the roads and likely paths by which he can come, but none may be nearer to the post office than two hundred yards. The dispatch runner is allowed to use any disguise and any method of travelling that he can hit upon.

In the country the game may similarly be played, the scout being directed to go to a certain house or other specified spot.

KIM'S GAME*

PLACE about twenty or thirty small articles on a tray, or on the table or floor, such as two or three different kinds of buttons, pencils, corks, rags, nuts, stones, knives, string, photos—anything you can find—and cover them over with a cloth or coat.

Make a list of these, and make a column opposite the list for each boy's replies. Like this:

List	*Jones*	*Brown*	*Smith*	*Atkins*	*Green*	*Long*
Walnut						
Button						
Black button						
Red rag						
Yellow rag						
Black rag						
Knife						
Red pencil						
Black pencil						
Cork						
String knot						
Plain string						
Blue bead						

Then uncover the articles for one minute by your watch, or while you count sixty at the rate of 'quick march'. Then cover them over again.

Take each boy separately and let him whisper to you each of the articles that he can remember, and mark it off on your scoring sheet.

The boy who remembers the greatest numbers wins the game.

MORGAN'S GAME

(Played by the 21st Dublin Co. Boys' Brigade.)

In Town

Scouts are ordered to run to a certain hoarding where an umpire is already posted to time them. They are each allowed to look at this for one minute, and then to run back to headquarters and report to the instructor all that was on the hoarding in the way of advertisements.

DEBATES, TRIALS, ETC.

A good exercise for a winter's evening in the clubroom is to hold a debate on any subject of topical interest, the Instructor acting as chairman. He will see that there is a speaker on one side prepared before hand to introduce and support one view of the subject, and that there is another speaker prepared to expound another view. After hearing them, he will call on the others present in turn to express their views. And in the end he takes the votes for and against the motion.

At first boys will be very shy of speaking unless the subject selected by the Instructor is one which really interests them and takes them out of themselves.

After a debate or two they get greater confidence, and are able to express themselves coherently; and also pick up the proper procedure for public meetings, such as seconding the motion, moving amendments, obeying chairman's ruling, voting, according votes of thanks to chair—etc., etc.

In place of a debate a mock trial may be of interest as a change.

For instance, the story of the murder given in Part I might form the subject of trial.

The Instructor would appoint himself to act the judge, and detail boys to the following parts:

Prisoner . . William Winter.
Witness . . Boy, Robert Hindmarsh.
" . . Police Constable.
" . . Villager.
" . . Old woman (friend of the murdered woman).
Counsel for prisoner.
" " prosecution.
Foreman and jury (if there are enough scouts).

Follow as nearly as possible the procedure of a court of law. Let each make up his own evidence, speeches, or cross-examination according to his own notions and imagination, the evidence to be made up on the lines of the story, but in greater detail. Do not necessarily find the prisoner guilty unless the prosecution prove their case to the jury.

In your summing up bring out the fact of the boy (Hindmarsh) having carried out each part of the duty of a scout, in order to bring home its lesson to the boys.

SCOUT'S WAR DANCE*

SCOUTS form up in one line with leader in front, each holding his staff in the right hand, and his left on the next man's shoulder.

Leader sings the Ingonyama song. Scouts sing chorus, and advance to their front a few steps at a time, stamping in unison on the long notes.

At the second time of singing they step backwards.

At the third, they turn to the left, still holding each other's shoulders, and move round in a large circle, repeating the chorus until they have completed the circle.

They then form into a wide circle, into the centre of which one steps forward and carries out a war dance, representing how he tracked and fought with one of his enemies. He goes through the whole fight in dumb show, until he finally kills his foe. The scouts meantime still singing the Ingonyama chorus, and dancing on their own ground. So soon as he finishes the fight, the leader starts the 'Be Prepared' chorus, which they repeat three times in honour of the scout who has just danced.

Then they recommence the Ingonyama chorus, and another scout steps into the ring, and describes in dumb show how he stalked and killed a wild buffalo. While he does the creeping up and stalking the animal, the scouts all crouch and sing their chorus very softly, and as he gets more into the fight with the beast, they similarly spring up and dance and shout the chorus loudly. When he has slain the beast, the leader again gives the 'Be Prepared' chorus in his honour, which is repeated three times, the scouts banging their staffs on the ground at the same time as they stamp 'Bom! bom!'

At the end of the third repetition, 'Bom! bom!' is repeated the second time.

The circle then close together, turn to their left again, grasping shoulders with the left hand, and move off, singing the Ingonyama chorus, or, if it is not desired to move away, they break up after the final 'Bom! bom!'

SCOUTS' PLAY

POCAHONTAS; OR, THE CAPTURE OF CAPTAIN JOHN SMITH*

SCENE: *In the jungle, Virginia, in 1607.*

ENTER: *A band of Red Indians,* R., *scouting. The leading scout suddenly signals to the others to halt and hide, and remains himself keenly looking ahead. The* PATROL LEADER *creeps nearer to him, and they speak in a loud whisper.*

PATROL LEADER (Eagle's Wing). Ho! Silver Fox! What dost thou see?

SILVER FOX (the leading scout). My leader, I saw but just now a strange figure ahead—but for the moment I see it not. There was an Indian, one of the hated Assock tribe, and close by him was a being who looked like a man yet not a man. He wore no feathers, no war paint. But his body was all hidden in skins or cloths, and his head was covered with a huge kind of protector. He had, it is true, two arms and legs, but his face was of a horrible colour—not bronze like ours, but an awful white, like that of a dead man, and half covered with a bush of hair.

EAGLE'S WING. It must be either a medicine man or devil.

SILVER FOX (*still gazing ahead*). Look there, he moves! (PATROL LEADER *springs forward and crouches near* SILVER FOX.) Close to yonder birch tree. What is it he carries? A heavy shining staff of iron. See he is pointing at those ducks with it. Ah!

(*Report of gun in the distance.*)

PATROL LEADER. Scouts! There is the devil before us. He spits fire and smoke from an iron staff.

SILVER FOX. Aye, and see how the birds fall dead before him.

PATROL LEADER. Yes, he is a very devil. What a prize for us if we can kill him and take his scalp.

SCOUTS. Nay, nay. He is a devil. He will kill us!

SILVER FOX. Yes, that is true. There is a saying, 'Let dogs that sleep lie sleeping, then they harm you not.' Let us leave this devil so he harm us not.

SCOUTS. Aye, aye.

EAGLE'S WING. Scouts! What woman's talk is this? Are ye no longer scouts and warriors when ye see a foe? The worse the foe the greater the glory of defeating him. Are four Sioux scouts afraid of one, even though he be the devil himself? Begone to your lodges, but never call yourselves warriors more. Ye be dogs! Curs but to harbour such thoughts. For me I am going to have that scalp—devil or no devil, I am going to have that scalp!

SILVER FOX. Pardon, my leader! I am no cur. Any man I will fight, but a witch or the devil is more than I had thought on. But if you mean to face him, why, then, so do I.

SCOUTS. Ay, and so do all of us.

EAGLE'S WING. 'Tis well, my scouts. But soft, he is coming this way. What luck! Better than scalping him, we will catch him alive, and present him living to our King. Hide. Hide yourselves. Lie close around his path, and, when I give the call, then rush upon him and secure him. (*All hide*, R.)

(*Enter* CAPT. JOHN SMITH, L., *accompanied by Indian guide, who is tied to* SMITH'S *left arm by his wrist by means of a garter—coloured tape*).

SMITH. How now, my untruthful friend? You have just told me that there are no Indians in this part of the country, and here are

Princess Pocahontas

footmarks of several quite fresh, and see where the grass quite newly trod down is still giving out juice. They must be quite close by. Lucky that I have thee tied to me, else could you run away and leave me guideless; but whatever befalls us now we share the risks together. How like you that, my red cocksparrow? (*An arrow whizzes past.*) Ha! They're not far off. Behold, they come, but they'll find one Briton is stouter stuff than the foes that they're accustomed to.

(*The Red Indians are heard shouting their war cries without. Arrows fly past.* JOHN SMITH *fires, loads, and fires again, talking all the time, while his native guide crouches back alarmed.*)

SMITH (*laughing*). Ha! ha! They like not my rifle-fire. They run, the dogs! Another bites the dust. (*Patting his rifle.*) Well done, thou trusty Bess—thou art a good lass! There! Have at them again. (*Fires.*) Good; another falls! But now they rally and come on again—their leader gives them heart. Well, and we will give them lead. (*Fires again. To his guide, who is very frightened.*) Cheer up.

Gadzooks, but I like their leader—that last ball struck him, still he fainteth not. He leads them on again. By my head! but we shall yet have a decent fight of it. Aid me, St George, and let me show what stuff an Englishman is made of. (*As he presses forward the guide in his fear slips down and accidentally drags* SMITH *down with him.*) How now—fool? You have undone me.

(*Indians rush in from all sides and spring on to* SMITH, *and after a severe struggle capture and bind his arms behind his back. He stands panting and smiling. The Indians stand back to either side while* EAGLE'S WING—*with one arm bleeding—addresses him.*)

EAGLE'S WING. So, devil, we have thee caught at last. Four good warriors hast thou sent to their happy hunting grounds, but our turn has come and we have thee fast—a prize, for kings—and for our King.

Captain John Smith

SMITH. Well, 'twas a good fight, and you deserve to win for facing rifle-fire, which you had never seen before. I should like to shake you by the hand had I a hand free to do it with. But by St George, had it not been for this white-livered knave who dragged me down, there would have been more of you to join your hunting-party down below. But who is this who comes?

(*Scouts chorus heard without 'Ingonyama', etc. Scouts all raise their hands and join in the chorus, looking off to the* R.)

(*Enter* KING POWHATTAN, R., *with his chiefs and warriors.*)

King Powhattan

KING. How now! Eagle's Wing, what have you here?

EAGLE'S WING. My lord, we have just fought and foiled a very devil. We killed him not in order that you, our liege, might have him to see and question and to kill yourself. (*Brings gun.*) He used the lightning and the thunder of Heaven with this engine, so that he killeth those he hateth. Four of us lie yonder stricken dead therewith. He is a very devil.

KING (*to* SMITH). So! What be you? Devil or witch or Indian painted white? What do you here?

SMITH. Hail, King! I am no witch nor devil—nothing but a man—an Englishman, which is something more than a mere man. I came across the seas. Five moons it took me; so far away my country is. But here I am, and where I am there follow others. And we come to tell you of a greater King than thou. *Our* King who is now to be your king also.

KING (*very angry*). What! a greater King than I? Knave, how dare you, whether devil or no—how dare thou speak like this?

KING.* Aye, I have heard of these white folk. Art not afraid?

SMITH. Nay. I have faced the seas and storms, the anger of the elements, beside which the rage of men is very small. (*Laughing.*) Forget not—I am an Englishman—an Englishman knows not fear.

KING. Ho! Say you so? We'll soon put that beyond all question by a proof. (*Draws dagger, rushes on* SMITH *with a yell, as if to stab him, and stops the knife only as it touches* SMITH'S *breast.* SMITH *does not flinch.*) Ah!

SMITH. A joke was it. (*Laughs.*) By St George, I thought you meant to kill me.

(*Enter* PRINCESS POCAHONTAS* *the* KING'S DAUGHTER. R. *Aside.*)

What is this strange being?. A man, yet not a red man. He has a noble look. Alas! that he should fall into my father's power, for he will surely slay him.

KING (*to* SMITH). And thou wert not afraid?

SMITH. Nay. Why should I be? I have long ago thought out how to meet my fate. Death and I have looked at each other face to face before now, and death has a kindly smile for anyone who has never wilfully done ill to a fellow creature; to such an one he is no longer a dreaded demon, but a kindly host.

KING. Well! he'll have a guest before long now; for since you say he is a friend of yours it proves that you are, as my people first told me, some kind of witch or devil yourself. Therefore, it will be well for the land that we do slay thee. Besides, I have not seen a man's red blood for many days, and I am tired of the blood of the Assocks. (POCAHONTAS *shrinks down, holding her ears.*) I shall dearly like to see how looks the blood of a white half-man, half-devil. But first I want to see him cower, and squeal for mercy; for therein lies the joy of killing. (*Calls to his* WARRIORS.) Ho! there! Stretch out this devil on the ground, and let him learn that death is not the joy he thinks it is.

(*They drag* SMITH *down, and lay him on his back on the ground,* C. *One holds his feet, but the rest, finding that he does not struggle, stand back; two prepare to use their battle-axes on him, while the rest dance weird dances; singing Ingonyama chorus round him. The executioners make false blows at his head—but he never flinches.*)

POCAHONTAS (*kneeling beside the* KING. R.). Oh! King—I have not often asked for gifts from you—and now I pray you, on my bended knee, to grant me this request. I have no slave to guard me when I walk abroad. It is not seemly that I take a young brave of our tribe, and the old ones are so very old and slow. Now here; a slave of whom one may be proud—one strange to see, yet strong and great and brave. Ah! give him to thy child instead of unto death.

KING. Nay! nay! my child. If you don't like the scene, withdraw, for he shall die. 'Tis sport for me to see how long he lasts before he cries for mercy. And when he does he dies. (*To* WARRIORS.) Now stand him up, and try some new device to make him quail.

(POCAHONTAS *shrinks back. They raise* SMITH, *and he stands boldly facing them.*)

KING. Death now comes to thee, and thou hast no chance of escaping him. Art thou not now afraid of him?

JOHN SMITH. Nay. Why should I be? We men are born not for ourselves but as a help to others; and if we act thus loyally we know our God will have us in his care both now and after death.

KING. But *after* death you're dead!

JOHN SMITH. Not so. A Christian lives again.

KING (*to* SMITH). Well now your hour has come. I know not what has brought you to this land, but you shall know that witch or no, your spells can have no power on me; and you will die, and I shall smile to see you die.

SMITH. What brought me here was duty to my King and God and countrymen; to spread his powerful sway over all the earth, that you and yours may know of God, that trade may spread to carry peace and wealth throughout the world. If you accept these views all will be well; if you accept them not then do your worst, but use your haste; our mission is to *clean* the world! Kill me, but that will not avail, for where I fall a thousand more will come. Know this, O Savage King, a Briton's word is trusted over all the world; his first care is for others—not himself; he sticks to friend through thick and thin; he's loyal to his King. And though you threat with death or pains, he'll do his duty to the end.

KING (*springs angrily forward*). I'll hear no more. You offer terms to ME, the King! Down, dog, upon your knees, and meet the death you feign to smile at. (*To* WARRIORS.) Strike, strike, and smash this vermin from my path.

(PRINCESS POCAHONTAS, *who has been cowering in the background, runs forward and places herself close in front of* Capt. JOHN SMITH, *so as to protect him from the* WARRIORS, *who are preparing*, R. and BACK, *to rush at him with their spears and axes*).

PRINCESS POCAHONTAS. Hold! Warriors—I am your Princess, and to get at him you have to kill me first. (*To* KING.) O King—I call you no more 'Father'. O *King* your rule has been a time of blood and murder. I was too young to think before, but now I know that all your works are cruel, bad, not just. (WARRIORS *lower their weapons, and whisper among themselves, as if saying*, '*Yes. She's quite right.*') And I have been obedient as your child till now. But now my eyes are opened, and I see that as King you are neither just nor kind towards your tribe—or other men.

To bring it home to you, I swear that if you slay this man you also slay your daughter! For I'll not leave him thus to die alone. (*To* WARRIORS.) Now, braves, come on and do your work.

(*They hang back.*)

How now—you never feared an enemy, so why fear me?

EAGLE'S WING (*bowing*). Nay, sweet Princess, it may not be. We care not what of men we kill in fighting for our land, but this we cannot do—to raise a hand against a woman, and she our own Princess.

Warrior

KING (*furious*). How now! What talk is this? Ye speak as though you had no King and no commands. Slay on—strike true, and spare not man nor maid, for she no longer is a child of mine.

(*Braves still hesitate.*)

Ye will not? Dogs, wouldst have me do it for myself? I will, and, what is more, I'll slay you Eagle's Wing for this, and you too——

(*Enter a warrior scout,* L., *who rushes up to the* KING *and kneels while shots are heard outside.*)

SCOUT. O King! There be more white devils over there. They're pressing on, and none can stand against them.

KING to WARRIORS. Stand firm, and kill these devils as they come. To every brave who takes a white man's scalp I'll give the noblest feather for his head. Stand firm! Bend well your bows.

(*While the* KING *and* WARRIORS *are looking off* L. *towards the fight*, POCAHONTAS *takes* SMITH R., *draws a dagger and cuts* JOHN SMITH'S *arms loose. He shakes hands with her. Taking the dagger, he rushes to the* KING, *and seizing his hair with one hand, and threatening him with the dagger with the other, he leads him* C.)

SMITH. Now yield thee, King, as prisoner, or I will send thee quick to other hunting grounds. (*To Warriors who rush forward to rescue the* KING.) Nay, stand you there: another step, and lo! your King will die. (*A pause. All stand quite still.*) I will not harm if he lists to me. (*Leads* KING *to front*, C., *and then lets go his hold of him.* WARRIORS *remain at back. Distant noise of fighting, cries and shots heard all the time.* WARRIORS *keep looking off to see how the fight is going on.*)

(SMITH *standing* L., *facing* KING, C. POCAHONTAS, R., WARRIORS, *back.*)

SMITH. If you would live in peace, your only way is now to join with us. Our God is stronger than your idols, and our King is king of many tribes far greater and more powerful than your own. But if you join with us your wicked ways must cease; no more to kill your people for no crime, no more to steal their goods or beasts, no more to make them slaves against their will. Beneath the British flag all men are free. (WARRIORS *whisper among themselves.* SMITH *turns to them.*) What say you? Will you join and serve our King, and live in peace, or will you go on being slaves of cruel chiefs, to life a life of fear and poverty?

EAGLE'S WING. Nay. We should like to join you well, but we have aye been faithful to our King, and what he says, why that is what we'll do.

SMITH. You're right in being faithful to your King. Now, King, what say you? Will you join our mighty King with all your braves, or will you face his power and be destroyed?

KING (*sullenly*). You talk as though you were a king yourself and conqueror, instead of but a prisoner in my hands. You must be mad or very brave, since I could kill thee at one stroke.

SMITH. Well, mad or brave, it matters not; but there are others just as mad or brave out there, who even now (*points off* L.) are pressing back your men; and were your men to kill off all of us, a thousand more will come for each one killed, and in the end you too would meet your fate. Know this, that Britain, once she puts her hand to the plough for doing noble work, does not withdraw, but presses on till peace and justice are set up, and cruel wrongs redressed. You would yourself remain as King among your people, but beneath the friendly wing of Britain's world-wide power.

KING (*to* WARRIORS). My braves! I never asked your will before; but ye have heard what this brave man has said. What think ye? Should we yield or fight this white man's power?

EAGLE'S WING. My King, we all say 'yield', and join this mighty power, whereby we shall ourselves be strong.

POCAHONTAS (*kneeling to* KING, R.). Once more I call thee Father, and I pray, for all the wives and children of our tribe, that you will take this noble man's advice, and bring true peace at last into our land. (*Kisses* KING'S *hands and remains kneeling while he speaks.*)

KING. 'Tis well. Fair, sir, we yield; and on our oath we swear allegiance to your King for aye and ever, weal or woe. We will be true (*holding up right hand in scout's sign*).

WARRIORS (*holding up right hands in scout's salute*). We will be true.

SMITH (*taking St George's flag from under his coat, and lying it on to a scout's staff, holds it aloft.*) Behold your flag—the flag of St George and Merry England!

WARRIORS *salute and sing Ingonyama Chorus. Band plays 'Rule Britannia'!*

CURTAIN.

DRESSES

WARRIORS.—Band or tape round head, with plait of hair over ear, and four goose feathers with black tips.

Naked body coloured red brick-dust colour.

Trousers: light-coloured if possible, with strips of coloured rag and goose feathers stitched all down the outside seam of the leg.

Bare feet.

Bow and arrows and staff.

KING.—Like warriors, but with red blanket or shawl over one shoulder, and headdress made of linen band with goose feathers, some upright in it and continued down the back.

POCAHONTAS.—Headdress band of linen, with three upright goose feathers and two drooping on each side; also a plait of hair over each shoulder.

Brass curtain-rings tied with thread round each ear as earrings.

Necklace of beads, also bracelets.

A skirt.

Coloured short petticoat under it.

Bare feet.

JOHN SMITH.—Big hat with pheasant's tails feathers.

Beard and moustache and long hair of tow or crepe hair. Could all be stitched to hat if desired. Steel gorget or wide soft linen collar; long brown or yellow coat, with big belt.

Bagging knickerbockers.

Stockings.

Shoes with big buckles.

Old-fashioned flint-lock gun.

SCENERY.—Strips of brown paper, 1 ft. to 1½ ft. wide, and 2 ft. to 3 ft. wide at the bottom will represent trees if stuck up on the back wall, and marked with charcoal and chalk to represent rough bark.

PART II

CONTENTS: CHAPTER II

TRACKING;

or, Noticing and Reading the Meaning of Small Signs

HINTS TO INSTRUCTORS

Instruction in the art of observation and deduction is difficult to lay down in black and white. It must be taught by practice. One can only give a few instances and hints, the rest depends upon your own powers of imagination and local circumstances.

The importance of the power of observation and deduction to the young citizen is great. Children are proverbially quick in observation, but it dies out as they grow older, largely because first experiences catch their attention, which they fail to do on repetition.

OBSERVATION is, in fact, a habit to which a boy has to be trained. TRACKING is an interesting step towards gaining it. DEDUCTION is the art of subsequently reasoning out and extracting the meaning from the points observed.

When once observation and deduction have been made habitual in the boy, a great step in the development of 'character' has been gained.

CONTENTS: CHAPTER III

(Commences on page 97)

WOODCRAFT;

or, Knowledge of Animals and Nature

HINTS TO INSTRUCTORS

HOW TO TEACH NATURAL HISTORY

If in London take your scouts to the Zoological Gardens and to Natural History Museum, South Kensington. Take them to certain animals on which you are prepared to lecture to them. About half a dozen animals would be quite enough for one day.

If in the country, get leave from a farmer or carter to show the boys how to put on harness, etc., and how to feed and water the horse; how he is shod, etc. How to catch hold of a runaway horse in harness. How to milk a cow.

Study habits of cows, rabbits, birds, water-voles, trout, etc., by stalking them and watching all that they do.

Take your scouts to any menagerie, and explain the animals.

CHAPTER II

TRACKING;

or,

Noticing and Reading the meaning of small Signs.—Camp Fire Yarns on Observation—Spooring—Reading 'Sign'

CAMP FIRE YARN.—No. 5

OBSERVATION OF 'SIGN'

Noticing 'sign'—Details of People—Sign round a dead body—Details in the Country—Use of eyes, ears, and nose by Scouts—Night Scouting—Hints to Instructors—Practices and Games in Observation—Books on Observation.

NOTICING SIGN

'SIGN' is the word used by scouts to mean any little details such as footprints, broken twigs, trampled grass, scraps of food, a drop of blood, a hair, and so on; anything that may help as clues in getting the information they are in search of.

Mrs Smithson,* when travelling in Kashmir last year, was following up with some native Indian trackers the 'pugs' of a panther which had killed and carried off a young buck. He had crossed a wide bare slab of rock which, of course, gave no mark of his soft feet. The tracker went at once to the far side of the rock where it came to a sharp edge; he wetted his finger, and just passed it along the edge till he found a few buck's hairs sticking to it. This showed him where the panther had passed down off the rock dragging the buck with him. Those few hairs were what scouts call 'sign.'

Mrs Smithson's tracker also found bears by noticing small 'sign'. On one occasion he noticed a fresh scratch in the bark of a tree evidently made by a bear's claw, and on the other he found a single black hair sticking to the bark of a tree, which told him that a bear had rubbed against it.

One of the most important things that a scout has to learn, whether he is a war scout or a hunter or peace scout, is *to let nothing escape his attention*; he must notice small points and signs, and then make out the meaning of them: but it takes a good deal of practice before a tenderfoot can get into the habit of really noting everything and letting nothing escape his eye. It can be learnt just as well in a town as in the country.

And in the same way you should notice any strange sound or any peculiar smell and think for yourself what it may mean. Unless you learn to notice 'signs' you will have very little of 'this and that' to put together and so you will be no use as a scout; it comes by practice.

Remember, a scout always considers it a great disgrace if an outsider discovers a thing before he has seen it for himself, whether that thing is far away in the distance, or close by under his feet.

If you go out with a really trained scout you will see that his eyes are constantly moving, looking out in every direction near and far, noticing everything that is going on, just from habit, not because he wants to show off how much he notices.

I was walking with one the other day in Hyde Park in London. He presently remarked 'that horse is going a little lame'—there was no horse near us, but I found he was looking at one far away across the Serpentine: the next moment he picked up a peculiar button lying by the path. His eyes, you see, were looking both far away and near.

In the streets of a strange town a scout will notice his way by the principal buildings, and side-streets, and in any case he will notice what shops he passes and what is in their windows; also what vehicles pass him and such details as whether the horses' harness and shoes are all right; and most especially what people he passes, what their faces are like, their dress, their boots, and their way of walking, so that if, for instance, he should be asked by a policeman, 'Have you seen a man with dark overhanging eyebrows dressed in a blue suit, going down this street,' he should be able to give some such answer as 'Yes—he was walking a little lame with the right foot, wore foreign-looking boots, was carrying a parcel in his hand, he turned down Gold Street, the second turning on the left from here, about three minutes ago.'

Information of that kind has often been of greatest value in tracing out a criminal, but so many people go along with their eyes shut and never notice things.

In the story of 'Kim', by Rudyard Kipling, there is an account of two boys being taught 'observation' in order to become detectives, or scouts, by means of a game in which a trayful of small objects was shown to them for a minute and was then covered over and they had to describe all the things on it from memory.

We will have that game, as it is excellent practice for scouts.

There was a revolutionary society in Italy called the Camorra* who used to train their boys to be quick at noticing and remembering things. When walking through the streets of the city, the Camorrist would suddenly stop and ask his boy—'How was the woman dressed who sat at the door of the fourth house on the right in the last street?' or, 'What were the two men talking about whom we met at the corner of the last street but three?' or, 'Where was the cab ordered to drive to, and what was its number?' 'What is the height of that house and what is the width of its upper floor window?' and so on. Or the boy was given a minute to look in a shop window and then he had to describe all that was in it. Captain Cook, the great explorer and scout, was trained in the same way as a boy, and so was Houdini* the great conjurer.

Every town scout should know, as a matter of course, where is the nearest chemist's shop (in case of accidents), the nearest police 'fixed point', police-station, hospital, fire alarm, telephone, ambulance station, etc.

The scout must also have his eyes on the ground especially along the edge of the pavement against the houses or in the gutter. I have often found valuable trinkets that have been dropped, and which have been walked over by numbers of people, and swept to one side by ladies' dresses without being noticed.

DETAILS OF PEOPLE

When you are travelling by train or tram always notice every little thing about your fellow travellers; notice their faces, dress, way of talking and so on so that you could describe them each pretty accurately afterwards; and also try and make out from their appearance and behaviour whether they are rich or poor (which you can generally tell from their boots*), and what is their probable business, whether they are happy, or ill, or in want of help.

But in doing this you must not let them see you are watching them, else it puts them on their guard. Remember the shepherd-boy

How the wearing of a hat shows character

who noticed the gipsy's boots, but did not look at him and so did not make the gipsy suspicious of him.*

Close observation of people and ability to read their character and their thoughts is of immense value in trade and commerce, especially for a shop-assistant or salesman in persuading people to buy goods, or in detecting would-be swindlers.

It is said that you can tell a man's character from the way he wears his hat. If it is slightly on one side, the wearer is good-natured: if it is worn very much on one side, he is a swaggerer: if on the back of his head, he is bad at paying his debts: if worn straight on the top, he is probably honest but very dull.

The way a man (or a woman) walks is often a good guide to his character—witness the fussy, swaggering little man paddling along with short steps with much arm-action, the nervous man's hurried, jerky stride, the slow slouch of the loafer, the smooth-going and silent step of the scout, and so on.

I was once accused of mistrusting men with waxed moustaches. Well, so, to a certain extent, I do. It often means vanity and sometimes drink.

Certainly the 'quiff' or lock of hair which some lads wear on their forehead is a sure sign of silliness. The shape of the face gives a good guide to the man's character.

Perhaps you can tell the character of these gentlemen?

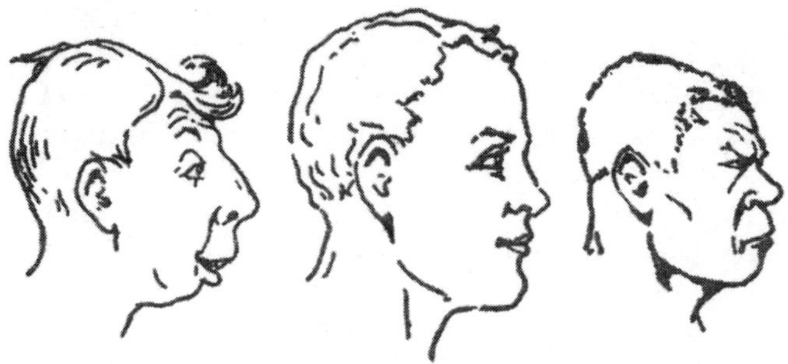

I was speaking with a detective not long ago about a gentleman we had both been talking to, and we were trying to make out his character. I remarked—'well, at any rate, he was a fisherman,' but my companion could not see why: but then he was not a fisherman himself. I had noticed a lot of little tufts of cloth sticking upon the left cuff of his coat.

A good many fishermen, when they take their flies off the line, stick them into their cap to dry: others stick them into their sleeve. When dry they pull them out, which often tears a thread or two of the cloth.

It is an amusing practice when you are in a railway carriage or omnibus with other people to look only at their feet and guess without looking any higher what sort of people they are, old or young, well to do or poor, fat or thin, and so on, and then look up and see how near you have been to the truth.

Mr Nat Goodwin,* the American actor, once described to me how he went to see a balloon ascent at a time when he happened to be suffering from a stiff neck. He was only able to look down instead of up—and he could only see the feet of the people round him in the crowd so he chose among the feet those that he felt sure belonged to an affable kind-hearted man who would describe to him what the balloon was doing.

I once was able to be of service to a lady who was in poor circumstances, as I had guessed it from noticing, while walking behind her, that though she was well dressed the soles of her shoes were in the last stage of disrepair. I don't suppose she ever knew how I guessed that she was in a bad way.*

But it is surprising how much of the sole of the boot you can see when behind a person walking—and it is equally surprising how much meaning you can read from that boot.* It is said that to wear out soles and heels equally is to give evidence of business capacity and honesty; to wear your heels down on the outside means that you are a man of imagination and love of adventure; but heels worn down on the inside signify weakness and indecision of character, and this last sign is more infallible in the case of man than in that of woman.

Remember how 'Sherlock Holmes'* met a stranger and noticed that he was looking fairly well-to-do, in new clothes with a mourning band on his sleeve, with a soldierly bearing, and a sailor's way of walking, sunburnt, with tattoo marks on his hands, and he was carrying some children's toys in his hand. What should you have supposed that man to be? Well! Sherlock Holmes guessed, correctly, that he had lately retired from the Royal Marines as a Sergeant, and his wife had died, and he had some small children at home.

SIGNS ROUND A DEAD BODY

It may happen to some of you that one day you will be the first to find the dead body of a man, in which case you will remember that it is your duty to examine and note down the smallest signs that are to be seen on and near the body before it is moved or the ground disturbed and trampled down. Besides noticing the exact position of the body (which should if possible be photographed exactly as found) the ground all round should be very carefully examined—without treading on it yourself more than is absolutely necessary, for fear of spoiling existing tracks. If you can also draw a little map of how the body lay and where the signs round it were, it might be of value.

Twice lately bodies have been found which were at first supposed to be those of people who had hanged themselves—but close examination of the ground round them, in one case some torn twigs and trampled grass, and in the other a crumpled carpet, showed that murder had been committed, and that the bodies had been hung after death to make it appear as though they had committed suicide.

Finger-marks should especially be looked for on any likely articles and if they do not correspond to those of the murdered man they may be those of his murderer, who could then be identified by comparing the impression with his fingers. Such a case occurred in India, where a man was found murdered and a bloody finger-mark on his clothes. The owner of the finger-mark was found, tried, and convicted.

In St Petersburg in Russia a banker was found murdered. Near the body was found a cigar-holder with an amber mouthpiece. This mouthpiece was of peculiar shape and could only be held in the mouth in one position, and it had two teeth marks in it. These marks showed that the two teeth were of different lengths.

The teeth of the murdered man were quite regular, so the cigar-holder was evidently not his. But his nephew had teeth which corresponded to the marks on the mouthpiece, so he was arrested, and then further proof came up and showed that he was the murderer.

[*Compare the story in 'Sherlock Holmes' Memoirs' called 'The Resident Patient'* in which a man was found hanging and was considered to be a suicide till Sherlock Holmes came in and showed various signs such as cigar ends bitten by different teeth, footprints, and that three men had been in the room with the dead man for some time previous to his death and had hanged him.*]

DETAILS IN THE COUNTRY

If you are in the country you should notice landmarks, that is objects which help you to find your way or prevent you getting lost, such as distant hills, church towers, and nearer objects such as peculiar buildings, trees, gates, rocks, etc.

And remember in noticing such landmarks that you may want to use your knowledge of them some day for telling someone else how to find his way, so you must notice them pretty closely so as to be able to describe them unmistakably and in their proper order. You must notice and remember every by-road and footpath.

Then you must also notice smaller signs such as birds getting up and flying hurriedly which means somebody or some animal is there; dust shows animals, men, or vehicles moving.

Of course when in the country you should notice just as much as in town all passers-by very carefully—how they are dressed, what their faces are like, and their way of walking, and examine their footmarks—and jot down a sketch of them in your notebook, so that you would know the footmark again if you found it somewhere else —(as the shepherd boy did in the story at the beginning of this book).

And notice all tracks—that is footmarks of men, animals, birds, wheels, etc., for from these you can read the most important information, as Captain d'Artagnan* did in the story of the secret duel, of which I shall tell you later.

This track-reading is of such importance that I shall give you a lecture on that subject by itself.

USING YOUR EYES

LET nothing be too small for your notice, a button, a match, a cigar ash, a feather, or a leaf, might be of great importance.*

A scout must not only look to his front but also to either side and behind him, he must have 'eyes at the back of his head' as the saying is.

Often by suddenly looking back you will see an enemy's scout or a thief showing himself in a way that he would not have done had he thought you would look round.

There is an interesting story by Fenimore Cooper called 'The Pathfinder'* in which the action of a Red Indian scout is well described. He had 'eyes at the back of his head', and after passing some bushes he caught sight of a withered leaf or two among the fresh ones which made him suspect that somebody might have put the leaves there to make a better hiding place, and so he discovered some hidden fugitives.

NIGHT SCOUTING

A SCOUT has to be able to notice small details just as much by night as by day and this he has to do chiefly by listening, occasionally by feeling or smelling.

In the stillness of the night sounds carry further than by day. If you put your ear to the ground or place it against a stick, or especially against a drum, which is touching the ground, you will hear the shake of horses' hoofs or the thud of a man's footfall a long way off. Another way is to open a knife with a blade at each end, stick one blade into the ground and hold the other between your teeth and you will hear all the better. The human voice, even though talking low, carries to a great distance and is not likely to be mistaken for any other sound.

I have often passed through outposts at night after having found where the picquets were posted by hearing the low talking of the men or the snoring of those asleep.*

BOOKS TO READ ON OBSERVATION

'Criminal Investigation', by Dr Gross.* Edited by John Adam. 30s.
'Aids to Scouting'* 1s. (Gale and Polden.)

An alarm bell in Mafeking—'Look out for shells!'

HINTS TO INSTRUCTORS*

HOW TO TEACH OBSERVATION IN PRACTICE

PRACTICES

In Towns: Practise your boys first in walking down a street to notice the different kinds of shops as they pass and to remember them in their proper sequence at the end.

Then to notice and remember the names on the shops.

Then to notice and remember the contents of a shop window after two minutes' gaze. Finally to notice the contents of several shop windows in succession with half a minute at each.

The boys must also notice prominent buildings as landmarks; the number of turnings off the street they are using; names of other streets; details of horses and vehicles passing by; and—especially—details of the people as to dress, features, gait; numbers on motor cars, policemen, etc.

Take them the first time to show them how to do it; and after that send them out and on their return question them, as below.

Make them learn for themselves to notice and remember the whereabouts of all chemists' shops, fire, alarms, police fixed points, ambulances, etc., etc.*

IN THE COUNTRY: Take the patrol out for a walk and teach the boys to notice distant prominent features as landmarks such as hills, church steeples, and so on, and as nearer landmarks such things as peculiar buildings, trees, rocks, gates, etc. By-roads or paths, nature of fences, crops; different kinds of trees, birds, animals, tracks, etc., also people, vehicles, etc. Also any peculiar smells of plants, animals, manure, etc.

Then send them out on a certain walk, and on their return have them in one by one and examine them verbally, or have them all in and let them write their answers on, say, six questions which you give them with reference to certain points which they should have noticed.

It adds to the value of the practice if you make a certain number of small marks in the ground beforehand, or leave buttons or matches, etc., for the boys to notice or to pick up and bring in (as a means of making them examine the ground close to them as well as distant objects).

TELLING CHARACTER: Send scouts out for half an hour to look for, say, a brutish character, or a case of genteel poverty, etc.

The scout must on his return be able to describe the person accurately, and give the reasons which made him think the person was of the character he reports.

He should also state how many other characters he passed in his search, such as silly, good-natured, deceitful, swaggering, wax-moustached, and so on, judging of course, by their faces, their walk, their boots, hats, and clothing, etc.

GAMES IN OBSERVATION

THIMBLE FINDING (Indoors)

SEND the patrol out of the room.

Take a thimble, ring, coin, bit of paper, or any small article, and place it where it is perfectly visible but in a spot where it is not likely to be noticed. Let the patrol come in and look for it. When one of them sees it he should go and quietly sit down without indicating to the others where it is.

After a fair time he should be told to point it out to those who have not succeeded in finding it.

[This ensures his having really seen it.]

SHOP WINDOW (Outdoors in town)

UMPIRE takes a patrol down a street past six shops. Gives them half a minute at each shop, then, after moving them off to some distance, he gives each boy a pencil and card, and tells him to write from memory, or himself takes down what they noticed in, say, the third and fifth shops. The one who sets down most articles correctly wins. It is useful practice to match one boy against another in heats—the loser competing again, till you arrive at the worst. This gives the worst scouts the most practice.

SIMILAR GAME (Indoors)

SEND each scout in turn into a room for half a minute; when he comes out take down a list of furniture and articles which he noticed. The boy who noticed most wins.

The simplest way of scoring is to make a list of the articles in the room on your scoring paper with a column for marks for each scout against them, which can then easily be totalled up at foot.

SPOTTING THE SPOT (Indoors—town or country)

SHOW a series of photos or sketches of objects, in the neighbourhood such as would be known to all the scouts if they kept their eyes open—such, for instance, as cross-roads, curious window, gargoyle or weathercock, tree, reflection in the water (guess the building causing it), and so on.

A pair of scouts can play most of the above competitions off between themselves, if they like, as a matter of practice.

Patrol leaders can match one pair of their scouts against another pair in the game, and thus get them really practised at it, and when they become really good he can challenge other patrols to compete against his.

Follow the Trail

Send out a 'hare', either walking or cycling, with a pocketful of corn, nutshells, confetti paper or buttons, etc., and drop a few here and there to give a trail for the patrol to follow.

Or go out with a piece of chalk and draw the patrol sign on walls, gateposts, pavements, lamp-posts, trees, etc., every here and there, and let the patrol hunt you by these marks. Patrols should wipe out all these marks as they pass them for tidiness, and so as not to mislead them for another day's practice.

The other road signs should also be used, such as closing up certain roads as not used, and hiding a letter at some point, giving directions as to the next turn.

Scout's Nose (Indoors)

Prepare a number of paper-bags, all alike, and put in each a different smelling article such as chopped onion in one, tan in another, roseleaves, leather, aniseed, violet powder, orange-peel, etc. Put these packets in a row a couple of feet apart and let each competitor walk down the line and have five seconds' sniff at each. At the end he has one minute in which to write down or to state to the umpire the names of the different objects smelled, from memory, in their correct order.

Far and Near (For town or country)

Umpire goes along a given road or line of country with a patrol in patrol formation. He carries a scoring card with the name of each scout on it.

Each scout looks out for the details required and directly he notices one he runs to the umpire and informs him or hands in the article if it is an article he finds. The umpire enters a mark accordingly against his name. The scout who gains most marks in the walk, wins.

Details like the following should be chosen, to develop the scout's observation and to encourage him to look far and near, up and down, etc.

The details should be varied every time the game is played; and about 8 or 10 should be given at a time.

Every match found	1 mark
Every button found	1 mark
Birds' foot tracks	2 marks
Patch noticed on stranger's clothing or boots	2 marks
Grey horse seen	2 marks
Pigeon flying	2 marks
Sparrow sitting	1 mark
Ash-tree	2 marks
Broken chimney pot	2 marks
Broken window	1 mark

CAMP FIRE YARN.—No. 6

SPOORING

Men's Tracks—Animals' Tracks—How to Learn 'Spooring'—Hints to Instructor—Tracking Games—Books on Spooring.

MEN'S TRACKS

GENERAL DODGE,* of the American Army, describes how he once had to pursue a party of Red Indians who had been murdering some people.

The murderers had nearly a week's start and had gone away on horseback. But General Dodge got a splendid tracking-scout named Espinosa to help him. The Indians were all riding unshod horses, except one, and after Espinosa had been tracking them for many miles he suddenly got off his horse and pulled four horseshoes out of a hidden crevice in the rocks. The Indian had evidently pulled them off so that they should not leave a track.

For six days they pursued the band, and for a great part of the time there was no sign visible to an ordinary eye, and after going for 150 miles they eventually overtook and captured the whole party. But it was all entirely due to Espinosa's good tracking.

On another occasion some American troops were following up a number of Indians, who had been raiding and murdering whites, and they had some other Red Indian scouts to assist them in tracking. In order to make a successful attack, they marched by night, and the trackers found the way in the darkness by feeling the tracks of the enemy with their hands, and they went at a fairly good pace for many miles, merely touching the track with their fingers; but suddenly they halted and reported that the track they had been following had been crossed by a fresh track, and on the commanding officer going up, he found the Indians still holding the track with their hands, so that there should be no mistake. A light was brought and it was found that the new track was that of a bear which had walked across the trail of the enemy! So the march continued without further incident, and the enemy were surprised, and caught in the early hours of the morning.

The scout, Burnham,* in South Africa, who was with Wilson's party when they were massacred on the Shangani River in Matabeleland, was sent away with a dispatch shortly before they were surrounded. He travelled during the night to escape observation of the enemy. He found his way by feeling for the tracks left in the mud by the column when it marched up there in the morning.

I myself led a column through an intricate part of the Matopo Mountains in Rhodesia by night to attack the enemy's stronghold which I had reconnoitred the previous day. I found the way by feeling my own tracks, sometimes with my hands and sometimes through the soles of my shoes which had worn very thin; and I never had any difficulty in finding the line.*

Tracking, or following up tracks, is called by different names in different countries. Thus, in South Africa you would talk only of 'spooring', that is, following up the 'spoor'; in India it would be following the 'pugs', or 'pugging'; in America it is 'trailing'.

It is one of the principal ways by which scouts gain information, and hunters find their game. But to become a good tracker you must begin young, and practise it at all times when you are out walking, whether in town or country.

If at first you constantly remind yourself to do it you will soon find that you do it as a habit without having to remind yourself. And it is a very useful habit, and makes the dullest walk interesting.

Hunters when they are looking about in a country to find game first look for any tracks, old or new, to see if there are any animals in the country; then they study the newer marks to find out where the animals are hiding themselves; then, after they have found a fresh track, they follow it up till they find the animal and kill him; and afterwards they often have to retrace their own tracks to find their way back to camp. And war scouts do much the same as regards their enemies.

First of all you must be able to distinguish one man's footmark from that of another, by its size, shape, and nails, etc. And similarly the prints of horses and other animals.

From a man's track, that is, from the size of his foot and the length of his stride, you can tell, to a certain extent, his height.

In taking notes of a track you should pick out a well-marked print, very carefully measure its length, length of heel, with widest point of tread, width at waist, width of heel, number of rows of nails, and number of nails in each row, heel and toe-plates or nails, shape of nail-heads, etc.

It is best to make a diagram of the foot-print thus—nails missing.

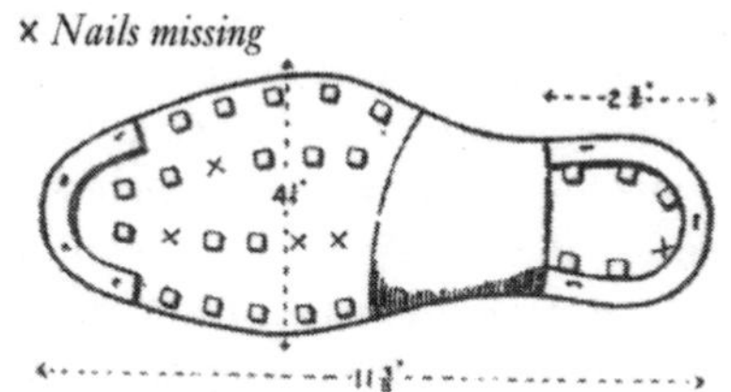

The way in which the diagram of a boot-track should be drawn

You should also measure very carefully the length of the man's stride from the toe of one foot to the heel of the other.

NOTE TO INSTRUCTOR: *Make each scout take off his own boot and draw a diagram of it on paper, putting in all nails and other points. Or, out of doors, give each scout the outline ready drawn of a foot-mark, and then let him find a foot-mark (or make his own) and fill in the details of nail-marks, etc.*

Also, he should note down the length of stride taken, and how much the feet point outwards from the straight direction of their path.

A man was once found drowned in a river. It was supposed that he must have fallen in accidentally, and that the cuts on his head were caused by stones, etc., in the river. But someone took a drawing of his boots, and after searching the river bank came on his tracks, and followed them up to a spot where there had evidently been a struggle, the ground being much trampled and bushes broken down to the water's edge, and the track of two other men's feet. And though these men were never found, it showed the case to be one of probable murder, which would not otherwise have been suspected.

A scout must learn to recognise at a glance at what pace the maker of the tracks was going, and so on.

A man walking puts the whole flat of his foot on the ground, each foot a little under a yard from the other. In running the toes are more deeply dug into the ground, and a little dirt is kicked up, and the feet are more than a yard apart. Sometimes men walk backwards in order to deceive anyone who may be tracking, but a good scout can generally tell this at once by the stride being shorter, the toes more turned in, and the heels being tightly impressed.

With animals, if they are moving fast, their toes are more deeply dug into the ground, and they kick up the dirt, and their paces are longer than when going slowly.

You ought to be able to tell the pace at which a horse has been going directly you see the tracks.

At a walk the horse makes two pairs of hoof prints—the near (left) hind foot close in front of near forefoot mark, and the off (right) forefoot similarly just behind the print of the off hindfoot.

At a trot the track is similar but the stride is longer.

The hind feet are generally longer and narrower in shape than the forefeet.

Native trackers boast that not only can they tell a person's sex and age by their tracks, but also their characters. They say that people who turn out their toes much are generally 'liars'.

It was a trick with highwaymen of old, and with horse stealers more recently, to put their horses' shoes on wrong way round in order to deceive trackers who might try to follow them up, but a good tracker would not be taken in. Similarly, thieves often walk backwards for the same reason, but a clever tracker will very soon recognise the deception.

HORSES' TRACKS

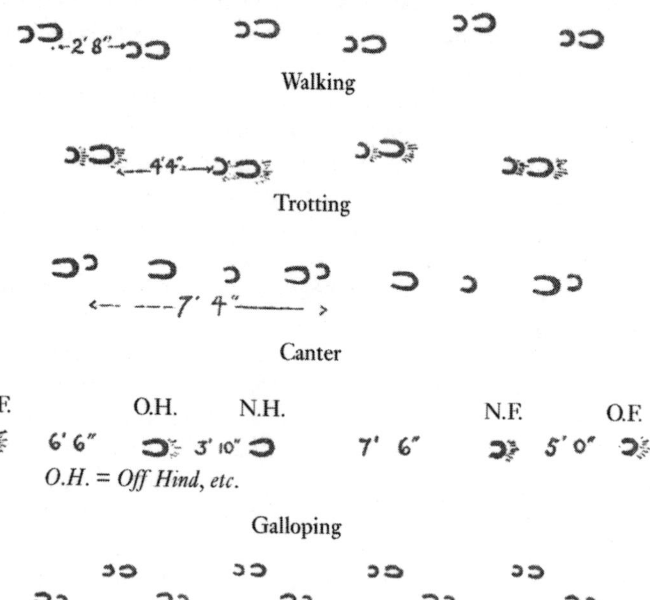

Lame horse walking: Which leg is he lame in?
N.B.—The long feet are the hind feet

These are the tracks of two birds on the ground. One lives generally on the ground, the other in bushes and trees. Which track belongs to which bird?

Wheel tracks should also be studied till you can tell the difference between the track of a gun, a carriage, a country cart, motor-car, or a bicycle, *and the direction they were going in*. [*See diagram.*]

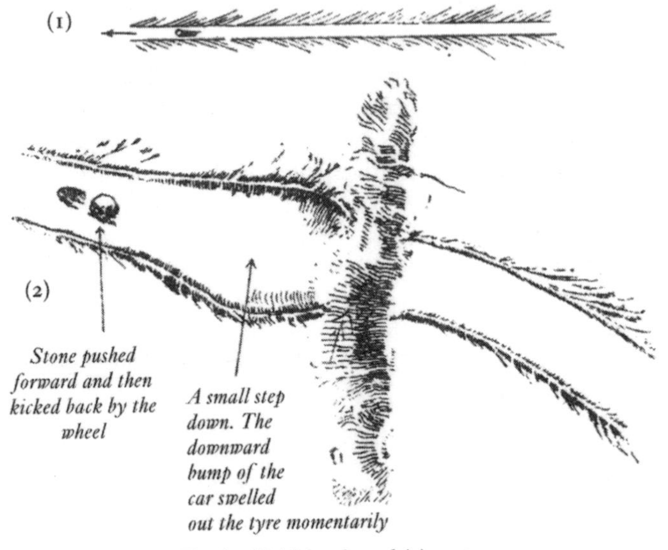
(1)
(2)
Stone pushed forward and then kicked back by the wheel
A small step down. The downward bump of the car swelled out the tyre momentarily

Track of (1) bicycle and (2) motor

In addition to learning to recognise the pace of tracks, you must get to know how old they are. This is a most important point, and requires a very great amount of practice and experience before you can judge it really well.

So much depends on the state of the ground and weather, and its effects on the 'spoor'. If you follow one track, say on a dry, windy day, over varying ground, you will find that when it is on light, sandy soil it will look old in a very short time, because any damp earth that it may kick up from under the surface will dry very rapidly to the same colour as the surface dust, and the sharp edges of the footmark will soon be rounded off by the breeze playing over the dry dust in which they are formed. When it gets into damp ground, the same track will look much fresher, because the sun will have only partially dried up the upturned soil, and the wind will not, therefore, have bevelled off the sharp edges of the impression, and if it gets into damp clay, under shade of trees, etc., where the sun does not get at it, the same track, which may have looked a day old in the sand, will here look quite fresh.

Of course, a great clue to the age of tracks will often be found in spots of rain having fallen on them since they were made (if you know at what time the rain fell), dust or grass seeds blown into them (if you noticed at what time the wind was blowing), or the crossing of other tracks over the original ones, or where the grass has been trodden down, the extent to which it has since dried or withered. In following a horse, the length of time since it passed can also be judged by the freshness, or otherwise, of the droppings—due allowance being made for the effect of sun, rain, or birds, etc., upon them.

Having learnt to distinguish the pace and age of spoor, you must next learn to follow it over all kinds of ground. This is an accomplishment that you can practise all you life, and you will still find yourself learning at the end of it—you will find yourself continually improving.*

Then there is a great deal to learn from the ashes of fires—whether they are still warm or cold, scraps showing what kind of food the people were eating, whether plentiful or scarce.

You must not only keep a sharp look out for scout signs made by your own scouts, but also for those made by hostile scouts. Foreign scouts also have their private signs—as also do tramps. The following are some of the signs made by tramps on walls or fences near houses where they have been begging which they chalk up to warn others of their class:

⊙	Very bad: they give you in charge here	⋋	No good
△	Too many tramps been here already	□	Bad people

There are very good native trackers in the Soudan and Egypt, and I saw some of their work there.

The Colonel of the Egyptian Cavalry had had some things stolen out of his house, so a tracker was sent for from the neighbouring Jaalin tribe.

He soon found the footprints of the thief and followed them a long way out on to the desert, and found the spot where he had buried the stolen goods. His tracks then came back to the barracks.

So the whole of the regiment was paraded without shoes on for the tracker to examine. And at the end when he had seen every man walk, he said, 'No the thief is not there.' Just then the Colonel's native servant came up to him with a message, and the tracker who was standing by said to the Colonel 'That is the man who buried the stolen things.'

The servant, surprised at being found out, then confessed that it was he who had stolen his master's property, thinking that he would be the last man to be suspected.*

Mr Deakin,* the Premier of Australia, told me how he travelled on board ship with a number of natives of Australia who were on the sea for the first time in their lives.

When the ship got out to sea he noticed all these natives had got into the bows and were lying flat on the deck with their heads over the side staring intently into the water ahead of the ship. So interested were they in the water that for some time he could not get any reply to his question as to what they were looking at, till at length one of them said: 'We cannot understand how the ship is finding its way across the sea; we cannot see the trail that it is following; we know that our eyes are sharp enough on shore and often when we are guiding white men along a trail they say they cannot see the tracks which to us are clear enough—their eyes are different to ours. But here at sea the English sailors evidently can see tracks ahead of them, otherwise they would not know which way to send the ship, and yet we, who are so good at seeing on shore, cannot see any sign of a track or mark on the water.'

When getting on to very fresh spoor of man or beast, the old scout will generally avoid following it closely because the hunted animal will frequently look back to see if it is being followed. The tracker therefore makes a circle, and comes back on to where he would expect to find the spoor again. If he finds it, he makes another circle further ahead till he finds no spoor. Then he knows he is ahead of his game so he gradually circles nearer and nearer till he finds it. See diagram.

HINTS TO SPOORING

SOME trackers of Scinde* followed up a stolen camel from Karachi to Sehwan, 150 miles over sand and bare rock. The thieves, to escape detection, drove the camel up and down a crowded street, in order to get the trail mixed up with others—but the trackers foresaw this and made a 'cast' round the town, and hit on the outgoing spoor on the far side, which they successfully followed up.

In tracking where the spoor is difficult to see, such as on hard ground, or in grass, note the direction of the last foot-print that you can see, then look on in the same direction, but well ahead of you, say 20 or 30 yards, and in grass you will generally see the blades bent or trodden, and on hard ground, possibly stones displaced or scratched, and so on, small signs which, seen in a line one behind the other, give

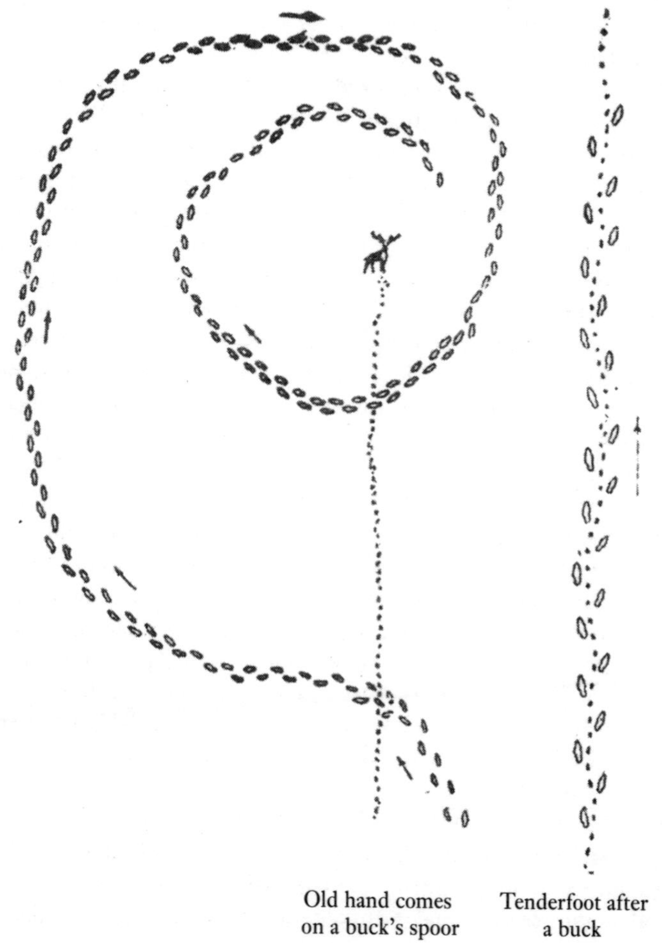

Old hand comes on a buck's spoor

Tenderfoot after a buck

a kind of track that otherwise would not be noticed. I once tracked a bicycle on a hard macadam road where it really made no impression at all, but by looking along the surface of the road for a long distance ahead of me, under the rising sun as it happened, the line it had taken was quite visible through the almost invisible coating of dew upon the ground. Standing on the track and looking upon it close to my feet I could not see the slightest sign of it. The great thing is to look for a difficult track *against* the sun, so that the slightest dent in the ground throws a shadow.

If you lose sight of the track you must make a 'cast' to find it again. To do this put your handkerchief, staff, or other mark at the first footmark that you noticed, then work round it in a wide circle, say 30, 50 or 100 yards away from it as a centre—choosing the most favourable ground, soft ground if possible, to find signs of the outward track. If you are with a patrol it is generally best for the patrol to halt while one or perhaps two men make the cast. If everybody starts trying to find the spoor they very soon defeat their object by treading it out or confusing it with their own footmarks—too many cooks easily spoil the broth in such a case.

In making a cast use your common-sense as to which direction the enemy has probably taken, and try it there. I remember an instance of tracking a boar which illustrates what I mean. The boar had been running through some muddy inundated fields, and was easy enough to follow until he turned off over some very hard and stony ground, where after a little while not a sign of his spoor was to be seen. A cast had accordingly to be made. The last footmark was marked, and the tracker moved round a wide circle, examining the ground most carefully, but not a sign was found. Then the tracker took a look round the country, and, putting himself in place of the pig, said 'Now which direction would I have gone in?' Some distance to the front of him, as the original track led, stood a long hedge of prickly cactus; in it were two gaps. The tracker went to one of these as being the line the boar would probably take. Here the ground was still very hard, and no footmark was visible, but on a leaf of the cactus in the gap was a pellet of wet mud; and this gave the desired clue; there was no mud on this hard ground, but the pig had evidently brought some on his feet from the wet ground he had been travelling through. This one little sign enabled the tracker to work on in the right direction to another and another, until eventually he got on to the spoor again in favourable ground, and was able to follow up the boar to his resting place.*

I have watched a tracker in the Soudan following tracks, where for a time they were quite invisible to the ordinary eye in this way. While the track was clear he made his own stride exactly to fit that of the track, so that he walked step for step with it, and he tapped the ground with his staff as he walked along—ticking off each footprint as it were. When the footprints disappeared on hard ground, or had been buried by drifting sand he still walked on at the same place tap-tapping the ground with his staff at the spot where there ought to have been a footprint. Occasionally one saw a slight depression or mark which showed that there had been a footprint there, and thus he knew he was still on the right line.

HINTS TO INSTRUCTORS

PRACTICES IN TRACKING

1. The Instructor should make his scouts prepare a well-rolled or flattened piece of ground (about ten or fifteen yards square) and make one boy walk across it, then run, and then bicycle across it. Part of the ground should be wet as if by rain, the other part dry.

He can then explain the difference in the tracks so that scouts can tell at once from any tracks they may see afterwards whether a person was walking or running.

If possible, a day later make fresh tracks alongside the old and notice the difference in appearance so that the scouts can learn to judge the age of tracks.

Then make tracks of various kinds overrunning each other, such as a bicycle meeting a boy on foot, each going over the other's tracks, and let the scouts read the meaning.

2. Send out a boy with 'Tracking Irons' on and let the patrol track him and notice when any other tracks override his, showing what people or animals have passed since.*

N.B. Tracking irons are an invention of Mr Thompson Seton's and can be strapped on to soles of scout's boots (like a pair of skates) so that wherever he goes he leaves a track similar to that of a deer.

TRACKING GAMES

PRACTICES AND GAMES IN SPOORING

Track Memory

MAKE a patrol sit with their feet up so that other scouts can study them. Give the scouts, say, three minutes to study the boots. Then leaving the scouts in a room or out of sight let one of the patrol make some foot-marks in a good bit of ground. Call up the scouts one by one and let them see the track and say who made it.

Track Drawing

TAKE out a patrol; set them on to one foot-track. Award a prize to the scout who makes the most accurate drawing of one of the foot-prints of the track. The scouts should be allowed to follow up the track till they get to a bit of ground where a good impression of it can be found.

FOR HONOURS

Spot the Thief

GET a stranger to make a track unseen by the scouts. The scouts study his track so as to know it again.

Then put the stranger among eight or ten others and let them all make their tracks for the boys to see, going by in rotation. Each scout then in turn whispers to the umpire which man made the original track—describing him by his number in filing past. The scout who answers correctly wins; if more than one answers correctly, the one who then draws the best diagram, from memory, of the foot-print wins.

This game may also be carried out as a test for marks towards a badge of honour. Correct detection of the thief counts two marks; if good diagram is also drawn another mark may be added.

'Smugglers Over the Border'

THE 'Border' is a certain line of country about four hundred yards long, preferably a road or wide path or bit of sand, on which foot-tracks can easily be seen. One patrol watches the border with sentries posted along this road, with a reserve posted further inland. This should be about half-way between the 'border' and the 'town', the 'town' would be a base marked by trees, buildings, or flags, etc., about half a mile distant from the border. A hostile patrol of smugglers assembles about half a mile on the other side of the border. They will all cross the border, in any formation they please, either singly or together or scattered, and make for the town, either walking or running, or at scout's pace. Only one among them is supposed to be smuggling, and he wears tracking irons, so that the sentries walk up and down their beat (they may not run till after the 'alarm'), waiting for the tracks of the smuggler. Directly a sentry sees the track, he gives the alarm signal to the reserve and starts himself to follow up the track as fast as he can. The reserve thereupon cooperate with them and try to catch the smuggler before he can reach the town. Once within the boundary of the town he is safe and wins the game.

BOOKS TO READ ON SPOORING

'Lectures on Tracking': *Cavalry Journal* Office, Whitehall, S.W.

'Scouting and reconnaissance in Savage Countries': Captain Stigand.

'Tracks of Wild Animals.'

CAMP FIRE YARN.—No. 7

READING 'SIGN' OR DEDUCTION

Putting this and that together—Sherlock-Holmesism—Instances of Deduction—Hints to Instructors—Practice in Deduction—Books on Deduction.

WHEN a scout has learned to notice 'sign', he must then learn to 'put this and that together', and so read a *meaning* from what he has seen. This is called 'deduction'. Here is an example of what I mean which was lately given in the 'Forest and Stream',* which shows how the young scout can read the meaning from 'sign' when he has been trained to it.

A cavalry soldier had got lost and some of his comrades were hunting all over the country to find him, when they came across a native boy, and asked him if he had seen the lost man. He immediately said: 'Do you mean a very tall soldier, riding a roan horse that was slightly lame?'

They said, 'Yes; that was the man. Where did you see him?'

The boy replied 'I have not seen him, but I know where he has gone.'

Thereupon they arrested him, thinking that probably the man had been murdered and made away with, and that the boy had heard about it.

But eventually he explained that he had seen tracks of the man which he could point out to them.

Finally he brought them to a place where the signs showed that the man had made a halt. The horse had rubbed itself against a tree, and had left some of its hairs sticking to the bark which showed that it was a roan horse; its hoof marks showed that it was lame, that is, one foot was not so deeply indented on the ground and did not take so long a pace as the other feet. That the rider was a soldier was shown by the imprint of his boot which was an army boot. Then they asked the boy 'How could you tell that he was a tall man?' and the boy pointed out to where the soldier had broken a branch from the tree which would have been out of reach of a man of ordinary height. Deduction is exactly like reading a book.

A boy who has never been taught to read and who sees you reading from a book would ask 'How do you do it?' and you would point out to him that a number of small signs on a page are letters; these letters when grouped form words; and words form sentences; and sentences give information.

Similarly a trained scout will see little signs and tracks, he puts them together in his mind and quickly reads a meaning from them such as an untrained man would never arrive at.

And from frequent practice he gets to read the meaning at a glance just as you do a book without the delay of spelling out each word, letter by letter.*

I was one day, during the Matabele war [*Show on map**] with a native out scouting near to the Matopo Hills over a wide grassy plain.* Suddenly we crossed a track freshly made in grass, where the

From 'Sketches in Mafeking and East Africa'. By permission of Messrs. Smith & Elder

blades of grass were still green and damp though pressed down; all were bending one way which showed the direction in which the people had been travelling; following up the track for a bit it got on to a patch of sand, and we then saw that it was the spoor of several women (small feet with straight edge, and short steps), and boys (small feet, curved edge and longer strides) walking not running, towards the hills, about five miles away; where we believed the enemy to be hiding.

Then we saw a leaf lying about ten yards off the track—there were no trees for miles, but we knew that trees having this kind of leaf grew at a village fifteen miles away, in the direction from which the footmarks were coming. It seemed likely therefore that the women had come from that village, bringing the leaf with them, and had gone to the hills.

On picking up the leaf we found it was damp, and smelled of native beer. The short steps showed that the women were carrying loads. So we guessed that according to the custom they had been carrying pots of native beer on their heads, the mouths of the pots being stopped up with bunches of leaves. One of these leaves had fallen out; but we found it ten yards off the track, which showed that at the time it fell a wind was blowing. There was no wind now *i.e.*, seven o'clock, but there had been one about five o'clock.

So we guessed from all these little signs that a party of women and boys had brought beer during the night from the village 15 miles away and had taken it to the enemy on the hills, arriving there soon after six o'clock.

The men would probably start to drink the beer at once (as it goes sour in a few hours), and would, by the time we could get there, be getting sleepy and keeping a bad look-out, so we should have a favourable chance of looking at their position.

We accordingly followed the women's track, found the enemy, made our observations and got away with our information without any difficulty.

And it was chiefly done on the evidence of that one leaf. So you see the importance of noticing even a little thing like that.

INSTANCES OF DEDUCTION

Mr Tighe Hopkins* writing in 'World's Work'* describes how by noticing very small signs detectives have discovered crimes.

In one case a crime had been committed and a stranger's coat was found which gave no clue to the owner. The coat was put into a stout bag and beaten with a stick. The dust was collected from the bag and examined under a powerful magnifying glass and was found to consist of fine sawdust which showed that the owner of the coat was probably a carpenter, or sawyer, or joiner. The dust was then put under a more powerful magnifying glass—called a microscope—and it was then seen that it also contained some tiny grains of gelatine and powdered glue. These things are not used by carpenters or sawyers, so the coat was shown to belong to a joiner, and the police got on the track of the criminal.

Dust out of pockets, or in the recesses of a pocket-knife, and so on, if closely examined, tells a great deal.

Then on another occasion a murder was committed, and close by a cap was found which did not belong to the victim, so probably it belonged to the murderer. Two hairs were found sticking to the lining of the cap; they were carefully taken to Dr Emile Pfaff, a celebrated observer. He examined the hairs under a microscope and was able to read from them that the owner of the cap was 'A man of middle age, strong, inclined to be fat; black hair with some grey among it, getting bald; lately had his hair cut.'

In this way a clue was got to the appearance of the murderer.

Dr Bell* of Edinburgh is said to be the original from whom Sir Conan Doyle drew his idea of Sherlock Holmes.

The doctor was once teaching a class of medical students at a hospital how to doctor people. A patient was brought in, so that the doctor might show how an injured man should be treated. The patient in this case came limping in, and the doctor turned to one of the students and asked him:

'What is the matter with this man?'

The student replied, 'I don't know, sir. I haven't asked him yet.'

The doctor said, 'Well, there is no need to ask him, you should see for yourself—he has injured his right knee; he is limping on that leg: he injured it by burning it in the fire; you see how his trouser is burnt away at the knee. This is Monday morning. Yesterday was fine; Saturday was wet and muddy. The man's trousers are muddy all over. He had a fall in the mud on Saturday night.'

Then he turned to the man and said, 'You drew your wages on Saturday and got drunk, and in trying to get your clothes dry by the fire when you got home you fell on the fire and burnt your knee—Isn't that so?'

'Yes, sir,' replied the man.

I saw a case in the paper last week where a judge at the county court used his powers of 'noticing little things,' and 'putting this and that together'. He was trying a man as a debtor.

The man pleaded that he was out of work, and could get no employment.

The judge said—'Then what are you doing with that pencil behind your ear if you are not in business?'

The man had to admit that he had been helping his wife in her business, which, it turned out, was a very profitable one, and the judge thereupon ordered him to pay his debt.

Dr Reiss, of the Police Department of the University of Lausanne, records how the police read spoor.

A burglary had taken place in a house, and the thief's footprints were found in the garden. Those going towards the house were not so deeply impressed as those coming away from it nor were they so close together; from this the police gathered that the burglar had carried away with him a heavy load which made him take short steps and he was fully weighted down so that they sank deeply in the ground.

HINTS TO INSTRUCTORS

HOW TO TEACH DEDUCTION IN PRACTICE

*Read aloud a story in which a good amount of observation of details occurs, with consequent deductions, such as in either the 'Memoirs' or the 'Adventures of Sherlock Holmes'.**

Then question the boys afterwards as to which details suggested certain solutions, to see that they really have grasped the method.

Follow up ordinary tracks and deduce their meaning. For examples of daily practice see my book of 'Aids to Scouting'.

EXAMPLE OF PRACTICE IN DEDUCTION

A SIMPLE deduction from signs noticed in my walk one morning on a stony mountain path in Kashmir.

Sign Observed—Tree-stump, about three feet high, by the path. A stone about the size of a cocoanut lying near it, to which were sticking some bits of bruised walnut rind, dried up. Some walnut rind also lying on the stump. Further along the path, 30 yards to the south of the stump, were lying bits of walnut shell of four walnuts. Close by was a high sloping rock, alongside the path. The only walnut tree in sight was 150 yards north of the stump.

At the foot of the stump was a cake of hardened mud which showed the impression of a grass shoe.

What would you make out from those signs? My solution of it was this:

A man had gone southward on a long journey along the path two days ago, carrying a load; and had rested at the rock while he ate walnuts.

My deductions were these:

It was a man carrying a load, because carriers when they want to rest do not sit down, but rest their load against a sloping rock and lean back. Had he had no load he would probably have sat down on the stump, but he preferred to go 30 yards further to where the rock was. Women do not carry loads there, so it was a man. But he first broke the shells of his walnuts on the tree-stump with the stone, having brought them from the tree 150 yards north. So he was travelling south, and he was on a long journey, as he was wearing shoes, and not going barefooted as he would be if only strolling near his home. Three days ago there was rain, the cake of mud had been picked up while the ground was still wet—but it had not been since rained upon and was now dry. The walnut rind was also dry and confirmed the time that had elapsed.

There is no important story attached to this, but it is just an example of everyday practice which should be carried out by scouts.

GAMES AND COMPETITIONS IN DEDUCTION

Get some people who are strangers to the boys to come along as passers-by in the street or road, and let the boys separately notice all about them; and after an interval ask each for a full description of each of the passers-by as to appearance, peculiar recognisable points, and what he guesses his business to be; or let each boy have two minutes' conversation with your friend and try to find out what he can about him in that time by questioning and observation.

Set a room or prepare a piece of ground with small signs, tracks, etc., read aloud the story of the crime up to that point and let each boy or each patrol in turn examine the scene for a given time and then privately give each his solution of it.

The very simplest, most elementary schemes should be given at first, and they can gradually be elaborated. For instance take a number of footmarks and spent matches by a tree showing where a man had difficulty in lighting his pipe, etc.

For a more finished theme take a mystery like that in 'Memoirs of Sherlock Holmes' called 'The Resident Patient'. Set a room to represent the patient's room where he was found hanging, with footprints of muddy boots on the carpet, cigar ends bitten or cut in the fireplace, cigar ashes, screw-driver and screws, etc. Put down a strip or 'stepping stones' of stuff, handkerchiefs, or paper on which the competitors shall walk (so as not to confuse existing tracks). Let each scout (or patrol) come in separately and have three minutes in which to investigate. Then to go out and give in his solution, written or verbal, half an hour later.

Let one patrol make tracks by carrying out such a series as that which D'Artagnan elucidated. The other patrol then acts as detectives and endeavours to unravel the mystery from the tracks and other sign.*

PLAY

Any one of Sherlock Holmes stories makes a good play.

BOOKS TO READ

'Memoirs of Sherlock Holmes'.

'Adventures of Sherlock Holmes'.

'The Thinking Machine' which contains a number of stories like Sherlock Holmes.

'Criminal Investigation', by Dr Gross. Edited by J. Adam. (Published by Specialist Press, London.)

CHAPTER III

WOODCRAFT;

or,

Knowledge of Animals and Nature

CAMP FIRE YARN.—No. 8

STALKING

As an aid to Observation—How to hide yourself—How to learn Stalking—Games—Book on Stalking.

AT some manœuvres lately, two hostile patrols of soldiers were approaching, looking for each other, till the ground between them became very open, and it seemed hopeless for a scout to cross it without being seen. However, a small ditch about two feet deep and overgrown with bushes ran across part of the open plain from the point where one patrol was lying hidden. They noticed two claves which came out on to the plain from the opposite side and walked across the open till they got to the end of this ditch, and here they stopped and separated and began browsing.

A scout now started to make use of this ditch by crawling along it till he should get to the far end near the calves, and there he hoped to find some way of getting on further, or of at least peeping out and getting a nearer view of the possible position of the enemy. When about half-way along the ditch he was suddenly fired at by an enemy's scout already there, in the ditch.

When the umpire rode up and asked him how he had got there without being seen, the hostile scout said that finding he could not reach the ditch without being seen if he went across the plain, he seized two calves which he had found among the bushes where his patrol were hiding, and stepping between them, he drove the pair of them, by holding their tails across the open ditch; here he let them go and slid himself into the ditch without being noticed.

HOW TO HIDE YOURSELF

When you want to observe wild animals you have to stalk them, that is, to creep up to them without their seeing or smelling you.

A hunter when he is stalking wild animals keeps himself entirely hidden, so does the war scout when watching or looking for the enemy; a policeman does not catch pickpockets by standing about in uniform watching for them, he dresses like one of the crowd and as often as not gazes into a shop window and sees all that goes on behind him reflected as if in a looking-glass.

If a guilty person finds himself being watched it puts him on his guard, while an innocent person becomes annoyed. So when you are observing a person don't do so by openly staring at them but notice the details you want to at one glance or two, and if you want to study them more, walk behind them; you can learn just as much from a backview, in fact, more than you can from a frontview, and, unless they are scouts and look round frequently, they do not know that you are observing them.

War scouts and hunters stalking game always carry out two important things when they don't want to be seen.

One is—they take care that the ground behind them, or trees, or buildings, etc., are of the same colour as their clothes.

And the other is—if an enemy or a deer is seen looking for them they remain perfectly still without moving so long as he is there.

In that way a scout even though he is out in the open will often escape being noticed.*

In choosing your background, consider the colour of your clothes; thus, if you are dressed in khâki, don't go and stand in front of a white-washed wall, or in front of a dark-shaded bush, but go where there is khâki-coloured sand or grass or rocks behind you—and remain perfectly still. It will be very difficult for an enemy to distinguish you even at a short distance.

If you are in dark clothes, get among dark bushes, or in the shadow of trees, or rocks, but be careful that the ground beyond you is also dark—if there is light-coloured ground beyond the trees under which you are standing, for instance, you will stand out clearly defined against it.

If you are in red, try and get against red brick buildings, or red earth or rocks, and so on.

Stalking attitudes

In making use of hills as lookout places be very careful not to show yourself on the top or sky-line. That is the fault which a Tenderfoot generally makes.

It is quite a lesson to watch a Zulu scout making use of a hill-top or rising ground as a look-out place. He will crawl up on all fours, lying flat in the grass; on reaching the top he will very slowly raise his head, inch by inch, till he can see the view. If he sees the enemy on beyond, he will have a good look, and, if he thinks they are watching him, will keep his head perfectly steady for an immense time, hoping that he will be mistaken for a stump or a stone. If he is not detected he will very gradually lower his head, inch by inch, into the grass again, and crawl quietly away. Any quick or sudden movement of the head on the sky-line would be very liable to attract attention, even at a considerable distance.

At night keep as much as possible in low ground, ditches, etc., so that you are down in the dark while an enemy who comes near will be visible to you outlined against the stars on higher ground.

By squatting low in the shadow of the bush at night, and keeping quite still, I have let an enemy's scout come and stand within three feet of me, so that when he turned his back towards me I was able to stand up where I was and fling my arms round him.

A point also to remember in keeping hidden while moving, especially at night, is to walk quietly; the thump of an ordinary man's heel on the ground can be heard a good distance off, but a scout or hunter always walks lightly, on the ball of his foot not on his heels; and this you should practise whenever you are walking by day or by night, indoors as well as out, so that it becomes a habit with you—so as to walk as lightly and silently as possible. You will find that as you grow into it your power of walking long distances will grow, you will not tire so soon as you would if clumping along in the heavy-footed manner of most people.

Remember always that to stalk a wild animal, or a good scout, you must keep down-wind of him even if the wind is so slight as to be merely a slight air.

Before starting to stalk your enemy then you should be sure which way the wind is blowing, and work up against it. To find this out you should wet your thumb all round with your tongue, and then hold it up and see which side feels coldest, or you can throw some light dust, or dry grass or leaves in the air, and see which way they drift.

The Red Indian Scouts when they wanted to reconnoitre an enemy's camp, used to tie a wolf's skin on their backs and walk on all fours, and, imitating the howl of a wolf, prowled round the camps at night.

In Australia the natives stalk emus—which are great birds something like an ostrich—by putting an emu's skin over themselves and walking with body bent and one hand held up to represent the bird's head and neck.

American scouts when peeping over a ridge or any place where their head might be seen against the sky-line put on a cap made of wolf's head skin with ears on it—so that they may be mistaken for a wolf if seen.*

Our scouts also when looking out among grass etc., tie a string or

From 'Sketches in Mafeking and East Africa'. By permission of Messrs. Smith & Elder

band round their head and stick a lot of grass in it, some upright some dropping over their face, so that their head is very invisible.

When hiding behind a big stone or mound, etc., they don't look over the top but round the side of it.

HOW TO TEACH STALKING

Demonstrate the value of adapting colour of clothes to background, by sending out one boy about 500 yards to stand against different backgrounds in turn, till he gets one similar in colour to his own clothes.

The rest of the patrol to watch and to notice how invisible he becomes when he gets a suitable background. e.g. a boy in a grey suit standing in front of dark bushes, etc., is quite visible—but becomes less so if he stands in front of a grey rock or house; a boy in dark suit is very visible in a green field but not when he stands in an open door-way against dark interior shadow.

GAMES IN STALKING

Scout Hunting

One scout is given time to go out and hide himself, the remainder then start to find him. He wins if he is not found, or if he can get back to the starting point within a given time without being touched.

Dispatch Running

A scout is told to bring a note into a certain spot or house from a distance within a given time: other hostile scouts are told to prevent any message getting to this place and to hide themselves at different points to stop the dispatch carrier getting in with it.

To count as a capture two scouts must touch the dispatch runner before he reaches the spot for delivering the message.

Stalking

Instructor acts as a deer—not hiding but standing, moving a little now and then if he likes.

Scouts go out to find and each in his own way tries to get up to him unseen.

Directly the instructor sees a scout he directs him to stand up as having failed. After a certain time the instructor calls 'time', all stand up at the spot which they have reached and the nearest wins.

The same game may be played to test the scouts in stepping lightly—the umpire being blindfolded. The practice should preferably be carried out where there are dry twigs lying about, and gravel, etc. The scout may start to stalk the blind enemy at 100 yards distance, and he must do it fairly fast—say in one minute and a half—to touch the blind man before he hears him.

Stalking and Reporting

The umpire places himself out in the open and sends each scout or pair of scouts away in different directions about half a mile off. When he waves a flag, which is the signal to begin, they all hide and then proceed to stalk him, creeping up and watching all he does. When he waves the flag again, they rise, come in, and report each in turn all that he did, either by handing in a written report or verbally as may be ordered. The umpire meantime has kept a look-out in each direction, and, every time he sees a scout, he takes two points off that scout's score. He, on his part, performs small actions, such as sitting down, kneeling up, and looking through glasses, using handkerchief, taking hat off for a bit, walking round in a circle a few times, to give scouts something to note and report about him. Scouts are given three points for each act reported correctly. It saves time if the umpire makes out a scoring card beforehand, giving the name of each scout, and a number of columns showing each act of his and what mark that scout wins, also a column of deducted marks for exposing themselves.

BOOK ON STALKING

'Deer Stalking'. Badminton Library Series.

CAMP FIRE YARN.—No. 9

ANIMALS

The calling of Wild Animals—Animals—Birds—Reptiles—Fish—Insects—Practical Instruction about Animals—Games—A Play about Animals—Books to read.

SCOUTS in many parts of the world use the calls of wild animals and birds for communicating with each other, especially at night or in thick bush, or in fog, etc., but it is also very useful to be able to imitate the calls if you want to watch the habits of the animals. You can begin by calling chickens; or by talking to dogs in dog language and you very soon find you can give the angry growl or the playing growl of a dog. Owls, woodpigeons, and curlews are very easily called.

In India I have seen a certain tribe of gipsies who eat jackals. Now a jackal is one of the most suspicious animals that lives and is very difficult to catch in a trap, but these gipsies catch them by calling them in this way.

Several men with dogs hide themselves in a grass and bushes round a small field. In the middle of this open place one gipsy imitates the call of the jackals calling to each other; he gets louder and louder till they seem to come together; then they begin to growl and finally tackle each other with violent snapping, snarling and yelling, and at the same time he shakes a bundle of dried leaves which sounds like the animals dashing about among grass and reeds. Then he flings himself down on the ground and throws up dust in the air so that he is completely hidden in it, still growling and fighting. If any jackal is within sound of this he comes tearing out of the jungle and dashes into the dust to join in the fight. When he finds a man there he comes out again in a hurry; but meantime the dogs have been loosed from all sides, and they quickly catch him and kill him.

Mr William Long in his very interesting book, called 'Beasts of the Field',* describes how he once called a moose. The moose is a very huge kind of stag with an ugly, bulging kind of nose. He lives in the forests of North America and Canada, and is very hard to get near; and is pretty dangerous when he is angry.

Mr Long was in a canoe fishing when he heard a moose bull calling in the forest—so just for fun he went ashore and cut a strip of bark of a birch tree and rolled it up into a cone or trumpet shape so as to make a kind of megaphone (about fifteen inches long, five inches wide at the larger end, and about an inch or two at the mouth-piece). With this he proceeded to imitate the roaring grunt of the bull-moose. The effect was tremendous; the old moose came tearing down and even came into the water and tried to get at him—and it was only by hard paddling that in the end he got away.

Indian gypsy calling jackals

One of the best things in scouting is the hunting of big game—that is going after elephants, lions, rhino, wild boar, deer, and those kind of animals; and a fellow has to be a pretty good scout if he hopes to succeed at it.

You get plenty of excitement and plenty of danger too; and all that I have told you about observation and tracking and hiding yourself comes in here. And in addition to these you must know all about animals and their habits and ways if you want to be successful.

I have said the 'hunting' or 'going after big game is one of the best things in scouting'. I did not say shooting or killing the game was the best part; for as you get to study animals you get to like them more and more, and you will soon find that you don't want to kill them for the mere sake of killing, and that the more you see of them the more you see the wonderful work of God in them.

All the fun of hunting lies in the adventurous life in the jungle, the chance in many cases of the animal hunting *you* instead of you hunting the animal, the interest of tracking him up, stalking him and watching all that he does and learning his habits. The actual shooting the animal that follows is only a very small part of the fun.

No scout should ever kill an animal unless there is some real reason for doing so, and in that case he should kill it quickly and effectively, so as to give it as little pain as possible.

In fact many big-game hunters nowadays prefer to shoot their game with the camera instead of with the rifle—which gives just as interesting results—except when you and your natives are hungry, then you must, of course, kill your game.

My brother* was lately big game shooting in East Africa and had very good sport with the camera, living in the wilds, and tracking and stalking and finally snap-shotting elephants, rhinoceros and other big animals.

One day he had crept up near to an elephant and had set up his camera and had got his head under the cloth focussing it, when his native cried, 'Look out, sir!' and started to run. My brother poked his head out from under the cloth and found a great elephant coming for him, only a few yards off. So he just pressed the button, and then lit out and ran too. The elephant rushed up to the camera, stopped, and seemed to recognise that it was only a camera after all and smiling at his own irritability lurched off into the jungle again.

Mr Schillings' book 'With Flashlight and Rifle in Africa'* is a most interesting collection of instantaneous photos of wild animals, most of them taken by night by means of flashlight, which was set going by the animals themselves striking against wires which he had put out for the purpose. He got splendid photos of lions, hyaenas, deer of all sorts, zebras, and other beasts. There is one of a lion actually in the air springing on to a buck.

The boar is certainly the bravest of all animals; he is the real 'King of Jungle', and the other animals all know it. If you watch a drinking pool in the jungle at night, you will see the animals that come to it all creeping down nervously, looking out in every direction for hidden enemies. But when the boar comes he simply swaggers down with his great head and its shiny tusks swinging from side to side: he cares for nobody, but everybody cares for him; even a tiger drinking at the pool will give a snarl and sneak quickly out of sight.

I have often lain out on moonlight nights to watch the animals, especially wild boars, in the jungle; and it is just as good fun as merely going after them to kill them.

And I have caught and kept a young wild boar and a young panther, and found them most amusing and interesting little beggars. The boar used to live in my garden, and he never became really tame though I got him as a baby.*

He would come to me when I called him—but very warily; he would never come to a stranger, and a native he would 'go for' and try and cut him with his little tusks.

He used to practise the use of his tusks while turning at full speed round an old tree stump in the garden, and he would gallop at this and round it in a figure-of-eight continuously for over five minutes at a time, and then fling himself down on his side, panting with his exertions.

My panther was also a beautiful and delightfully playful beast, and used to go about with me like a dog; but he was very uncertain with his dealings with strangers.

I think one gets to know more about animals and to understand them better by keeping them as pets at first, and then going and watching them in their wild natural life.

But before going to study big game in the jungles everybody must study all animals wild and tame at home. It would be a very good thing if every scout kept some kind of animal such as a pony or a dog, or even birds, rabbits, or even live butterflies.

Every boy scout ought to know all about the tame animals which he sees every day. You ought to know all about grooming, feeding, and watering a horse, about putting him into harness or taking him out of harness and putting him in the stable, and know when he is going lame and should not therefore be worked.

And when you harness a horse I hope you will show more knowledge of the animal and more kindness towards him than do half the carriage coachmen in London—by not putting bearing reins on him.

Prince Edward of Wales was reported a short time ago to have said as follows:—

'When I am King I shall make three laws:

1. That no one shall cut puppies' tails, because it must hurt them so.
2. That there shall be no more sin in the country.
3. That nobody shall use bearing-reins because they hurt the horses.'

These laws not only show us that King Edward VIII, will be a kind and humane monarch, but that he is farseeing, for the last one at any rate might well be a law of the country now. It is much needed.

Bearing reins are small extra reins which are hooked on to the horse's collar to hold up his head. They are generally put on so tightly as to cause him pain the moment he droops his head at all; when put on loosely they do not cause him to hold up his head and therefore are not of any use.

There are no better drivers than the London cabbies and 'busmen, and they do not use bearing reins, and their horses are more handy than those usually seen in carriages.

Sometimes you see them used on horses in heavy carts; they are then called 'Hame-reins'—but they are cruel on the horse if tightly tied. A horse when pulling a heavy cart wants to lean forward with his head down, just as you or I would do when pulling a garden roller—but this hame-rein pulls at the corners of his mouth and forces him to keep his head up.

I saw lately a man in charge of a loaded cart whose horse was thus tied up. He wanted to get the cart through some heavy mud (it was

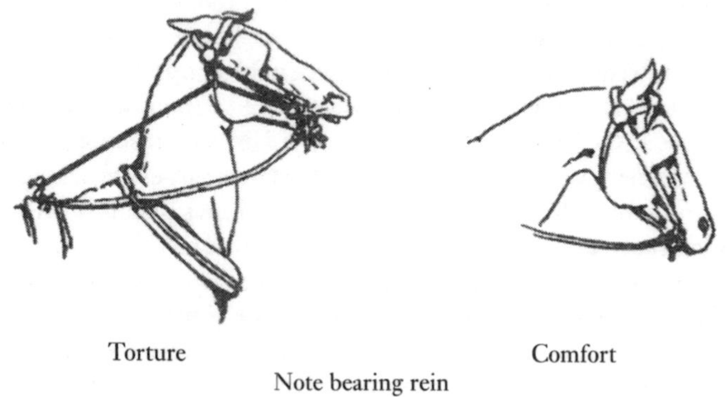

Torture — Comfort

Note bearing rein

on the new Mall from Buckingham Palace to Charing Cross) and the horse tried to lean forward to pull but could not. The man beat him for not trying—the poor beast in his pain and terror reared up on his hind legs, and the man beat him again for 'showing temper'.

When I saw it I felt inclined to beat the man, but I went up and said I thought I could make the horse do it. The man grinned while I was undoing the hame-rein and said I should have to get another horse to do it then. But when the horse found his head free and I smacked him on the back, he flung the whole of his weight into the collar with his head well down, and with both hind toes dug into the ground he heaved the cart forward a few inches, and then again a few more, and not many seconds later had it all safe on the hard road.

Often you can help a horse struggling with a load on a slippery road by scattering a few handfuls of sand or ashes. Miss Lisette Rest used to do this in London and when she died she left money for that purpose.

Other tame animals to understand are, of course, dogs. And a good dog is the very best companion for a scout, who need not think himself a really good scout till he has trained a young dog to do all he wants of him. It requires great patience and kindness, and genuine sympathy with the dog.

A dog is the most human of all animals and, therefore the best companion for a man. He is always courteous, and always ready for a game—full of humour, and very faithful and loving.

Of course a scout who lives in the country has much better chances of studying animals and birds than one who lives in a town.

Still if you live in London there are lots of different kinds of birds in the parks, ducks and waterfowl of every kind, pelicans, wood-pigeons, woodpeckers, and most of the English birds; there is almost every animal under the sun to be seen alive in the Zoological Gardens, or stuffed and set up in the Natural History Museum at South Kensington—so that a Boy Scout in London ought to know as much about all animals as most people. And even in Leadenhall Market you can see a number of different kinds of live animals for sale, as well as in the many animal shops about London or any other big town.

In other towns it is perhaps a little more difficult, but most of them have their Natural History Museum where a fellow can learn the appearance and names of many animals; and you can do a lot of observing in the parks or by starting a feeding-box for birds at your own window. And, best of all, by going out into the country whenever you can get a few hours for it by train, or bicycle or on your own flat feet, and there to stalk such animals as rabbits, hares, water-rats, birds, fish, etc., and watch all they do, and get to know their different kinds and their names, and also what kind of tracks they make on the ground, their nests and eggs, and so on.

If you are lucky enough to own a camera you cannot possibly do better than start making a collection of photos of animals and birds taken from life. Such a collection is ten times more interesting than the ordinary boy's collection of stamps, or crests, or autographs, which any ass can accomplish by sitting at home and bothering other people to give.

And cameras can be got very cheaply now: it only means saving up money in a money-box for a short time.

The wild animals I shall talk of now are those which you find in Great Britain. Any scouts who live in the Colonies or elsewhere must make up their own lists for themselves.

As a scout you should study the habits of as many of these animals as you can:—

Red Deer	Badgers	Otters	Hedgehogs
Hares	Foxes	Fallow Deer	Voles
Rabbits	Mice	Bats	Squirrels
Rats	Weasels	Moles	Polecats
	Stoats		

Every animal is interesting to watch and it is just as difficult to stalk a weasel as it is to stalk a lion. Even the humble hedgehog can be a hero among animals. Here is a description of a fight between a hedgehog and a viper by Mr Millais in his book on the 'Mammals of Great Britain and Ireland'.* (Mammals mean animals that have 'Mammas'—that is, they are born alive, not like chickens in eggs that have to be hatched—birds are not mammals.)

'Everyone knows that the hedgehog is a sworn enemy of reptiles in general and of the viper in particular; but few, perhaps, are aware in what way he overcomes so dangerous an enemy.

'My keeper was going his rounds this summer in a wood which was infested by vipers when he espied an enormous one asleep in the sun. He was on the point of killing it with a charge of shot, when he perceived a hedgehog coming cautiously over the moss and noiselessly approaching the reptile. He then witnessed a curious sight. As soon as the hedgehog was within reach of his prey, he seized it by the tail with his teeth and as quick as thought rolled himself into a ball. The viper, awakened by the pain, at once turned and made a terrific dart at him. The hedgehog did not wince. The viper, infuriated, extended itself, hissed and twisted in fearful contortions. In five minutes it was covered with blood, its mouth one large wound (from the spines of the hedgehog), and it lay exhausted on the ground.

'A few more starts, and then a last convulsive agony, and it expired.

'When the hedgehog perceived that it was quite dead he let go his hold and quietly unrolled himself. He was just about to begin his meal and devour the reptile when the sight of my keeper, who had approached during the struggle, alarmed him, and he rolled himself up again till the man had retreated into the wood.'

We are apt to think that all animals are guided in their conduct by instinct, that is, by a sort of idea that is born in them. For instance, we imagine that a young otter swims naturally directly he is put into water, or that a young deer runs away from a man from a natural inborn fear of him.

Mr W. Long in his book 'The School of the Woods'* shows that animals largely owe their cleverness to their mothers who teach them while yet young. Thus he has seen an otter carry two of her young upon her back into the water, and after swimming about for a little while she suddenly dived from under them and left them struggling in the water. But she rose near them and helped them to swim back to the shore. In this way she gradually taught them to swim.

I once saw a lioness in East Africa sitting with her four little cubs all in a row watching me approaching her. She looked exactly as though she were teaching her young ones how to act in the case of a man coming.

She was evidently saying to them, 'Now, cubbies. I want you all to notice what a white man is like. Then, one by one, you must jump up

Teaching the youngsters

and skip away, with a whisk of your tail. The moment you are out of sight in the long grass you must creep and crawl till you have got to leeward (down-wind) of him; then follow him, always keeping him to windward, so that you can smell whereabouts he is and he cannot find you.'

In 'The School of the Woods', Long writes:*

'Watch, say, a crow's nest. One day you will see the mother bird standing near the nest and stretching her wings over her little ones. Presently the young stand up and stretch their wings in imitation. That is the first lesson.

'Next day, perhaps, you will see the old bird lifting herself to tip-toe and holding herself there by vigorous flapping. Again the young imitate and soon learn that their wings are a power to sustain them. Next day you may see both parent birds passing from branch to branch about the nest aided by their wings in the long jumps. The little ones join the play and lo! they have learned to fly without even knowing that they were being taught.'

BIRDS

A MAN who studies birds is called an ornithologist. Mark Twain,* the amusing, yet kind-hearted, American writer, says: 'There are fellows who write books about birds and love them so much that they'll go hungry and tired to find a new kind of bird—and kill it.

'They are called "ornithologers".

'I could have been an "ornithologer" myself, because I always loved birds and creatures. And I started out to learn how to be one. I see a bird sitting on a dead limb of a high tree, singing away with his head tilted back and his mouth open—and before I thought I fired my gun at him; his song stopped all suddenly, and he fell from the branch, limp like a rag, and I ran and picked him up—and he was dead: his body was warm in my hand, and his head rolled about this way and that, like as if his neck was broke, and there was a white skin over his eyes, and one drop of red blood sparkled on the side of his head—and—laws! I couldn't see nothing for the tears. I haven't ever murdered no creature since then that warn't doing me no harm—and I ain' agoing to neither.'

A good scout is generally a good 'ornithologer' as Mark Twain calls him. That is to say he likes stalking birds and watching all that they do. He discovers by watching them where and how they build their nests.

He does not, like the ordinary boy, want to go and rob them of their eggs, but he likes to watch how they hatch out their young and teach them to feed themselves and to fly. He gets to know every species of bird by its call and by its way of flying; and he knows which birds remain all the year round and which only come at certain seasons; and what kind of food they like best, and how they change their plumage; what sort of nests they build, where they build them, and what the eggs are like.

There are 177 different kinds of birds in Great Britain. Here are some of the commoner birds which a scout should know by sight and sound:

Wood pigeon	Heron	Jackdaw
Pheasant	Wren	Rook
Partridge	Wagtail	Crow
Grouse (Scotland)	Swallow	Raven
Cuckoo	Martin	Thrush
Skylark	Woodpecker	Blackbird
Snipe	Gull	Tit
Wild duck	Tern	Finch
Plover	Owl	Woodcock
Wild goose	Hawk	Curlew
Robin	Falcon	Kingfisher
Starling	Moorhen	

A good deal of natural history can even be studied by keeping birds in your houses, or watching them in your neighbourhood, especially if you feed them daily in winter. It is interesting to note, for instance, their different ways of singing, how some sing to make love to the hen birds, while others, like the barndoor cock, crow or sing to challenge another to fight. A herring gull makes an awful ass of himself, when he tries to sing and to show himself off to the ladies, and an old crow is not much better. Then it is interesting to watch how the young birds hatch out; some appear naked with no feathers and their eyes shut and their mouths open. Others, with fluffy kind of feathers all over them, are full of life and energy. Young moorhens, for instance, swim as soon as they come out of the egg; young chickens start running about and hunting flies within a very few minutes; while a young sparrow is useless for days, and has to be fed and coddled by his parents.

There are over forty different kinds of birds which visit England from abroad, especially from India and Africa, at certain times of the year, chiefly in April, such as the sand martin, swallow, house martin, nightingale, hobby falcon, cuckoo, corncrake, and swift.

A good many birds are almost dying out in Great Britain, because so many boys bag all their eggs when they find their nests.

Birds'-nesting is very like big game shooting—you look out in places that, as a hunter, you know are likely places for the birds you want; you watch the birds fly in and out and you find the nest. But do not then go and destroy the nest and take all the eggs. If you are actually a collector, take one egg and leave the rest, and, above all, don't pull the nest about, otherwise the parent birds will desert it, and all those eggs which might have developed into jolly young birds will be wasted.

Far better than taking the eggs is to take a photo or make a sketch of the hen sitting on her nest, or to make a collection of pictures of the different kinds of nests, made by the different kinds of birds.

Aberdeen in Scotland is supposed to be specially well off for skylarks, for the following reason.

A few years ago there came a very severe gale and snowstorm late in March—and all the high ground inland was so buried under snow and ice, that the birds were all driven to the lower land near the coast. The fields by the seashore were covered with them.

Numbers of people went out to catch them with birdlime, nets, snares, and guns. Large numbers were taken alive to be sent to market in London and other towns.

One gentleman found a man selling a big cage full of them. They were crowded up to a fearful extent and all fluttering with terror at their imprisonment, struggling over each other in their frantic desire to escape. He felt so sorry for them that he bought the whole lot and took them to his warehouse where he was able to give them plenty of room and food and water.

Then he offered to buy all the larks that were being captured for the market at market prices. In this way he received over a thousand—and these he put in a big room where they had comparative freedom and plenty of food. It is said that the noise of their singing in the morning was almost deafening and crowds of birds used to gather over the house to hear them.

At last the bad weather passed off, the sun shone out again and the fields became green and bright, and then the kind man who had housed the birds opened the windows of the room and all the birds flew out in a happy crowd chirping and singing as they mounted into the bright warm air or fluttered off to the adjoining fields and woods. And there they built their nests and hatched out their young so that to-day the song of the lark is to be heard everywhere round Aberdeen.

Through ignorance of natural history many keepers and others see no difference between sparrow-hawks, merlins, and kestrels, and destroy all of them as mischievous to game. Sparrow-hawks and merlins do, no doubt, kill young game, but a kestrel hardly ever, if ever. He lives principally on field mice. You can tell him by his flight—he spends much of his time hovering in the air looking out with his sharp eyes for a mouse upon which to swoop down. The sparrow-hawk flits in and out round rocks and over fences hoping thus to come on prey by surprise. The merlin is a very small but very plucky little hawk and hunts down his prey by fast flying.

REPTILES AND FISHES

THE more usual reptiles in Great Britain are:—

Grass Snake	Toad
Viper	Lizard
Frog	

The commoner fishes are:—

Trout	Dace	Pike
Grayling	Chub	Minnow
Perch	Bream	Salmon
Roach		

and a number of sea fish.

Every scout ought to be able to fish in order to get food for himself. A tenderfoot who starved on the bank of a river full of fish would look very silly, yet it might happen to one who had never learnt to catch fish.

And fishing brings out a lot of the points in scouting, especially if you fish with a fly. To be successful you must know a lot about the habits and ways of the fish, what kind of haunt he frequents, in what kind of weather he feeds, and at what time of day, which kind of food he likes best, how far off he can see you, and so on. Without knowing these you can fish away until you are blue in the face and never catch one.

A fish generally has his own particular haunt in the stream and when once you discover a fish at home you can go and creep near and watch all that he does.

Then you have to be able to tie very special knots with delicate gut—which is a bit of a puzzler to any boy whose fingers are all thumbs.

And you have to have infinite patience; your line gets caught up in bushes and reeds, or your clothes—or when it can't find any other body it ties itself up in a knot round itself. Well, it's no use getting angry with it. There are only two things to do—the first is to grin a smile,* and the second is to set to work, very leisurely, to undo it. Then you will have loads of disappointments in losing fish through the line breaking, or other mishaps; but remember those are what happen to everybody when they begin fishing and are the troubles that in the end make it so very enjoyable when you have got over them.

And when you catch your fish, do as I do—only keep those you specially want for food or as specimens; put back the others the moment you have landed them. The prick of the hook in their leathery mouth does not hurt them permanently, and they swim off quite happily to enjoy life in their water again.

If you use a dry fly, that is keeping your fly sitting on top of the water instead of sunk under the surface, you have to really stalk your fish just as you would deer or any other game, for a trout is very sharp-eyed and shy.

You can also catch fish by netting, or, as scouts often have to do, by spearing them with a very sharp three-pronged spear. I have done it many a time, but it requires practice to be successful.

A scout, of course, has to look at animals of all sorts, partly with an eye to their being useful to him sometime or another for food. Reptiles don't look tempting as food but, once you have tasted frogs legs nicely cooked, you will want more of them.

I believe that fried snake, like fried eel, is not half bad.

I have eaten the huge kind of lizard called an iguana. He had his head and tail cut off to enable him to go into the cooking pot, and when he was boiled and put on the table he looked exactly like a headless baby with his arms and legs and little hands. And when we ate him he tasted just like a baby too. Well—you know what a baby tastes like—sort of soft chicken flavoured with violet-powder!

As far as snakes go, there are not, fortunately, many poisonous ones in England—only the viper is poisonous. It is differently marked from other snakes having a black V or arrow-head mark on

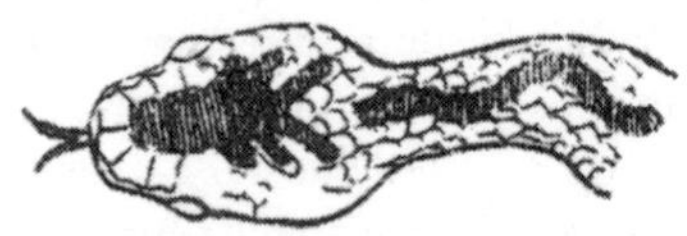

A viper (or adder) has this marking on his head and neck; other snakes have none—in Great Britain

its head and a dark zig-zag line along its back. It is generally dark brown in colour. The viper is sometimes called adder.

Of course a scout ought to know about snakes because in almost all wild countries you come across plenty of them and many of them dangerous.

They have a horrid knack of creeping into tents and under blankets, or into boots. You will always notice an old hand in camp before he turns in at night look very carefully through his blankets, and in the morning before putting on his boots he will carefully shake them out. I even find myself doing it now in my bedroom at home, just from habit.

Snakes don't like crawling over anything rough as a rule; so in India you often construct a kind of path made of sharp jagged stones all round a house to prevent snakes crawling into it from the garden.

And on the prairie hunters sometimes lay a hair rope on the ground in a circle round their blankets.

A hair rope has so many tiny spikes sticking out of it that it tickles the snake's tummy to such an extent he cannot go over it.

I used to catch snakes when I was at school, by using a long stick with a small fork at the end of it. When I saw a snake I stalked him, jammed the fork down on his neck, and then tied him up the stick with strips of old handkerchief, and carried him back to sell to anybody who wanted a pet. But they are not good things to make pets of as a rule because so many people have a horror of them, and it is not fair, therefore, to have them about in a house where servants or others might get frightened by them.

Poisonous snakes carry their poison in a small kind of bag inside their mouths. They have two fangs or long pointed teeth, which are on a kind of hinge; they lie flat along the snake's gums till he gets angry and wants to kill something; then they stand on end, and he dives his head forward and strikes them into his enemy. As he does so the poison passes out of the poison bag, or gland as it is called, into the two holes in your skin made by the fangs. This poison then gets into the veins of the man who has been bitten and is carried by the blood all over the body in a few seconds, unless steps are at once taken to stop it by sucking the wound and binding the veins up very tightly.

INSECTS

INSECTS are very interesting animals to collect, or to watch, or to photograph.

Also for a scout who fishes, or studies birds, or reptiles, it is most important that he should know a certain amount about the insects which are their favourite food at different times of the year or different hours of the day.

The usual insects about which a scout ought to know something, are:—

Moths	Spiders
Gnats	Glow-worms
Beetles	Butterflies
Grasshoppers	Lice
Ants	Bees and Wasps

About bees alone whole books have been written—for they have wonderful powers in making their honeycomb, in finding their way for miles—sometimes as far as six miles—to find the right kind of flowers for giving them the sugary juice for making honey, and getting back with it to the hive.

They are quite a model community, for they respect their Queen and kill their unemployed.

Then some insects are useful as food. Ants make a substitute for salt. Locusts—a big kind of grasshopper—are eaten in India and South Africa. We were very glad to get a flight or two of them over Mafeking. When they settled on the ground we went, and with empty sacks, beat them down as they tried to rise. They were then dried in the sun and pounded up and eaten.

HINTS FOR INSTRUCTOR

PRACTICES

Set your scouts to find out by observation, and to report on such points as these:

IN COUNTRY: *How does a wild rabbit dig his hole? When a lot of rabbits are alarmed does a rabbit merely run because the others do, or does he look round and see what is the danger before he goes, too?*

Does a woodpecker break the bark away to get at insects on a tree trunk, or does he pick them out of holes, or how does he get at them?

Does a trout when disturbed by people passing along the bank, go up or down stream? Does he go away altogether, or return to his place? How long does he stay away? etc.

IN TOWN: *Make your scouts go out and report if they see a lame horse or one with collar gall or sore mouth or tight bearing-rein.*

Patrol to make a beehive or two, and put in queen bees or swarms, and start bee-farming for profit.

Scouts make lures, traps, snares, etc., and set them (not on preserved ground) to catch birds and animals for food.

HONOURS

THE following marks can be gained in this section by First Class Scouts towards Badge of Honour.

For drawing correctly the foot-tracks of twelve different animals or birds, 3 marks.

Name twelve different kinds of fish and describe the points by which they may be recognised, up to 2 marks. The same illustrated by drawings, or models in clay, up to 4 marks.

Photos or sketches from life of twelve wild animals, birds, reptiles, &c., with short description of about twenty words each. Taken and developed, or drawn by the scout himself, up to 5 marks.

LION HUNTING*

A LION is represented by one scout who goes out with tracking irons on his feet, and a pocketful of corn or peas, and six tennis balls. He is allowed half an hour's start, and then the patrol go after him, following his spoor, each armed with one tennis ball with which to shoot him, when they find him. The lion may hide or creep about or run just as he feels inclined, but whenever the ground is hard or very grassy, he must drop a few grains of corn, every few yards to show the trail.

If the hunters fail to come up to him neither wins the game. When they come near to his lair the lion fires at them with his tennis balls, and the moment a hunter is hit he must fall out dead and cannot throw his tennis ball. If the lion gets hit by a hunting tennis ball he is wounded, and if he gets wounded three times he is killed.

Tennis balls may only be fired once; they cannot be picked up and fired again in the same fight.

Each scout must collect and hand in his tennis balls after the game. In winter if there is snow, this game can be played without tracking irons, and using snow-balls instead of tennis balls.

BOOKS TO READ

'Every Boy's Book of British Natural History', by W. P. Westall. (Pub. Religious Tract Society, London.)

'With Flashlight and Rifle in East Africa', by Schilling.

'Duty', by S. Smiles. (Chap. XIII, XIV.) 2s. 6d.

'A Year with Nature', by Westall. Giving the habits of animals and birds of the British Isles according to the months.

'Beasts of the Field', by William J. Long. (Pub. Ginn & Co.).

'Countryside', weekly, illustrated, 1d.

'Wild Sports of the Highlands', by C. St. John. (Murray.)

'I Go A-walking Through Lanes and Meadows'. Photos and short accounts of English birds. Rev. C. Johns. (Foulis.)

'The Jungle Book', by Rudyard Kipling.

'Jock of the Bushveld', by Sir Percy Fitzpatrick.* A story of big game hunting in S. Africa, and the active part that 'Jock' the terrier played in it.

PLAY

'The Wild Animal Play', by Mrs E. Thompson Seton. A musical play in which the parts of Lobo, Waahb, and Vixen are taken by boys and girls. Price 6d. Published by Doubleday, Page & Co., 133 East 16th Street, New York City, U.S.A.

CAMP FIRE YARN.—No. 10

PLANTS

Trees and their leaves—Eatable Plants—Practices and games connected with Plants—Books about Plants.

TREES

ALTHOUGH they are not animals, trees are things about which scouts should know something. Very often a scout has to describe country which he has seen, and if he says it is 'well-wooded' it would often be of great importance that the reader of his report should know what kind of trees the woods were composed of.

For instance, if the wood were of fir or larch trees it would mean you could get poles for building bridges; if it were palm trees you know you could get cocoa-nuts (or dates if they were date palms), and the palm juice for drinking. Willow trees mean water close by.

Or if pine woods or sugar bush or gum-trees it would mean lots of good fuel. And he must know a poplar tree by sight, so as not to use poplar wood in camp if there are any old scouts present—they have a superstition that poplar brings bad luck.*

A scout should, therefore, make a point of learning the names and appearances of the trees in his country.

He should get hold of a leaf of each kind and compare it with the leaf on the tree.*

Horse chestnut is not so called because horses like the chestnuts, but because it has on the bark of its smaller branches small marks like horse-shoes with all the nails in them.* And then get to know the

Oak

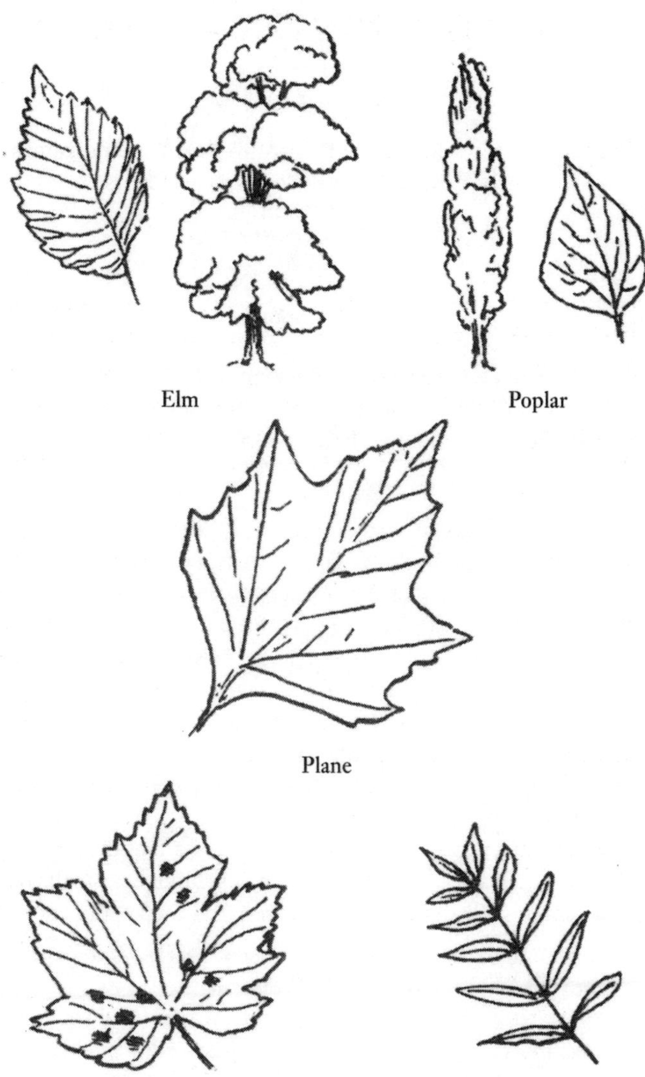

Elm

Poplar

Plane

Sycamore

Ash

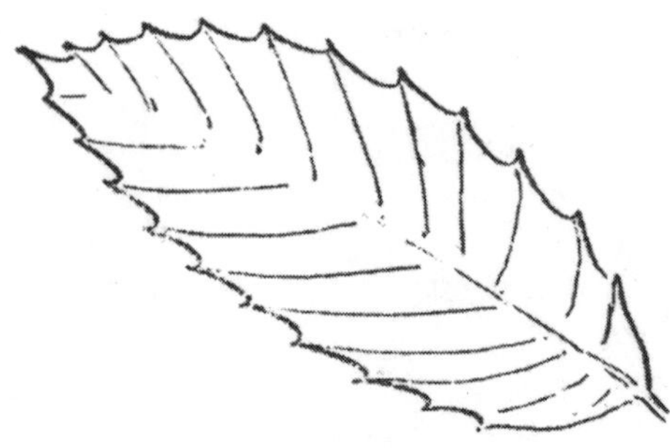

Spanish Chestnut

general shape and appearance of each kind of tree, so as to be able to recognise it at a distance, and not only in summer, but also in winter.

The common trees in Great Britain which a scout should know by sight are:

Oak	Poplar	Holly	Beech
Elm	Pine	Horse Chestnut	Birch
Plane	Sycamore	Ash	Spanish Chestnut
Cedar	Larch	Lime	Walnut
Fir	Willow		

PLANTS

But especially you ought to know which kinds of plants are useful to you in providing you with food. Supposing you were out in a jungle without any food, as very often happens; if you knew nothing about plants you would probably die of starvation, or of poisoning, from not knowing which fruit or roots were wholesome and which dangerous to eat.

There are numbers of berries, nuts, roots, barks, and leaves that are good to eat.

The same with crops of different kinds of corn and seed, vegetable roots, and even grasses and vetches. Seaweed is much eaten in Ireland (Sloke) and Scotland. Certain kinds of moss are also used as food.

HINTS FOR INSTRUCTOR

PRACTICES

Take out scouts to get specimens of leaves, fruits, or blossoms of various trees, shrubs, etc., and observe the shape and nature of the tree both in summer and in winter.

Collect leaves of different trees; let scouts make tracings of them and write the name of the tree on each.

In the country make scouts examine crops in all stages of their growth so that they know pretty well by sight what kind of crop is coming up.

Start gardens, if possible, either a patrol garden or individual scout's garden. Let them grow flowers and vegetables for profit to pay for their equipment, etc.

Show all the wild plants which may be made use of for food.

COMPETITIONS AND GAMES

Marks towards a Badge of Honour may be awarded to first-class scouts for collection of not less than twenty-five kinds of leaf—pressed, with names neatly written against them. Marks, 3; or the leaves may be drawn on paper. Marks awardable, 4.

Prize for best window-box of flowers planted and grown by the scout himself.

GAMES

Plant Race

Start off your scouts, either cycling or on foot, to go in any direction they like, to get a specimen of any ordered plant, say a sprig of yew, a shoot of ilex, a horseshoe mark from a chestnut-tree, a briar rose, or something of that kind, whichever you may order, such as will tax their knowledge of plants and will test their memory as to where they noticed one of the kind required, and will also make them quick in getting there and back.

BOOK TO READ

'School Gardening', by W. E. Watkins, 2s. (Philip & Son.)

PLAY

THE DIAMOND THIEF

(Best performed in the open air and in dumbshow.)

A PARTY of prospectors have been out into the wild country in South Africa, and have found a magnificent diamond. They are now making their way back to civilisation with it. Horse-sickness has killed off their horses, and so they are doing the journey on foot, carrying their blankets, food, and cooking pots.

As the heat of the day comes on they camp for the day, meaning to push on again at night. They rig up blanket-tents and light fires and cook their food, weave mattresses, sing songs of home, play cards, etc. The diamond is taken out of the sardine tin in which it is kept for all to look at and admire. It is then put carefully back. The box is placed out in the open where it can be seen and one man is told off as a sentry to guard it. The remainder have their food, and then gradually lie down to sleep. When the camp is all still, the sentry gets tired of standing and presently sits down and begins to nod.

While he is dozing the diamond thief sneaks into sight, creeps near to the camp, and crouches, watching the sleeping man; when the sentry wakes up for a moment with a start the thief crouches flat.

Eventually the sentry reclines and goes to sleep. Inch by inch the thief creeps up, till he stealthily removes the sentry's gun (or pistol) out of his reach; then he swiftly glides up to the diamond-box, seizes it, and sneaks quickly away, without being discovered, dodges about, walks backward, and wipes out his tracks as he goes in order to confuse pursuers.

The leader wakes with a yawn, and, when looking round, starts when he sees there is no sentry standing about. He springs up, rushes to the sleeping sentry, shakes him up, and asks him where is the diamond. Sentry wakes up confused and scared. Remainder wake and crowd angrily together threatening and questioning the sentry.

When one suddenly sees the footprints of the thief he follows in jerks of a few paces; along the trail the rest follow and help to pick it up, first one and then another finding it till they go off the scene. The leader is about to follow them when he stops and waves them onward, and then turns back to the sentry who is standing stupefied. He hands him a pistol and hints to him that having ruined his friends by his faithlessness, he may as well shoot himself. The leader then turns to follow the rest, looking about for them. A shout is heard in the distance just as the guilty sentry is putting the pistol to his head—the leader stops him from shooting himself. And both stand listening to shouts in the distance.

Remainder of the men return bringing in with them the thief and the diamond all safe.

They then sit round in a semicircle, the leader on a mound or box in the centre with the diamond in front of him. The thief standing with arms bound, is tried and condemned to be shot. He goes away a few paces and sits down with his back to the rest and thinks over his past life.

They then try the sentry, and condemn him as a punishment for his carelessness to shoot the thief.

All get up. They start to dig a grave. When ready, the thief is made to stand up, his eyes are bound. The sentry takes a pistol and shoots him. Remainder then bring a blanket and lift the dead man into it and carry him to the grave—to the opposite side from the audience so that everyone can see the 'body' lowered into the grave. They then withdraw the blanket, fill in the grave, and trample the earth down. All shake hands with the sentry to show that they forgive him.

Pack up camp, put out fire, and continue their journey with the diamond.

N.B.—The grave is managed thus: A hole must be previously prepared rather near to the edge of the scena. Then a tunnel must be made by which the 'corpse' can creep out of the grave and get away underground. This is done by digging a trench and roofing it with boards or hurdles and covering it over with earth and turf again, so that the audience will not notice it. The grave, too, is made in the same way, but shallower and partly filled up with sods: the diggers remove the top earth, then, hidden by the rest crowding round, they remove the board and pile up the sods on the surface. As soon as the corpse is lowered into the grave he creeps away down the tunnel, and so goes off the scene. The diggers throw in some earth, jump down and trample it, then pile up the sods on top till they make a nice-looking grave.

The whole thing wants careful rehearsing beforehand but is most effective when well done, especially if accompanied by sympathetic music.

It is a good thing to use for an open-air show to attract a crowd when raising funds for your troop.

PART III

CONTENTS: CHAPTER IV

CAMP LIFE

CONTENTS: CHAPTER V

(Commences on page 152)

CAMPAIGNING

CHAPTER IV

CAMP LIFE

CAMP FIRE YARN.—No. 11

PIONEERING

Knot-tying—Hutmaking—Felling Trees—Bridging—Measurements—Handicrafts.

PIONEERS are men who go ahead to open up a way in the jungles or elsewhere for those coming after them.

When I was on service on the West Coast of Africa* I had command of a large force of native scouts, and, like all scouts, we tried to make ourselves useful in every way to our main army. So not only did we look out for the enemy and watch his moves, but we also did what we could to improve the road for our own army, since it was merely a narrow track through thick jungle and swamps. That is, we became pioneers as well as scouts. In the course of our march, we built nearly two hundred bridges of timber over streams. But when I first set the scouts to do this most important work I found that, out of the thousand men, a great many did not know how to use an axe to cut down the trees, and, except one company of about sixty men, none knew how to make knots—even bad knots. So they were quite useless for building bridges, as this had to be done by tying poles together.

So every scout ought to be able to tie knots.

To tie a knot seems to be a simple thing, and yet there are right ways and wrong ways of doing it, and scouts ought to know the right way. Very often it may happen that lives depend on a knot being properly tied.

The right kind of knot to tie is one which you can be certain will hold under any amount of strain, and which you can always undo easily if you wish to.

A bad knot, which is called a 'granny', is one which slips away when a hard pull comes on it, or which gets jammed so tight that you cannot untie it.

The following are useful knots which every scout ought to know, and ought to use whenever he is tying string or rope, etc.*

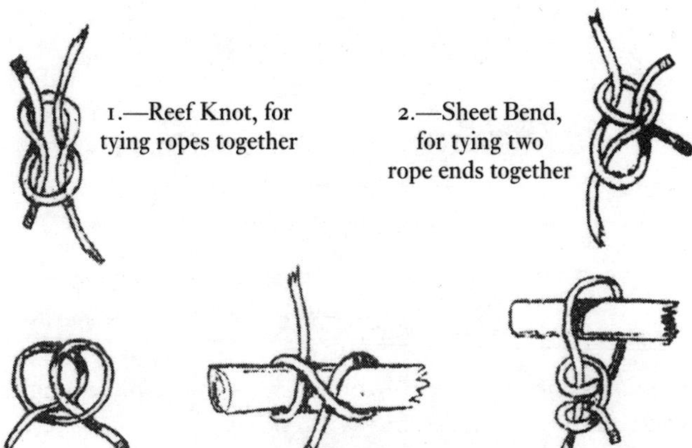

1.—Reef Knot, for tying ropes together

2.—Sheet Bend, for tying two rope ends together

3.—Clove Hitch, for fastening rope to a pole

4.—Two Half-Hitches, to make a rope fast to a pole with a sliding loop

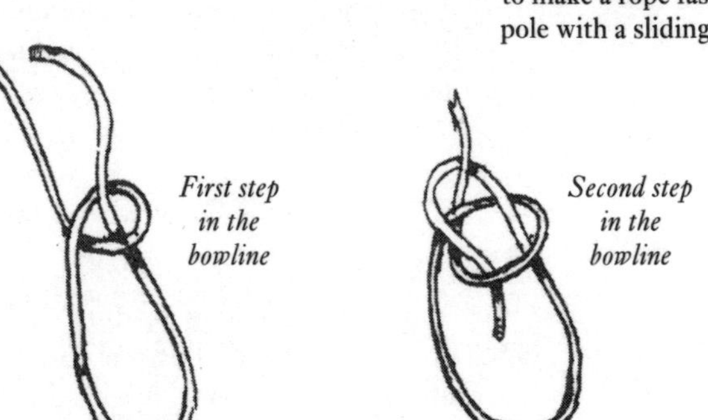

First step in the bowline

Second step in the bowline

5.—Bowline, for making a loop that will not slip, such as you tie round a man when you want to rescue him from fire, etc.

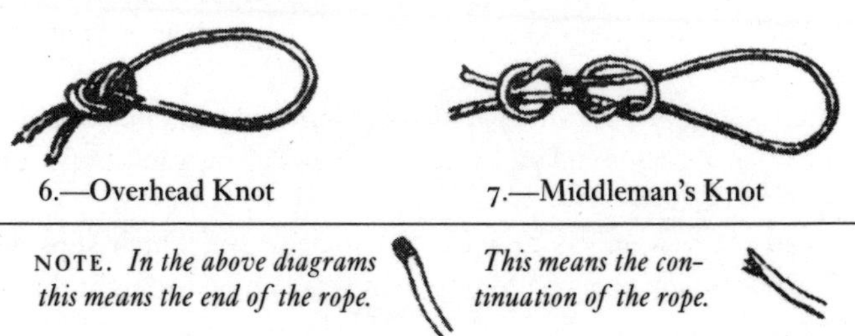

6.—Overhead Knot

7.—Middleman's Knot

NOTE. *In the above diagrams this means the end of the rope.* *This means the continuation of the rope.*

Pioneering scouts in Ashanti

We had no rope with us in West Africa, so we used the strong creeping plants, and also used thin withes or long whippy sticks which we made still more pliant or bendable by holding one end under foot and twisting the other round and round with our hands. The best wood for withes in England is willow or hazel. You see them used for binding faggots of wood together. You cannot tie all knots with them as with rope—but they can generally make a timber hitch; or this withe knot.

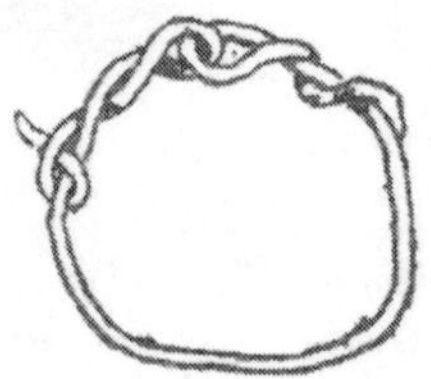

HUT BUILDING

To live comfortably in camp a scout must know how to make a bivouac shelter for the night, or a hut if he is going to be for a long time in camp.

It all depends on the country and weather as to what sort of shelter you put up.

In making your roof, whether of branches of fir-trees, or of grass or reeds, etc., put them on as you would do tiles or slates, beginning at the bottom so that the upper overlap the lower ones and thus run off the rain without letting it through.

Notice which direction the wind generally blows from and put the back of your shelter that way with your fire in front of it.

The simplest shelter is to plant two forked sticks firmly in the ground, and rest a cross bar on them as ridge-pole. Then lean other poles against it, or a hurdle or branches, and thatch it with grass, etc.

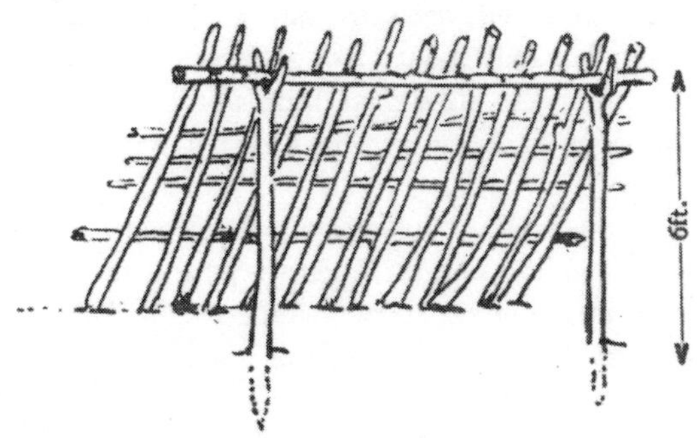

Framework of a bivouac shelter, to be thatched with brushwood or grass. A second lean-to roof on opposite side of ridge pole will then make a hut

Or another good way, and quicker, is to cut one pole only and lean it against a tree, binding its end there; then thatch it with branches or brushwood, etc.

Where you have no poles available you can do as the South African natives do—pile up a lot of brushwood, heather, etc., into a small wall made in semi-circle to keep out the cold wind; and make your fire in the open part.

If your tent or hut is too hot in the sun, put blankets or more

Hut

straw, etc., over the top. The thicker the roof the cooler is the tent in summer. If it is too cold, make the bottom of the walls thicker, or build a small wall of sods about a foot high round the foot of the wall outside. Never forget to dig a good drain all round your hut, so that if heavy rain comes in the night your floor will not get flooded from outside.

Zulus make their huts by planting in the ground a circle of long whippy sticks standing upright, then they bend the tops all down towards the centre and tie them together, then they weave more whippy sticks round in and out of the uprights horizontally until they have made a kind of circular bird-cage, this they then cover with a straw mat or thatch, or with straw woven into the sticks. Sometimes a small hole is left at the top where all the sticks join, to act as a chimney.

The Red Indians make their 'Tee Pee' with several poles tied together in the form of a pyramid, and over these they pass a piece of canvas, which at a little distance looks like a bell tent.

FELLING TREES

A SCOUT must know how to use an axe or bill-hook for chopping down small trees and branches.

The way to cut down a tree is first to chop out a chunk of wood near the bottom of the stem on that side to which you want the tree

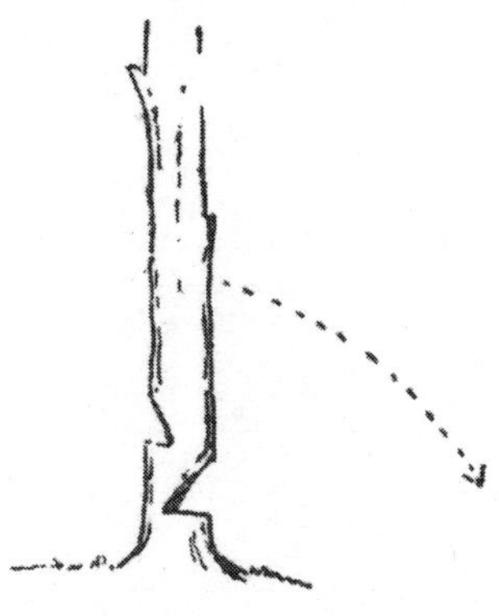

How to fell a tree

to fall, then go round to the other side, and chop away on the opposite side of the stem a few inches above the first cut until the tree topples over. It is a matter of practice to become a wood-cutter, but you have to be very careful at first lest in chopping you miss the tree and chop your own leg.

HOW TO MAKE BRIDGES

As I told you before, my scouts in Ashanti, when also acting as pioneers, had to build nearly two hundred bridges—and they had to make them out of any kind of material that they could find on the spot.

There are many ways of making bridges. In the Army they are generally made of poles lashed together. In India, in the Himalaya Mountains, the natives make bridges out of three ropes stretched across the river and connected together every few yards by V-shaped sticks, so that one rope forms the footpath and the other two make the handrail on each side. They are jumpy kind of bridges to walk across, but they take you over; and they are easily made.

The simplest way for bridging a narrow, deep stream is to fell a tree, or two trees side by side, on the bank, so that they fall across the stream. With an adze you then flatten the topside; put up a hand-rail, and there you have a very good bridge.

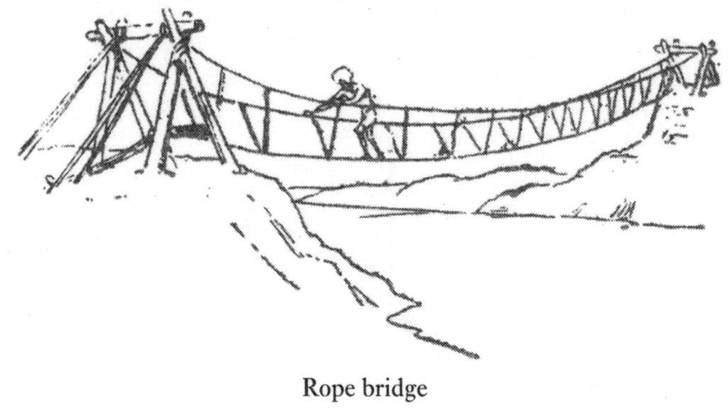

Rope bridge

Rafts, too, can be used. You build your raft alongside the bank, in the water if the river is shallow; on the bank if deep. When it is finished you hold on to the down-stream end, push the other out from the bank and let the stream carry it down into position.

SELF MEASURES

EVERY pioneer should know his exact personal measurement in the following details (of which I give the average man's measure):

Nail joint of forefinger, or breadth of thumb	1 inch.
Span of thumb and forefinger	8 inches.
Span of thumb and little finger or other finger	9 inches.
(This also gives you the length of your foot.)	
Wrist to elbow	10 inches.
Elbow to tip of forefinger (called 'cubit')	17 inches.
Middle of kneecap to ground	18 inches.

Extended arms, from finger-tip to finger-tip, is called a fathom and nearly equals your height.

Pulse beats about 75 times a minute: each beat is a little quicker than a second.

Pace: A pace is about 2½ feet: about 120 paces equal 100 yards. Fast walking paces are shorter than when going slow.

Fast walking you walk a mile in 16 minutes, or nearly four miles an hour.

THE SCOUT IS ALWAYS A HANDY-MAN

PIONEERS are always 'handy-men'. In the Army the Regimental Pioneers are the men who in war make bridges and roadways for the troops to get along; they destroy the enemy's bridges and railways so that he cannot get away; and they blow up his fortifications so that the rest of the soldiers can rush in and capture the place, and so on. In peace-time the pioneers do all the useful jobs in barracks, such as carpentering, doing plumbers' and painters' work, bricklaying and metal work, making chairs, tables, bookshelves, etc. So scouts, if they want to be handy pioneers, should also learn this kind of work: and it will always be useful to them afterwards.

Also scouts must know how to mend and even to make themselves clothes and boots. I have made myself boots as well as shoes out of all sorts of materials, but always wished I had, while a boy, learned to do a bit of boot-mending from a cobbler.

HINTS TO INSTRUCTORS

Start a carpentry class, or instruction in electricity, or plumbing, elementary engineering, etc., with a view to teaching the boys handicrafts that may be of real use to them in their future life. If you do not know enough about it yourself, get a friend to come and demonstrate with models or instruments for a few evenings.

Get leave to take the scouts over a factory to study the engines, etc.

Teach the boys to chop firewood. If they learn to chop up old packing cases, etc., and make the billets into bundles for the trade, they can earn a good deal towards their funds.

Teach them to make wooden mechanical toys (from one or two penny ones as models). Thereby teaching them elementary mechanics, and handiness with tools.

PRACTICES

Knot-tying should be practised against time, by knot-tying races between scouts in heats, the losers to pair off again for further heats till the slowest knot-tyer is found. In this way (which should be used in other branches of instruction also) the worst performers get the most practice—and the emulation is just as great to avoid being the worst, as it would be in striving to be the best, and win a prize.

Knot-tying races should also be carried out in the dark, the instructor turning out the light for a few seconds on naming the knot to be tied.

Hurdle-making by planting a row of upright stakes and weaving in withes.

Make models of bridges with scouts' staves, cords, planks out of old packing cases.

BOOKS TO READ

'Manual of Military Engineering': War Office Publication.

'Active Service Pocket Book', by Mr Bertrand Stewart, 3s. 6d. (Clowes and Son.)

'Romance of Engineering and Mechanism', 5s. (Published by Seely and Co.)

'How it Works'. Showing how such things work as steam engines, motors, vacuum brakes, telephones, telegraphs, etc.

1s. books on Carpentering, Joinery, Engine-driving, etc.

CAMP FIRE YARN.—No. 12

CAMPING

Comfort in Camp—Useful Tricks and Dodges—Camp Fires and all about them—Tidiness.

COMFORT IN CAMP

SOME people talk of 'roughing it' in camp.* Those people are generally 'tenderfoots'; an old backwoodsman doesn't rough it, he knows how to look after himself and to make himself comfortable by a hundred little dodges.* For instance, if there are no tents he doesn't sit down to shiver and grouse, but at once sets to work to rig up a shelter or a hut for himself. He chooses a good spot for it where he is not likely to be flooded out if a storm of rain were to come on. Then he lights up a camp fire and makes himself a comfortable mattress of ferns or straw. An old scout is full of resource, that is he can find a way out of any difficulty or discomfort. He is full of 'dodges', like the

Resourcefulness in doing a good turn

boy who had to rap on the door with the knocker which he could not reach. He showed resourcefulness.

A bivouac is a halt without tents and generally is not meant to last for many hours; a camp generally means a resting place with tents or huts to live in.

There are many ways of making a comfortable bed in camp, but always if possible have some kind of covering over the ground between your body and the earth, especially after wet weather. Cut grass or straw or bracken are very good things to lay down thickly where you are going to lie, but if you cannot get any of these and are obliged to lie on the ground, do not forget before lying down to make a small hole about the size of a teacup in which your hip joint will rest when you are lying on your side; it makes all the difference for sleeping comfortably. A very comfortable bed, almost a spring mattress, is made in Canada by cutting a large number of tops of the fir-tree branches and planting them upright in the ground as close together as possible, like bristles in a brush, so close that when you lie down on them they form a comfortable and springy couch.

Remember when sleeping in camp the secret of keeping warm is to have as many blankets *underneath* you as you have above you.

If a patrol were sleeping round a fire you would all lie with your feet towards it like the spokes of a wheel. If your blankets do not keep you sufficiently warm, put straw or bracken over yourselves and newspapers if you have them. It is also a good tip in cold weather, if you have not sufficiently warm clothing, to put a newspaper under your coat or waistcoat up your back and round your body, it will be as good as a greatcoat in giving you extra warmth.

To make a bed, cut four poles—two of seven feet, two of three—lay them on the ground so as to form the edges.

Cut four pegs, two feet long, and sharpen, drive them into the ground at the four corners to keep the poles in place.

Bed

Cut down a fir tree, cut off all branches and lay them overlapping each other like slates on a roof till a thick bed of them is made; the outside ones underlapping the poles. Cover with a blanket.

To make a mattress you first set up a camp loom (see 'Hints to Instructors', page 144) and weave a mattress out of bracken, ferns, heather, straw, or grass, etc., six feet long and two feet nine inches across.

With this same loom you can make grass or straw mats, with which to form tents, or shelters, or walls, or carpets, etc.

Camp candlesticks can be made by bending a bit of wire into a small spiral spring; or by using a cleft stick stuck in the wall; or a glass candle shade can be made by cutting the bottom off a bottle and sticking it upside down in the ground with a candle stuck into the neck.

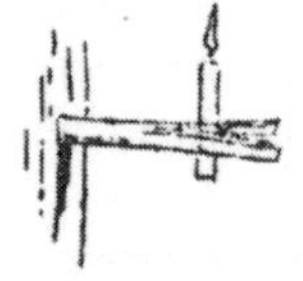

Camp candlesticks

The bottom of the bottle may be cut off either by putting about an inch or an inch and a half of water into the bottle and then standing it in the embers of the fire till it gets hot and cracks at the water-level. Or it can be done by passing a piece of string round the body of the bottle, and drawing it rapidly to and fro till it makes a hot line round the bottle which then breaks neatly off with a blow or on being immersed in cold water.

Camp forks can also be made out of wire sharpened at the points.

Camp fork

It is something to know how to sit down in a wet camp. You 'squat' instead of sitting. Natives in India squat on their heels, but this is a tiring way if you have not done it as a child; though it comes easy if you put a sloping stone or chock of wood under your heels.

Boers and other camp men squat on one heel. It is a little tiring at first.

Buttons are always being lost in camp, and it adds greatly to your comfort to know how to make buttons out of bootlaces or string. This will be shown to you. Scouts should also be able to carve collar studs out of wood, bone, or horn.

A great secret of sleeping comfortably in camp is to have a canvas bag about two feet long by one foot wide into which you pack odds and ends—or carry empty and fill up with grass or underclothing to form your pillow at night.

CAMP FIRES—THE RIGHT WAY OF MAKING THEM

Before lighting your fire remember always to do as every backwoodsman does, and that is to cut away or burn all bracken, heather, grass, etc., round the fire to prevent its setting light to the surrounding grass or bush. Many bad bush-fires have been caused by young tenderfoots fooling about with blazes which they imagined to be camp fires. In burning the grass for this purpose (or 'ring-burning' as it is called), burn only a little at a time and have branches of trees or old sacks ready with which you can beat it out again at once when it has gone far enough.

Scouts should always be on the look-out to beat out a bush-fire that has been accidentally started at any time as a 'good turn' to the owner of the land or to people who may have herds and crops in danger.

It is no use to learn how to light a fire by hearsay, the only way is to pay attention to the instructions given you, and then practise laying and lighting a fire yourself.

In the book called 'Two Little Savages', instructions for laying a fire are given in the following rhyme:—

> First a curl of birch bark as dry as it can be,
> Then some twigs of soft wood dead from off a tree,
> Last of all some pine knots to make a kettle foam,
> And there's a fire to make you think you're sitting right at home.*

Remember to begin your fire with a small amount of very small chips or twigs of really dry dead wood lightly heaped together and a little straw or paper to ignite it; about this should be put little sticks leaning together in the shape of a pyramid, and above this bigger sticks similarly standing on end. When the fire is well alight bigger sticks can be added, and, finally, logs of wood. A great thing for a cooking fire is to get a good pile of red-hot wood ashes, and if you use three large logs they should be placed lying on the ground, star-shaped, like the spokes of a wheel, with their ends centred in the fire. A fire made in this way need never go out, for as the logs burn away you keep pushing them towards the centre of the fire, always making fresh red-hot ashes there. This makes a good cooking fire, and also one which gives very little flame or smoke for the enemy to detect from a distance.

To leave your fire alight at night, cover it over with a heap of ashes and it will smoulder all night ready for early use in the morning, when you can easily blow it into a glow.

Star fire ready to light

If you want to keep a fire going all night to show or to warm you, put good-sized logs end-to-end star shaped—and one long one reaching to your hand so that you can push it in from time to time to the centre without trouble of getting up to stoke the fire.

If coals or wood are difficult to get for making fires at home, don't forget that old boots which you often find lying about on dustheaps, make very good fuel.

You can do a good turn to any poor old woman in winter time by collecting old boots and giving them to her for firing.

Another way to make a good cooking fire is one they use in America.

Drive two stout stakes into the ground about four feet apart, both leaning a bit backwards. Cut down a young tree with a trunk some fifteen feet high and ten inches thick; chop it into five-foot lengths; lay three logs, one on top of another, leaning against the upright stakes. This forms the back of your fireplace. Two short logs are then laid as fire-dogs, and a log laid across them as front bar of the fire, Inside this 'grate' you build a pyramid-shaped fire, which then gives out great heat. The 'grate' must, of course, be built so that it faces the wind.

Camp grate

Tongs are useful about a camp-fire, and can be made from a rod of beech or other tough wood, about four feet long and one inch thick. Shave it away in the middle to about half its proper thickness, and put this part into the hot embers of the fire for a few moments, and bend the stick over till the two ends come together. Then flatten away the inside edges of the ends so that they have a better grip—and there are your tongs.

A besom is also useful for keeping the camp clean, and can easily be made with a few sprigs of birch bound tightly round a stake.

DRYING CLOTHES.—You will often get wet through on service, and you will see recruits remaining in their wet clothes until they get dry again; no old scout would do so, as that is the way to catch fever and get ill. When you are wet, take the first opportunity of getting your wet clothes off and drying them, even though you may not have other clothes to put on, as happened to me many a time. I have sat naked under a waggon while my one suit of clothes was drying over a fire. The way to dry clothes over a fire is to make a fire of hot ashes, and then build a small beehive-shaped cage of sticks over the fire, and then to hang your clothes all over this cage, and they will very quickly dry. Also, in hot weather it is dangerous to sit in your clothes when they have got wet from your perspiration. On the West Coast of Africa I always carried a spare shirt, hanging down my back, with the sleeves tied round my neck; so soon as I halted I would take off the wet shirt I was wearing and put on the dry, which had been hanging out in the sun on my back. By these means I never got fever when almost everyone else went down with it.

TIDINESS

THE camp ground should at all times be kept clean and tidy, not only (as I have pointed out*) to keep flies away, but also because if you go away to another place, and leave an untidy ground behind you, it gives so much important information to enemy's scouts. For this reason scouts are always tidy, whether in camp or not, as a matter of habit. If you are not tidy at home you won't be tidy in camp; and if you're not tidy in camp you will be only a tenderfoot and no scout.

A scout is tidy also in his tent or room, because he may yet be suddenly called upon to go off on an alarm, or something unexpected: and if he does not know exactly where to lay his hand on his things he will be a long time in turning out, especially if called up in the middle of the night. So on going to bed, even when at home, practise the habit of folding up your clothes and putting them where you can at once find them in the dark and get into them quietly.

A scout even ties his shoe laces neatly—in fact they are not tied, but are wove through the eyelet holes from top of the boot downwards, and so need no tying.

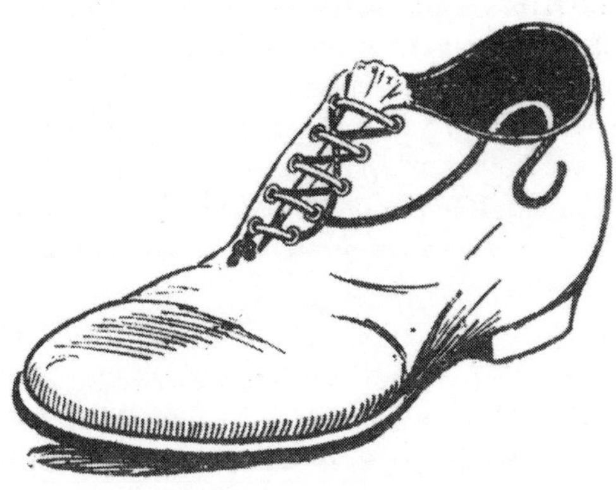

Left shoe laced in the scout's way

One end of the lace is knotted under the lowest outside hole, and the lace is brought through and threaded downwards through the opposite hole; it is then taken up to the top. The dotted part of the lace is the part which lies underneath the shoe and is not visible

HINTS TO INSTRUCTORS

CAMP ORDERS

In going into camp it is essential to have a few 'Standing Orders' published, which can be added to from time to time if necessary. These should be carefully explained to patrol leaders, who should then be held fully responsible that their scouts carry them out exactly.

Such orders might point out that each patrol will camp separately from the others, and there will be a comparison between the respective cleanliness and good order of tents and surrounding ground.

Patrol leaders to report on the good work or otherwise of their scouts, which will be recorded in the scoutmaster's book of marks.

Rest time for one hour and a half in middle of day.

Bathing under strict supervision to prevent non-swimmers getting into dangerous water.

'Bathing piquet of two good swimmers will be on duty while bathing is going on, and ready to help any boy in distress. This piquet will be in the boat (undressed) with greatcoats on. They may only bathe when the general bathing is over and the last of the bathers has left the water.'

Orders as what is to be done in case of fire alarm.

Orders as to boundaries of grounds to be worked over, damages to fences, property, etc.

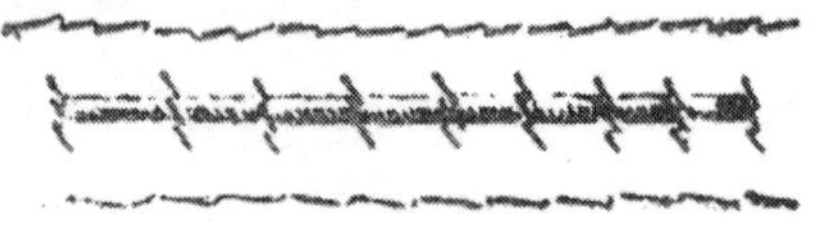

Latrine, with screens across

CAMP LATRINES.—*A simple trench should be dug, one foot wide, two and a half feet deep, for the user to squat astride. Straw mats or canvas screens to be put up across the trench every four feet to secure privacy between the users. (N.B.—This is an important point in education.) Side screens to hide the latrine from outside view.*

PRACTICES

TO MAKE A CAMP LOOM.—Plant a row of five stakes, 2ft. 6in., firmly in the ground; opposite to them, at a distance of 6ft. to 7ft., drive in a row of from two to five stakes. Fasten a cord or gardener's twine to the head of each stake in No. 1 row and stretch it to the corresponding stake in No. 2 and make it fast there, then carry the continuation of it back over No. 1 row for some 5ft. extra, and fasten it to a loose crossbar or 'beam' at exactly the same distances apart from the next cord as it stands at the stakes. This beam is then moved up and down at slow intervals by one scout, while the remainder lay bundles of fern or straw, etc., in layers alternately

Camp loom, for making mats and mattresses

under and over the stretched strings, which are thus bound in by the rising or falling on to them.

If in camp, practise making different kinds of beds.

If indoors, make camp candlesticks, lamps, forks, tongs, buttons, besoms.

If outdoors, practise laying and lighting fires.

Make scouts lace shoes neatly on the principle given.

CAMP FIRE YARN.—No. 13

CAMP LIFE

Cooking, Right Ways and Wrong Ways—Bread-making—Driving Cattle—Cleanliness—Water.

COOKING

EVERY scout must, of course, know how to cook his own meat and vegetables and to make bread for himself without regular cooking utensils. For boiling water a scout would usually have his tin 'billy', and in that he can boil vegetables or stew his meat, and often he will want it for drinking and will cook his meat in some other way. This would usually be done by sticking it on sharp sticks and hanging it close to the fire so that it gets broiled; or the lid of an old biscuit tin can be used as a kind of frying-pan. Put grease or water in it to prevent the meat getting burnt before it is cooked.

Meat can also be wrapped in a few sheets of wet paper or in a coating of clay and put in the red-hot embers of the fire, where it will cook itself. Birds and fish can also be cooked in this manner, and there is no need to pluck the bird before doing so if you use clay, as the feathers will stick to the clay when it hardens in the heat, and when you break it open the bird will come out cooked, without its feathers, like the kernel out of a nutshell.

Another way is to clean out the inside of the bird, get a pebble about the size of its inside, and heat it till nearly red-hot, place it inside the bird, and put the bird on a gridiron or on a wooden spit over the fire.

Birds are most easily plucked immediately after being killed.

Don't do as I did once when I was a tenderfoot. It was my turn to cook, so I thought I would vary the dinner by giving them soup. I had some pea-flour, and I mixed it with water and boiled it up, and served it as pea-soup; but I did not put in any stock or meat juice of any kind. I didn't know that it was necessary or would be noticeable. But they noticed it directly—called my beautiful soup a 'wet peas-pudding', and told me I might eat it myself—not only told me I *might*, but they jolly well *made* me eat it. I never made the mistake again.

To boil your 'billy' or camp kettle you can either stand it on the logs (where it often falls over unless care is taken), or, better, stand it on the ground among the hot embers of the fire, or else rig up a triangle of three green poles over the fire, tying them together at the

Camp kitchen

top and hanging the pot by a wire or chain from the poles. But in making this tripod do not, if there is an old scout in camp, use poplar sticks for poles, because, although they are easy to cut and trim for the purpose, old-fashioned scouts have a fancy that they bring bad luck to the cooking. Any other kind of wood will do better.

This is as good a kind of camp kitchen as any, it is made with two lines of sods, bricks, stones, or thick logs, flattened at the top, about six feet long, slightly splayed from each other, being four inches apart at one end and eight inches at the other—the big end towards the wind.

Another way, when there are several 'billies' to cook, is to put them in two lines a few inches apart, one end of the line facing towards the wind. Lay your fire of small wood between the two lines, and put a third row of 'billies' standing on top of the first two rows—so that a small tunnel is made by the 'billies'. In the windward end of this tunnel start your fire; the draught will carry its heat along the tunnel, and this will heat all the pots. The fire should be kept up with small split chunks of wood.

When boiling a pot of water on the fire, do not jam the lid on too firmly, as when the steam forms inside the pot it must have some means of escape or it will burst the pot.

To find out when the water is beginning to boil, you need not take off the lid and look, but just hold the end of a stick, or knife, etc., to the pot, and if the water is boiling you will feel it trembling.

Kabobs.—Cut your meat up into a slice about half or three-quarters of an inch thick; cut this up into small pieces about one to one and a half inches across. String a lot of these chunks on to a stick or iron rod, and plant it in front of the fire, or suspend it over the hot embers for a few minutes till the meat is roasted.

Hunter's Stew.—Chop your meat into small chunks about an inch or one and a half inches square.

Scrape and chop up any vegetables, such as potatoes, carrots, onions, etc., and put them into your 'billy'.

Add clean water or soup till it is half full.

Mix some flour, salt, and pepper together, and rub your meat well in it, and put this in the 'billy'.

There should be enough water just to cover the food—no more.

Let the 'billy' stand in the embers and simmer for about one hour and a quarter.

The potatoes take longest to cook. When these are soft (which you try with a fork) enough not to lift out, the whole stew is cooked.

BREAD MAKING

To make bread, the usual way is for a scout to take off his coat; spread it on the ground, with the inside uppermost (so that any mess he makes in it will not show outwardly when he wears his coat afterwards); then he makes a pile of flour on the coat and scoops out the centre until it forms a cup for the water which he then pours in hot; he then mixes the dough with a pinch or two of salt, and of baking-powder or of Eno's Fruit Salt, and kneads and mixes it well together until it forms a lump of well-mixed dough. Then with a little fresh flour sprinkled over the hands to prevent the dough sticking to them, he pats it and makes it into the shape of a large bun or several buns.

Then he puts it on a gridiron over hot ashes, or sweeps part of the fire to one side, and on the hot ground left there he puts his dough, and piles hot ashes round it and lets it bake itself.

Only small loaves like buns can be made in this way.

If real bread is required, a kind of oven has to be made, either by using an old earthenware pot or tin box, and putting it into the fire and piling fire all over it, or by making a clay oven, lighting a fire inside it, and then when it is well heated raking out the fire and putting the dough inside, and shutting up the entrance tightly till the bread is baked.

Another way is to cut a stout club, sharpen its thin end, peel it and heat it in the fire. Make a long strip of dough, about two inches wide and half an inch thick: wind it spirally down the club; then plant the club close to the fire and let the dough toast itself, just giving the club a turn now and then.

Ration Bags.—Very often on service they serve you out with a double handful of flour instead of bread or biscuits, a bit of meat, a spoonful of salt, one of pepper, one of sugar, one of baking-powder, and a handful of coffee or tea. It is rather fun to watch a tenderfoot get this ration and see how he carries it away to his bivouac.

How would you do it?

Of course you could put the pepper into one pocket, the salt into another, the sugar into another, the flour into your hat, and carry that in one hand, the bit of beef in the other hand, and the coffee in the other.

Only if you are in your shirt sleeves, as you generally are, you haven't many pockets, and if, like some people, you have only two hands, it is a difficult job.

The old campaigner, therefore, always has his three 'ration bags', little bags which he makes himself out of bits of shirt tails or pocket-handkerchiefs, or other such luxuries; and into one he puts the flour and baking-powder, into No. 2 his coffee and sugar, into No. 3 his salt and pepper.

Very often just after we had got our rations we would have to march at once. How do you suppose we made our flour into bread in one minute?

We just mixed it with a lot of water in a mug and drank it! It did just as well in the end.

CATTLE-DRIVING AND SLAUGHTERING

BEFORE you cook your hare you've got to catch him. So with mutton or beef—you have to bring the sheep or ox to the place where you want him. Then you have to kill him and cut him up before you can cook him and eat him.

Scouts ought to know how to drive sheep and cattle and horses. Tenderfoots always forget to send someone in front of the herd to draw them on.

Sheep are apt to crowd up too much together so that those in the middle of the flock soon get half suffocated in dust and heat, and then they faint. It is often therefore advisable for one driver to keep moving in the centre of the flock to make an occasional opening for air, and it keeps the whole flock moving better. If you come to an obstacle like a stile or wall with sheep, lift one or two over it and the rest will soon follow, but they should not be too hurried.

Scouts should also know how to kill and cut up their cattle.

Cattle are generally poleaxed, or a spike is driven into the forehead with a mallet, or a shot or blank cartridge is fired into the forehead, or a big sharp knife is driven into the spine just behind the horns, the animal's head having first been securely tied down to a cart wheel or fence.

Sheep are generally killed either by being laid on their side and having their head drawn back and throat cut with a big sharp knife, or by being shot in the forehead with a revolver or blank cartridge of a rifle.

The animal should then be gutted by having the belly slit open and the inside taken out, liver and kidneys being kept.

To skin the beast, lay the carcase on its back and slit the skin down the centre with a sharp knife, slit up the inside of the legs, and pull the skin off, helping it with the knife where it sticks to the body, first one side and then the other down to the back bone.

The carcase is split in half in the case of a big beast; with a sheep it is cut into two, and the forequarters and hindquarters are then again divided into joints.

A scout should know how to milk a cow or a goat, else he may go thirsty when there is lots of milk available. A goat is not so easy to milk as you might think. You have to keep hold of its head with one hand, its hind leg with the other, and milk it with the other if you had a third. The way a native does it is to catch hold of its hind leg between his big toe and the next, and thus he has a hand to spare to milk with.

CLEANLINESS

ONE thing to remember in camp is that if you get sick you are no use as a scout, and are only a burden to others, and you generally get ill through your own fault. Either you don't change into dry clothes when you get wet, or you let dirt get into your food, or you drink bad water.

So, when cooking your food, always be careful to clean your cooking pots, plates, forks, etc., very thoroughly.

Flies are most dangerous, because they carry about seeds of disease on their feet, and if they settle on your food they will often leave the poison there for you to eat—and then you wonder why you get ill. Flies generally live best where there is dirt, and scraps of food are left lying about.

For this reason you should be careful to keep your camp very clean, so that flies won't come there. All slops and scraps should be thrown away into a properly-dug hole, where they can be buried, and not scattered about all over the place. Patrol leaders must be very careful to see that this is always done.

WATER

GOOD drinking water is one of the most important of all things in campaigning, in order to make sure of your being healthy.

All water has a large number of tiny animals floating about in it, too small to be seen without the help of a microscope. Some of them are poisonous, some are not; you can't tell whether the poisonous ones are there, so the safest way is to kill them all before you drink any water; and the way to kill them is to boil the water, and let it cool again before drinking it. In boiling the water don't let it merely come to a boil and then take it off, but let it boil fully for a quarter of an hour, as these little beasts, or microbes as they are called, are very tough customers, and take a lot of boiling before they get killed.

For the same reason it is very dangerous to drink out of streams, and especially out of ponds, when you feel thirsty, for you may suck down any amount of poison in doing so. If a pond is your only water-supply, it is best to dig a small well, three feet deep, about ten feet away from the pond, and the water will ooze through into it, and will be much more healthy to drink.

We did this in Mafeking, when the Boers cut off our regular water-supply, and so had no sickness from bad water.

HINTS TO INSTRUCTORS

Practise in mixing dough and baking; it is useful. If possible, get a baker to give a lesson. But let each scout mix his own dough with the amount of water he thinks right. Let him make his mistakes at first to get experience.

A visit to a slaughter-house and butcher's shop to see the cutting up is useful for boys.

Get scouts to make their own linen ration bags.

Issue raw rations, and let each scout make his own fire and cook his own meal.

CAMP GAMES

HOCKEY, Rounders, Football, Basket Ball, which is practically football played only with the hands, with a basket seven feet above ground as goal. A small bit of ground or a room or court will do for the game.

'Bang the Bear'* from Mr Thompson Seton's 'Birchbark Roll of the Woodcraft Indians'. One big boy is bear, and has three bases, in which he can take refuge and be safe. He carries a small air balloon on his back. The other boys are armed with clubs of straw rope twisted, with which they try to burst his balloon while he is outside the base. The bear has a similar club, with which he knocks off the hunters' hats. The hat represents the hunter's life. A good game for introducing strange or shy boys to each other.

Songs, recitations, small plays, etc., can be performed round the camp fire, and every scout should be made to contribute something to the programme, whether he thinks he is a performer or not. A different patrol may be told off for each night of the week to provide for the performance; they can thus prepare it beforehand.

BOOK TO READ

'Woodcraft', by Nessmuk. 2s. (Pub.: Forest and Stream, New York.)

CHAPTER V

CAMPAIGNING

CAMP FIRE YARN.—No. 14

LIFE IN THE OPEN

Outdoor Training—Exploration—Boat Cruising—Watermanship —Mountaineering—Patrolling—Nightwork—Weather Wisdom.

THE native boys of the Zulu and Swazi tribes learn to be scouts before they are allowed to be considered men, and they do it in this way: when a boy is about fifteen or sixteen he is taken by the men of his village, stripped of all clothes and painted white from head to foot, and he is given a shield and one assegai or small spear, and he is turned out of the village and told that he will be killed if anyone catches him while he is still painted white. So the boy has to go off into the jungle and mountains and hide himself from other men until the white paint wears off, and this generally takes about a month; so that all this time he has to look after himself and stalk game with his one assegai and kill it and cut it up; he has to light his fire by means of rubbing sticks together in order to cook his meat; he has to make the skin of the animal into a covering for himself; and he has to know what kind of wild root, berries, and leaves are good for food as vegetables. If he is not able to do these things, he dies of starvation, or is killed by wild animals. If he succeeds in keeping himself alive, and is able to find his way back to his village, he returns when the white paint has worn off and is then received with great rejoicings by his friends and relations, and is allowed to become a soldier of the tribe since he has shown that he is able to look after himself.*

It is a pity that all British boys cannot have the same sort of training before they are allowed to consider themselves men—and the training which we are now doing as scouts is intended to fill that want as far as possible. If every boy works hard at this course and really learns all that we try to teach him, he will, at the end of it, have some claim to call himself a scout and a man, and will find if ever he goes on service, or to a colony, that he will have no difficulty in looking after himself and in being really useful to his country.

There is an old Canadian scout and trapper, now over eighty years of age, still living, and, what is more, still working at his trade of trapping. His name is Bill Hamilton.* In a book which he lately wrote, called 'My Sixty Years in the Plains', he describes the dangers of that adventurous line of life. The chief danger was that of falling into the hands of the Red Indians. 'To be taken prisoner was to experience a death not at all to be desired. A slow fire is merciful beside other cruelties practised by the Indians. I have often been asked why we exposed ourselves to such danger? My answer has always been that there was a charm in the open-air life of a scout from which one cannot free himself after he has once come under its spell. Give me the man who has been raised among the great things of Nature; he cultivates truth, independence, and self-reliance; he has generous impulses; he is true to his friends, and true to the flag of his country.'

I can fully endorse what this old scout has said, and, what is more, I find that those men who come from the furthest frontiers of the Empire, from what we should call a rude and savage life, are among the most generous and chivalrous of their race, especially towards women and weaker folk. They become 'gentle men' by their contact with nature.

Mr Roosevelt,* the President of the United States of America, also is one who believes in outdoor life, and he indulges in it himself on every possible occasion when his duties allow. He writes:

'I believe in outdoor games, and I do not mind in the least that they are rough games, or that those who take part in them are occasionally injured. I have no sympathy with the overwrought sentiment which would keep a young man in cotton wool. The out-of-doors man must always prove the better in life's contest. When you play, play hard; and when you work, work hard. But do not let your play and your sport interfere with your study.'

I knew an old Boer who after the war said that he could not live in the country with the British, so he went off to take service with the German troops which were at that time fighting in the neighbouring district of South West Africa. But after some months he came back and said that after all he preferred to be with the British.

He said that one of his reasons for disliking the British was that when they arrived in the country they were so 'stom' as he called it—*i.e.* so utterly stupid when living on the veldt that they did not know how to look after themselves, to make themselves comfortable in camp, to kill their food or to cook it, and they were always losing their way on the veldt; he allowed that after six months or so the English soldiers got to learn how to manage for themselves fairly well. But when he went to the Germans he found that they were even more 'stom' than the British, with the great difference that they went on being 'stom', no matter how long they remained in the country. He said they were 'stom' till they died, and they generally died through blundering about at the business end of a mule.

The truth is that, being brought up in a civilised country like England, soldiers and others have no training whatever in looking after themselves out on the veldt, or in the backwoods, and the consequence is that when they go out to a colony or on a campaign they are for a long time perfectly helpless and go through a lot of hardship and trouble which would not occur had they learnt, while boys, how to look after themselves both in camp and when on patrol. They are just a lot of 'Tenderfoots'.

They have never had to light a fire, or to cook their own food; that has always been done for them. At home, if they wanted water they merely had to turn on the tap, and had no idea of how to set about finding water in a desert place by looking at the grass, or bush, or by scratching at the sand till they began to find signs of dampness; and if they lost their way, or did not know the time, they merely had to 'ask a policeman'. They had always found houses to shelter them, and beds to lie in. They had never to manufacture these for themselves, nor to make their own boots or clothing. That is why a 'tenderfoot' talks of 'roughing in camp'; but living in camp for a scout who knows the game is by no means 'roughing it'. He knows how to make himself comfortable in a thousand small ways, and then when he does come back to civilisation, he enjoys it all the more for having seen a contrast; and even there he can do very much more for himself than the ordinary mortal who has never really learned to provide for his own wants. The man who has had to turn his hand to many things, as the scout does in camp, finds that when he comes into civilisation he is more easily able to obtain employment, because he is ready to turn his hand to whatever kind of work may turn up.

EXPLORATION

A GOOD form of scout work can be got in Great Britain by scouts going about either as patrols on an exploring expedition, or in pairs like knight-errants of old on a pilgrimage through the country to find people wanting help and to help them. This can equally well be done with bicycles, or, in the winter, by skating along the canals.

Scouts in carrying out such a tramp should never, if possible, sleep under a roof—that is to say, on fine nights they would sleep in the open wherever they may be, or, in bad weather, would get leave to occupy a hay loft or barn.

You should on all occasions take a map with you, and find your way by it, as far as possible, without having to ask the way of passers-by. You would, of course, have to do your daily good turn whenever opportunity presented itself, but besides that, you should do good turns to farmers and others who may allow you the use of their barns, and so on, as a return for their kindness.

As a rule, you should have some object in your expedition, that is to say, if you are a patrol of town boys, you would go off with the idea of scouting some special spot, say a mountain in Scotland or Wales, or a lake in Cumberland, or, possibly, some old castle, or battle-field, or a sea-side beach. Or you may be on your way to join one of the larger camps.

If, on the other hand, you are a patrol from the country, you can make your way up to London, or to a big town, with the idea of going to see its buildings, and its Zoological Gardens, circuses, museums, etc. And you should notice everything as you go along the roads, and remember, as far as possible, all your journey, so that you could give directions to anybody else who wanted to follow that road afterwards. And make a map. Explorers, of course, keep a log or journal giving a short account of each day's journey, with sketches or photos of any interesting things they see.

BOAT CRUISING

INSTEAD of tramping or cycling, it is also an excellent practice for a patrol to take a boat and make a trip in that way through the country; but none should be allowed in the boat who is not a good swimmer, because accidents are pretty sure to happen, and if all are swimmers, it does not matter; in fact, it is rather a good experience than otherwise.

I once made such a cruise with two of my brothers.* We took a small folding-up canvas boat, and went as far up the Thames as we could possibly get till it became so narrow and small a stream that we were continually having to get out and pull our boat over fallen trees and stopped up bits of river. Then we took it on the Avon, which rises near the source of the Thames, but flows to the westward, and here, again, we began where the river was very small, and gradually worked our way down until it developed into a big stream, and so through Bath and Bristol on to the Severn. Then across the Severn, and up the Wye into Wales. We carried with us our tent, stores, and cooking apparatus, so that we were able to live out independent of houses the whole time. A more enjoyable trip could not be imagined, and the expense was very small.

WATERMANSHIP

It is very necessary for a scout to be able to swim, for he never knows when he may have to cross a river, to swim for his life, or to plunge in to save someone from drowning, so those of you that cannot swim should make it your business to begin at once and learn; it is not very difficult.

Also, a scout should be able to manage a boat, to bring it properly alongside the ship or pier, that is, either by rowing it or steering it in a wide circle so that it comes up alongside with its head pointing the same way as the bow of the ship or towards the current. You should be able to row one oar in time with the rest of the boat's crew, or to scull a pair of oars, or to scull a boat by screwing a single oar over the stern. In rowing, the object of feathering or turning the blade of the oar flat when it is out of the water, is to save it from catching the wind and thereby checking the pace of the boat. You should know how to throw a coil of rope so as to fling it on to another boat or wharf, or how to catch and make fast a rope thrown to you. Also you should know how to make a raft out of any materials that you can get hold of, such as planks, logs, barrels, sacks of straw, and so on, for often you may want to cross a river with your food and baggage where no boats are available, or you may be in a shipwreck where nobody can make a raft for saving themselves. You should also know how to throw a lifebuoy to a drowing man. These things can only be learnt by practice.

As a scout you must know how to fish, else you would find yourself very helpless, and perhaps starving, on a river which is full of food for you if you were only able to catch it.

MOUNTAINEERING

A GOOD deal of interesting mountaineering can be done in the British Isles if you know where to go; and it is grand sport, and brings out into practice all your scoutcraft to enable you to find your way, and to make yourself comfortable in camp.

You are, of course, continually losing your direction because, moving up and down in the deep gullies of the mountain side, you lose sight of the landmarks which usually guide you, so that you have to watch your direction by the sun, and by your compass, and keep on estimating in what direction your proper line of travel lies.

Then, again, you are very liable to be caught in fogs and mists, which are at all times upsetting to the calculations even of men who know every inch of the country. I had such an experience in Scotland last year when, in company with a Highlander who knew the ground, we got lost in the mist. But supposing that he knew the way, I committed myself entirely to his guidance, and after going some distance I felt bound to remark to him that I noticed the wind had suddenly changed, for it had been blowing from our left when we started, and was now blowing hard on our right cheek. However, he seemed in no way nonplussed, and led on. Presently I remarked that the wind was blowing behind us, so that either the wind, or the mountain, or we ourselves were turning round; and eventually it proved as I suggested, that it was not the wind that had turned, or the mountain, it was ourselves who had wandered round in a complete circle, and were almost back at the point we started from within an hour.

Then scouts working on a mountain ought to practise the art of roping themselves together, as mountaineers do on icy slopes to save themselves from falling into holes in the snow and slipping down precipices. When roped together in this way supposing that one man falls, the weight of the others will save him from going down into the depths.

When roped together each man has about 14ft. between himself and the next man. The rope is fastened round his waist by a loop or bowline, the knot being on his left side. Each man has to keep back off the man in front of him so as to keep the rope tight all the time; then if one falls or slips the others lean away from him with all their weight and hold him up till he regains his footing. A loop takes up about 4ft. 6in. of rope and should be a 'bowline' at the ends of the rope, and an 'overhead knot' or a 'middleman's loop' for central men on the rope.

PATROLLING

SCOUTS generally go about scouting in pairs, or sometimes singly; if more go together they are called a patrol. When they are patrolling the scouts of a patrol hardly ever move close together, they are spread out so as to see more country and so that if cut off or ambuscaded by an enemy they will not all get caught, some will get away to give information. A patrol of six scouts working in open country would usually move in this sort of formation: in the shape of a kite with the patrol leader in the centre, if going along a street or road the patrol would move in a similar way, but in this formation keep close to the hedges or walls. No. 2 scout is in front, Nos. 3 and 4 to the right and left, No. 5 to the rear, and No. 6 with the leader (No. 1) in the centre.

Patrols when going across open country where they are likely to be seen by enemies or animals should get over it as quickly as possible, *i.e.*, by moving at the scout's pace, walking and running alternately from one point of cover to another. As soon as they are hidden in cover they can rest and look round before making the next move. If as leading scout you get out of sight of your patrol, you should, in passing thick bushes, reeds, etc., break branches or stems of reed and

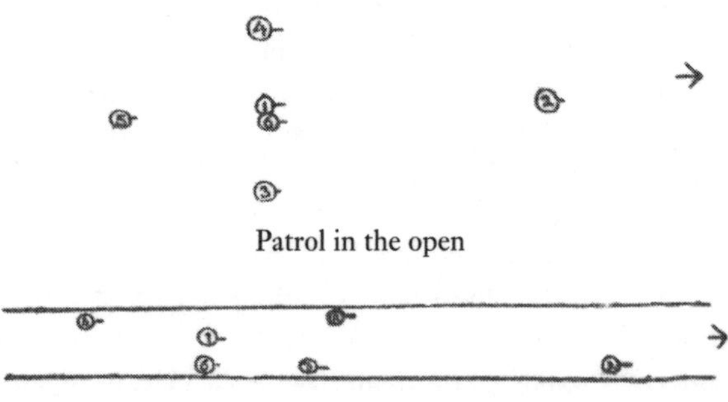

Patrol in the open

Patrol on a road or street

grass every few yards, making the heads point *forward* to show your path, for in this way you can always find your way back again, or the patrol or anyone coming after you can easily follow you up and they can judge from the freshness of the grass pretty well how long ago it was you passed that way. It is also useful to 'blaze' trees—that means take a chip out of the bark with your axe or knife, or chalk marks upon walls, or make marks in the sand, or lay stones, or show which way you have gone by the signs which I have given you.

NIGHT WORK

SCOUTS must be able to find their way equally well by night as by day. In fact, military scouts in the Army work mostly by night in order to keep hidden, and lie up during the day.

But unless they practise it frequently, fellows are very apt to lose themselves by night, distances seem greater, and landmarks are hard to see. Also, you are apt to make more noise than by day, in walking along, by accidently treading on dry sticks, kicking stones, etc.

If you are watching for an enemy at night you have to trust much more to your ears than to your eyes, and also to your nose, for a scout who is well-practised at smelling out things and who has not damaged his sense of smell by smoking, can often smell an enemy a good distance away. I have done it many times myself and found it of the greatest value.

When patrolling at night, scouts keep closer together than by day, and in very dark places, such as woods, etc., they should keep touch with each other by each catching hold of the end of the next scout's staff.

When working singly the scout's staff is most useful for feeling the way in the dark, and pushing aside dry branches, etc.

Scouts working apart from each other in the dark keep up communication by occasionally giving the call of their patrol-animal. Any enemy would thus not be made suspicious.

All scouts have to guide themselves very much by the stars at night.

WEATHER WISDOM

WEATHER.—Every scout ought to be able to read signs of the weather, especially when going mountaineering or cruising, and to read a barometer.

He should remember the following points:

Red at night shepherd's delight (*i.e.*, fine day coming).
Red in morning is the shepherd's warning (*i.e.*, rain).
Yellow sunset means wind.
Pale yellow sunset means rain.
Dew and fog in early morning means fine weather.
Clear distant view means rain coming or just past.
Red dawn means fine weather—so does low dawn.
High dawn is when sun rises over a bank of clouds; high above the horizon means wind.
Soft clouds, fine weather.
Hard edged clouds, wind.
Rolled or jagged, strong wind.

When the wind's before the rain,
Soon you may make sail again;
When the rain's before the wind,
Then your sheets and halyards mind.

HINTS TO INSTRUCTORS

PRACTICES

Practise roping scouts together for mountain climbing. Practise (if boats available) coming alongside, making fast, sculling, punting, laying oars, coiling ropes, etc., and other details of boat management. Read barometer.

GAMES IN LIFE IN THE OPEN

Night Patrolling

Practise scouts to hear and see by night by posting some sentries, who must stand or walk about, armed with rifles and blank cartridges, or with whistles. Other scouts should be sent out as enemies to stalk and kill them. If a sentry hears a sound he fires, calls, or whistles. Scouts must at once halt and lie still. The umpire comes to the sentry and asks which direction the sound came from, and, if correct, the sentry wins. If the stalker can creep up within 15 yards of the sentry without being seen, he deposits some article, such as a handkerchief, on the ground at that point, and creeps away again. Then he makes a noise for the sentry to fire at, and when the umpire comes up, he can explain what he has done.

GAMES

A Whale Hunt

THE whale is made of a big log of wood with a roughly shaped head and tail to represent a whale. Two boats will usually carry out the whale hunt, each boat manned by one patrol—the patrol leader acting as captain, the corporal as bowman or harpooner, the remainder of the patrol as oarsmen. Each boat belongs to a different harbour, the two harbours being about a mile apart. The umpire takes the whale and lets it loose about halfway between the two harbours, and on a given signal, the two boats race out to see who can get to the whale first. The harpooner who first arrives within range of the whale drives his harpoon into it, and the boat promptly turns round and tows the whale to its harbour. The second boat pursues, and when it overtakes the other, also harpoons the whale, turns round, and endeavours to tow the whale back to its harbour. In this way the two boats have a tug-of-war, and eventually the better boat tows the whale, and, possibly, the opposing boat into its harbour. It will be found that discipline and strict silence and attention to the captain's orders are very strong points towards winning the game. It shows, above all things, the value of discipline. The game is similar to one described in E. Thompson Seton's 'Birchbark Roll of the Woodcraft Indians'.*

A whale hunt

Mountain Scouting

THIS has been played by tourists' clubs in the Lake District, and is very similar to the 'Spider and Fly' game. Three hares are sent out at daybreak to hide themselves about in the mountains; after breakfast a party of hounds go out to find them before a certain hour, say 4 p.m. If they find them, even with field glasses, it counts, provided that the finder can say definitely who it was he spotted. Certain limits of ground must be given, beyond which anyone would be out of bounds, and therefore disqualified.

BOOKS ON LIFE IN THE OPEN

'A Woman Tenderfoot', by Mrs Ernest Thompson Seton.* 5s. (Published by Doubleday.) A book of outdoor adventures and hints for camping for women and girls.

'Two Little Savages', by Ernest Thompson Seton. 6s. (Published by A. Constable & Co.)

'Mountaineering'. Badminton Library Series.

CAMP FIRE YARN.—No. 15

PATHFINDING

Finding the Way—Judging Distances—Finding the North.

AMONG the Red Indian scouts the man who was good at finding his way in a strange country was termed a 'Pathfinder', which was with them a name of great honour, because a scout who cannot find his way is of very little use.

Many a tenderfoot has got lost in the veldt or forest, and has never been seen again, through not having learned a little scouting, or what is called 'eye for a country', when a boy. I have known many instances of it myself.

In one case a man got off a coach, which was driving through the bush in Matabeleland, for a few minutes, while the mules were being changed. He apparently walked off a few yards into the bush, and when the coach was ready to start they called for him in every direction, and searched for him, but were unable to find him; and at last, the coach being unable to wait any longer, pursued its journey, leaving word for the lost man to be sought for. Full search was made for him; his tracks were followed as far as they could be, in the very difficult soil of that country, but he was not found for weeks afterwards, and then his dead body was discovered nearly fifteen miles away from where he started, and close to the road.

It often happens that when you are tramping along alone through the bush, or even in a town, you become careless in noticing what direction you are moving in; that is, you frequently change it to get round a fallen tree, or some rocks, or some other obstacle, and having passed it, you do not take up exactly the correct direction again, and a man's inclination somehow is to keep edging to his right, and the consequence is that when you think you are going straight, you are really not doing so at all; and unless you watch the sun, or your compass, or your landmarks, you are very apt to find yourself going round in a big circle after a short time.

In such a case a tenderfoot, when he suddenly finds himself out of his bearings, and lost alone in the desert or forest, at once loses his head and gets excited, and probably begins to run, when the right thing to do is to force yourself to keep cool and give yourself something useful to do—that is, to track your own spoor back again; or, if you fail, start getting firewood for making signal fires to direct those who are looking for you.

The main point is not to get lost in the first instance.

Every old scout on first turning out in the morning notices which way the wind is blowing.

When you start out for a walk or on patrol, you should notice which direction, by the compass, you start in, and also notice which direction the wind is blowing, as that would be a great help to you in keeping your direction, especially if you have not got a compass, or if the sun is not shining.

Then you should notice all landmarks for finding your way, that is, in the country notice any hills or prominent towers, steeples, curious trees, rocks, gates, mounds, bridges, and so on; any points, in fact, by which you could find your way back again, or by which you could instruct anyone to go the same line which you have gone. If you notice your landmarks going out you can always find your way back by them, but you should take care occasionally to look back at them after passing them, so that you get to know their appearance for your return journey. The same holds good when you are in a town, or when you arrive in a new town by train; the moment you step out from the station notice where the sun is, or which way the smoke is blowing. Also notice your landmarks, which would be prominent buildings, churches, factory chimneys, names of streets and shops, etc., so that when you have gone down numerous streets you can turn round and find your way back again to the station without any difficulty. It is wonderfully easy when you have practised it a little, yet many people get lost when they have turned a few corners in a town which they do not know.

The way to find which way the wind is blowing if there is only very light air is to throw up little bits of dry grass, or to hold up a handful of light dust and let it fall, or to suck your thumb and wet it all round and let the wind blow on it, and the cold side of it will then tell you which way the wind is blowing. When you are acting as scout to find the way for a party you should move ahead of them and fix your whole attention on what you are doing, because you have to go by the very smallest signs, and if you get talking and thinking of other things you are very apt to miss them. Old scouts are generally very silent people, from having got into this habit of fixing their attention on the work in hand. Very often you see that a 'tenderfoot' out for the first time, thinking that the leading scout looks lonely, will go and walk or ride alongside of him and begin a conversation, until the scout shows him by his manner or otherwise that he does not particularly want him there. On Thames steamers you see a notice, 'Don't speak to the man at the wheel', and the same thing applies with a scout who is guiding a party. When acting as scout you must keep all your thoughts on the one subject, like Kim did when Lurgan tried to mesmerise him.

JUDGING HEIGHTS AND DISTANCES

EVERY scout must be able to judge distance from an inch up to a mile and more. You ought, first of all, to know exactly what is the span of your hand and the breadth of your thumb, and the length from your elbow to your wrist, and the length from one hand to the other with your arms stretched out to either side, and also the length of your feet; if you remember these accurately they are a great help to you in measuring things. Also it is useful to cut notches on your staff, showing such measurements as one inch, six inches, one foot, and one yard. These you can measure off with a tape measure before you use your staff, and they may come in very useful.

Judging the distance of objects from you is only gained by practice, and judging the distance of a journey is generally estimated by seeing how long you have been travelling, and at what rate; that is to say, supposing you walk at the rate of four miles an hour, if you have been walking for an hour and a half you know that you have done about six miles.

Distance can also be judged by sound; that is to say, if you see a gun fired in the distance, and you count the number of seconds between the flash and the sound of the explosion reaching you, you will be able to tell how far off you are from the gun.

Sound travels at the rate of 365 yards in a second; that is, as many yards as there are days in the year.

A scout must also be able to estimate heights, from a few inches up to two or three thousand feet or more, that is to say, he ought to be able to judge the height of a fence, the depth of a ditch, or the height of an embankment, of a house, tree, of a tower, or hill, or mountain. It is easy to do when once you have practised it for a few times, but it is very difficult to teach it by book.

You must also know how to estimate weights, from a letter of an ounce, or a fish, or a potato of one pound, or a sack of bran, or a cartload of coals; and also the probable weight of a man from his appearance—these, again, are only learnt by practice, but as a scout you should take care to learn them for yourself.

Also you should be able to judge of numbers; that is to say, you should be able to tell at a glance *about* how many people are in a group, or on a 'bus, or in a big crowd, how many sheep in a flock, how many marbles on a tray, and so on. These you can practise for yourself at all times in the street or field.

In the German Army instructions for judging distance are given as follows:

At fifty yards, mouth and eyes of the enemy can be clearly seen.

At 100 yards, eyes appear as dots; 200 yards, buttons and details of uniform can still be seen. At 300 yards, face can be seen; at 400 yards, the movement of the legs can be seen; at 500 yards the colour of the uniform can be seen.

For distances over these, think out for yourself which point is halfway to the object. Estimate how far this may be from you, and then double it to obtain the distance. Or another way is to estimate the furthest distance that the object can be away, and then the very nearest it could be, and strike a mean between the two.

Objects appear nearer than they really are: first, when the light is bright and shining on the object; secondly, when looking across water or snow, or looking uphill or down. Objects appear further off when in the shade; across a valley; when the background is of the same colour; when the observer is lying down or kneeling; when there is a heat haze over the ground.

FINDING THE NORTH

EVERY sailor boy knows the points of the compass by heart and so should a scout. I have talked a good deal about the north, and you will understand that it is a most important help to a scout in path-finding to know the direction of the north.

If you have not a compass the sun will tell you by day where the north is, and the moon and the stars by night.

At six o'clock in the morning the sun is due east, at nine o'clock he is south-east, at noon he is south, at three o'clock in the afternoon he is south-west, and at six o'clock he is due west. In winter he will have

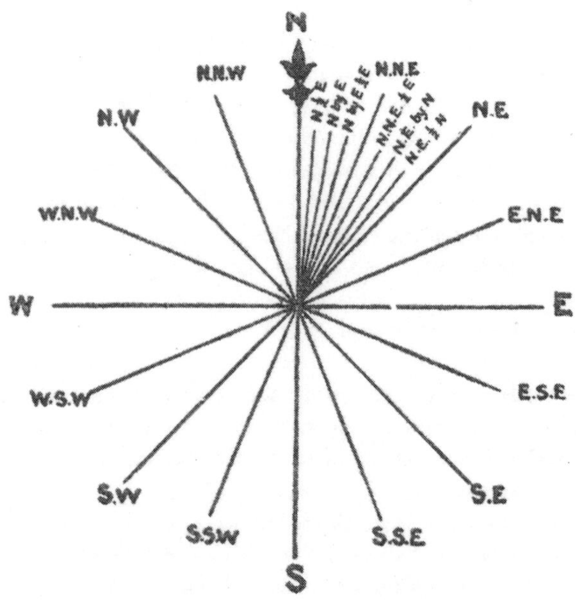

set long before six o'clock, but he will not have reached due west when he is set.

The Phoenicians who sailed round Africa in ancient times noticed that when they started the sun rose on their left-hand side—they were going south. Then they reported that they got to a strange country where the sun got up in the wrong quarter, namely, on their right-hand. The truth was that they had gone round the Cape of Good Hope and were steering north again up the east side of Africa.

To find the south at any time of day by the sun—hold your watch flat, face upwards, so that the sun shines on it. Turn it round till the hour hand points at the sun. Then, without moving the watch, lay the edge of a piece of paper or a pencil across the face of the watch so that it rests on the centre of the dial and points out halfway between the Figure XII and the hour hand. The line given by that pencil will be the true south and north line.

(Instructor should make each boy find the south for himself with a watch.)

THE STARS.—The stars appear to circle over us during the night, which is really due to our earth turning round under them.

There are various groups which have got names given to them because they seem to make some kind of pictures or 'sky-signs' of men and animals.

The 'Plough' is an easy one to find, being shaped something like a plough. And it is the most useful one for a scout to know, because in the northern part of the world it shows him exactly where the north is. The Plough is also called the 'Great Bear', and the four stars in the curve make its tail. It is the only bear I know of that wears a long tail.

The two stars in the Plough called the 'Pointers' point out where the North or Pole Star is. All the stars and constellations move round, as I have said, during the night, but the Pole Star remains fixed in the north. There is also the 'Little Bear' near the Great Bear, and the last star in his tail is the North or Pole Star.

The sky may be compared to an umbrella over you. The pole star is where the stick goes through the centre of it.

A real umbrella has been made with all the stars marked on it in their proper places. If you stand under it and twist it slowly round

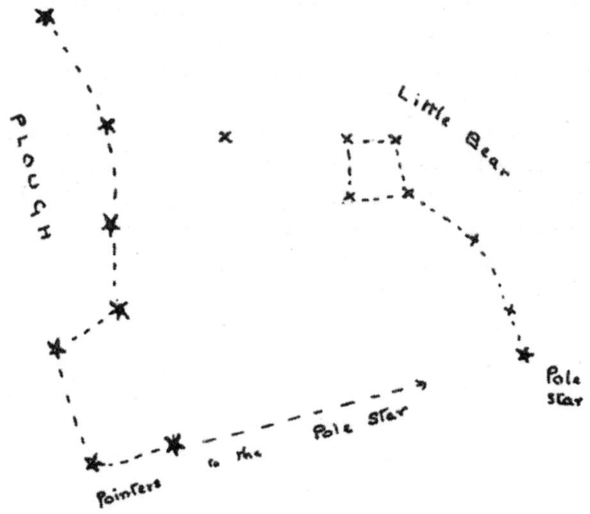

you see exactly how the stars quietly go round, but the Pole Star remains steady in the middle.

Then another set of stars or 'constellation', as it is called, represents a man wearing a sword and belt, and is named 'Orion'. It is easily recognised by the three stars in line, which are the belt, and three smaller stars in another line close by, which are the sword. Then two stars to right and left below the sword are his feet, while two more above the belt are his shoulders, and a group of three small stars between them make his head.

Now the great point about Orion is that by him you always can tell which way the north or Pole Star lies, and which way the south, and you can see him whether you are in the south or the north part of the world. The Great Bear you only see when you are in the north, and the Southern Cross when you are in the south.

If you draw a line, by holding up your staff against the sky, from the centre star of Orion's belt through the centre of his head, and carry that line on through two big stars till it comes to a third, that third one is the North or Pole star.

Then if you draw a line the other way, beginning again with the centre star of the belt, and passing through the centre star of the sword your line goes through another group of stars shaped like the letter L. And if you go about as far again past L, you come to the South Pole, which unfortunately is not marked by any star.

Roughly, Orion's sword—the three small stars—points north and south.

The Zulu scouts call Orion's belt and sword the 'Ingolubu',* or three pigs pursued by three dogs. The Masai in East Africa say that the three stars in Orion's belt are three bachelors being followed by three old maids. You see scouts all know Orion, though under different names.

On the south side of the world, that is in South Africa, South

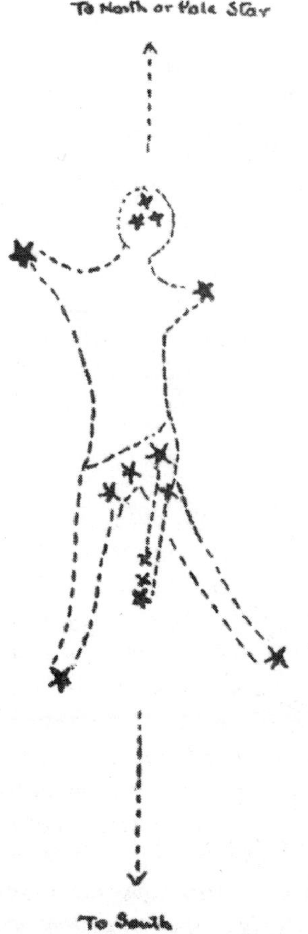

Orion and his sword always point North and South

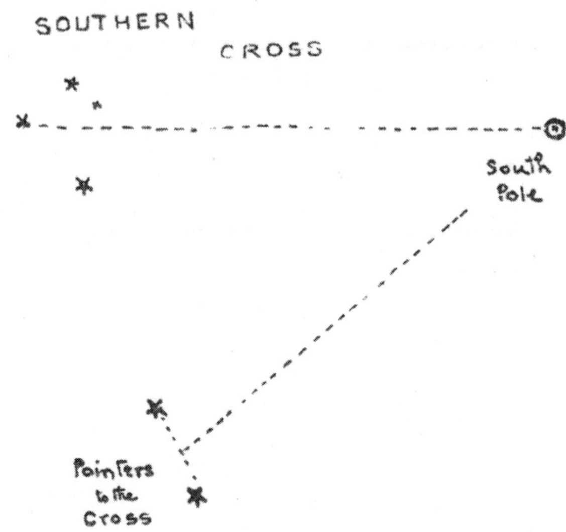

America, and Australia, the Plough or Great Bear is not visible, but the Southern Cross is seen. The Southern Cross is a good guide as to where the exact south is, which, of course, tells a scout just as much as the Great Bear in the north pointing to the North Star.

HINTS TO INSTRUCTORS

PRACTICES IN PATHFINDING

Teach the boys to recognise the Great Bear and the Pole Star, and Orion; to judge time by the sun; find the south by the watch. Practise map reading and finding the way by the map; and mark off roads by blazing, broken branches, and signs drawn on the ground. Practise judging distance, heights and weights, and numbers.

*The way to estimate the distance across a river is to take an object X, such as a tree or rock on the opposite bank; start off at right angles to it from A, and pace, say, ninety yards along your bank; on arriving at sixty yards, plant a stick or stone, B; on arriving at C, thirty yards beyond that, that is ninety from the start, turn at right angles and walk inland, counting your paces until you bring the stick and the distant tree in line; the number of paces that you have taken from the bank C D will then give you the half distance across A X.**

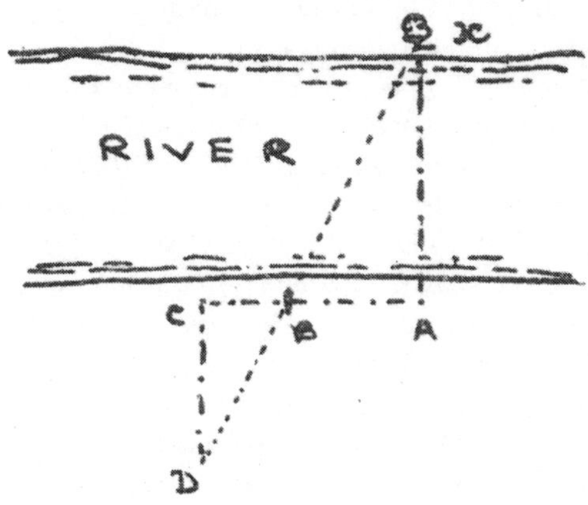

To find the height of an object, such as a tree (A X), or a house, pace a distance of, say, eight yards away from it, and there at B plant a stick, say, six feet high; then pace on until you arrive at a point where the top of the stick comes in line C with the top of the tree; then the whole distance A C from the foot is to A X, the height of the tree, the same as the distance B C, from the stick, is to the height of the stick; that is if the whole distance A C is thirty-three feet, and the distance B C from the stick is nine (the stick being six feet high), the tree is twenty-two feet high.

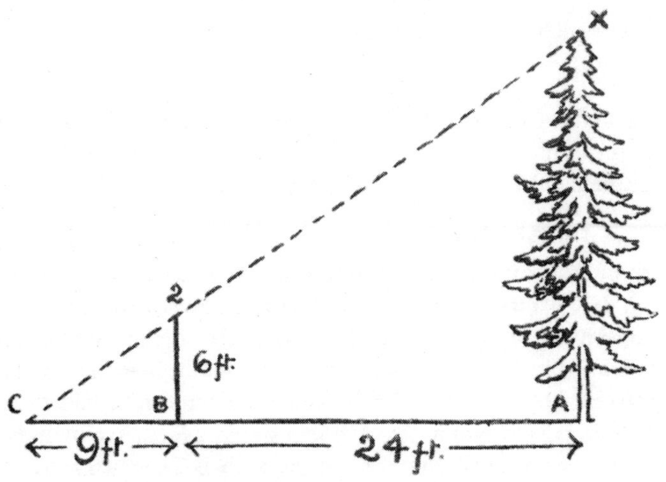

Mr G. L. Boundy,* of Exeter, has been practising his boys in judging distances in the following manner:

He has a board put up on which are given the actual distances and heights and measurements of the various streets and buildings round about with which they are well acquainted. This gives the boys a standard to work upon, and they then go out and guess heights and distances, and other objects given to them by Mr Boundy, who has previously ascertained their correct measurements by inquiry or otherwise. In this way they are able to learn a good deal of the subject in the immediate neighbourhood in the middle of the town.

It is often useful for the instructor, if he has a bicycle, to measure a number of distances beforehand by running over them and counting the revolutions of his wheel. He can them make the boys guess those distances, and can check them, knowing the correct distance himself.

GAMES IN PATHFINDING

INSTRUCTOR takes a patrol in patrolling formation into a strange town or into an intricate piece of strange country, with a cycling map. He then gives instructions as to where he wants to go to, makes each scout in turn lead the patrol, say for seven minutes if cycling, fifteen minutes if walking. This scout is to find the way entirely by the map, and marks are given for ability in reading, that is to say, each scout is given ten marks on starting, and one is deducted for every mistake that he makes. If he makes no mistake at all throughout the exercise, his ten small marks will count as one real scout mark towards a badge 'of merit'.

STAR-GAZING.—Take out the scouts on clear nights and post them separately, and let each find the North Star and Orion, etc., and point them out to you as you come round.

JUDGING DISTANCE.—Take a patrol and station its members about in different directions and with different background, according to the colour of their clothes; then take another patrol to judge distance of these points. Two competitors are sent in turn to three different points. At the first point they are merely given the compass bearing of the next one, which is some three hundred yards distant, and so on in succession. At each point each pair of scouts notices regarding the enemy—first, how many visible; second, how far off;

third, what is their compass direction; fourth, how they are clothed. The best answers win provided they are within the specified time. The time allowed should be one minute for observation at each station, and half a minute for each bit of running.

Find the North.—Scouts are posted thirty yards apart, and each lays down his staff on the ground pointing to what he considers the exact north (or south), without using any instrument. The umpire compares each stick with the compass; the one who guesses nearest wins. This is a useful game to play at night or on sunless days as well as sunny days.

Other Games.—For further games in 'Pathfinding', see 'Scouting Games', Part VI.

BOOKS TO READ

'Guide to the Umbrella Star Map', by D. MacEwan, member of the British Astronomical Association, 1s.

'The Umbrella Star Map', made by Reid & Todd, 215, Sauchiehall Street, Glasgow. (An ordinary umbrella with all the stars in their proper places on the inside. This map can be correctly set for any day in the year and any hour, showing the approximate positions of the stars.)

'The Science Year Book', by Major Baden-Powell. 5s. King, Sell & Olding, 27, Chancery Lane.

'An Easy Guide to the Constellations', by the Rev. James Gall. 1s. (Gall & Inglis.) Contains diagrams of the constellations.

'Astronomy for Everybody', by Simon Newcomb. 6s. (Publisher, Isbister.) Also books on astronomy by Professors Ball, Heath, Maunder, and Flammarion.

CAMP FIRE YARN.—No. 16

INFORMATION BY SIGNAL

Hidden Dispatches—Signalling—Whistle and Flag-Signals.

Scouts have to be very clever at passing news secretly from one place to another, or signalling to each other; and if it should ever happen that an enemy got into England, the Boy Scouts would be of greatest value if they have practised this art.

Before the siege of Mafeking commenced, I received a secret message from some unknown friend in the Transvaal, who sent me news of the Boers' plans against the place, and the numbers that they were getting together of men, horses, and guns. This news came to me by means of a very small letter which was rolled up in a little ball, the size of a pill, and put inside a tiny hole in a rough walking stick, and plugged in there with wax. The stick was given to a native, who merely had orders to come into Mafeking and give me the stick as a present. Naturally, when he brought me this stick, and said it was from another white man, I guessed there must be something inside it, and soon found this very important letter.

Also I received another letter from a friend, which was written in Hindustani language, but in English writing, so that anybody reading would be quite puzzled as to what language it was written in; but to me it was all as clear as daylight.

Then when we sent letters out from Mafeking, we used to give them to natives, who were able to creep out between the Boer outposts, and once through the line of sentries, the Boers mistook them for their own natives, and took no further notice of them. They carried their letters in this way. The letters were all written on thin paper in small envelopes, and half a dozen letters or more would be crumpled up tightly into a little ball, and then rolled up into a piece of lead paper, such as tea is packed in. The native scout would carry a number of these little balls in his hand, and hanging round his neck loosely by strings. Then, if he saw he was in danger of being captured by a Boer, he would drop all his balls on the ground, where they looked exactly like so many stones, and he would notice landmarks from two or three points round about him, by which he would be able again to find the exact spot where the letters were lying; then he would walk boldly on until accosted by the Boer, who, if he searched him, would have found nothing suspicious about him. He would then wait about for perhaps a day or two until the coast was clear, and come back to the spot where the landmarks told him the letters were lying.

'Landmarks', you may remember, mean any objects, like trees, mounds, rocks, or other details which do not move away, and act as signposts for a scout who notices and remembers them.

SIGNALLING

Captain John Smith* was one of the first to make use of signals to express regular words, three hundred years ago.

He was then fighting on the side of the Austrians against the Turks. He thought it wicked for Christian men to fight against Christians if it could possibly be avoided, but he would help any Christian, although a foreigner, to fight against a heathen; so he joined the Austrians against the Turks.

He invented a system of showing lights at night with torches, which when held in certain positions with each other meant certain words.

Several officers in the Austrian forces practised these signals till they knew them.

On one occasion one of these officers was besieged by the Turks. John Smith brought a force to help him, and arrived on a hill near the town in the night. Here he made a number of torch signals, which were read by the officer inside, and they told him what to do when Smith attacked the enemy in the rear; and this enabled the garrison to break out successfully.

In the American Civil War, Captain Clowry, a scout officer, wanted to give warning to a large force of his own army that the enemy were going to attack it unexpectedly during the night, but he could not get to his friends, because there was a flooded river between them which he could not cross, and a storm of rain was going on.

What would you have done if you had been him?

A good idea struck him. He got hold of an old railway engine that was standing near him. He lit the fire, and got up steam in her, and then started to blow the whistle with short and long blasts—what is called the Morse alphabet. Soon his friends heard and understood, and answered back with a bugle. And he then spelt out a message of warning to them, which they read and acted upon. And so their force of 20,000 men was saved from surprise.

Lieutenant Boyd Alexander* describes in his book 'From the Niger to the Nile', how a certain tribe of natives in Central Africa signal news to each other by means of beats on a drum. And I have known tribes in the forests of the West Coast of Africa who do the same.

Every scout ought to learn the 'dot and dash' or Morse method of signalling, because it comes in most useful whenever you want to send messages some distance by flag signalling, as in the Army and Navy, and it is also useful in getting you employment as a telegraphist. It is not difficult to learn if you set about it with a will. I found it most useful once during the Boer War.* My column had been trying to get past a Boer force who was holding a pass in the mountains. Finding they were too strong for us, we gave it up late in the evening, and leaving a lot of fires alight as if we were in camp in front of them, we moved during the night by a rapid march right round the end of the mountain range, and by daylight next day we were exactly in rear of them without their knowing it. We then found a telegraph line evidently leading from them to their headquarters some fifty miles

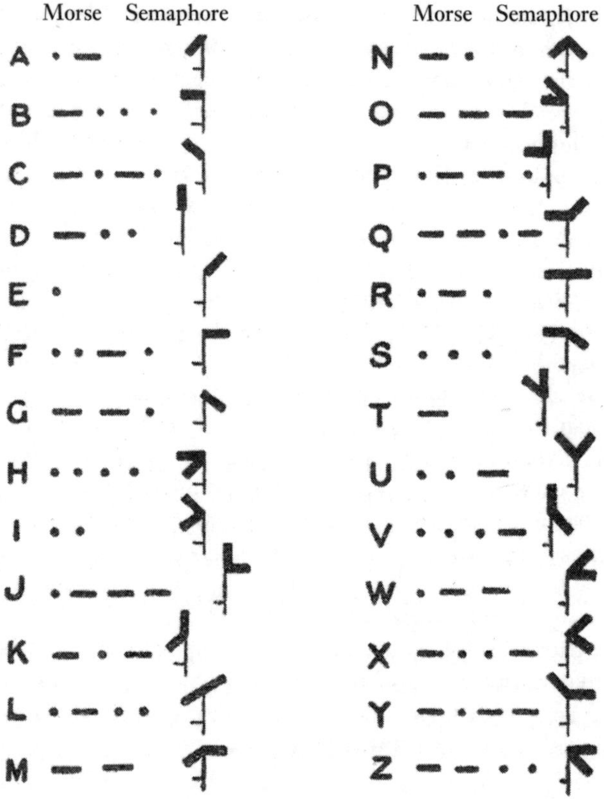

further off, so we sat down by the telegraph wire and attached our own little wire to it and read all the messages they were sending, and they gave us most valuable information. But we should not have been able to do that had it not been that some of our scouts could read the Morse code.

Then the semaphore signalling, which is done by waving your arms at different angles to each other, is most useful and quite easy to learn, and is known by every soldier and sailor in the service. Here you have all the different letters, and the different angles at which you have to put your arms to represent those letters, and though it looks complicated in the picture, when you come to work it out, you will find it is very simple.

For all letters from A to G the right arm only is used, making a quarter of a circle for each letter in succession. Then from H to N (except J), the right arm stands at A, while the left moves round the circle again for the other letters. From O to S the right arm stands at B, and the left arm moves round as before. For T, V, Y, and the 'annul' the right arm stands at C, the left moving to the next point of the circle successively.

The letters A to K also mean figures 1 to 9, if you first make the sign

to show that you are going to send numbers.

If you want to write a dispatch that will puzzle most people to read, use the Morse or Semaphore letters in place of the ordinary alphabet. It will be quite readable to any of your friends who understand signalling.

Also if you want to use a secret language in your patrol you should all set to work to learn 'Esperanto'.* It is not difficult, and is taught in a little book costing one penny. This language is being used in all countries so that you would be able to get on with it abroad now.

WHISTLE AND FLAG SIGNALS

EACH patrol leader should provide himself with a whistle and a lanyard or cord for keeping it. The following commands and signals should be at your finger ends, so that you can teach them to your patrol, and know how to order it properly.

Words of Command

'Fall in' (in line).

'Alert' (stand up smartly).

'Easy' (stand at ease).

'Stand easy' (sit or lie down without leaving the ranks).

'Dismiss' (break off).

'Right' (or left); (each scout turns accordingly).

'Patrol right' (or left); (each patrol with its scouts in line wheels to that hand).

'Quick march' (walk smartly, stepping off on the left foot).

'Double' (run at smart pace, arms hanging loose).

'Scout's Pace' (walk fifty yards and run fifty yards alternately).

Signals and Signs

When a scoutmaster wants to call his troop together he makes his bugler sound 'The Scout's Call'.

Patrol leaders thereupon call together their patrols by sounding their whistles, followed by their patrol (animal) war cry. Then they double their patrol to the scoutmaster.

Whistle Signals are these: One long blast means; 'Silence'; 'Alert'; 'Look out for my next signal'.

1. A succession of long slow blasts means: 'Go out'; 'Get further away'; or 'Advance'; 'Extend'; 'Scatter'.

2. A succession of short, sharp blasts means: 'Rally'; 'Close in'; 'Come together'; 'Fall in'.

3. A succession of short and long blasts alternately means: 'Alarm'; 'Look out'; 'Be ready'; 'Man your alarm posts'.

4. Three short blasts followed by one long one, from scoutmaster calls up the patrol leaders—*i.e.* 'Lĕadĕrs cŏme here!'

Any whistle signal must be instantly obeyed at the double as fast as ever you can run—no matter what other job you may be doing at the time.

Hand Signals, which can also be made by patrol leaders with their patrol flags when necessary:

Hand waved several times across the face from side to side, or flag waved horizontally from side to side opposite the face means: 'No; Never mind; As you were.'

Hand or flag held high, and waved very slowly from side to side at full extent of arm, or whistle a succession of slow blasts means: 'Extend; Go further out; Scatter.'

Hand or flag held high and waved quickly from side to side at full extent of arm, or whistle a succession of short, quick blasts means: 'Close in; Rally; Come here.'

Hand or flag pointing in any direction means: 'Go in that direction.'

Hand or flag jumped rapidly up and down several times, means: 'Run'.

Hand or flag held straight up over head, means: 'Stop'; 'Halt'.

When a leader is shouting an order or message to a scout who is some way off, the scout, if he hears what is being said, should hold up his hand level with his head all the time. If he cannot hear he should stand still making no sign. The leader will then repeat louder or beckon to the scout to come in nearer.

The following signals are made by a scout with his staff when he is sent out to reconnoitre within sight of his patrol, and they have the following meanings: Staff held up horizontally, that is flat with both hands above the head, means 'a few enemy in sight'.

The same, but with staff moved up and down slowly, means 'a number of enemy in sight, a long way off'.

The same, staff moved up and down rapidly means 'a number of enemy in sight, and close by'.

The staff held straight up over the head means 'no enemy in sight'.

PRACTICES IN SIGNALLING

Practise laying, lighting, and use of signal fires of smoke or flame.

Practise whistle and drill signals.

Teach Semaphore and Morse Codes; also Esperanto if feasible.

Encourage competitive ingenuity in concealing dispatches on the person.

HINTS TO INSTRUCTORS

In all games and competitions, it should be arranged as far as possible that all the scouts should take part, because we do not want to have merely one or two brilliant performers, and the others no use at all. All ought to get practice, and all ought to be pretty good. In competitions where there are enough entries to make heats, ties should be run off by losers instead of the usual system of by winners, and the game should be to find out which are the worst instead of which are the best. Good men will strive just as hard not to be worst, as they would to gain a prize, and this form of competition gives the bad man most practice.

MARKS TOWARDS BADGES OF HONOUR IN CAMPAIGNING

MAKING a complete model bridge. Up to four marks.

Lay and light the following fires separately, using only six matches for the whole: First, cooking fire, and cook a bannock. Second, flame signal fire and make signals. Third, smoke signal fire and make signals. Marks up to three.

To measure without instruments, within ten per cent of correctness, three different widths of river, or impassable ground, without crossing it. Heights of three different trees or buildings. Number of sheep in a flock, stones on a table, etc. Weights of four different things from one ounce up to one hundred pounds. Four distances between one inch and one mile. Marks up to five for the whole lot.

DISPATCH RUNNING

A SCOUT is given a dispatch to take to the headquarters of a besieged town, which may be a real town (village, farm, or house), and he must return with a receipt for it. He must wear a coloured rag 2ft. long pinned on to his shoulder. He must start at least four miles away from the town he is going to. Besiegers who have to spot him can place themselves where they like, but must not go nearer to the headquarters' building than three hundred yards. (Best to give certain boundaries that they know or can recognise.) Anyone found within that limit by the umpire will be ruled out as shot by the defenders at headquarters. The dispatch runner can use any ruse he likes, except dressing up as a woman, but he must always wear the red rag on his shoulder. To catch him, the enemy must get the red rag from him. Ten hours may be allowed as the limit of time, by which the dispatch runner should get his message to headquarters and get back again to the starting-point with the receipt. This game may also be made a life-and-death venture in which case any scout who volunteers to risk his life (*i.e.* his scout's badge) in getting through with a dispatch, gains the badge 'For Merit' if he wins; but if he fails, he loses his scout's badge (fleurs-de-lis), and cannot get it again, although he may still remain a member of the corps. The enemy win three marks each if they spot him, and lose three marks if he succeeds. To win a badge of merit there must be not less than two patrols out against him. A similar game can be played in a city, but requires modifications to suit the local conditions.

For Exploration Practice, see 'Scouting Games', Part VI, for imitating exploring expeditions in Africa, Arctic regions, etc.

DISPLAY

ACT a scene of castaways on a desert island. They make camp fire: pick seaweed, grass, roots, etc., and cook them: Make pots, etc., out of clay: Weave mats out of grass: Build raft, and if water is available get afloat in it: put up a mast and grass mat sail, etc.: and punt or sail away, or can be rescued by sighting ship and making smoke signals or getting a boat's crew of sailors to come and fetch them.

PART IV

CONTENTS: CHAPTER VI

ENDURANCE FOR SCOUTS;

Or, How to be Strong

CONTENTS: CHAPTER VII

(Commences on page 212)

CHIVALRY of the KNIGHTS

ENDURANCE FOR SCOUTS

HINTS TO INSTRUCTORS

HOW TO HELP IN A GREAT NATIONAL WORK

Recent reports on the deterioration of our race ought to act as a warning to be taken in time before it goes too far.

One cause which contributed to the downfall of the Roman Empire was the fact that the soldiers fell away from the standard of their forefathers in bodily strength.

Our standard of height in the Army was 5ft. 6in. in 1845; it was FOUR INCHES *less in 1895. In 1900 forty-four men in every thousand recruits weighed under 7st. 12lbs.; in 1905 this deficiency had increased to seventy-six per thousand.*

This year our recruits were two inches below the standard height of men of their age, viz., eighteen to nineteen, and six pounds under the average weight.

Three thousand men were sent home from the South African War on account of bad teeth.

Reports on school children, made by the London County Council, show that out of 700 examined only twenty had sound teeth, 323 had more than five teeth decayed.

Out of 1,521 examined for adenoids in the throat 29 per cent had enlargements, 10 per cent required operation. Out of 1,000 boys of thirteen, sons of rich or well-to-do persons, examined by Dr Clement Dukes, 526 had knock-knees, 445 had curvature of the spine, 329 flat feet, 126 pigeon-breasts—all preventable deformities. In this case, however, the teeth were well cared for.

Deafness from adenoids and weak eyesight are also very prevalent among them.

Dr Wright Thomson, in the 'British Medical Journal', September 14th, 1907, shows how town children suffer greatly from defective sight, which might be, to a great extent, remedied by special exercises for the eyes and by good feeding.

The report [see Blue Book C. D. 3637] last year on the school children of Glasgow showed their average weight and height were very much below the standard; and these varied almost exactly according to the number of rooms occupied by the family, that is, according to the air space available.

These and the many similar reports show that much PREVENTABLE *deterioration is being allowed to creep in among the rising generation.*

Then there is also prevalent a great amount of illness resulting from self-abuse and venereal disease, as well as from drink. Also much pauper over-population due to want of self-restraint on the part of men and women.

The training of Boy Scouts would be therefore incomplete if it did not endeavour to help in remedying these evils. Some idea is much needed among boys of their personal hygiene. It has been stated on good authority that half our losses in the Boer War from sickness might have been avoided had our men and officers had any knowledge of personal care of their health.

No doubt it is the same in peace time, as numbers of men are thrown out of work by sickness, which might be avoided if they knew how to look after themselves, and took reasonable precautions.

Since most of these causes of physical decay are preventable, they open to instructors a field for doing a work of national value.

For these reasons the following chapter suggests the instruction of boys in being PERSONALLY RESPONSIBLE for their own Strength, Health and Sanitary Surroundings.

CHAPTER VI

ENDURANCE for SCOUTS;

or,

How to be Strong

CAMP FIRE YARN.—No. 17

HOW TO GROW STRONG

Need for Scouts to be strong—Exercises—Care of Body—Nose—Ears—Eyes—Teeth—Practices.

A SCOUT'S ENDURANCE

A SCOUT lay sick in hospital in India with that most fatal disease called cholera. The doctor told the native man in attendance on him that the only chance of saving his life was to violently warm up his feet and keep the blood moving in his body by constantly rubbing him. The moment the doctor's back was turned the native gave up rubbing and squatted down to have a quiet smoke. The poor patient, though he could not speak, understood all that was going on—and he was so enraged at the conduct of his native attendant, that he resolved then and there that he would get well if only to give the native a lesson. Having made up his mind to get well he *got* well.

A scout's motto is 'Never say die till you're dead'—and if he acts up to this it will pull him out of many a bad place when everything seems to be going wrong for him. It means a mixture of pluck, patience, and strength, which we call 'Endurance'.

The great South African hunter and scout, F. C. Selous*, gave a great example of scout's endurance when on a hunting expedition in Barotseland north of the Zambesi River some years ago. In the middle of the night his camp was suddenly attacked by a hostile tribe who fired into it at close range and charged in.

He and his small party of natives scattered at once into the darkness and hid themselves away in the long grass. Selous himself had snatched up his rifle and a few cartridges and got safely into the grass. But he could not find any of his men, and seeing that the enemy had got possession of his camp and that there were still a few hours of darkness before him in which to make his escape, he started off southward, using the stars of the Southern Cross as his guide.

He crept past an outpost of the enemy whom he overheard talking, and then swam across a river and finally got well away, only dressed in a shirt, and shorts and shoes. For the next few days and nights he kept walking southward, having frequently to hide to avoid hostile natives. He shot deer for food.

But one night going into what he thought was a friendly village he had his rifle stolen from him, and was again a fugitive without any means of protecting himself or of getting food. However, he was not one to give in while there was a chance of life left, and he pushed on and on till at length he reached a place where he met some of his men who had also escaped, and after further tramping they got safely back into friendly country.

But what a terrible time they must have had!

Three weeks had passed since the attack, and the great part of that time Selous had been alone—hunted, starving, and bitterly cold at night, and in sweltering heat by day.

None but a scout with extraordinary endurance could have lived through it, but then Selous is a man who as a lad had made himself strong by care and exercise; and he neither drinks nor smokes. And he kept up his pluck all the time.

It shows you that if you want to get through such adventures safely when you are a man you must train yourself up to be strong, healthy, and active as a lad.

EXERCISES AND THEIR OBJECT

There is a great deal of nonsense in fashion in the way of bodily exercises; so many people seem to think that their only object is to make huge muscle. But to make yourself strong and healthy it is necessary to begin with your inside and to get the blood into good order and the heart to work well; that is the secret of the whole thing, and physical exercises should be taken with that intention. This is the way to do it:

(*a*) Make the heart strong, in order to pump the blood

properly to every part of the body and so to build up flesh, bone, and muscle.

Exercise: The 'Struggle' and 'Wrist Pushing.' See Pages 193, 194.

(*b*) MAKE THE LUNGS STRONG, in order to revive the blood with fresh air.

Exercise: 'Deep breathing'. See Page 201.

(*c*) MAKE THE SKIN PERSPIRE, to get rid of the dirt from the blood.

Exercise: Bath, or dry rub with a damp towel every day.

(*d*) MAKE THE STOMACH WORK, to feed the blood.

Exercise: 'Cone', or 'Body Bending', and 'Twisting'. See Pages 209–10.

(*e*) MAKE THE BOWELS ACTIVE, to remove the remains of food and dirt from the body.

Exercise: 'Body Bending' and 'Kneading the Abdomen'. Drink plenty of good water. Regular daily 'rear'.*

(*f*) WORK MUSCLES IN EACH PART OF THE BODY, to make the blood circulate to that part, and so increase your strength.

Exercise: Running and walking, and special exercises of special muscles, such as 'Wrist Pushing', etc.

The secret of keeping well and healthy is to keep your blood clean and active. These different exercises will do that if you will use them everyday. Someone has said, 'If you practise body exercises every morning you will never be ill: and if you also drink a pint of hot water every night you will never die.'

The blood thrives on simple good food, plenty of exercise, plenty or fresh air, cleanliness of the body both inside and out, and proper rest of body and mind at intervals.

The Japs* are particularly strong and healthy, as was shown in the late war with Russia. There was very little sickness among them and those who were wounded generally very quickly recovered because their skin was clean and their blood was in a healthy, sound condition. They are the best example that we can copy. They keep themselves very clean by having two or three baths every day.

They eat very plain food, chiefly rice and fruit, and not much of it. They drink plenty of water, but no spirits. They take lots of exercise. They make themselves good-tempered and do not worry their brain. They live in fresh air as much as possible day and night.

Their particular exercise is 'Ju-Jitsu', which is more of a game than drill and is generally played in pairs. And pupils get to like the game so much that they generally go on with it after their course of instruction has finished.

By Ju-Jitsu, the muscles and body are developed in a natural way in the open air as a rule. It requires no apparatus, and once the muscles have been formed by it they do not disappear again when you cease the practices as is the case in ordinary gymnastics.

Admiral Kamimura, the great Admiral of our friends the Japanese, strongly recommends all young men and lads to practise Ju-Jitsu, as it not only makes them strong, but also quick in the mind.

THE NOSE

A SCOUT must be able to smell well in order to find his enemy by night. If he always breathes through the nose and not through the mouth this helps him considerably. But there are other reasons more important than that for always breathing through the nose. Fifty years ago, Mr Catlin* in America wrote a book called 'Shut your mouth and save your life', and he showed how the Red Indians for a long time had adopted that method with their children to the extent of tying up their jaws at night to ensure their only breathing through their nose.

Breathing through the nose prevents germs of disease getting from the air into the throat and stomach, it also prevents a growth in the back of the throat called 'adenoids' which are apt to stop the breathing power of the nostrils, and also to cause deafness.

For a scout nose-breathing is also specially useful.

By keeping the mouth shut you prevent yourself from getting thirsty when you are doing hard work. And also at night if you are in the habit of breathing through the nose it prevents snoring, and snoring is a dangerous thing if you are sleeping anywhere in an enemy's country. Therefore practise keeping your mouth shut and breathing through your nose at all times.

EARS

A SCOUT must be able to hear well. Generally the ears are very delicate and once damaged are apt to become incurably deaf. People are too apt to fiddle about with their ears in cleaning them by putting the corners of handkerchiefs, hairpins and so on into them, and also stuffing them up with hard cotton wool, all of which are dangerous with such a delicate organ as the ear, the drum of the ear being a very delicate, tightly-stretched skin which is easily damaged. Very many children have had the drums of their ears permanently injured by getting a box on the ear.

EYES

A SCOUT, of course, must have particularly good eyesight; he must be able to see anything very quickly and to see at a long way off. By practising your eyes in looking at things at a great distance they will grow stronger. While you are young you should save your eyes as much as possible, or they are not strong when you get older: therefore avoid reading by lamplight as much as possible and also sit with your back or side to the light when doing any work during the day; if you sit facing the light it strains your eyes.

The strain of the eyes is a very common failure with growing boys, although very often they do not know it, and headaches come most frequently from the eyes being strained; frowning on the part of a boy is very generally a sign that his eyes are being strained.

A scout, besides having good eyesight, must be able to tell the colour of things which he sees. Colour blindness is a great infliction which some boys suffer from. It takes away a pleasure from them, and it also makes them useless for certain trades and professions.

For instance, a railway signalman or engine-driver or a sailor would not be much good if he couldn't tell the difference between red and green.

It can very often be cured, and a simple way of doing this, if you find you are rather colour blind, is to get a collection of little bits of wool, or paper, of every different kind of colour, and pick out which you think is red, blue, yellow, green, and so on, and then get someone to tell you where you were right and where wrong. Then you go at it again, and in time you will find yourself improving, until you have no difficulty in recognising the right colours. It is better still to practise by looking at coloured lights at night in chemists' shops, railway signals, etc.

TEETH

A WOULD-BE recruit came up to the recruiting officer to be enlisted during the Boer War. He was found to be a sufficiently strong and well-made man but when they came to examine his teeth they found that these were in bad condition, and he was told that he could not be accepted as a soldier. To this he replied: 'But, sir, that seems hard lines. Surely we don't have to eat the enemy when we've killed them, do we?'

A scout with bad teeth is no use at all for scouting work, because he has to live on hard biscuits and hard meat which he cannot possibly eat or digest if his teeth are not good, and good teeth depend upon how you look after them when you are young, it means that you should keep them very carefully clean. At least twice a day they should be brushed, when you get up in the morning and when you go to bed, both inside and out, with a tooth-brush and tooth powder; and should be rinsed with water if possible after every meal but especially after eating fruit or acid food.

Scouts in the jungle cannot always find tooth-brushes, but they make substitutes out of dry sticks which they fray out at the end and make an imitation of a brush.

Three thousand men had to be sent away from the war in South Africa because their teeth were so bad that they could not chew the hard biscuits, etc., on which they had to live there.

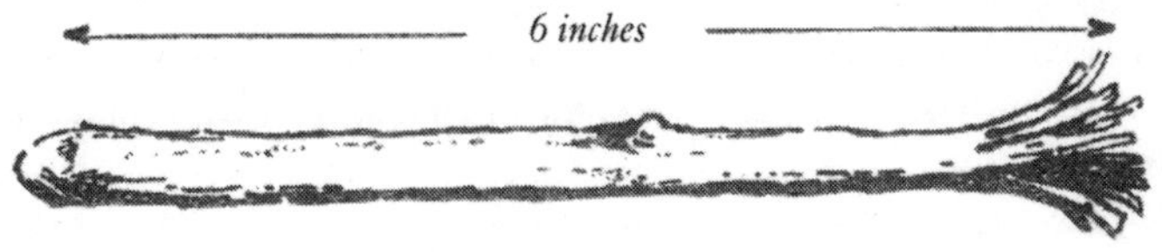

Camp tooth-brush

'Out West', in America, cowboys are generally supposed to be pretty rough customers, but they are in reality peace scouts of a high order. They live a hard life doing hard and dangerous work far away from towns and civilisation—where nobody sees them. But there is one civilised thing that they do—they clean their teeth every day, morning and evening.

Years ago I was travelling through Natal on horseback, and I was anxious to find a lodging for the night, when I came across a hut evidently occupied by a white man, but nobody was about. In looking round inside the hut, I noticed that though it was very roughly furnished there were several tooth-brushes on what served as a wash-hand stand, so I guessed that the owner must be a decent fellow, and I made myself at home until he came in, and I found that I had guessed aright.

HINTS TO INSTRUCTORS

PRACTICES IN DEVELOPING STRENGTH

Measurement of the Boy

It is of paramount importance to teach the young citizen to assume responsibility for his own development and health.

Physical drill is all very well as a disciplinary means of development, but it does not give the lad any responsibility in the matter.

It is therefore deemed preferable to tell each boy, according to his age, what ought to be his height, weight, and various measurements (such as chest, waist, arm, leg, etc.). He is then measured, and learns in which points he fails to come up to the standard. He can then be shown which exercises to practise for himself in order to develop those particular points. Encouragement must afterwards be given by periodical measurements, say every three months or so.

Cards can be obtained from the 'Boy Scouts' Office, Henrietta Street, London, W.C., which, besides giving the standard measurements for the various ages, give columns to be filled in periodically showing the boy's re-measurements and progress in development. If each boy has his card it is a great incentive to him to develop himself at odd times when he has a few minutes to spare.

Teach how to make camp tooth-brushes out of sticks. 'Dragon-root' sticks for cleaning teeth can be got at chemists' shops as samples.

GAMES TO DEVELOP STRENGTH

Boxing, wrestling, rowing, skipping, cock-fighting, are all valuable health aids to developing strength.

'Old Spotty-face' (To develop eyesight).—Prepare squares of cardboard divided into about a dozen small squares. Each scout should take one, and should have a pencil and go off a few hundred yards, or, if indoors, as far as space will allow. The umpire then takes a large sheet of cardboard, with twelve squares ruled on it of about three inch sides if in the open, or one and a half to two inches if indoors. The umpire has a number of black paper discs (half an inch diameter) and pins ready, and sticks about half a dozen on to his card, dotted about where he likes. He holds up his card so that it can be seen by the scouts. They then gradually approach, and as they get within sight they mark their cards with the same pattern of spots. The one who does so at the farthest distance from the umpire wins. Give five points for every spot correctly shown, deduct one point for every two inches nearer than the furthest man. This teaches long sight.

'Spotty-face' for strengthening the eyesight

'QUICK SIGHT' can also be taught with the same apparatus, by allowing the scouts to come fairly close, and then merely showing your card for five seconds, and let them mark their cards from memory. The one who is most correct wins.

'THE STRUGGLE'.—Two players face each other about a yard

apart, stretch arms out sideways, lock fingers of both hands, and lean towards each other till their chests touch, push chest to chest, and see who can drive the other back to the wall of the room or on to a goal line. At first a very short struggle is sufficient to set their hearts pumping, but after practice for a few days the heart grows stronger and they can go on for a long time.

The 'Struggle' for strengthening the heart

'Wrist Pushing' by one man alone. Stand with both your arms to the front about level with the waist, cross your wrists so that one hand has knuckles up, the other knuckles down. Clench the fists.

Now make the lower hand press upwards and make the upper hand press downwards.

Press as hard as you can with both wrists gradually, and only after great resistance let the lower push the upper one upwards till opposite your forehead, then let the upper press the lower down, the lower one resisting all the time.

These two exercises, although they sound small and simple, if carried out with all your might, develop most muscles in your body and especially those about the heart. They should not be carried on too long at a time, but should be done at frequent intervals during the day for a minute or so.

'Wrist Pushing' can also be played by two boys half facing each other, each putting out the wrist nearest to his opponent, at arm's length; pressing it against the other's wrist and trying to turn him round backwards.

BOOKS TO READ

'Cassell's Physical Educator', by E. Miles (Cassell & Co.). A complete compendium of all kinds of Physical Training for boys and girls.

'Ju-jitsu.' Price 6d. (Published by Richard Fox.)

'School Games', by T. Chesterton. (Educational Supply Association.)

'Boxing', by A. J. Newton. 1s. (C. A. Pearson Ltd.)

CAMP FIRE YARN.—No. 18

HEALTH-GIVING HABITS

Keep Clean—Don't Smoke—Don't Drink—Avoid Self-Abuse*—
Rise Early—Laugh and Grow Fat.

HOW TO KEEP HEALTHY

ALL the great peace-scouts who have succeeded in exploring or hunting expeditions in wild countries have only been able to get on by being pretty good doctors themselves; because diseases, accidents, and wounds are always being suffered by them or their men, and they don't find doctors and chemists' shops in the jungles to cure them. So that a scout who does not know something about doctoring would never get on at all; he might just as well stay at home for all the good he will be.

Therefore, practise keeping healthy yourself, and then you will be able to show others how to keep themselves healthy too.

In this way you can do many good turns.

David Livingstone* the great missionary and peace-scout, endeared himself to the natives by his cleverness as a doctor.

Also, if you know how to look after yourself you need never have to pay for medicines. The great English poet, Dryden* in his poem,

'Cymon and Iphigenia', wrote that it was better to trust to fresh air and exercise than to pay doctors' bills to keep yourself healthy:

> Better to hunt in fields for health unbought
> Than fee the doctor for a nauseous draught;
> The wise, for cure, on exercise depend;
> God never made his work for man to mend.

KEEP YOURSELF CLEAN

In the war in South Africa we lost an enormous number of men dying from disease as well as from wounds. The Japs, in their war, lost very few from sickness, and a very small proportion of those who were wounded. What made the difference? Probably a good many things. Our men were not so particular as to what water they drank as the Japs were, and they ate more meat than the Japs; but, also, they did not keep themselves or their clothes very clean—it was often difficult to find water. The Japs, on the other hand, kept themselves very clean, with baths every day.

If you cut your hand when it is dirty it is very likely to fester, and to become very sore; but if your hand is quite clean and freshly washed no harm will come of it, it heals up at once. It was the same with wounds in the war; they became very bad in the case of men who had not kept themselves clean.

Cleaning your skin helps to clean your blood. The Japs say that half the good of exercise is lost if you do not have a bath immediately after it.

It may not be always possible for you to get a bath every day, but you can at any rate rub yourself over with a wet towel, or scrub yourself with a dry one, and you ought not to miss a single day in doing this if you want to keep fit and well.

You should also keep clean in your clothing, both your underclothing as well as that which shows. Beat it out with a stick every day before putting it on.

And to be healthy and strong you *must* keep your blood healthy and clean inside you. This is done by breathing in lots of pure, fresh air, by deep breathing, and by clearing out all dirty matter from inside your stomach, which is done by having a 'rear' daily, without fail; many people are the better for having it twice a day. If there is any difficulty about it one day, drink plenty of good water, both morning and evening, and practise body-twisting exercises, and all should be well.

Never start work in the morning without some sort of food inside you, if it is only a cup of hot water.

Never bathe in deep water very soon after a meal, it is very likely to cause cramp, which doubles you up, and so you get drowned.

SMOKING

A SCOUT does not smoke. Any boy can smoke; it is not such a very wonderful thing to do. But a scout will not do it because he is not such a fool. He knows that when a lad smokes before he is fully grown up it is almost sure to make his heart feeble, and the heart is the most important organ in a lad's body. It pumps the blood all over him to form flesh, bone, and muscle. If the heart does not do its work the body cannot grow to be healthy. Any scout knows that smoking spoils his eyesight, and also his sense of smell, which is of greatest importance to him for scouting on active service.

The boy who apes the man by smoking will never be much good

A strong and healthy boy has the ball at his feet

Sir William Broadbent* the great doctor, and Professor Sims Woodhead* have both told us what bad effects tobacco smoking has on the health of boys. Numerous well-known sportsmen and others in all kinds of professions have given up the use of tobacco as they find they can do better without it. Lord Roberts and Lord Wolseley as soldiers, Lord Charles Beresford as a sailor, the Archbishop of

Canterbury, the judge, Sir William Grantham, all do not smoke, nor do Dr Grace the cricketer, Mr Noble and seven of the chief Australian cricketers, Mr Eustace Miles* the champion tennis player, Basset the football player, Hanlon the sculler, Weston the pedestrian, Taylor the golf player, Burnham the scout, Selous the hunter, and very many other celebrated men. They are all non-smokers.

The railway and post office authorities in America will not employ boys who smoke. I know one big employer who not only does not smoke, but will not employ a boy who does. So with a great many other employers in Great Britain. In Japan no boy under twenty is allowed to smoke, and if he does his parents are taken up and fined.

Professor Osler* in speaking against tobacco, said it would be a good thing if all the beer and spirits in England could be thrown into the sea one day, and if, on the second day, you dumped all the tobacco there too it would be very good for everyone in England—although unhealthy for the fish.

No boy ever began smoking because he liked it, but generally because either he feared being chaffed by the other boys as afraid to smoke, or because he thought that by smoking he would look like a great man—when all the time he only looks like a little ass.

So don't funk, but just make up your own mind for yourself that you don't mean to smoke till you are grown up; and stick to it. That will show you to be a man much more than any slobbering about with a half-smoked cigarette between your lips. The other fellows will in the end respect you much more, and will probably in many cases secretly follow your lead. If they do this you will already have done a good thing in the world, although you are only a boy. From that small start you will most probably go on and do big things as you grow up.

DRINKING

A PRIEST in the East End of London has lately stated that out of a thousand cases of distress known to him only two or three were not caused by drink.

A soldierly-looking man came up to me one night and brought out his discharge certificates, showing that he had served with me in South Africa. He said he could get no work, and he was starving. Every man's hand was against him, apparently because he was a soldier. My nose and eyes told me in a moment another tale, and that was the real cause of his being in distress.

A stale smell of tobacco and beer hung about his clothes, his finger-tips were yellow with cigarette smoke, he had even taken some kind of scented lozenge to try and hide the whisky smell in his breath. No wonder nobody would employ him, or give him more money to drink with, for that was all that he would do with money if he got it.

Very much of the poverty and distress in this country is brought about by men getting into the habit of wasting their money and time on drink. And a great deal of crime, and also of illness, and even madness is due to the same habit of drinking too much. Liquor—that is beer or spirits—is not at all necessary to make a man strong and well. Quite the contrary. The old saying, 'Strong drink makes weak men', is a very true one.

Yet £166,400,000 were spent last year alone on drink in the United Kingdom—enough to have made every family in the country better off by £15 if they had drunk water. And this £15 would be increased to £22 if the men gave up tobacco.

It would be simply impossible for a man who drinks to be a scout. Keep off liquor from the very first, and make up your mind to have nothing to do with it. Water, tea, or coffee are quite good enough drinks for quenching your thirst or for picking you up at any time, or if it is very hot lemonade or a squeeze of lemon are much better refreshment.

A good scout trains himself pretty well to do without liquid. It is very much a matter of habit. If you keep your mouth shut when walking or running, or chew a pebble (which also makes you keep your mouth shut), you do not get thirsty like you do when you go along with your mouth open sucking in the air and dry dust. But you must also be in good, hard condition. If you are fat from want of exercise you are sure to get thirsty and want to drink every mile. If you do not let yourself drink the thirst wears off after a short time. If you keep drinking water on the line of march, or while playing games, it helps to tire you and spoils your wind.

It is often difficult to avoid taking strong drinks when you meet friends who want to treat you, but they generally like you all the better if you say you don't want anything, as then they don't have to pay for it; if they insist you can take a gingerbeer or something quite harmless. But it is a stupid fashion when, in order to prove that you are friends, you have to drink with each other. Luckily it is dying out now; the best men do not do it because they know it does them no good. Wasters like to stand about a bar talking and sipping—generally at the other fellow's expense, but they are wasters, and it is as well to keep out of their company, if you want to get on and have a good time.

EARLY RISING

THE scout's time for being most active is in the early morning, because that is the time when wild animals all do their feeding and moving about; and also in war the usual hour for an attack is just before dawn, when the attackers can creep up unseen in the dark, and get sufficient light to enable them to carry out the attack suddenly while the other people are still asleep.

So a scout trains himself to the habit of getting up very early; and when once he is in the habit it is no trouble at all to him, like it is to some fat fellows who lie asleep after the daylight has come.

The Emperor Charlemagne,* who was a great scout in the old days, used always to get up in the middle of the night.

The Duke of Wellington, who, like Napoleon Bonaparte, preferred to sleep on a little camp bed, used to say, 'When it is time to turn over in bed it is time to turn out'.

Many men who manage to get through more work than others in a day, do so by getting up an hour or two earlier. By getting up early you also can get more time for play.

If you get up one hour earlier than other people you get thirty hours a month more of life than they do; while they have twelve months in the year you get 365 extra hours, or thirty more days—that is, thirteen months to their twelve.

The old rhyme has a lot of truth in it when it says,

> Early to bed and early to rise,
> Makes a man healthy, and wealthy, and wise.

SMILE

WANT of laughter means want of health. Laugh as much as you can: it does you good; so whenever you can get a good laugh on. And make other people laugh too, when possible, as it does them good.

If you are in pain or trouble make yourself smile at it: if you remember to do this, and force yourself, you will find it really does make a great difference.

If you read about great scouts like Captain John Smith, the 'Pathfinder', and others, you will generally find that they were pretty cheery old fellows.

The ordinary boy is apt to frown when working hard at physical exercises, but the boy scout is required to smile all the time: he drops a mark off his score whenever he frowns.

HOW TO KEEP HEALTHY

PRACTICES

DEEP BREATHING.—Deep breathing is of the greatest importance for bringing fresh air into the lungs to be put into the blood, and for developing the size of the chest, but it should be done carefully, according to instructions, and not overdone, otherwise it is liable to strain the heart. The Japs always carry on deep breathing exercise for a few minutes when they first get up in the morning, and always in the open air. It is done by sucking air in through the nose until it swells out your ribs as far as possible, especially at the back; then, after a pause, you breathe out the air slowly and gradually through the mouth until you have not a scrap of air left in you, then after a pause draw in your breath again through the nose as before.

Singing, if carried out on a system like that of Mr Tomlin's, develops simultaneously proper breathing and development of heart, lungs, chest, and throat, together with dramatic feeling in rendering the song.

'Japanese cock fighting' to strengthen the legs

For instance, his method of 'Hooligan Taming' is to get a large crowd of wild lads together, and to start shouting a chorus to piano accompaniment—say, 'Hearts of Oak'. He shouts the suggestion of a story as they go along with it; how they are marching boldly to attack a fort which they mean to carry in style for the glory of themselves and their country, when suddenly they become aware that the enemy does not know of their approach, so they must creep and crawl, 'in a whisper', as they stealthily get nearer to the fort. Closer and closer they come with gradually increasing tone. Now charge on up the hill, through shot and shell, a scramble, a rush and a fight, and the fort is theirs. But there are wounded to be picked up tenderly, and the dead to be laid out reverently with quiet and measured song, solemn and soft.

And then they pick up their arms again, and with the prisoners and spoils of war they march gaily away in triumph, at the full power of their lungs.

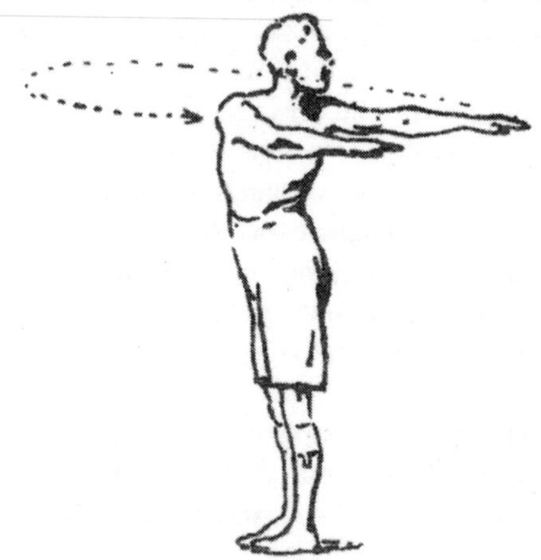

'Body twisting' for stomach muscles

Old English Morris Dances, too, are excellent practice for winter evenings, with their quaint music and movements.

BOOKS TO READ

'What's the Harm in Smoking?', by B. McCall Barbour. 1d. (Published by S. W. Partridge.)

'In My Youth'. Same series. Practical Hints on Purity. (B. M. Barbour, 37 Chambers Street, Edinburgh.)

'What a Young Boy ought to Know', by Sylvanus Stall* 4s. Giving information and warning to boys regarding the organs of reproduction.

'A Note for Parents', by J. H. Bradley. 3d. (Ballantyne Press. London.) Suggestions for teaching children about reproduction.

CAMP FIRE YARN.—No. 19

PREVENTION OF DISEASE

Camp doctoring—Microbes and how to fight them—Proper food—Clothing—Use of drill and exercise.

CAMP DOCTORING

SOME years ago,* when I was in Kashmir, Northern India, some natives brought to me a young man on a stretcher who they said had fallen off a high rock and had broken his back and was dying. I soon found that he had only dislocated his shoulder and had got a few bruises, and seemed to think that he ought to die.

So I pulled off my shoe, sat down alongside him facing his head, put my heel in his arm-pit, got hold of his arm, and pulled with all my force till the bone jumped into its socket. The pain made him faint and his friends thought I really had killed him. But in a few minutes he recovered and found his arm was all right. Then they thought I must be no end of a doctor, so they sent round the country for all the sick to be brought in to be cured; and I had an awful time of it for the next two days. Cases of every kind of disease were carried in and I had scarcely any drugs with which to treat them, but I did the best I could, and I really believe that some of the poor creatures got better from simply *believing* that I was doing them a lot of good.

But most of them were ill from being dirty and letting their wounds get poisoned with filth; and many were ill from bad drainage, and from drinking foul water, and so on.

Pulling in a dislocated shoulder—an incident in Kashmir

This I explained to the headmen of the villages, and I hope that I did some good for their future health.

At any rate, they were most grateful, and gave me a lot of help ever afterwards in getting good bear-hunting and in getting food, etc.

If I had not known a little doctoring I could have done nothing for these poor creatures.

MICROBES AND HOW TO FIGHT THEM

DISEASE is carried about in the air and in water by tiny invisible insects called 'germs' or 'microbes', and you are very apt to breathe them in through the mouth or to get them in your drink or food and to swallow them, and then they breed disease inside you. If your blood is in really good order it generally does not matter, no harm results; but if your blood is out of order from weakness or constipation—that is, not going regularly to the 'rear'—these microbes will very probably make you ill. A great point is, therefore, to abolish the microbes if possible. They like living in dark, damp, and dirty places. And they come from bad drains, old dustbins, and rotting flesh, etc.; in fact, generally where there is a bad smell. Therefore, keep your room, or your camp, and your clothes clean, dry, and as sunny as possible and well aired; and keep away from places that smell badly.

Before your meals you should always wash your hands and finger-nails, for they are very apt to harbour microbes which have come from anything that you may have been handling in the day.

You frequently see notices in omnibuses and public places requesting you not to spit. The reason for this is that many people spit who have diseased lungs and from their spittle the microbes of their diseases get in the air and are breathed by healthy people into their lungs, and they become also diseased. Often you may have a disease in you for some years without knowing it and if you spit you are liable to communicate that disease to sound people; so you should not do it for their sake.

But you need not be afraid of diseases if you breathe through your nose and keep your blood in good order. It is always well on coming out of a crowded theatre, church or hall, to cough and blow your nose in order to get rid of microbes which you might have breathed in from other people in the crowd. One in every thirty of people that you meet has got the disease of consumption on him—and it is very catching. It comes very much from living in houses where the windows are kept always shut up. The best chance of getting cured of it if you get the disease is to sleep always out of doors.

A scout has to sleep a great deal in the open air, therefore when he is in a house he sleeps with the windows as wide open as possible, otherwise he feels stuffy; and also if he gets accustomed to sleeping in warm atmosphere he would catch cold when he goes into camp, and nothing could be more ridiculous or more like a tenderfoot than a scout with a cold in his head. When once he is accustomed to having his windows open he will never catch cold in a room.

FOOD

A GOOD many illnesses come from over-eating or eating the wrong kind of food.

A scout must know how to take care of himself, else he is of no use. He must keep himself light and active. Once he has got the right kind of muscles on he can remain fit without further special exercising of those muscles, provided that he eats the right kind of food.

Eustace Miles* the tennis and racket champion, does not go into training before he plays his matches; he knows he has got his muscles rightly formed, and he simply lives on plain, light food always, and so is always fit to play a hard game. He never eats meat.

In the siege of Mafeking, when we were put on short commons, those of the garrison who were accustomed to eat very little at their meals did not suffer like some people, who had been accustomed to do themselves well in peace time; these became weak and irritable. Our food there towards the end was limited to a hunk of pounded-up oats, about the size of a penny bun, which was our whole bread-supply for the day, and about a pound of meat and two pints of 'sowens', a kind of stuff like bill-stickers' paste that had gone wrong.

English people as a rule eat more meat than is necessary, in fact they could do without it altogether if they tried, and would be none the worse. It is an expensive luxury. The Japanese are as strong as us, but they do not eat any meat, and only eat small meals of other things.

The cheapest and best foods are Dried Peas, 2d. per lb; Flour, 1s. 4d. per stone; Oatmeal, 2d. per lb.; Potatoes, 1/2d. per lb.; Hominy, 1½d. per lb.; Cheese at 6d. per lb. Other good foods are fruit, vegetables, fish, eggs, nuts, rice, and milk, and one can live on these perfectly well without meat; bananas are especially good food, they are cheap, have no seeds nor pips to irritate your inside, their skin protects them from germs of disease and their flesh is of a wholesome kind and satisfying.

The natives of the West Coast of Africa eat very little else all their lives and they are fat and happy.

If you have lots of fresh air you do not want much food, if on the other hand you are sitting indoors all day much food makes you fat and sleepy, so that in either case you are better for taking a little; still, growing boys should not starve themselves but, at the same time, they need not be like that little hog at the school-feast who, when asked, 'Can't you eat any more?' replied, 'Yes, I could *eat* more, but I've no room to *swallow* it.'

A great cause of illness nowadays is the amount of medicine which fellows dose themselves with when there is no reason for taking any medicine at all. The best medicine is open-air and exercise and a big cup of water in the early morning if you are constipated, and a pint of hot water on going to bed.

CLOTHING

A SCOUT'S clothing should be of flannel or wool as much as possible, because it dries easily. Cotton next the skin is not good unless you change it directly it gets wet—it is so likely to give you a chill, and a scout is no use if he gets laid up.

One great point that a scout should take care about, to ensure his endurance and being able to go on the march for a long time, is his boots.

A scout who gets sore feet with much walking becomes useless.

You should therefore take great care to have good, well-fitting, roomy boots, and fairly stout ones, and as like the natural shape of your bare feet as possible with a straighter edge on the inside than bootmakers usually give to the swagger boot. Scouts have no use for swagger boots.

The feet should be kept as dry as possible; if they are allowed to get wet the skin is softened and very soon gets blistered and rubbed raw where there is a little pressure of the boot.

Of course they get wet from perspiration as well as from outside wet. Therefore to dry this it is necessary to wear good woollen socks.

If a man wears thin cotton or silk socks you can tell at once that he is no walker. A fellow who goes out to a Colony for the first time is called a 'Tender-foot' because he generally gets sore feet until by experience he learns how to keep his feet in good order. It is a good thing to soap or grease your feet and the inside of your socks before putting them on.

If your feet always perspire a good deal it is a useful thing to powder them with powder made of boric acid, starch, and oxide of zinc in equal parts. This powder should be rubbed in between the toes so as to prevent soft corns forming there. Your feet can be hardened to some extent by soaking them in alum and water, or salt and water.

Keep your boots soft with lots of grease, mutton fat, dubbin, or castor oil—especially when they have got wet from rain, etc. Wash the feet every day.

PRACTICES

Drill

Scouts have to drill to enable them to be moved quickly from one point to another in good order. Drill also sets them up, and makes them smart and quick.

It strengthens the muscles which support the body and by keeping the body upright the lungs and heart get plenty of room to work, and

How not to sit

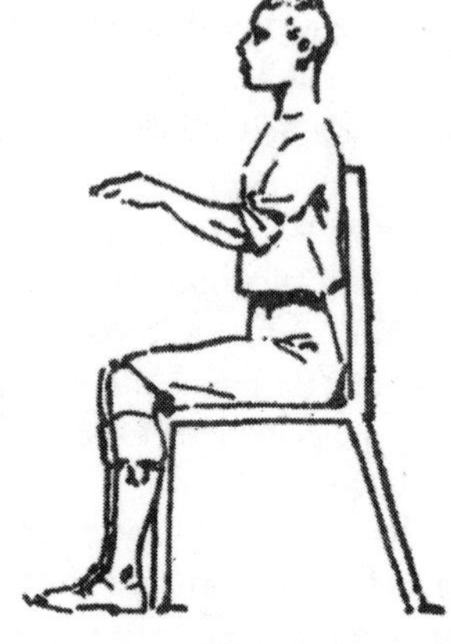

How to sit

the inside organs are kept in the proper position for proper digestion of food and so on.

A slouching position on the other hand depresses all the other organs and prevents them doing their work properly, so that a man in that position is generally weak and often ill.

Growing lads are very apt to slouch and should therefore do all they can to get out of the habit by plenty of physical exercises and drill.

Stand upright when you are standing and when you are sitting down sit upright with your back well into the back part of the chair. Alertness of the body whether you are moving, standing, or sitting means alertness of mind and it is a paying thing to have because many an employer will select an alert-looking boy for work and pass over a sloucher. When you have to stoop over writing at a table or even tying a boot-lace do not round your back but tuck in the small of your back which thus helps to strengthen your body.

DRILL.—On the word 'Alert' the scout stands upright with both feet together, hands hanging naturally at the sides, fingers straight, and looking straight to his front.

On the word 'Easy' he carries the right foot away six inches to the right, and clasps his hands behind his back, and can turn his head about. At the word 'Sit Easy' he squats down on the ground in any position he likes. 'Sit Easy' should usually be given whenever you don't want the boys to be at the 'Alert', provided that the ground is dry.

1 2 3

Walking for exercise

1.—The right way 2.—A common way 3.—A very usual way

-----> *Direction of eyes*

On the command 'Quick March', boys move off with the left foot leading, at a smart pace, swinging the arms freely, as this gives good exercise to the body and muscles and interior organs.

At the command 'Double' boys run at a jog-trot with short, sharp steps, hands swinging loosely, not tucked up at the side.

On the command 'Scout Pace' the boys march at the quick march for fifty paces then double fifty paces, and so on alternately running and walking, until the word is given 'Quick March' or 'Halt'.

'Right turn'—each boy turns to the right.

'Follow Your Leader'. 'Leader Right Turn'—the leading man turns to his right, the remainder move up to the place where he turned and then follow after him.

'Front Form' (when 'following the leader'). Those in rear run up and form in line alongside the leader on his left.

'Cone Exercises'.—Standing at the 'Alert' raise both hands as high as possible over the head, and link fingers, lean backwards, then sway the arms very slowly round in the direction of a cone so that the hands make a wide circle above and round the body, the body turning from the hips, and leaning over to one side, then to the front, then to the other side and then back; this is to exercise the muscles of the waist and stomach, and should be repeated say six times to either hand. With the eyes you should be trying to see all that goes on behind you during the movement.

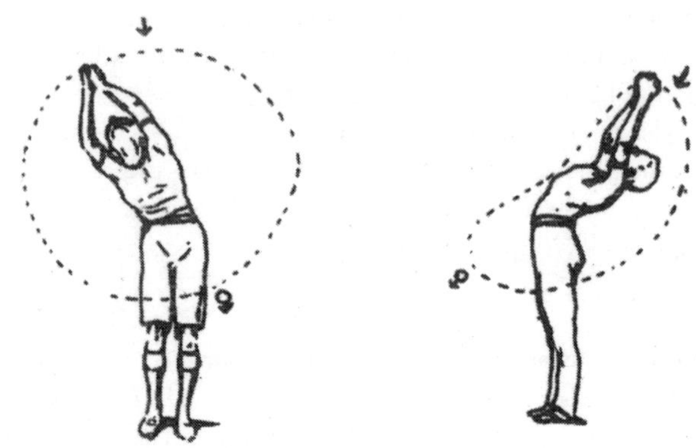

'Body-bending' or 'Cone' exercise

Note.—The arrow → means when to draw in breath; the O→ means when to breathe out

'TOUCH THE TOES'.—From the position of 'Alert' raise the hands above the head then bend slowly forward and touch the toes with the fingers, or knuckles of clenched fists, then slowly rise to the original position and continue the motion a dozen times, the knees not to be bent in performing this exercise. This makes the body supple, and strengthens the back and legs.

'SQUATTING EXERCISE'.—From the position of the 'Alert' bend the knees and slowly lower the body into a squatting position, the back being kept upright; after a momentary pause slowly rise to the standing position again, repeat this a dozen times standing on the toes throughout. The hands may be resting on the hips or held out straight to the front in line with the shoulders. This exercise strengthens the leg and feet muscles.

'LEG RAISING FROM THE BACK'.—Lie on your back and slowly raise the legs till they are upright above you, then slowly lower them almost to the ground and raise them again, several times in succession. This stengthens the stomach muscles.

GAMES

'Ju-jitsu'—contains numerous interesting games to teach grips and holds, and development of muscles.

'Doctoring'—each scout in turn acts as an explorer or missionary, with a few simple remedies. Three patients are brought to him in succession to be treated, each having a different disease or injury. He has to advise or show what treatment should be carried out.

All ordinary boys' games, where all are players and none lookers-on, are good for health and cheerfulness—'Leap-frog', 'Rounders', 'Squash-football', 'Tip-and-run'.

BOOKS TO READ

'Japanese Physical Training', by Irving Hancock. (Pub. Putnam.)

'How to be well and strong', by W. Edwards, 4d. (Melrose.)

'Walking', by C. Lang Neil. 1s (C. A. Pearson Ltd.) Useful hints on walking, training, mountain-climbing, food, etc.

'Modern Physical Culture', by C. Lang Neil. 1s. (C. A. Pearson Ltd.) Gives summary of various systems: Curative exercises; hints on food, on organs of the body, etc.

'Health and Strength'. Monthly Journal. 2d.

CHAPTER VII

CHIVALRY of the KNIGHTS

HINTS TO INSTRUCTORS

One aim of the Boy Scouts scheme is to revive amongst us, if possible, some of the rules of the knights of old, which did so much for the moral tone of our race, just as the Bushido of the ancient Samurai Knights has done, and is still doing, for Japan. Unfortunately, chivalry with us has, to a large extent, been allowed to die out, whereas in Japan it is taught to the children, so that it becomes with them a practice of their life, and it is also taught to children in Germany and Switzerland with the best results. Our effort is not so much to discipline the boys, as to teach them to discipline themselves.

It is impossible in so short a space as I have at my disposal to do more than touch upon subjects which the instructor may elaborate for himself. The different qualities which the Knight's Code demanded are here grouped under the three heads:—

1.—*Chivalry to Others.*
2.—*Discipline of Self.*
3.—*Self-Improvement.*

CAMP FIRE YARN.—No. 20

CHIVALRY TO OTHERS

Knights Errant—Helpfulness to Others—Courtesy to Women.

'In days of old, when knights were bold'* it must have been a fine sight to see one of these steel-clad horsemen come riding through the dark green woods in his shining armour, with shield and lance and waving plumes, bestriding his gallant war-horse, strong to bear its load, and full of fire to charge upon an enemy. And near him rode his squire, a young man, his assistant and companion, who would some day become a knight.

Behind him rode his group, or patrol of men-at-arms—stout, hearty warriors, ready to follow their knight to the gates of death if need be. They were the tough yeomen of the old days, who won so many of her fine fights for Britain through their pluck and loyal devotion to their knights.

In peace time, when there was no fighting to be done, the knight would daily ride about looking for a chance of doing a good turn to any wanting help, especially woman or child who might be in distress. When engaged in thus doing good turns he was called a 'Knight Errant'. His patrol naturally acted in the same way as their leader, and a man-at-arms was always equally ready to help the distressed with his strong right arm. The knights of old were the patrol leaders of the nation, and the men-at-arms were the scouts.

You patrol leaders and scouts are therefore very like the knights and their retainers, especially if you keep your honour ever before you in the first place and do your best to help other people who are in trouble or who want assistance. Your motto is, 'Be Prepared' to do this, and the motto of the knights was a similar one, 'Be Always Ready'.

Chivalry—that is, the order of the knights—was started in England some 1,500 years ago by King Arthur.

On the death of his father, King Uther Pendragon, he was living with his uncle, and nobody knew who was to be King. He did not himself know that he was son of the late King.

Then a great stone was found in the churchyard, into which a sword was sticking, and on the stone was written:

'Whosoever pulleth this sword out of this stone is the rightwise King born of all England.'

All the chief lords had a try at pulling it out, but none could move it.

That day there was a tournament at which Arthur's cousin was to fight, but when he got to the ground he found he had left his sword at home, and he sent Arthur to fetch it. Arthur could not find it, but remembering the sword in the churchyard he went there and pulled at it, and it came out of the stone at once; and he took it to his cousin. After the sports he put it back again into the stone; and again they all tried to pull it out, but could not move it, but when he tried he drew it out quite easily. So he was proclaimed King.

He afterwards got together a number of knights, and used to sit with them at a great round table, and so they were called the 'Knights of the Round Table'. The table is still to be seen at Winchester.

ST GEORGE

THEY had as their patron saint St George, because he was the only one of all the saints who was a horseman. He is the patron saint of cavalry and scouts all over Europe.

St George is the special saint of England. The battle-cry of the knights used to be, 'For Saint George and Merrie England!'

St George's Day is 23rd April, and on that day all good scouts wear a rose in his honour and fly their flags. Don't forget it on the next 23rd April.

THE KNIGHTS' CODE

THE laws of the knights were these:

> *Be Always Ready*, with your armour on, except when you are taking your rest at night.
> Defend the poor, and help them that cannot defend themselves.
> Do nothing to hurt or offend anyone else.
> Be prepared to fight in the defence of England.
> At whatever you are working try and win honour and a name for honesty.
> Never break your promise.
> Maintain the honour of your country with your life.
> Rather die honest than live shamelessly.
> Chivalry requireth that youth should be trained to perform the most laborious and humble offices with *cheerfulness* and grace; and to do good unto others.

These are the first rules with which the old knights started, and from which the scout laws of to-day come.

A knight (or scout) is at all times a gentleman. So many people seem to think that a gentleman must have lots of money. That does not make a gentleman. A gentleman is anyone who carries out the rules of chivalry of the knights.

A London policeman, for instance, is a gentleman, because he is well disciplined, loyal, polite, brave, good-tempered, and helpful to women and children.

UNSELFISHNESS

CAPTAIN JOHN SMITH,* the old English adventurer of three hundred years ago, was a pretty tough customer to deal with, as he had fought in every part of the world and had been wounded over and over again; but he also had a good, kind heart within him. He was as good a type of scout as you could find anywhere. One of his favourite expressions was, 'We were born, not for ourselves, but to do good to others,' and he carried this out very much in his life, for he was the most unselfish of men.

SELF-SACRIFICE

KING RICHARD I,* who was one of the first of the Scouts of the Empire, left his kingdom, his family, and everything to go and fight against the enemies of the Christian religion, and very nearly lost his kingdom by doing so, for he was absent for some years, and in the meantime his brother tried to usurp his place. On his way home from the wars in Palestine he was caught by the King of Austria, and was put by him in prison, where he lingered for twelve months. He was discovered by his minstrel, Blondel, who knowing that he must have been captured somewhere went about Europe singing his favourite songs outside the prisons until he was answered from inside; and so he found him and procured his release.

(See 'The Talisman', by Sir Walter Scott.*)

But self-sacrifice is also to be found among us to-day. Only the other day a lad of eighteen named Currie saw a little girl playing on the railway line at Clydebank in front of an approaching train. He tried to rescue her, but he was lame from an injury he had got at football, and it delayed him in getting her clear. The train knocked both of them over, and both were killed.

But Currie's gallant attempt is an example of chivalry for scouts to follow. It was sacrifice of himself in the attempt to save a child.

KINDNESS

'KINDNESS and gentleness are great virtues', says an old Spanish proverb, and another says, 'Oblige without regarding whom you oblige', which means be kind to anyone, great or small, rich or poor.

The great point about a knight was that he was always doing kindnesses or good turns to people. His idea was that everyone must die, but you should make up your mind that before your time comes you will do something good. Therefore, do it at once, for you never know when you may be going off.

So, with the scouts, it has been made one of our laws that we do a good turn to somebody every day. It does not matter how small that good turn may be, if it were only to help an old woman lift her bundle, or to guide a child across a crowded street, or to put a halfpenny in the poor-box. Something good ought to be done each day of your life, and you should start to-day to carry out this rule, and never forget it during the remaining days of your life. Remember the knot in your necktie and on your scout's badge—they are reminders to you to do a good turn. And do your good turn not only to your friends, but to strangers and even to your enemies.

When the Russians were besieged in Port Arthur by the Japanese in 1905, the Japs got close up to their forts by digging long, deep trenches, into which the Russians were not able to shoot. On one occasion they were so close that a Russian soldier was able to throw a letter into the Japanese trench. In this letter he said that he wanted to send a message to his mother in Russia, as she was very anxious about him; but as Port Arthur was now cut off from all communication he begged that the Japs would send the message for him; and he enclosed a note for his mother and a gold coin to pay the cost.

The Japanese soldier who found the note, instead of tearing up the letter and keeping the money, did what every scout would do, took it to his officer, and the officer telegraphed the Russian's message to his mother, and threw a note back into the enemy's fort to tell him that he had done so.

This, with other instances of chivalry on both sides, is described in Mr Richmond Smith's book, 'The Siege and Fall of Port Arthur'.

GENEROSITY

SOME people are fond of hoarding up their money and never spending it. It is well to be thrifty, but it is also well to give away money where it is wanted; in fact, that is part of the object of saving up your money. In being charitable, be careful that you do not fall into the mistake of false charity. That is to say, it is very easy and comforting to you to give a penny to a poor beggar in the street, but you ought not to do it. That poor beggar is ninety-nine times out of a hundred an arrant old fraud, and by giving your penny you are encouraging him and others to go on with that trade. There may be, probably are, hundreds of really poor and miserable people hiding away, whom you never see and to whom that penny would be a godsend. The Charity Organisation Society knows where they are, and which they are, and if you give your penny to them, they will put it into the right hands for you.

You need not be rich in order to be charitable. Many of the knights were poor men. At one time some of them wore as their crest two knights riding on one horse, which meant that they were too poor to afford a horse apiece.

TIPS

THEN 'tips' are a very bad thing.

Wherever you go, people want to be tipped for doing the slightest thing which they ought to do out of common good feeling. A scout will never accept a tip, even if it is offered him. It is often difficult to refuse, but for a scout it is easy. He has only to say, 'Thank you very much, but I am a scout, and our rules don't allow us to accept anything for doing a good turn.'

'Tips' put you on a wrong footing with everyone.

You cannot work in a friendly way with a man if you are thinking how much 'tip' you are going to get out of him, or he is thinking how much he'll have to 'tip' you. And all scouts' work for another ought to be done in a friendly way.

Of course, proper pay that is earned by your work is another thing, and you will be right to accept it.

FRIENDLINESS

THE great difference in a Colonial bushman and a stay-at-home Briton is that the Colonial is in shirt-sleeves while the other is buttoned up in his coat, and their characters are much the same. The Colonial is open and cheery with everybody at once, while the Briton is rather inclined to shut himself up from his neighbours inside his coat, and takes a deal of drawing out before he becomes friendly. The free, open-air, shirt-sleeve habits of the Colonial do away with this, and life becomes much more pleasant to everybody all round. A boy scout should remember that he is like the Colonial, and, like Kim, the 'friend of all the world'.

But don't let your friendliness lead you into that foolery that is too common in England, namely, throwing away your hard-earned savings in 'standing treat' to your friends.

POLITENESS

ONE of the stories that the knights used to tell as an example of politeness was that Julius Caesar, when he was entertained to supper by a poor peasant, was so polite that when the man gave him a dish of pickles to eat, thinking they were the sort of vegetables that a high-born officer would like, Caesar ate the whole dish, and pretended to like them, although they burnt his mouth and disagreed with him considerably.

In Spain you ask a man the way—he does not merely point it out, but takes off his hat, bows, and says that it will be a great pleasure to him to show it, and walks with you till he has set you properly upon it. He will take no reward.

A Frenchman will take off his hat when he addresses a stranger, as you may often see him do in London, even when he asks a policeman the way.

The Dutch fishermen, big and brawny as they are, take up the whole street when walking down it; but when a stranger comes along they stand to one side, and smilingly take off their caps to let him pass.

A lady told me that when in one of the far west Canadian townships she met a group of wild-looking cowboys walking down the street, she felt quite alarmed. But as they got near they stood to one side, and took off their hats with the greatest respect, and made way for her.

COURTESY TO WOMEN

THE knights of old were particularly attentive in respect and courtesy to women.

Sir Nigel Loring in 'The White Company'* is a type of a chivalrous knight of the old times. Although very small, and half-blind by reason of some lime which an enemy had thrown in his eyes early in his career, he was an exceedingly brave man, and at the same time very humble, and very helpful to others.

But above all things he reverenced women. He had a big, plain lady as his wife, but he always upheld her beauty and virtue, and was ready to fight anybody who doubted him.

Then with poor women, old or young, he was always courteous and helpful. And that is how a scout should act.

King Arthur, who made the rules of chivalry, was himself chivalrous to women of whatever class.

One day a girl rushed into his hall crying for help. Her hair was streaming and smeared with mud, her arms were torn with brambles, and she was dressed in rags. She had been ill-treated by a band of robbers who roved the country, doing all the harm they could. When he heard her tale King Arthur sprang on to his horse and rode off himself to the robbers' cave, and even at the risk of his own life he fought and defeated them, so that they could no more trouble his people.

When walking with a lady or a child, a scout should always have her on his left side, so that his right is free to protect her.

This rule is altered when walking in the streets: then a man will walk on the side of her nearest to the traffic, to protect her against accident, or mud-splashes, etc.

In meeting a woman or a child, a man should, as a matter of course, always make way for her, even if he has to step off the pavement into the mud.

So also in riding in a crowded tram or railway carriage no man worthy of the name will allow a woman or a child to stand up if he has a seat. He will at once give it up to the woman and stand himself. As a scout, you should set an example in this by being the first man in the carriage to do it. And in doing so, do it cheerfully, with a smile, so that she may not think you are annoyed at having to do it.

When in the street always be on the look out to help women and children. A good opportunity is when they want to cross a street, or to find the way, or to call a cab or 'bus. If you see them, go and help them at once—and don't accept any reward.

The other day I saw a boy help a lady out of a carriage, and as he shut the door after her, she turned to give him some money, but he touched his cap, and smilingly said, 'No, thank you, Marm; it's my duty,' and walked off. So I shook hands with him, for I felt that although he had not been taught, he was a scout by nature.

This is the kind of courtesy one wants to see more amongst boys of to-day. Only the other day in London, a girl who had been robbed ran after a thief and pursued him till he dashed down into a narrow alley, where she could not follow, but she waited for him; so did the crowd. And when he came out again, she collared him and struggled to prevent him escaping; but not one of the crowd would help her, although there were men and boys present there. They must have been a poor lot not to help a girl!

Of course, in accidents men and boys will always see that the women and children are safely got out of danger, before they think of going themselves. In two wrecks which occurred in 1906 on the south coast of England, viz., the *Jebba*, and the *Suevic*, it was very noticeable how carefully arrangements were made for saving the women and children and old people, before any idea was given as to how the men were to be rescued. You should carry your courtesy on with ladies at all times. If you are sitting down and a lady comes into the room, stand up, and see if you can help her in any way before you sit down.

A scout looking out ready to help others

Scout's uniform—Scout hat; Handkerchief (not a white one) round neck; Shirt (not white); Belt, with pouch; Shorts, with hip pocket; Stockings, with coloured garters; Boots or shoes, with good nails; Long stick for feeling way; Whistle; Haversack, with food; Coat rolled, with dry socks and vest inside in pockets

Don't lark about with a girl whom you would not like your mother or sister to see you with.

Don't make love to any girl unless you mean to marry her.

Don't marry a girl unless you are in a position to support her, and to support some children.

PRACTICES

OTHER ways of doing good turns, are such small things as these: sprinkle sand on a frozen road where horses are liable to slip; remove orange or banana skins from the pavement, as they are apt to throw people down; don't leave gates open, and don't injure fences or walk over crops in the country; help old people in drawing water or carrying fuel, etc., to their homes; help to keep the streets clean by removing scraps of paper.

HINTS TO INSTRUCTORS

HOW TO PRACTISE CHIVALRY

Make each scout tie a knot in his necktie every morning as a reminder to carry out his idea of doing a good turn every day, till it becomes a habit with him.

Take your boys to an armoury, such as the Tower of London or South Kensington Museum, and explain to them the armour and weapons of the knights.

Make a scout bring in a boy, who is a total stranger, as his guest for the evening to play in club games, and hear camp yarns, etc.

GAMES

'KNIGHT ERRANTRY'.—Scouts go out singly, or in pairs, or as a patrol. If in a town, to find women or children in want of help, and to return and report, on their honour, what they have done. If in the country call at any farms or cottages and ask to do odd jobs—for nothing. The same can be made into a race called a 'Good Turn' race.

PLAY

'King Arthur and the Round Table'. See Part VI.*

Also other stories of chivalry, as in 'Stories of King Arthur'.

BOOKS TO READ

'Ivanhoe', by Sir Walter Scott.
'Stories of King Arthur'. Cutler. 3s. 6d.
'The White Company', by Sir Conan Doyle, 1s.
'The Broad Stone of Honour', by Kenelm Digby.
'Fifty-two stories of Chivalry'.
'Puck of Pook's Hill', by Rudyard Kipling.

CAMP FIRE YARN.—No. 21

SELF-DISCIPLINE

Honour—Obedience—Courage—Cheeriness.

TO INSTRUCTORS

The self-disciplined man is described by Browning as:*

One who never turned his back but marched breast forward;
Never doubted clouds would break;
Never dreamed, though right were worsted, wrong would triumph;
Held we fall to rise, are baffled to fight better,
Sleep—to wake.

Lycurgus said that the wealth of a state lay not so much in money as in men who were sound in body and mind, with a body fit for toil and endurance, and with a mind well disciplined, and seeing things in their proper proportions.*

HONOUR

THE true knight placed his honour before all things. It was sacred, and he will never do a dishonourable action, such as telling an untruth or deceiving his superiors or employers. A man who is honourable is always to be trusted, and always commands the respect of his fellow men. His honour guides him in everything that he does. A captain sticks to the ship till the last, in every wreck that was ever heard of. Why? She is only a lump of iron and wood; his life is as valuable as that of any of the women and children on board, but he makes everybody get away safely before he attempts to save his more valuable life. Why? Because the ship is his ship, and he has been taught that it is his duty to stick to it, and he considers it would be dishonourable in him to do otherwise; so he puts honour before safety. So also a scout should value his honour most of anything.

FAIR PLAY.—Britons, above all other people, insist on fair play.

If you see a big bully going for a small or weak boy, you stop him because it is not 'fair play'.

And if a man, in fighting another, knocks him down, he must not hit or kick him while he is down; everybody would think him an awful beast if he did. Yet there is no law about it; you could not get him imprisoned for it. The truth is that 'fair play' is an old idea of Chivalry that has come down to us from the knights of old, and we must always keep up that idea.

Other nations are not all so good.

Often we hear of wounded men being again shot and killed in battle when they are lying helpless on the ground. In the South African War, when Major MacLaren,* now our Manager in the Boy Scouts, was lying helpless, with his thigh broken by a bullet and his horse shot on top of him, a Boer came up and finding him alive, fired two more shots into him. Luckily he recovered and is alive to-day. But that Boer had no Chivalry in him.

HONESTY.—Honesty is a form of Honour. An honourable man can be trusted with any amount of money or other valuables with the certainty that he will not steal it.

Cheating at any time is a sneaking, underhand thing to do.

When you feel inclined to cheat in order to win a game, or feel very distressed when a game in which you are playing is going against you, just say to yourself, 'After all, it is only a game. It won't kill me if I do lose. One can't win always, though I will stick to it in case of a chance coming.'

If you keep your head in this way, you will very often find that you win after all from not being over-anxious or despairing.

And don't forget, whenever you *do* lose a game, if you are a true scout, you will at once cheer the winning team or shake hands with and congratulate the fellow who has beaten you.

This rule will be carried out in *all* games and competitions among Boy Scouts.

LOYALTY.—Loyalty was, above all, one of the distinguishing points about the knights. They were always devotedly loyal to their King and to their country, and were always ready and eager to die in their defence. In the same way a follower of the Knights should be loyal not only to the King but also to everyone who is above him, whether his officers or employers, and he should stick to them through thick and thin as part of his duty.

He should also be equally loyal to his own friends and should support them in evil times as well as in good times.

Loyalty to duty was shown by the Roman soldier of old who stuck to his post when the city of Pompeii was overwhelmed with ashes and lava from the volcano Vesuvius. His remains are still there, with his hand covering his mouth and nose to prevent the suffocation which in the end overcame him.

His example was followed at some manœuvres not long ago by a cadet of Reigate Grammar School who when posted as sentry was accidentally left on his post when the field day was over. But though night came on and it was very cold—in November last—the lad stuck to his post till he was found in the middle of the night, half-perished with cold, but alive and alert.

OBEDIENCE AND DISCIPLINE

DISCIPLINE and obedience are as important as bravery for scouts and for soldiers.

The *Birkenhead** was a transport-ship carrying troops. She had on board 630 soldiers with their families and 130 seamen. Near the Cape of Good Hope one night, she ran on to some rocks, and began to break up. The soldiers were at once paraded on deck. Some were told off to get out the boats, and to put the women and children into them, and others were told off to get the horses up out of the hold, and to lower them overboard into the sea in order that they might have a chance of swimming ashore. When this had all been done it was found that there were not enough boats to take the men, and so the men were ordered to remain in their ranks. Then the ship broke in half and began to go down. The Captain shouted to the men to jump over and save themselves, but the Colonel, Colonel Seaton, said 'No, keep your ranks.' For he saw that if they swam to the boats and tried to get in they would probably sink them too. So the men kept their ranks and as the ship rolled over and sank they gave a cheer and went down with her. Out of the whole 760 on board, only 192 were saved, but even those would probably have been lost had it not been for the discipline and self-sacrifice of the others.

Last year a British Training Ship, the *Fort Jackson*, full of boy-sailors was run into by a steamer, but just as on the *Birkenhead* there was no panic or crying out. The boys fell in quickly on parade, put on their lifebelts, and faced the danger calmly and well. And not a life was lost.

DISCIPLINE.—Gibraltar* is a great big fortified rock which belongs to England, down on the South Coast of Spain. One hundred and twenty years ago it was besieged by the Spanish and French armies together.

The Spanish Army attacked Gibraltar on the land side, while the French attacked it by sea, but though they fought hard and with greatest endurance for over three years, the British troops defending the place were a match for them and held out successfully until they were relieved by the Fleet from home.

General Elliot, who had been a Cavalry officer in the 15th Hussars, commanded the troops at Gibraltar, and it was largely owing to his strict discipline that the Garrison succeeded in holding out. Every man had learnt to obey orders without any hesitation or question.

One day a man disobeyed an order, so General Elliot had him up before him and explained that for a man to be insubordinate at such a time showed that he could not be in his right senses; he must be mad. So he ordered that his head should be shaved and that he should be blistered, bled, and put into a strait-waistcoat and should be put in the cells, with bread and water, as a lunatic, and should also be prayed for in church!

HUMILITY.—Humility or being humble was one of the things which was practised by the knights, that is to say that, although they were generally superior to other people in fighting or campaigning, they never allowed themselves to swagger about it. So Don't Swagger.

And don't imagine that you have got rights in this world except those that you earn for yourself. You've got the right to be believed if you earn it by always telling the truth, and you've got the right to go to prison if you earn it by thieving; but there are lots of men who go about howling about their rights who have never done anything to earn any rights. Do your duty first and you will get your rights afterwards.

FORTITUDE.—Then the knights were men who never said 'Die' till they were dead; they were always ready to stick it out till the last extremity, but it is a very common fault with men to give in to trouble or fear long before there is any necessity. They often give up working because they don't get success all at once, and probably if they stuck to it a little longer, success would come. A man must expect hard work and want of success at first.

COURAGE

VERY few men are born brave, but any man can make himself brave if he tries—and especially if he begins trying when he is a boy.

The brave man dashes into danger without any hesitation, when a less brave man is inclined to hang back. It is very like bathing. A lot of boys will come to a river to bathe, and will cower shivering on the bank, wondering how deep the water is, and whether it is very cold—but the brave one will run through them and take his header into the water,* and will be swimming about happily a few seconds later.

The thing is, when there is danger before you, don't stop and look at it—the more you look at it the less you will like it—but take the plunge, go boldly in at it, and it won't be half so bad as it looked, when you are once in it.

In the late war between Japan and Russia some Japanese pioneers had been ordered to blow up the gate of a Russian fort so that the attackers could get in. After nearly all of them had been shot down, a few of them managed to get to the gate with their charges of powder. These had to be 'tamped' or jammed tight against the door somehow, and then fired. The Japs 'tamped' them by pushing them against the door with their chests; they then lit their matches, fired the charge, and blew up the gates, but blew up themselves in doing so. But their plucky self-sacrifice enabled their comrades to get in and win the place for the Emperor.

GOOD TEMPER AND CHEERINESS

THE knights laid great stress on being never out of temper. They thought it bad form to lose their temper, and to show anger. Captain John Smith, of whom I spoke just now, was himself a type of a cheerful man. In fact, towards the end of his life two boys (and he was very fond of boys) to whom he told his adventures, wrote them down in a book, but they said that they found great difficulty in hearing all that he said, because he roared with laughter so over his own descriptions of his troubles. But it is very certain, that had he not been a cheery man, he never could have got through half the dangers with which he was faced at different times in his career.

Over and over again he was made prisoner by his enemies—sometimes savage enemies—but he managed always to captivate them with his pleasant manner and become friends with them, so that often they let him go, or did not trouble to catch him when he made his escape.

If you do your work cheerfully, your work becomes much more of a pleasure to you, and also if you are cheerful it makes other people cheerful as well, which is part of your duty as a scout. Mr J. M. Barrie* writes: 'Those who bring sunshine to the lives of others, cannot keep happiness from themselves,' which means, if you make other people happy, you make yourself happy.

If you are in the habit of taking things cheerfully, you will very seldom find yourself in serious trouble, because if a difficulty or annoyance or danger seems very great, you will, if you are wise, force yourself to laugh at it, although I will allow it is very difficult to do so at first. Still, the moment you do laugh, most of the difficulty seems to disappear at once, and you can tackle it quite easily.

Good temper can be attained by a boy who wants to have it, and it will help him in every game under the sun, and more especially in difficulty and danger, and will often keep him in a situation where a short-tempered fellow gets turned out, or leaves in a huff.

Bad language and swearing are generally used, like smoking, by boys who want to try and show off how manly they are, but it only makes them look like fools. Generally, a man who swears is a man easily upset, and loses his head in a difficult situation, and he is not, therefore, to be depended upon. You want to be quite undisturbed under the greatest difficulties; and so when you find yourself particularly anxious or excited, or angry, don't swear, force yourself to smile, and it will set you right in a moment.

Captain John Smith, who neither smoked nor swore, had a way of dealing with swearers, which is also adopted by our scouts. He says in his diary that when his men were cutting down trees, the axes blistered their tender fingers, so that at about every third blow, a loud oath would drown the echo of the axe. To remedy this he devised a plan of having every man's oath noted down, and at night, for every oath, he had a can of water poured down the swearer's sleeve, 'with which an offender was so washed, that a man would scarce hear an oath in a week'.

BOOKS TO READ

'Courage', by Charles Wagner. (Published by T. Fisher Unwin, London.)

'Golden Deeds'. (Macmillan.)

'Parents and Children'. Miss Charlotte Mason.

'Duty', by Samuel Smiles, 2s. (Murray.) (Published by Kegan Paul.)

PRACTICE IN SELF-DISCIPLINE

PRACTICE unselfishness by a picnic to which all contribute what they are able to, according to their means. No remarks to be allowed on the amounts given.

GAMES

CALL for volunteers for some dangerous enterprise, such as 'Dispatch Running', or some other game made dangerous by the condition that if the scout selected to do the dangerous job fails he will lose his life; that is, will forfeit his scout's badge permanently. If he succeeds he may get up to 15 marks towards a badge of merit.

Any games such as football, basketball, etc., where rules are strictly enforced, are good for teaching discipline and unselfishness.

Ju-jitsu has many excellent points, too, in that direction.

'Bowmanship'—Crossbow shooting. Scouts should, if possible, make their own crossbows.

'Longbowmanship' as by the archers of the Middle Ages. Scouts to make their own bows and arrows if possible. Read Aylward's doings in 'The White Company'.

'Quarter Staff Play' with scouts' staves, as played by the yeomen and apprentices in old days.

CAMP FIRE YARN.—No. 22

SELF-IMPROVEMENT

Religion—Thrift—How to get on.

TO INSTRUCTORS

This camp fire yarn opens to instructors a wide field for the most important work of all in this scheme of Boy Scouts, and gives you an opportunity for doing really valuable work for the nation.

The prevailing want of religion should be remedied by a practical working religion rather than a too spiritual one at first.

SELF-IMPROVEMENT.—*A great amount of poverty and unemployedness results from boys being allowed to run riot outside the school walls as loafers, or from being used early in life as small wage-earners, such as errand boys, etc., and then finding themselves at the commencement of manhood without any knowledge of a trade to go on with, and unable to turn their hand to any work out of their one immediate line. They are helpless and unemployable. It is here that as instructor you can do invaluable work for the boy, by getting each in turn to talk privately over his future, and to map out a line for himself, and to start preparing himself for it. Encourage him to take up 'hobbies' or handicrafts.*

The suggestions offered here are, owing to the want of space, very limited in number, but your own experience or imagination will probably provide many more.

DUTY TO GOD

AN old British chieftain, some thirteen hundred years ago, said:

Our life has always seemed to me like the flight of a sparrow through the great hall, when one is sitting at meals with the log-fire blazing on the hearth, and all is storm and darkness outside. He comes in, no one knows from where, and hovers for a short time in the warmth and light, and then flies forth again into the darkness. And so it is with the life of a man; he comes no one knows from where; he is here in the world for a short time till he flies forth again, no one knows whither. But now you show us that if we do our duty during our life we shall not fly out into darkness again when life is ended, since Christ has opened a door for us to enter a brighter room, a Heaven where we can go and dwell in peace for ever.*

This old chief was speaking for all the chiefs of northern England when King Edwin had introduced to them a knowledge of the Christian religion; and they adopted it then and there as one more comforting to them than their old Pagan worship of heathen gods; and ever since those days the Christian religion has been the one to rule our country.

Religion is a very simple thing:

1st. To believe in God.
2nd. To do good to other people.

The old knights, who were the scouts of the nation, were very religious. They were always careful to attend church or chapel, especially before going into battle or undertaking any serious difficulty. They considered it was the right thing always to Be Prepared for death. In the great church of Malta you can see to-day where the old knights used to pray, and they all stood up and drew their swords during the reading of the Creed, as a sign that they were prepared to defend the gospel with their swords and lives. Besides worshipping God in church, the knights always recognised His work in the things which He made, such as animals, plants, and scenery. And so it is with peace scouts to-day that wherever they go they love the woodlands, the mountains, and the prairies, and they like to watch and know about the animals that inhabit them and the wonders of the flowers and plants. No man is much good unless he believes in God and obeys His laws. So every scout should have a religion.

There are many kinds of religion such as Roman Catholics, Protestants, Jews, Mohammedans, and so on, but the main point about them is that they all worship God, although in different ways. They are like an army which serves one king, though it is divided into different branches, such as cavalry, artillery, and infantry, and these wear different uniforms. So, when you meet a boy of a different religion from your own, you should not be hostile to him, but recognise that he is like a soldier in your own army, though in a different uniform, and still serving the same king as you.

In doing your duty to God, always be grateful to Him. Whenever you enjoy a pleasure or a good game, or succeed in doing a good thing, thank Him for it, if only with a word or two, just as you say grace after a meal. And it is a good thing to bless other people. For instance, if you see a train starting off, just pray for God's blessing on all that are in the train and so on.

In doing your duty towards man, be helpful and generous and also always be grateful for any kindness done to you, and be careful to show that you are grateful.

Remember that a present given to you is not yours until you have thanked for it. While you are the sparrow flying through the Hall, that is to say, while you are living your life on this earth, try and do something good which may remain after you. One writer says:*

> I often think that when the sun goes down the world is hidden by a big blanket from the light of Heaven, but the stars are little holes pierced in that blanket by those who have done good deeds in this world. The stars are not all the same size; some are big, some little, and some men have done great deeds and others have done small deeds, but they have made their hole in the blanket by doing good before they went to Heaven.

Try and make your hole in the blanket by good work while you are on the earth.

It is something to *be* good, but it is far better to *do* good.

THRIFT

It is a funny thing that out of you boys who now read these words, some of you are certain to become rich men, and some of you may die in poverty and misery. And it just depends on your own selves which you are going to do.

And you can very soon tell which your future is going to be.

The fellow who begins making money as a boy will go on making it as a man. You may find it difficult to do at first, but it will come easier later on; but if you begin and if you go on, remember, you are pretty certain to succeed in the end—especially if you get your money by hard work.

If you only try to make it by easy means—that is by betting, say, on a football match or a horse-race—you are bound to lose after a time. Nobody who makes bets ever wins in the end; it is the bookmaker, the man who receives the bets, that scores over it. Yet there are thousands of fools who go on putting their money on because they won a bit once or hope to win some day.

Any number of poor boys have become rich men—but in nearly every case it was because they meant to do so from the first; they worked for it, and put every penny they could make into the bank to begin with.

So each one of you has the chance if you like to take it. The great owner of millions of pounds, J. Astor,* began his career as a poor boy-pedlar with seven German flutes as his stock-in-trade. He sold them for more than he gave and went on increasing his business.

The knights of old were ordered by their rules to be thrifty, that is to save money as much as possible, not to expend large sums on their own enjoyment, but to save it in order that they might keep themselves and not be a burden to others, and also in order that they might have more to give away in charity; and if they had no money of their own, they were not allowed to beg for it, they must work and make it in one way or another. Thus money-making goes with manliness, hard work, and sobriety.

Boys are not too young to work for money.

Mr Thomas Holmes, the police-court missionary, tells us how hundreds of poor boys in London are working pluckily and well at making their living, even while doing their school work. They get up early, at half-past four in the morning, and go round with milk or bakers' barrows till about eight, and after that off to school; back in the afternoon to the shop to clean the pails and cans. They save up their money every day; those who have mothers, hand it over to them; those who have not, store it up or bank it. They are regular men before they are twelve years of age, and good examples to other boys wherever they may be.

HOW TO MAKE MONEY

THERE are many ways by which a scout, or a patrol working together, can make money, such as:

CARPENTERING.—Making arm-chairs, recovering old furniture, etc. is a very paying trade. Fretwork and carving, picture-frames, birdcages, cabinets, carved pipe-bowls, can be sold through a shop.

HOW TO MAKE BUTTONS OUT OF BOOTLACES

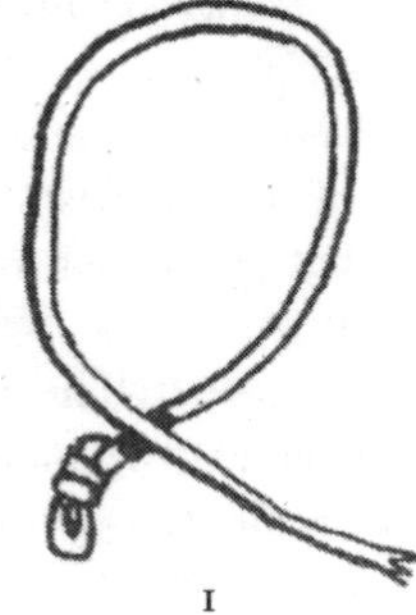

1

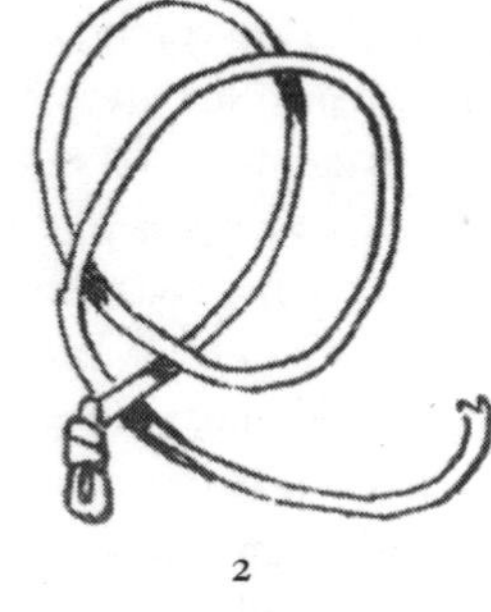

2

3

4
Continue till you have the whole knot doubled or trebled

5
The loop for attaching the button is moved from its original position to hang from the centre of the knot

6
Pull all tight, cut off loose end, and the button is complete

Get permission to cut certain sticks in hedges or woods and trim them into walking-sticks, after hanging them with weights attached to straighten and dry them. Breeding canaries, chickens, rabbits, or dogs pays well. Beekeeping brings in from £1 to £2 a year per hive, after you have paid for hive and queen bee or swarm.

You can make novel sets of buttons out of bootlaces. Collect old packing cases and boxes and chop them into bundles of firewood. Make nets, besoms, etc., for gardeners. Keeping goats and selling their milk will pay in some places. Basket making, pottery, book-binding, etc., all bring money. Or a patrol working together can form themselves into a corps of messenger-boys in a country town, or they can get an allotment garden and work it for selling vegetables and flowers, or they can make themselves into a minstrel troupe, or perform scouting displays or pageants, etc., like those shown in this book, and take money at the doors.

These are only a few suggestions; there are loads of other ways of making money which you can think out for yourselves, according to the place you are in.

But in order to get money you must expect to work. The actor, Ted Payne, used to say in one of his plays, 'I don't know what is wrong with me, I eat well, I drink well, and I sleep well, but somehow whenever anybody mentions the word "Work" to me I get a cold shudder all over me.' That is what happens to a great many men in England, I am afraid. There are a good many other chicken-hearted fellows, who, when any work faces them, 'get a cold shudder all over them'; or when trouble comes, they go and take to drink, instead of facing it and working it off.

Start a money-box, put any money you can make into that, and when you have got a fair amount in it, hand it over to a bank, and start an account for yourself. As a scout, you have to have a certain amount in the savings bank before you can become entitled to wear a badge. Save your pence and you'll get pounds.

(Scouts' Money Boxes can be obtained from Manager Boy Scouts, Henrietta Street, London, W.C.)

HOW TO GET ON

A FEW years ago the American Government was at war with rebels in the island of Cuba.* *(Point out on map.)*

America, as you know, is ruled by a President and not by a King.

The late President, McKinley,* wanted to send a letter to Garcia, the chief of the rebels in Cuba, but did not know how to get it taken to him, as the rebels were a savage lot inhabiting a wild and difficult country.

When he was talking it over with his advisers, someone said: 'There's a young fellow called Rowan who seems to be able to get anything done that you ask him. Why not try him?'

So Rowan was sent for, and when he came in the President explained why he had sent for him, and, putting the letter in his hand, said: 'Now, I want that letter sent to Garcia.'

The lad simply smiled and said, 'I see,' and walked out of the room without saying another word.

Some weeks passed and Rowan appeared again at the President's door and said, 'I gave your letter to Garcia, sir,' and walked out again. Of course, Mr McKinley had him back and made him explain how he had done it.

It turned out that he had got a boat and sailed away in her for some days; had landed on the coast of Cuba, and disappeared into the jungle; in three weeks' time he reappeared on the other side of the island having gone through the enemy and found Garcia, and given him the letter.

He was a true scout, and that is the way a scout should carry out an order when he gets it. No matter how difficult it may seem he should tackle it, with a smile; the more difficult it is the more interesting it will be to carry out.

Most fellows would have asked a lot of questions—first as to how they were to set about it, how they could get to the place, where were they to get food from, and so on; but not so Rowan: he merely learnt what duty was wanted of him, and *he* did the rest without a word; any fellow who acts like that is certain to get on.

We have a lot of good scouts already in England among the District Messenger Boys in London. These lads, from having difficult jobs frequently given them and being *expected* to carry them out successfully, take them on with the greatest confidence in themselves; and, without asking a lot of silly questions, they start off in a businesslike way, and do them.

That is the way to deal with any difficulty in life. If you get a job or a trouble that seems to you to be too big for you, don't shirk it: smile, think out a way by which you might get successfully through with it, and then go at it.

Remember that 'a difficulty is no longer a difficulty when once you laugh at it—and tackle it'.

Don't be afraid of making a mistake. Napoleon said 'Nobody ever made anything who never made a mistake.'

MEMORY.—Then practise remembering things. A fellow who has a good memory will get on because so many other people have bad memories from not practising them.

At the Olympic Theatre, Liverpool, the forgetfulness on the part of the people in the audience gradually made it necessary for the manager to keep a special room and ledgers for all lost articles left behind in the theatre after each performance. But the happy idea struck him of putting a notice on the curtain by means of a bioscope lantern a few minutes before the end of the performance saying, 'Please look under your seat before leaving.'

This has made a great difference in the number of things left behind.

People used to leave every kind of thing, even medicine bottles, and false teeth; and once a cheque for £50 was left.

A great coral island is build up of tiny sea insects blocking themselves together; so also great knowledge in a man is built up by his noticing all sorts of little details and blocking them together in his mind by *remembering* them.

LUCK.—If you want to catch a tramcar when it is not at a stopping station you don't sit down and let it run past you and then say, 'How unlucky I am'; you run and jump on. It is just the same with what some people call 'luck'; they complain that luck never comes to them. Well, luck is really the chance of getting something good or of doing something great; the thing is to look out for every chance and seize it—run at it and jump on—don't sit down and wait for it to pass you. Opportunity is a tramcar which has very few stopping places.

CHOOSE A CAREER.—'Be Prepared' for what is going to happen to you in the future. If you are in a situation where you are earning money as a boy what are you going to do when you finish that job? You ought to be learning some proper trade to take up; and save your pay in the meantime, to keep you going till you get employment in your new trade.

And try to learn something of a second trade in case the first one fails you at any time, as so very often happens.

If you want to serve your King and Country there is the Royal Navy open to you, a fine service with its grand traditions, its splendid ships, guns, and seamen. It takes you across the seas to our great Colonies and to foreign lands, from the frozen Arctic to the tropical coasts of Africa.

Or there is the Army, with cavalry, infantry, artillery, engineers, and other branches, in which you can wear the uniform of your country and do good work in every climate under the sun.

In either service a good and honourable career is open to you—for you have everything found for you, food, housing, clothing, and hospital, with good pay and the certainty of promotion and pension for the rest of your life if you make up your mind to serve loyally, steadily, and well. In such a career you have plenty of adventure and you are among good comrades and friends. And if you start early to save your pay, and not to throw it away as too many do, you can easily put by £25 a year in the bank.

[*The instructor should similarly give advice on other trades and professions, especially those in the neighbourhood.*]

PRACTICES IN SELF-IMPROVEMENT

MARKET GARDENING.—The patrol or troop can work an allotment or other garden and sell the produce for their fund.

FOR A TROOP OR A NUMBER OF TROOPS.—Offer a good prize for the best article made by a scout with materials which have not cost more than 2s. Entrance fee to competition 3d.

Have an exhibition of these, coupled with displays and scenes, etc., by the scouts, and take money at the doors.

At the end sell the articles by auction: the articles which fetch the highest prices win the prizes.

INSTRUCTION CLASSES in Esperanto, Bookkeeping, Mechanics, Electricity, and, especially, Shorthand.

ARMY CLASS.—At the Home Office School, Stoke Farm, boys are put through the same examination as in the Army Schools for promotion certificates. They thus know their classification should they then go into the Army.

MEMORIZING.—Read something to the boys, a line or two at a time, to see who can repeat it best. To concentrate the mind and develop memory.

Mr G. L. Boundy of Exeter has had great success in developing intelligence amongst his lads by taking parties of them round to see the different factories in Exeter. They all take notes and rough drawings as they go along and reproduce them the following meeting, and report on what they have seen.

INFORMATION ON PROFESSIONS, ETC.

CONDITIONS of service in the Royal Navy, Army, Post, Telegraph, or Police can be obtained at the nearest Post Office or Police Station.

Conditions of service in the Mercantile Marine or Training for it can be obtained from the Navy League: Lancashire Sea Training Home for boys from 13½ to 15½, 28 Chapel Street, Liverpool.

Post Office Savings Bank, Penny Banks and Benefit Societies exist in all leading towns and will give full information. As an example:

National Deposit Friendly Society, 37 Queen Square, Southampton Row, London. Payments for children from 6d, a month, adults 2s. 3d. and entitles them to sick pay, pension, funeral expenses, in addition to their own cash capital.

So soon as it becomes possible organise an employment agency for getting your boys in touch with employers, etc.

BOOKS TO READ

'Thrift', by Samuel Smiles. 2s. (John Murray.)

'One Hundred and One Ways of Making Money'. (Sell & Odling, London.)

'Do It Now', by Peter Keary. 1s. (C. A. Pearson Ltd.)

'Rabbits for Profit', by J. Brod. 1s.

'The Secrets of Success', by Peter Keary. 1s. (C. A. Pearson Ltd.)

'Bees for Pleasure and Profit', by Swanson. 1s.

'Esperanto for the Million'. 1d. (Stead, 39 Whitefriars Street, London, E.C.)

'Cassell's Handbooks'. 1s. 6d. each. Joinery, Pottery, Painters' Work, etc.

'Work Handbooks' series. 1s. each. On Harness-making, Tinplate, Pumps, Bookbinding, Signwriting, Beehives, etc.

'How to Make Baskets', by Miss White. 1s.

'Rafia Work', by M. Swannell. 2s. (Geo. Philip & Son, Fleet Street.) ['Rafia' or 'Bast' is the inner bark of a tree and is used for making baskets, mats, hats, etc.]

'Self Help', by S. Smiles.* 2s. (John Murray.)

See also 'Papers on Trades for Boys' in Boys Brigade Gazette.

Sobriety—Practise Observation—Fortitude—Notes to Instructors*

SOBRIETY

REMEMBER that drink never yet cured a single trouble; it only makes troubles grow worse and worse the more you go on with it. It makes a man forget for a few hours what exactly his trouble is, but it also makes him forget everything else. If he has wife and children it makes him forget that his duty is to work and help them out of the difficulties instead of making himself all the more unfit to work.

A man who drinks is generally a coward—and one used to see it very much among soldiers. Nowadays they are a better class and do not drink.

Some men drink because they like the feeling of getting half stupid, but they are fools, because once they take to drink no employer will trust them, and they soon become unemployed and easily get ill, and finally come to a miserable end. There is nothing manly about getting drunk. Once a man gives way to drink it ruins his health, his career, and his happiness, as well as that of his family. There is only one cure for this disease, and that is—never to get it.

PRACTISE OBSERVATION

A WELL-KNOWN detective, Mr Justin Chevasse, describes how with a little practice in observation you can tell pretty accurately a man's character from his dress.

He tells the story* of a Duke who used to dress very shabbily. One day this nobleman was travelling by train with a friend of his, Lord A. A commercial traveller who was in the carriage got into conversation with them. At one station the Duke got out, and after he was gone the commercial traveller asked 'Who is the gentleman who has just got out?' 'Oh,' said Lord A. 'that is the Duke of X.' The commercial traveller was quite taken aback and said, 'Fancy that! Fancy him talking so affably to you and me. I thought all the time that he must be a gardener.'

I expect that that commercial traveller had not been brought up as a scout and did not look at people's boots: if he had he would probably have seen that neither the Duke's nor Lord A's were those of a gardener.

The boots are very generally the best test of all the details of clothing. I was with a lady the other day in the country, and a young lady was walking just in front of us. 'I wonder who she is,' said my friend. 'Well,' I said, 'I should be inclined to say I wonder whose maid she is.' The girl was very well dressed but when I saw her boots I guessed that the dress had belonged to someone else, had been given to her and refitted by herself—but that as regards boots she felt more comfortable in her own. She went up to the house at which we were staying—to the servants' entrance—and we found that she was the maid of one of the ladies staying there.

Dr Gross* relates the story of a learned old gentleman who was found dead in his bedroom with a wound in his forehead and another in his left temple.

Very often after a murder the murderer, with his hands bloody from the deed and running away, may catch hold of the door, or a jug of water to wash his hands.

In the present case a newspaper lying on the table had the marks of three blood-stained fingers on it.

The son of the murdered man was suspected and was arrested by the police.

But careful examination of the room and the prints of the finger-marks showed that the old gentleman had been taken ill in the night—had got out of bed to get some medicine, but getting near the table a new spasm seized him and he fell, striking his head violently against the corner of the table and made the wound on his temple which just fitted the corner. In trying to get up he had caught hold of the table and the newspaper on it and had made the bloody finger-marks on the newspaper in doing so. Then he had fallen again, cutting his head a second time on the foot of the bed.

The finger-marks were compared with the dead man's fingers, and were found to be exactly the same. Well, you don't find two men in 64,000,000,000,000 with the same pattern on the skin of their fingers. So it was evident there had been no murder, and the dead man's son was released as innocent.

FORTITUDE

In Japan, whenever a child is born, the parents hang up outside the house either a doll or a fish, according as the child is a girl or boy. It is a sign to the neighbours: the doll means it is a girl, who will some day have children to nurse; the fish means it is a boy, who, as he grows into manhood, will, like a fish, have to make his way against a stream of difficulties and dangers. A man who cannot face hard work or trouble is not worth calling a man.

Some of you may have heard the story of the two frogs. If you have not, here it is:

Two frogs were out for a walk one day and they came to a big jug of cream. In looking into it they both fell in.

One said: 'This is a new kind of water to me. How can a fellow swim in stuff like this? It is no use trying.' So he sank to the bottom and was drowned through having no pluck.

But the other was a more manly frog, and he struggled to swim, using his arms and legs as hard as he could to keep himself afloat; and whenever he felt he was sinking he struggled harder than ever, and never gave up hope.

Perseverance: frogs in the milk

At last, just as he was getting so tired that he thought he *must* give it up, a curious thing happened. By his hard work with his arms and legs he had churned up the cream so much that he suddenly found himself standing all safe on a pat of butter!

So when things look bad just smile and sing to yourself, as the thrush sings: 'Stick to it, stick to it, stick to it,' and you will come through all right.

DUTY BEFORE ALL.—You have all heard of 'Lynch-Law,' by which is meant stern justice by hanging an evil-doer.

The name came from Galway in Ireland where a memorial still commemorates the act of a chief magistrate of that city named Lynch who in the year 1493 had his own son Walter Lynch executed for killing a young Spaniard.

The murderer had been properly tried and convicted. His mother begged the citizens to rescue her son when he was brought out from the jail to suffer punishment, but the father foreseeing this had the sentence carried out in the prison, and young Lynch was hanged from the prison window.

The elder Lynch's sense of duty must have been very strong indeed to enable him to make his feelings as a father give way to his conscience as a magistrate.

General Gordon* sacrificed his life to his sense of duty. When he was besieged at Khartum he could have got away himself had he liked, but he considered it his duty to remain with the Egyptians whom he had brought there although he had no admiration for them. So he stuck to them and when at last the place was captured by the enemy he was killed.

NOTES TO INSTRUCTORS

RELIGION

CHARLES STELZLE, in his 'Boys of the Streets and How to Win Them', says:

> Sometimes we are so much concerned about there being enough religion in our plans for the boy that we forget to leave enough boy in the plans. According to the notions of some, the ideal boys' club would consist of prayer meetings and Bible classes, with an occasional missionary talk as a treat, and perhaps magic lantern views of the Holy Land as a dizzy climax.*

Religion can and ought to be taught to the boy, but not in a milk-and-watery way, or in a mysterious and lugubrious manner; he is very ready to receive it if it is shown in its heroic side and as a natural every-day quality in every proper man, and it can be well introduced to boys through the study of Nature; and to those who believe scouting to be an unfit subject for Sunday instruction, surely the study of God's work is at least proper for that day. There is no need for this instruction to be dismal, that is, 'all tears and texts'. Arthur Benson, writing in the *Cornhill Magazine*, says there are four Christian virtues, not three. They are—Faith, Hope, Charity—and Humour. So also in the morning prayer of Robert Louis Stevenson:

> The day returns and brings us the petty round of irritating concerns and duties. Help us to play the man—help us to perform them with laughter and kind faces. Let cheerfulness abound with industry. Give us to go blithely on our business all this day. Bring us to our resting beds weary and content and undishonoured, and grant us in the end the gift of sleep.*

THRIFT

A VERY large proportion of the distress and unemployedness in the country is due to want of thrift on the part of the people themselves; and social reformers, before seeking for new remedies, would do well to set this part of the problem right in the first place; they would then probably find very little more left for them to do. Mr John Burns,* in a recent speech, pointed out that there is plenty of money in the country to put everyone on a fair footing, if only it were made proper use of by the working man. In some places, it is true, there is thrift—workmen save their pay and buy their own houses, and become prosperous, contented citizens in happy homes. It is estimated that £500,000,000 of working-men's money is invested in savings banks and friendly societies. But there is a reverse to the medal. This great balance represents savings of many years, whereas it could be doubled in two or three years were men to give up drinking and smoking.

Where we deposit £4 per head per annum in savings banks, other countries deposit far more, although earning lower wages, and in Denmark such deposits amount, on an average, to £19 per head.

£166,000,000 were spent last year on drink, and £25,000,000 on tobacco. This alone would be enough, if divided amongst our thirty-five millions of poor, to give £22 a year to each family; and we know that this is only part of the extravagance of the nation. From £8,000 to £10,000 a week is estimated to go into the pockets of the bookmakers at Liverpool and its surrounding towns at football. Holiday, or 'Going Off' clubs, are common in Lancashire, where workers save up money to spend on their holidays. In Blackburn alone £117,000 was thus expended last year. At Oldham £25,000 was saved to be expended in festivities at the 'Wakes'.

The wastefulness in Great Britain is almost inconceivable, and ought to be made criminal. Men draw big wages of £3 and £4 on Saturday nights, but have nothing to show for it by Monday night. If they had thrift a large majority of our working-men and their families might be in prosperous circumstances to-day, but they have never been taught what thrift may be, and they naturally do as their neighbours do. If the rising generation could be started in the practice of economy, it would make a vast difference to the character and prosperity of the nation in the future.

In Manchester the school children are encouraged to save up their money by means of money-boxes, and 44,000 of them now have deposits in the savings banks. It has been found a very successful way of encouraging thrift. For this reason we have instituted money-boxes for Boy Scouts.

Politeness

An instance of politeness in war occurred at the Battle of Fontenoy,* when we were fighting against the French.

The Coldstream Guards coming up over a hill suddenly found themselves close up to the French Guards. Both parties were surprised, and neither fired a shot for a minute or two.

In those days when gallant men quarrelled, they used to settle their differences by fighting duels with pistols. At a duel both combatants were supposed to fire at the same moment when the word was given, but it often happened that one man, in order to show how brave he was, would tell his adversary to fire first. And so in this case. When both parties were about to fire, the officer commanding the British Guards, to show his politeness and fearlessness, bowed to the French commander, and said, 'You fire first, sir.'

When the French Guards levelled their rifles to fire, one of the soldiers of the Coldstreams exclaimed, 'For what we are going to receive may the Lord make us truly thankful.' In the volley that followed, a great number of our men fell, but the survivors returned an equally deadly volley, and immediately charged in with the bayonet, and drove the French off the field.

PART V

CONTENTS: CHAPTER VIII

SAVING LIFE;

or, How to Deal with Accidents

CONTENTS: CHAPTER IX

(Commences on page 273)

PATRIOTISM;

or, Our Duties as Citizens

CHAPTER VIII

SAVING LIFE;

or,

How to Deal with Accidents

CAMP FIRE YARN.—No. 23

BE PREPARED FOR ACCIDENTS

The Knights Hospitallers of St John—Boy Heroes and Girl Heroines—Life-Saving Medals.

HINTS TO INSTRUCTORS

The subjects in this chapter should not only be explained to the scouts, but should also, wherever possible, be demonstrated practically, and should be practised by each boy himself in turn.

Theoretical knowledge in these points is nothing without practice.

THE KNIGHTS OF ST JOHN

THE knights of old days were called Knights Hospitallers, because they had hospitals for the treatment of the sick poor and those injured in accidents or in war. They used to save up their money to keep these hospitals going, and they used to act as nurses and doctors themselves. The Knights of St John of Jerusalem especially devoted themselves to this work 800 years ago, and the St John's Ambulance Corps is to-day a branch which represents those knights. Their badge is an eight-pointed white cross on a black ground, and when worn as an Order it has a black ribbon.

Explorers and hunters and other scouts in out-of-the-way parts of the world have to know what to do in the case of accident or sickness, either to themselves or their followers, as they are often hundreds of miles away from any doctors. For these reasons boy scouts should, of course, learn all they can about looking after sick people and dealing with accidents.

My brother was once camping with a friend away in the bush in

Australia. His friend was drawing a cork, holding the bottle between his knees to get a better purchase. The bottle burst, and the jagged edge of it ran deeply into his thigh, cutting an artery. My brother quickly got a stone and wrapped it in a handkerchief to act as a pad, and he then tied the handkerchief round the limb above the wound, so that the stone pressed on the artery. He then got a stick, and, passing it through the loop of the handkerchief, twisted it round till the bandage was drawn so tight that it stopped the flow of blood. Had he not known what to do, the man would have bled to death in a few minutes. As it was, he saved his life by knowing what to do, and doing it at once.

[*Demonstrate how to bind up an artery, and also the course taken by the arteries, viz., practically down the inside seam of sleeves and trousers.*]

Accidents are continually happening, and Boy Scouts will continually have a chance of giving assistance at first aid. In London alone during the past year 212 people were killed and 14,000 were injured in street accidents.

We all think a great deal of any man who at the risk of his own life saves someone else's.

He is a hero.

Boys especially think him so, because he seems to them to be a being altogether different from themselves. But he isn't; every boy has just as much a chance of being a life-saving hero if he chooses to prepare himself for it.

It is pretty certain that nearly every one of you scouts will some day or another be present at an accident where, if you know what to do, and do it promptly, you may win for yourself the life-long satisfaction of having rescued or helped a fellow-creature.

Remember your motto, 'BE PREPARED'. Be prepared for accidents by learning beforehand what you ought to do in the different kinds that are likely to occur.

Be prepared to do that thing the moment the accident does occur.

I will explain to you what ought to be done in the different kinds of accidents, and you must practise them as far as possible.

But the great thing for you scouts to bear in mind is that wherever you are, and whatever you are doing, you should think to yourself, 'What accident is likely to occur here?' and, 'What is my duty if it occurs?'

You are then prepared to act.

And when an accident does occur, remember always that as a scout it is your business to be the first man to go to the rescue; don't let an outsider be beforehand with you.

Suppose, for instance, that you are standing on a crowded platform at a station, waiting for the train.

You think to yourself, 'Now, supposing someone fell off this platform on to the rails just as the train is coming in, what shall I do? I must jump down and jerk him off the track on to the far side into the six-foot way—there would be no time to get him up on to the platform again. Or if the train were very close the only way would be to lie flat and make him lie flat too between the rails, and let the train go over us both.'

Then, if this accident happened, you would at once jump down and carry out your idea, while everybody else would be running about screaming and excited and doing nothing, not knowing what to do.

Such a case actually happened last year. A lady fell off the platform at Finsbury Park Station just as the train was coming in; a man named Albert Hardwick jumped down and lay flat, and held her down, too, between the rails, while the train passed over both of them without touching them. The King gave him the Albert Medal for it.

When there is a panic among those around you, you get a momentary inclination to do as the others are doing. Perhaps it is to run away, perhaps it is to stand still and cry out 'Oh!' Well, you should check yourself when you have this feeling. Don't catch the panic, as you see others do; keep your head and think what is the right thing to do, and do it at once.

Then last year that disgraceful scene occurred on Hampstead Heath, where a woman drowned herself before a whole lot of people in a shallow pond, and took half-an-hour doing it, while not one of them had the pluck to go in and bring her out. One would not have thought it possible with Englishmen that a lot of men could only stand on the bank and chatter, but so it was—to their eternal disgrace.*

It was again a case of panic. The first man to arrive on the scene did not like going in, and merely called another. More came up, but finding that those already there did not go in, they got a sort of fear of something uncanny, and would not go in themselves, and so let the poor woman drown before their eyes.

Had one Boy Scout been there, there would I hope have been a very different tale to tell. It was just the opportunity for a Boy Scout to distinguish himself. He would have remembered his training.

Do your duty.

Help your fellow-creature, especially if it be a woman.

Don't mind if other people are funking.

Plunge in boldly and look to the object you are trying to attain, and don't bother about your own safety.

Boys have an idea that they are too young and too small to take any but an outside part in saving life. But this is a great mistake. In the Boys' Brigade last year nine boys got the Cross for saving life, eight of them for saving other people from drowning. All aged between 13 and 16.

Cyril Adion (13) and Newlyn Elliott (17) also saved lives from drowning last year, and a small boy only nine years old, David Scannell, was given a silver watch at St Pancras for saving a child's life at a fire.

In addition to this, a boy named Albert Abraham was recommended for the highest honour that any man can get for saving life, and that is the Albert Medal.

Three boys were climbing up some cliffs from the seashore, when one of them fell to the bottom and was very badly hurt. Another climbed up the rest of the cliff and ran away home, but told nobody for fear of getting into trouble. The third one, Albert Abraham, climbed down again to the assistance of the boy who had fallen, and he found him lying head downwards between two rocks, with his scalp nearly torn off and his leg broken.

Abraham dragged him up out of reach of the tide, for where he had fallen he was in danger of being drowned, and then replaced his scalp and bound it on, and also set his leg as well as he could, and bound it up in splints, having learned the 'First Aid' duties of the St John's Ambulance Society. Then he climbed up the cliff and gathered some ferns and made a bed for the injured boy.

He stayed with him all that day, and when night came on he still remained with him, nor did he desert him even when a great seal climbed on to the rocks close to him and appeared to be rather aggressive. He drove it off with stones.

Parties went out and eventually rescued both boys, but the injured one died soon after, in spite of the efforts that Albert Abraham had made to save him.

In talking of boys I may as well state that the same remark applies to women and girls, that they are not only capable of doing valuable work in saving life, but they have done so over and over again.

For the Albert Medal a small girl aged nine has been recommended. Kate Chapman endeavoured to rescue two small children from being run over by a runaway cart. She succeeded in doing so, but was herself run over and badly injured in the attempt.

Mrs Ann Racebottom was awarded the Albert Medal in 1881 for rescuing some school children when the roof of the schoolhouse had fallen in upon them and she got them out by crawling in under the falling ruins at the greatest risk to her own life.

Doris Kay, of Leytonstone, is only eight years old, but she was awarded the diploma for life saving by the Royal Humane Society last year.

LIFE-SAVING MEDALS

In war, as you know, the Victoria Cross is awarded to soldiers for performing acts of valour.

So, in peace, a decoration is given to anybody who distinguishes himself by bravery in saving life at the risk of his own.

The Albert Medal is the highest of these rewards.

The Royal Humane Society also give medals or certificates.

The Edward Medal is granted for gallantry in accidents which so frequently happen in mines.

In the Boys' Brigade medals are given for acts of daring and self-sacrifice in saving life or marked courage in the face of danger.

In the Boy Scouts we have a medal for gallantry, which is granted for similar acts.

But of all these the Albert Medal and the Edward Medal are the most valued, being given by the King himself, and only in very special cases.

So let every Boy Scout prepare himself to win one of these. Some day, most probably, an accident will happen before you to give you your chance. If you have learnt beforehand what to do, you can step forward at once and do the right thing; you may find yourself decorated with the medal. In any case, you will have what is far greater than a mere medal—you will have the satisfaction of having helped a fellow-creature at the risk of your own life.

PRACTICE FOR LIFE SAVING

Flinging the Squaler

The squaler is a piece of cane, 19 inches long, loaded at the butt with 1¾lb. of lead, and having attached to it at the other end a life-saving line of six-thread Italian hemp. The target is a crossbar and head, life-size, representing the head and arms of a drowning man, planted in the ground twenty yards away. Each competitor throws in turn from behind a line drawn on the ground; he may stand or run to make the throw. Whoever throws the furthest wins, provided that the line falls on some part of the dummy, so that it could be caught by the drowning man.

Or have heats to find out who is the worst thrower.

Practise throwing a life-belt in the same way.

Practise making two lines of bucket-men, for full and empty buckets. Each line to relieve the other frequently by exchanging duties.

Practise carrying, unrolling, and rolling up hose. Joining up lengths. Affixing to hydrants. Throwing on water, and directing its fall.

Practise use of ladders, poles, ropes, lowering people from window by ropes or bed-clothes. Jumping sheet and shoot-escape;* how to rig, hold, and use carpets or double blankets, but not flimsy ones or sheets.

CAMP FIRE YARN.—No. 24

ACCIDENTS AND HOW TO DEAL WITH THEM

Panic—Fire—Drowning—Runaway Horse—Mad Dog — Miscellaneous.

PANICS

Every year numbers of lives are lost by panics, which very often are due to the smallest causes, and which might be stopped if only one or two men would keep their heads. One evening, two years ago, on board a ferry-boat in New York, a man who had been catching some crabs thought it would be a good joke to let one of them loose on board the boat. This crab caught hold of the ship's cat and made it squeal, and it jumped into the middle of a crowd of schoolgirls, who at once scattered screaming. This started a panic among the hundreds of passengers on board; they rushed in every direction, and in a moment the railings broke and eight people fell overboard, and before anything could be done they were swept away by the tide and drowned.

In Germany, a girl who was bathing suddenly pretended to be drowning, just for fun. Three men sprang into the river to rescue her, but one began to sink, and another went to his help, and both were drowned. And only last September a tobacconist in a town in Russia, on opening his shop in the morning, saw a big black bomb lying on the counter. He rushed out into the street to get away from it, and a policeman seeing him running mistook him for a thief, and when he would not stop he fired at him. The bullet missed him, but hit another man who was a Jew; the remainder of the Jews* immediately collected and made a riot, and many lives were lost. After it was over, the tobacconist went back to his shop and found the bomb still on his counter, but it was not a bomb, it was only a black watermelon!

Only the other day occurred a case of panic among children in a theatre at Barnsley, when a crush and panic occurred from no cause at all except overcrowding, and eight children were crushed to death. More lives would certainly have been lost had not two men kept their heads and done the right thing. One man named Gray called to a number of the children in a cheery voice to come another way, while the man who was working a lantern-slide show threw a picture on the screen and so diverted the attention of the rest, and prevented them catching the panic. That is the great point in a panic. If only one or two men keep their heads and do the right thing on the spur of the moment, they can often calm hundreds of people and thus save many lives.

This is a great opportunity for a Boy Scout. Force yourself to keep calm and not to lose your head. Think what is the right thing to do and do it at once.

RESCUE FROM FIRE

INSTANCES of gallant rescues of people from burning houses are frequent. One sees them every day in the newspapers, and scouts should study each of these cases as they occur, and imagine to themselves what they would have done under the circumstances, and in this way you begin to learn how to deal with the different accidents. An instance occurred only the other day where a young sailor named George Obeney stationed at Chatham in H.M.S. *Andromeda* was walking along the Kingsland Road, when he suddenly saw a house on fire, and a woman on the second storey was screaming that she had some children there who could not get out. The sailor rushed from his friends and somehow scrambled up the face of the wall till he reached the window on the first storey and broke in that window so that he could obtain room to stand. The woman at the window above was then able to lower a child so that he could catch it, and he again passed it down to the ground. Child after child was thus handed down till he passed six of them to the ground, and finally two women, and then he, overcome by smoke himself, fell insensible, but was caught by the people below. His act was an example to you of how to do your duty AT ONCE without thinking of dangers or difficulties.

In January, 1906, at Enfield Hospital, the Children's Ward caught fire in the middle of the night, and a number of children would probably have been burnt before the firemen arrived on the spot had it not been that the matron, Miss Eardley, rushed over from her house in her nightdress and fixed up the fire-hose and played it on the flames while the two night nurses set to work and rescued twenty children out of the burning building.

The Boys' Life Brigade have taken up the instruction of boys in what to do in cases of fire.

DIRECTIONS

THESE are some of their directions:

If you discover a house on fire you should

1st. Alarm the people inside.
2nd. Warn the nearest policeman or fire brigade station.
3rd. Rouse neighbours to bring ladders, mattresses, carpets, to catch people jumping.

After arrival of fire engines the best thing boys can do is to help the police in keeping back the crowd out of the way of the firemen, hose, etc.

The Boys' Life Brigade are taught a certain drill called 'scrum' for keeping back the crowd. They form a line or double line, and pass their arms round each other's waists, and shove, head down, into the crowd, and so drive it back.

If it is necessary to go into a house to search for feeble or insensible people, the thing is to place a wet handkerchief or worsted stocking over your nose and mouth and walk in a stooping position, or crawl along on your hands and knees quite near the floor, as it is here that there is least smoke or gas. Also, for passing through fire and sparks, if you can, get hold of a blanket and wet it, and cut a hole in the middle through which to put your head, it forms a kind of fireproof mantle with which you can push through flames and sparks. [*Practise this.*]

Dragging insensible man: both heads down near the floor

When a fire occurs anywhere near the Boy Scouts should assemble their patrols as quickly as possible, and go off at scouts' pace to the fire, guided by the glare or the smoke. Then the patrol leader should report to the police or firemen, and offer the help of his patrol either to keep the crowd back or to run messages or guard property or to help in any way.

If you find a person with his clothes on fire, you should throw him flat on the floor, because flames only burn upwards, then roll him up in the hearthrug or carpet, coat or blanket, and take care in doing so that you don't catch fire yourself. The reason for doing this is that fire cannot continue to burn when it has no air. Then pour water over the patient to put out all sparks.

When you find an insensible person (and very often in their fright they will have hidden themselves away under beds and tables, etc.), you should either carry him out on your shoulder, or what is often more practicable in the case of heavy smoke, gas fumes, etc., harness yourself on to him with sheets or cords, and drag him out of the room along the floor, crawling on all fours yourself.

[*Practise this by tying a bowline round the patient's waist, another round his ankles, and another round your own neck. Turn your back to him, go on all fours with the rope underneath you, and thus drag him out. Also practise the 'Fireman's Lift' for getting an insensible person on to your shoulders.*]

RESCUE FROM DROWNING

THE list of Boys' Brigade heroes shows you what a large proportion of accidents are due to not knowing how to swim. It is therefore most important that every boy should learn to swim, and having done so to learn how to save others from being drowned.

Mr Holbein,* the great Channel swimmer, writing in *The Boy's Own Paper*, points out that a boy, when learning to swim, should learn first how to get in and out of a boat, *i.e.*, by climbing in over the stern. Secondly, how to support himself on an oar or plank, *i.e.*, by riding astride on it, or by catching hold of one end and pushing it before him and swimming with his legs. Thirdly, how to get into a floating lifebuoy, *i.e.*, by shoving the nearest side of it down under water and capsizing it over his head and shoulders, so that he is inside it when it floats. Fourthly, how to save life.

[*Practise these at swimming baths or bathing parade.*]

A moderate swimmer can save a drowning man if he knows how, and has practised it a few times with his friends. The popular idea that a drowning person rises three times before he finally sinks is all nonsense. He often drowns at once, unless someone is quick to help him. The important point is not to let the drowning person catch hold of you, or he will probably drown you too. Keep behind him always. If you find yourself clutched by the wrist, turn your wrist against his thumb, and force yourself free. Your best way in helping a drowning man is to keep behind and hold him up by the hair, or by the back of the neck, or by putting your arms under his armpits, and telling him to keep quiet and not to struggle; if he obeys, you can easily keep him afloat; but otherwise be careful that in his terror he does not turn over and catch hold of you. If he should seize you by the neck, Holbein says, 'Scrag him, and scrag him quickly. Place your arm round his waist, and the other hand, palm upwards, under his chin, with your finger-tips under his nose. Pull and push with all your might, and he must perforce let go.' But you will never remember this unless you practise it frequently with other boys first; each taking it in turns to be the drowning man or rescuer. [*Practise this.*]

Among the innumerable cases of saving life from drowning, Mr Scullion was recommended for the Albert Medal. He sprang into the river to save a boy from drowning who had fallen between the wharf and the ship's side. When he got hold of the boy there was no room for him to swim in that narrow space, and the tide was very strong, so he dived down, taking the boy with him, under the ship's bottom, and came up in open water on the other side of the ship, and then easily swam to a boat and thus rescued him. Had he not kept his head and dived under the ship, it is probable that both would have been drowned.

Any of you who cannot swim as yet, and who fall into the water out of your depth, remember that you need not sink if you can remember to do the following things. First, keep your mouth upwards by throwing the head well back. Secondly, keep your lungs full of air by taking in long breaths, but breathe out very little. Thirdly, keep your arms under water. To do this you should not begin to shout, which will only empty your lungs, and you should not throw your arms about or beckon for help, else you will sink.

[*Practise this position.*]

If you see a person fall into the water and begin to drown, and you yourself are unable to swim, you must throw him a rope, or an oar, or plank right over him, so that when he comes up again he may clutch at it and hold it. If a person falls through ice, and is unable to get out again because of the edges breaking, throw him a rope, and tell him not to struggle. This may give him confidence until you can get a long ladder or pole which will enable him to crawl out, or will allow you to crawl out to catch hold of him.

RESCUE FROM RUNAWAY HORSES

ACCIDENTS are continually recurring from runaway horses running over people. In fact, on an average, the number of runaway horses that are stopped by policemen during the year amounts to over two hundred; and it is well that everybody should know how to stop a runaway horse, and thus to save numerous accidents and injuries.

Private Davies, of the 16th Lancers, was awarded the Albert Medal, at Aldershot, for stopping the horses of an artillery wagon, which had become unmanageable and run away. The driver, who was riding one of them, had been thrown off, and the horses were careering down hill towards the married quarters of the cavalry barracks, where a number of children were at play, when Private Davies, seeing the danger to the children, ran to the horses, and seizing the off horse with his right hand, held on to the shaft with his left, and endeavoured to stop the wagon. He was dragged in that position for some yards when the chain fastening the shafts to the wagon gave way and let the shafts fall, bringing Davies also to the ground.

The wagon passed over his legs, and very severely injured him, and, though he did not actually succeed in stopping the horses, he so diverted them from their course that time was given for the children to be saved from being run over.

Not long ago a lady was being run away with by her horse in Hyde Park. The animal was tearing along quite mad with fright, and though she was a good rider and kept her head, she had no control over him whatever.

The danger was that the road on which he was galloping, though straight for a good distance, turned at the end very sharply, and was bounded by a high iron railing. Now a horse when he is thoroughly frightened seems to lose his sight as well as his wits; he will run over a cliff or into a wall without trying to stop, and on this occasion it seemed most likely that he would charge into the great iron railings at the end of the road, and the consequences to the girl on his back would have been too awful to think of.

In front of her as she came thundering along were two gentlemen riding quietly along talking together, heading in the same direction that she was going. One of them—it was the Hon. George Wyndham,* at that time Chief Secretary for Ireland—turned his head to see what was happening behind him, and in one moment he grasped the whole situation, saw what to do, and did it. He saw that a girl was being rushed to her death by the maddened horse if something were not done to stop it, or to make it turn round the corner at the end of the road which was now not far away.

Now what would any of you have done had you been in Mr Wyndham's place?

He saw that to put his horse across her path would be easy, but if he did so it would probably throw both horses down, and possibly kill both riders; so what he did was to put his own horse at once into a gallop, and for a moment it looked as if he were running away, with the lady chasing him at full speed. But it soon became evident what he was doing.

He gradually let the lady's horse overtake him until its head was abreast of him and close alongside him, then he gradually turned his own horse for taking the corner, and, pressing all the time against the shoulder of the lady's horse, forced it also gradually to turn with him till it was safely directed away from the railings and into the new direction of the road, and here, while still keeping partly ahead of it, he got hold of its reins, and in a short time succeeded in pulling it up and bringing it to its senses.

This is a lesson to everyone to BE PREPARED, even at most ordinary moments of strolling along, talking to a friend, to spring at once to the assistance of a fellow-creature who is in danger.

The other day I myself found a horse and cab running away over Westminster Bridge, but I stopped it without any difficulty. The way to stop a runaway horse is not to run out in front of it and wave your arms, as so many people do, but to try and race alongside it, catch hold of the shaft to keep yourself from falling, and seize the reins with the other hand, and drag the horse's head round towards you, and so turn him until you can bring him up against a wall or house, or otherwise compel him to stop. But, of course, for a boy, with his light weight, this is a very difficult thing to do. The share he would have in such an accident would probably be to look after the people injured by the runaway horse.

MISCELLANEOUS ACCIDENTS

ONE cannot go through the whole list of accidents that might come under your notice, but the point is that a scout should always remember to keep his head, and think what is the right thing to do at the moment, and be the man to do it, even under the most unexpected circumstances.

Police-Sergeant Cole was awarded the Albert Medal some years ago for removing a dynamite bomb, which he found in Westminster

Hall. It was already lit for exploding, and instead of running away and taking cover himself he snatched it up and rushed out of the place and flung it away, and very nearly lost his life in the explosion which followed immediately after. Had he hesitated to think what would be the best thing to do he would probably have lost his own life, and have allowed the place to be smashed up.

A man named John Smith was awarded the Albert Medal, because one day, when at his work in a steel-casting factory, a great, red-hot steel ingot, weighing 26 tons, was about to be hoisted out of a casting-pit, when one of the workmen named Stanley slipped, and fell into the pit, which was fifteen feet deep, alongside the ingot in a space of about two feet, which existed between the ingot and the wall of the pit. John Smith immediately got a ladder and ran down into the next pit, from which there was a passage communicating into the first one, and in this way he managed to get into the lower part of the ingot pit and drag Stanley out of it into the empty one. Stanley died of his burns two days later, but Smith, though badly burnt himself, recovered to wear the Albert Medal.

MAD DOG

A DOG that is mad runs along snapping at everybody in his path. Every scout should know what to do when there is a mad dog about, and should be prepared to do it.

Sir Thomas Fowell Buxton* was one day out for a ride when his dog, which was running with him, went mad, and started to run through the town.

Sir Thomas edged him off the road and drove him into a garden. He then jumped off his horse, ran at the dog, and succeeded in grabbing him by the neck without getting bitten. Then followed a tremendous struggle between man and dog.

At last the gardener came and brought a chain which Sir Thomas then clipped on, and only when the other end had been securely fastened to a tree he let go his hold of the dog. The dog was then raving mad and tore at his chain so badly that it was in danger of breaking, when Sir Thomas went at him again with a second and stronger chain, and pinning him down by the neck with a pitchfork he fastened it on to him. When this was done and the pitchfork removed the dog sprang at him with such force that it burst the old chain. Luckily the new one held. And soon after the dog died.

The way to prevent a dog biting you is to hold a stick, or even a handkerchief, in your two hands across your front, and the dog will generally try to paw it down before he actually bites you, and you may thus get a chance of landing him a kick under the jaw.

PRACTICES IN LIFE-SAVING

Practise scrum for keeping back crowd at fire.

Practise holding and wrestling with drowning men.

How to prevent a man shooting another with pistol.

Make ladders out of poles, twine, and cross sticks.

Instruct scouts to know the position of neighbouring fire plugs and hydrants, police points, fire alarms, fire stations, ambulances, hospitals, etc.

BOOKS TO READ

'Manual of Boys' Life Brigade': Life-saving Drill. Price 2d. (56 Old Bailey, London.)

Marksmanship
(Picture from 'Sketches in Mafeking', by the Author.
By Permission of Messrs Smith & Elder)

'Manual of Fire Drill' of London County Council. 1s. (P. King and Son, 9 Bridge Street, Westminster.)

'Swimming', by Prof. Holbein, 1s. (A. Pearson, Ltd.)

CAMP FIRE YARN.—No. 25

HELPING OTHERS

Rendering First Aid—Suicides—How to Carry a Patient.

RENDERING FIRST AID

[NOTE TO INSTRUCTOR.—*It is impossible in the short space at one's disposal to give all the details of First Aid. These can be found in any of the books mentioned at the end of this Camp Fire Yarn.*]

IN an accident when you are alone with the injured person, if he is unconscious lay him on his back with his head a little raised and on one side so that he does not choke, and so that any vomit or water, etc., can run out of his mouth. Loosen the clothing about his neck and chest. See where he is injured and treat him according to what you are taught in learning 'First Aid'.

If you have found the man lying insensible you should carefully examine the ground round him for any 'sign', and take note of it and of his position, etc., in case it should afterwards appear that he had been attacked by others.

[*Practise above, one boy as patient, the other to find him. Make 'sign' round the patient.*]

If you are out with a patrol and an accident happens, or you find an injured man, the patrol leader should direct one scout to go for a doctor; he himself will attend to the patient with one scout to help him. The corporal will use the other scouts in assisting by getting water or blankets, or making a stretcher, or keeping the crowd back.

As a rule, it is best to keep the patient quite quiet at first; unless it is necessary, do not try to move him; and don't bother him with questions until he recovers a bit.

[*Practise above.*]

Artificial Breathing.—To restore anyone who is apparently drowned, it is necessary at once to clear the water out of his lungs, for which purpose therefore you should incline him face downwards and head downwards, so that the water may run out of his mouth, and to help it you should open his mouth and pull forward his tongue; take off the wet clothing and wrap him in blankets if possible, and rub and move his limbs as much as possible to get back the

Artificial breathing: Schäfer system

circulation of the blood. After running the water out of the patient, place him on his side with his body slightly hanging down, and keep the tongue hanging out. If he is breathing let him rest; if he is not breathing, you must at once endeavour to restore breathing artificially. Lay him flat on his front with his arm bent and placed under his forehead to keep his nose and mouth off the ground. Put a folded coat or pillow under his chest and let his head hang down. In this way his tongue will not block his throat, and any water or slime can run out. Then either stand astride of him or kneel alongside him, and, placing both your hands on his lower ribs, press steadily down and forwards to drive any air out of his body for three or four seconds, and then ease up to let the air come in again through the throat, then press down again. Continue this pressing and easing, counting four to each movement, until the patient begins to breathe again. Sometimes this doesn't happen till you have been trying for an hour or even more.

This is called the Schäfer method, and can be used equally well for drowned people or for those overcome with smoke or gas fumes.

[*Make the scouts, in pairs, practise above.*]

SMOKE OR FUMES.—Accidents are continually occurring from escapes of gas in mines, sewers, and houses.

In endeavouring to rescue a person, keep your nose and month well covered with wet rags, and get your head as close to the floor as possible, and drag the insensible person out as I have suggested in case of a fire. Drag your patient as quickly as possible into the fresh air—(I say as quickly as possible, because if you delay about it you are very apt to be overcome by the noxious gas yourself)—then loosen all his clothing about the neck and chest, dash cold water in his face and apply burnt feathers under his nose. If you find that he is no longer breathing, then treat him as you would a drowned person, and try and work back the breath into his body.

BURNS.—In treating a man who has been burnt, remove his clothes, not by peeling them off, but by cutting them with a SHARP knife or scissors. If any part of the dress sticks to the skin from having been burnt there, do not tear it away but cut the cloth round it, then as quickly as possible protect the burnt parts from the air which causes intense pain. The best way to protect them is by dusting them with powdered chalk or flour, or by laying strips of lint well soaked in sweet oil or linseed oil, and covering the whole with cotton wool. Keep the patient warm, and give warm drinks, such as hot tea, hot milk, or spirits and water.

Major John Garroway, M.D., strongly recommends, instead of flour or oil to stop the pain of a burn, to put a piece of paper firmly over the wound, and the pain will be relieved in a few seconds.

ACID BURNING.—A case occurred only the other day of a woman throwing vitriol over a man's face. This is an awful acid which burns and eats away the flesh wherever it touches. Fortunately a policeman happened to be on the spot at the time and knew what to do. He at once applied water to wash off the acid, and then applied flour or whitening to protect the wound from the air and ease the pain.

BROKEN LIMBS.—You may get persons with broken limbs or stunned. In the case of broken limbs you would learn what to do in passing your ambulance course, which every boy scout ought to pass before he can be considered to be fully trained. You would there learn how to know when a limb was broken, and how to tie it up between splints made of pieces of wood, rolls of newspaper or rushes, bundles of twigs, walking sticks, or any other articles that will make a straight support for the limb. [*Practise this.*]

BLEEDING.—When a man is bleeding badly from a wound, squeeze the wound or the flesh just above it—that is, between the wound and the heart—press it hard with your thumb to try and stop the blood running in the artery. Then make a pad with something like a flat rounded pebble, and bind it over the wound. If bleeding violently, tie a handkerchief loosely round the limb above the wound and twist it tight with a stick. [*Demonstrate this.*] Keep the wounded part raised above the rest of the body if possible. Apply cold water, or ice if possible, wet rags, etc.

FAINTING.—If your patient faints and is pale—fainting comes from too little blood in the head—let him lie flat down with head on the ground. If his face is flushed raise the head—there is too much blood in it, as in apoplexy or sunstroke.

FITS.—A man cries out and falls, and twitches and jerks his limbs about, froths at the mouth, he is in a fit. It is no good to do anything to him but to put a bit of wood or cork between his jaws, so that he does not bite his tongue. Let him sleep well after a fit.

POISONING.—If a person suddenly falls very ill after taking food, or is known to have taken poison, the first thing to do is to make him swallow some milk or raw eggs. These seem to collect all the poison that is otherwise spread about inside him. Then, if the mouth is not stained or burnt by the poison, make him sick if possible by giving him salt and warm water, and try tickling the inside of his throat with a feather. Then more milk and eggs and weak tea. If the poison is an acid that burns, the patient should not be made to vomit, but milk or salad oil should be given. The patient should be kept awake if he gets drowsy.

BLOOD-POISONING.—This results from dirt being allowed to get into a wound. Swelling, pain, red veins appear. Fomenting with hot water is the best relief.

CHOKING.—Loosen collar; hold the patient's nose with one hand and with the forefinger of the other, or with the handle of a spoon try and pull out whatever is stuck in his throat. By pressing down the root of the tongue you may make him sick and throw out the obstruction. For slight choking make patient bend head well back and swallow small pills made of bread, and sip of water. Sometimes a good hard smack on the back will do him good.

SNAKE BITE

FORTUNATELY poisonous snakes are uncommon in England, but if you travel in a colony you are sure to come across them, and you ought always to know how to deal with bites from them. The same treatment does also for wounds from poisoned arrows, mad dogs, etc. Remember the poison from a bite gets into your blood and goes all through your body in a very few beats of your pulse. Therefore, whatever you do must be done immediately. The great thing is to stop the poison rushing up the veins into the body. To do this bind a cord or handkerchief immediately round the limb above the place where the patient has been bitten, so as to stop the blood flying back to the heart with the poison. Then try and suck the poison out of the wound, and, if possible, cut the wound still more, to make it bleed, and run the poison out. The poison, when sucked into the mouth, does no harm unless you have a wound in your mouth. The patient should also be given stimulants, such as coffee or spirits, to a very big extent, and not allowed to become drowsy, but should be walked about and pricked and smacked in order to keep his senses alive.

[*Practise this process in make-believe.*]

GRIT IN THE EYE

DO not let your patient rub the eye; it will only cause inflammation and swelling, and so make the difficulty of removing the grit all the greater.

If the grit is in the lower eyelid, draw down the lid as far as you can, and gently brush it out with the corner of a moistened handkerchief, or with a paintbrush, or feather.

If it is under the upper lid, pull the lid away from the eyeball and push the underlid up underneath the upper one. In this way the eyelashes of the lower lid will generally clean the inside of the upper one.

Another way, which every scout must practise, is to seat your patient and stand behind him yourself with the back of his head against your chest. Lay a card, match, or any flat substance under your own thumb on the upper part of the upper eyelid and then catch hold of the edge of the eylid and draw it upwards over the match so that it turns inside out; gently remove the grit with a feather or wet handkerchief, and roll the eyelid down again.

If the eye is much inflamed, bathe it with lukewarm weak tea.

If the grit is firmly embedded in the eye, drop a little oil (olive or castor oil) into the lower lid; close the eye and bandage it with a soft wet pad and bandage, and get a doctor to see it.

[*Practise above.*]

SUICIDES

I WAS once travelling in the train in Algeria, a part of North Africa which belongs to the French, and there was with me only one other passenger in the carriage, a French farmer, with whom I got into conversation.* He became very communicative, and told me that if I had not come into the carriage he would by this time have been a dead man, as he had got into the train with the intention of killing himself. So I asked him about his troubles, and, as he unfolded them to me, I was able to tell him various remedies which promised success for him in the future, for he was chiefly upset over his recent failures in farming. After we had been going on for some time, he quite cheered up, and told me that he was going to get out at the next station, and go back and set to work in the way suggested.

You may have opportunities of saving people who are thinking of killing themselves. The newspapers give cases of suicides almost every day, and go into details of them, because they know that so many people have a foolish love of reading horrors.

Most people at one time or the other of their lives get a feeling that they will kill themselves; as a rule they get over it in a day or two, and find that it comes from nothing worse than an attack of indigestion, liver, or influenza, or from disappointment, or over-anxiety; but there are others with weaker minds, who read these newspaper accounts, and brood over them till they can think of nothing else. They hug the idea to themselves, although with horror, and get panic-stricken. They think too much of their own trouble, without thinking how the rest of the world is doing.

It only needs a sympathising friend to come along and take command of the would-be suicide, and to give him something else to think about and to do. You can point out that suicide does no good to anybody; that it generally comes from something wrong with the bodily health, which makes the patient hysterical; that he has only got to command his own mind firmly, and the attack will pass off again. Then, if possible, try to get a Salvation Army officer to see him; he will probably set him right. In this way you may be able to save lives.

[*The Salvation Army have now a department which gives advice to people who are feeling inclined to kill themselves. This past year 1,125 men and 90 women have applied to their London office alone; and of these probably three-quarters would have killed themselves if it had not been for the sympathy and advice of the officers who reasoned with them, and found for them ways out of their difficulties. The official returns of suicides for the past year show a much smaller number than usual.*]

Where a man has gone so far as to attempt suicide, a scout should know what to do with him. In the case of a man cutting his throat, the great point is to stop the bleeding from the artery, if it be cut. The artery runs from where the collarbone and breast-bone join, up to the corner of the jaw, and the way to stop bleeding is to press hard with the thumb on the side of the wound nearest to the heart, and pressure should be kept up as hard as possible until assistance arrives. [*Demonstrate this.*] In a case where the would-be suicide has taken poison, give milk and make him vomit, which is done by tickling the inside of the throat with the finger or a feather, or pouring down his throat a tumbler of water mixed with a tablespoon of mustard or salt.

In the case of hanging, cut down the body at once, taking care to support it with one arm while cutting the cord. Cut the noose, loosen all tight clothing about the neck and chest. Let the patient have as much fresh air as possible, throw cold water on the face and chest, or cold and hot water alternately. Perform artificial breathing as in the case of apparently drowned people.

A tenderfoot is sometimes inclined to be timid about handling an insensible man or a dead man, or even of seeing blood. Well, he won't be much use till he gets over such nonsense; the poor insensible fellow can't hurt him, and he must force himself to catch hold of him; when once he has done this his fears will pass off. And if he visits a butcher's slaughterhouse he will soon get accustomed to the sight of blood.

At Reading, not long ago, two men were severely reprimanded by the coroner for being afraid to go and cut down a man who had hanged himself—they only ran and fetched someone else, and so he was killed. What would you have done had you been one of the men?

HOW TO CARRY A PATIENT

(See National Health Society's Manual.)

To Carry Single-handed an Unconscious Person.—Turn patient on his face. Raise him into a kneeling posture. Kneel, and place yourself across and under him, so that his stomach rests on your right shoulder. Pass your right arm between his thighs and behind his right thigh. With your left arm draw his left hand forwards under your left, and grasp the wrist with your right hand; then raise yourself to an erect position.

[*Make scouts practise this in pairs.*]

Lifting insensible man

With Two Helpers to Carry a Conscious Person. (See Manual.)

Stretchers may be arranged in some of the following ways:

(a) A hurdle, shutter, door, gate, covered well with straw, hay, clothing, sacking.

(b) A piece of carpet, blanket, sacking, tarpaulin, spread out, and two stout poles rolled up in the sides. Put clothes for a pillow.

(c) Two coats, with the sleeves turned inside out; pass two poles through the sleeves; button the coats over them.

(d) Two poles passed through a couple of sacks, through holes at the bottom corners of each.

In carrying a patient on a stretcher be careful that he is made quite comfortable before you start. Let both bearers rise together; they must walk *out of step*, and take short paces. It should be the duty of the hinder bearer to keep a careful watch on the patient.

[*Practise these different methods.*]

Carrying insensible man

HOW TO PRACTISE

In practising First Aid it is a great thing to bespatter the patient with blood to accustom the rescuer to the sight of it, otherwise it will often unnerve him in a real accident. Sheep's blood can be got from the butcher's shop.

Prepare a heavy smoke fire in a neighbouring room or building (if possible on the first floor), while you are lecturing in the club room. Secretly arrange with two or three boys that if an alarm of fire is given they should run about frightened and try to start a panic.

Have the alarm given either by getting someone to rush in and tell you of the fire, or by having some explosive bombs fired. Then let a patrol, or two patrols, tackle the fire under direction of their patrol leaders. They should shut windows and doors. Send scouts into different parts of the building to see if the fire is spreading, and to search for people in need of rescue.

These scouts should have wet handkerchiefs over their months and noses. 'Insensible' people (or sack dummies) should be hidden under tables, etc.

Scouts rescue them by shouldering or dragging them out and getting them down to the ground. Use jumping sheet, shoot, etc.

Other parties lay and connect the hose, or make lines for passing fire buckets.

Another party revive the rescued by restoring animation. Another party form 'scrum' to help the police and fire brigade by keeping the crowd back.

GAMES

'DRAGGING RACE'. A line of patients of one patrol are laid out at one hundred yards distance from start. Another patrol, each carrying a rope, run out, tie ropes to the patients, and drag them in. Time taken of last in. Patrols change places. The one which completes in shortest time wins. Knots must be correctly tied, and patients' coats laid out under their heads.

BOOKS TO READ

'Aid to the Injured or Sick'. H. W. Gell, M. B. Twopence. (Published by G. Gill & Sons, 13, Warwick Lane, London, E.C.)

National Health Society's Booklets, one penny, on hygiene and sanitation. Same publishers.

CHAPTER IX

PATRIOTISM;

or,

Our Duties as Citizens

CAMP FIRE YARN.—No. 26

OUR EMPIRE

How it Grew—How it Must be Held.

HINTS TO INSTRUCTORS

The use of a large Map of the Empire is very desirable for illustrating this. The Arnold-Forster or the Navy League or the League of the Empire Map are very good, and we hope to issue one specially designed for the Boy Scouts.*

Look up the local history of your neighbourhood, and give your scouts the more interesting and dramatic bits of it, on the actual scene of the events if possible.

OUR EMPIRE

Any of you who have travelled much about this country by train, going for your holidays and so on, know how two or three hours will take you a good long distance and six or eight hours will take you to the other end of England.

Well, if instead of hours you travelled for as many days, even six or eight days would take you a very little way over our Empire. It would get you into Canada, but you would want several more days—not hours—to get you across that country. Eighteen days' hard travelling day and night would get you to India or South Africa, but either of these are little more than half way to Australia. And all that distance off, across the seas, on the other side of the world, we have a British country into which you could put nine Great Britains and Irelands.

9	United Kingdoms	=	1 Australia.
10	,,	=	1 Canada.
6	,,	=	1 India and Burma.
5	,,	=	East Africa, Uganda, and Soudan.
5	,,	=	South Africa.
1	,,	=	New Zealand.
1½	,,	=	Nigeria.

Then there are numbers of smaller Colonies or Dependencies, such as Guiana (nearly as big as the United Kingdom), North Borneo, New Guinea, Somaliland, Straits Settlements, Gold Coast, West Indies, Tasmania, etc., and numbers of islands in every sea all over the world.

Our Colonies together are something like forty times the size of the United Kingdom at home.

Our fellow-subjects amount to four hundred millions, and comprise almost every known race. Almost every known species of wild animal occurs in British territory.

It is a magnificient Empire over which the Union Jack flies, but it is still only at the beginning of its development. The territories are there, but the people are only coming. The white population of all these Colonies only amounts to a little over a quarter of the population of our crowded little island. We have nearly forty-four millions here; they have among the Colonies a little over eleven millions.

Many of you scouts, as you grow up, will probably become scouts of the nation, and will find your way to some of the Colonies to help to push them up into big prosperous countries.* Your scout's training will come in very useful to you there. But when you go there you must be prepared to work, and to work hard, and to turn your hand to any kind of job.

HOW OUR EMPIRE GREW

All those vast Colonies did not come to England of themselves. They were got for us by the hard work and the hard fighting of our forefathers.

America.—When we first got to America it took Sir Walter Raleigh, Captain John Smith, and other great pioneers four or five months to get there in their little cockleshells of ships, some of them only 30 tons measurement—no bigger than a Thames barge. Nowadays you can get there in five or six days, instead of months, in steamers of 30,000 tons.

Think of the pluck of those men tackling a voyage like that, with a very limited supply of water and salt food. And, when they got to land with their handful of men, they had to overcome the savages, and in some cases other Europeans, like the Dutch, the Spaniards, and the French; and then they had hard work to till the ground, to build settlements, and to start commerce.

Hard sailoring, hard soldiering, hard colonising by those old British sea-dogs, Sir Francis Drake, Sir Walter Raleigh, Hawkins, Frobisher, and, best of all to my mind, Captain John Smith.*

He left Louth Grammar School in Lincolnshire to become a clerk in an office, but he soon went off to the wars. After two years' fighting he returned home.

He admitted he had gone out as a 'tenderfoot', and had not properly prepared himself as a boy for a life of adventure; so he set to work then and there to learn scouting. He built himself a hut in the woods, and learnt stalking game, and killing and cooking it for himself; he learnt to read maps and to draw them, and also the use of weapons; and then, when he had made himself really good at scoutcraft, he went off to the wars again.

He afterwards became a sailor, fought in some very tough sea-fights, and eventually, in 1607, he went with an expedition to colonise Virginia in America. They sailed from London in three ships, the biggest of which was only 100 tons, the smallest 30 tons. But they got there after five months, and started a settlement on the James River.

Here John Smith was captured by the Red Indians one day when out shooting (as you have seen by the play in Chapter 1), and they were proceeding to kill him when the King's daughter, Pocahontas, asked for him to be spared. After this the Red Indians and the Whites got on good terms with each other. Pocahontas became a Christian, and married Smith's lieutenant, Rolfe, and came to England. After many strange and exciting adventures in America, John Smith got much damaged by an accidental explosion of gunpowder, and came home ill. He eventually died in London.

He was a splendid character—and always did his duty in spite of all temptations to let it slide. He was a tremendous worker, very keen, and very brave. He was never defeated by any difficulty however great, because he was always cheery under the worst of circumstances. His motto was, 'We were born not for ourselves, but to do good to others,' and he acted up to it.

In South Africa we had to drive out the Dutch and then fight the natives for our foothold, which once gained we never let go—and though it has cost us thousands of lives and millions of money we have got it now.

Australia was got by our sailor-adventurers, like Captain Cook, outstripping all other nations in their plucky navigation of immense unknown oceans.

India was practically in possession of the French when Clive and Wellesley drove them out, and then in turn had to fight the hordes of fighting natives of the interior, and gradually, foot by foot, by dint of hard fighting, we have won that country for our Empire.

East Africa, Uganda, and the Soudan beyond Egypt, and Somaliland have also been fought for and won in quite recent times.

And now in all of these we are spreading the blessings of peace and justice, doing away with slavery and oppression, and developing commerce, and manufactures, and prosperity in those countries.

Other nations could formerly only look on and wonder, but now they too are pressing forward in the race for empire and commerce, so that we cannot afford to sit still or let things slide.

We have had this enormous Empire handed down to us by our forefathers, and we are responsible that it develops and goes ahead, and above all that we make ourselves fit and proper men to help it to go ahead. It won't do so of itself, any more than it would have become ours of itself. If we don't do this some other nation will take it from us.

If our island of England were attacked and taken, down comes our Empire like a house built of cards.

We have had this danger always, even before our Empire was a paying one and worth taking. Nowadays it is much more tempting for other people to take. We defeated determined attacks of the Dutch upon us in the old days. The Spaniards with their Armada attempted to invade us, when, largely thanks to a storm, we defeated them utterly. Then the French, after a long struggle to best us, had their invasion stopped by Nelson's victory at Trafalgar, and their harmfulness ended by Wellington at Waterloo. The French Emperor had been so sure of success that he had had medals got ready to commemorate the capture of England. And since helping in the defeat of the Russians in the Crimea we have been at peace with our Continental neighbours.

Let us hope that this peace will remain permanent.

HOW THE EMPIRE MUST BE HELD

PEACE cannot be certain unless we show that we are always fully prepared to defend ourselves in England, and that an invader would only find himself ramming his head against bayonets and well-aimed bullets if he tried landing on our shores.

The surest way to keep peace is to be prepared for war. Don't be cowards, and content yourselves by merely paying soldiers to do your fighting and dying for you. Do something in your own self-defence.

You know at school how if a swaggering ass comes along and threatens to bully you, he only does so because he thinks you will give in to him; but if you know how to box and square up to him he alters his tone and takes himself off. And it is just the same with nations.

It is much better that we should all be good friends—and we should all try for that—no calling each other names, or jeering; but if one of them comes along with the idea of bullying us, the only way to stop him is to show him that you *can* hit and *will* hit if he drives you to it.

Every boy should prepare himself, by learning how to shoot and to drill, to take his share in defence of the Empire, if it should ever be attacked. If our enemies saw that we were thus prepared as a nation, they would never dare to attack, and peace would be assured.

Remember that the Roman Empire 2,000 years ago was comparatively just as great as the British Empire of to-day. And though it had defeated any number of attempts against it, it fell at last, chiefly because the young Romans gave up soldiering and manliness altogether; they paid men to play their games for them, so that they themselves could look on without the fag of playing, just as we are doing in football now. They paid soldiers to fight their battles for them instead of learning the use of arms themselves; they had no patriotism or love for their grand old country, and they went under with a run when a stronger nation attacked them.

Well, we have got to see that the same fate does not fall upon our Empire. And it will largely depend upon you, the younger generation of Britons that are now growing up to be the men of the Empire. Don't be disgraced like the young Romans, who lost the Empire of their forefathers by being wishy-washy slackers without any go or patriotism in them.

Play up! Each man in his place, and play the game!* Your forefathers worked hard, fought hard, and died hard, to make this Empire for you. Don't let them look down from heaven, and see you loafing about with hands in your pockets, doing nothing to keep it up.

HINTS TO INSTRUCTORS

Teach the words and choruses of:

'The Maple Leaf' (Canada), 'The Song of Australia', and other Colonial songs.*
'God Bless the Prince of Wales'.
'Rule Britannia'.
'Hearts of Oak'.
'The Flag of Britain'.
'God Save the King'.
(J. S. Maddison, 32 Charing Cross.)

Apply to Secretary, League of the Empire, Caxton Hall, Westminster, S.W.

Explore Westminster Abbey, St Paul's Cathedral, the Temple Church, etc., with following books:

BOOKS TO READ

'St Paul's Cathedral' and 'Westminster Abbey', both by Mrs Frewen Lord, 1s. (Published by Clowes and Son, Charing Cross.)

(Excellent short histories of our famous men and their deeds.)

'Travels of Captain John Smith', by Dr Rouse. 6d. (Blackie.)

'The Story of Captain Cook', edited by John Lang. 1s. 6d.

'Deeds that Won the Empire', by Fitchett.*

'Heroes of Pioneering' (in America, India, Africa), by Sanderson. (Seeley.) 2s. 6d.

Excellent Lantern Slide Lectures can be got on hire from the League of the Empire, Caxton Hall, Victoria Street, London, on the history of our Colonies and Empire.

DISPLAY*

JOHN NICHOLSON was one of the finest among many fine Britons who helped to rule India. On one occasion he had a meeting of a number of chiefs at a time when they were beginning to show some signs of mutiny. The most important one of these chiefs was called Mehtab Singh, and just before the meeting he told the others that he for one was not afraid of the Englishman, and that he meant to swagger into the room with his shoes on. (It is the custom in India for natives to take off their shoes on entering the presence of a superior just as in England you take off your hat on coming in.) And he did so. He walked in before them all with his shoes on.

Nicholson did not appear to take any notice of it and went on with the meeting; but at the end of it, just as they were all leaving, he suddenly stopped Mehtab Singh, and ordered the others to wait. He then reprimanded him for his insolence, and ordered him to take off his shoes then and there and to walk out with them in his hand before all the other chiefs. And so he had to go, hanging his head with shame, disgraced and humbled by the firmness of the British ruler.

This makes a good subject for a display.

Scene in a great tent or hall in India.

Nicholson (with a black beard), in a dark suit, sitting on a throne in the centre, with several British and native officers in red tunics grouped behind him. Native princes, seated in chairs in semi-circle to either side of him, all with white socks or bare feet, except Mehtab Singh, who has black shoes on, put out well before him for all to see.

Nicholson rises, signs to the chiefs that they may go.

All rise and bow to him, with both hands to the forehead.

As they turn to go he stops them.

'Stay, gentlemen, one moment. I have a matter with you, Mehtab Singh! Thou camest here intent to show contempt for me, who represent your Queen. But you forget that you are dealing with a Briton—one of that band who never brooks an insult even from an equal, much less from a native of this land. Were I a common soldier it would be the same; a Briton, even though alone, amongst a thousand of your kind, shall be respected, though it brought about his death. That's how we hold the world. To plot against your master brings but trouble on yourself. Take off those shoes.'

Mehtab Singh

Face—Dark rouge, not black. Dress—Big turban, coloured dressing-gown and girdle, white socks, and black shoes.

[Mehtab starts, draws himself up, and glares at Nicholson angrily.]

Nicholson [very quietly and deliberately]—'Take—off—those—shoes.' [Points at them.]

A pause. Mehtab looks round as if for help, takes a step towards

Nicholson, but catches his eye, and stops. He sinks slowly on one knee, head down, and slowly takes off his shoes.

Rises, keeping his head down, slowly turns—Nicholson still pointing—and walks slowly out, shoes in hand.

[If a longer scene is required Nicholson might then address the chiefs on the might of Britain, which, though a small country, is all powerful for good of the world, and so he, as representing her, stands one among them for the good of the whole. And that if they want peace and prosperity they themselves must be loyal and true to the hand that is arranging it. Nicholson's words are splendidly rendered in the poem by Henry Newbolt.]

CAMP FIRE YARN.—No. 27

CITIZENSHIP

Duties of Scouts as Citizens—Duties as Citizen Soldiers—Marksmanship—Helping the Police.

SCOUT'S DUTY AS A CITIZEN

THERE are two ways by which every good Briton ought to be prepared to keep up our Empire.

The first is by peaceful means as a citizen.

If every citizen of the Empire were to make himself a really good useful man, our nation would be such a blessing to the civilised world, as it has been in the past, that nobody would wish to see it broken up by any other nation. No other nation would probably wish to do it. But to hold that position we must be good citizens and firm friends all round among ourselves in our country.

A house divided against itself cannot stand. If a strong enemy wants our rich commerce and Colonies, and sees us in England divided against each other, he would pounce in and capture us.

For this you must begin, as boys, not to think other classes of boys to be your enemies. Remember, whether rich or poor, from castle or from slum, you are all Britons in the first place, and you've got to keep England up against outside enemies. You have to stand shoulder to shoulder to do it.

If you are divided among yourselves you are doing harm to your country. You must sink your differences.

If you despise other boys because they belong to a poorer class than yourself you are a snob; if you hate other boys because they happen to be born richer and belong to higher-class schools than yourself, you are a fool.

We have got, each one of us, to take our place as we find it in this world and make the best of it, and pull together with the others around us.

We are very like bricks in a wall, we have each our place, though it may seem a small one in so big a wall. But if one brick gets rotten, or slips out of place, it begins to throw an undue strain on others, cracks appear, and the wall totters.

Don't be too anxious to push yourself on to good billets. You will get disappointments without end if you start that way.

Work for the good of the State, or of the business in which you are employed, and you will find that as you succeed in doing this you will be getting all the promotion and all the success that you want.

Try and prepare yourself for this by seriously taking up the subjects they teach you at school, not because it amuses you, but because it is your duty to your country to improve yourself. Take up your mathematics, your history, and your language—learning in that spirit, and you'll get on.

Don't think of yourself, but think of your country and your employers. Self-sacrifice pays all round.

DUTIES AS CITIZEN-SOLDIER

A CUTTLE-FISH is an animal with a small, round body and several enormously long arms which reach out in every direction to hold on to rocks to enable it to keep its position and to get food.

Great Britain has been compared to a cuttle-fish, the British Isles being the body and our distant Colonies the arms spread all over the world.

When anyone wants to kill a cuttle-fish he does not go and lop off one of its arms; the other arms would probably tackle him and hold him for the cuttle-fish to suddenly eat. No, the way to kill a cuttle-fish is to suddenly stab him in the heart, and then his arms fall helpless and dead.

Well, we have many powerful enemies round about us in Europe who want very much to get hold of the trade in our great manufacturing towns, and of the vast farmlands in our Colonies. If they tried to lop off one of our Colonies it would be like trying to lop off one of the arms of the cuttle-fish. All the rest would tackle him at once, as happened in the last war in South Africa.

Their only way—and they know it—is to stab suddenly at the heart of the Empire, that is to attack England. If they succeeded, the whole of the Empire must fall at once, because the different parts of it cannot yet defend themselves without help from home.

Cuttle fish

For this reason every Briton who has any grit in him will BE PREPARED to help in defending his country.

When Mafeking was attacked by the Boers, the boys of the town made themselves into a Cadet Corps, and did very useful work in the defence. It is quite likely that England will some day be attacked just as Mafeking was, unexpectedly, by a large number of enemies.

If this happens, every boy in the country should be prepared to take his place and help in the defence like those Mafeking boys did.

We don't think much of a fellow who is no good at cricket or football, and who only loafs about trying (without success) to look like a man by smoking cheap cigarettes. But we ought really not to think too much of any boy, even though a cricketer and footballer, unless he can also *shoot*, and *can drill* and *scout*.

That is the fellow who is going to be useful if England is attacked.

I hope that before long every eleven, whether football or cricket, will also make itself a good eleven for shooting and scouting and therefore useful for defence of our King and country when needed.*

In the Colonies boys think more of their shooting than of their games, because the shooting is for their *country* the games for *themselves*.

Mr Roosevelt,* President of the United States of America, writes:

'The qualities that make a good scout are, in large part, the qualities that make a good hunter. Most important of all is the ability to shift for one's self—the mixture of hardihood and resourcefulness which enables a man to tramp all day in the right direction, and, when night comes, to make the best of whatever opportunities for shelter and warmth may be at hand. Skill in the use of the rifle is another trait; quickness in seeing game, another; ability to take advantage of cover, yet another; while patience, endurance, keenness of observation, resolution, good nerves, and instant readiness in an emergency, are all indispensable to a really good hunter.'

Roosevelt is not, like certain men I know of, a man who pays others to do his fighting for him, but, when America went to war with Spain about Cuba, he went to the front as a soldier—like many good Britons did in South Africa—and was of greatest value to his side because he had begun life as a scout.

So make yourselves good scouts and good rifle shots in order to protect the women and children of your country if it should ever become necessary.

MARKSMANSHIP

LORD ROBERTS,* who has seen more of war than almost anybody alive, knows how terrible a thing it would be if war came into England, and he urges everybody to join in preventing it by becoming a good marksman with the rifle. Thanks to him, all those who have patriotism in them are taking it up everywhere.

The value of non-smoking again comes in rifle shooting. I used to smoke myself as a youngster, but I had to do some rifle shooting, and when in training I found my eyesight was better when I did not smoke. So I gave up smoking altogether, and am very glad I did.

The boys of the International Anti-Cigarette League bind themselves not to smoke, in order to make themselves better men for their country—that is the best reason for doing it.

I heard another reason given the other day for not smoking, and that was that St Paul did not smoke. I don't suppose he did. Tobacco wasn't invented in his time.

The Boers are all good shots, and so are the Swiss. In both countries the boys begin learning marksmanship at an early age by using crossbows. They have much the same action for the firer as the rifle, since they are aimed from the shoulder and fired by pulling a trigger when the aim is taken. Boys trained with the crossbow have no difficulty in shooting accurately with a rifle directly it is put in their hands.

Boer boys shooting with crossbows

To be able to shoot well, a great secret is to hold your rifle properly; if it leans over a little bit to one side or the other the bullet will fly low over to that side. Keep your left arm well underneath the rifle to support it, and hold it well into the shoulder with your left hand. The right hand should have the thumb on the top of the stock, and the forefinger as far round the trigger as you can get it; then in firing don't give a pull with your forefinger or you will pull the aim off the target just as you fire; you should squeeze the woodwork of the rifle between your thumb and forefinger, and that will fire it with steadiness.

Then when your rifle has gone off, don't throw up the muzzle in a hurry, but do like all old scouts, continue to look along your sights after firing to see how much you have jumped off your aim in firing, and try and correct it next time.

Shooting at a fixed target is only a step towards shooting at a moving one like a man. Firing at moving objects is, of course, more difficult, but more real, because you will not find a deer or an enemy as a rule kind enough to stand still while you shoot at him, he will be running and dodging behind cover, so you have to get your aim quick and to shoot quick.

The very best practice for this is always to be aiming at moving objects with your staff, using it as if it were a rifle.

Aim first at the man, then moving the muzzle a little faster than he is moving, and fire while moving it when it is pointing where he will be a second or two later, and the bullet will just get there at the same time as he does and will hit him.

HELPING POLICE

Boy Scouts can be of special use in assisting the police in towns. In the first place every Boy Scout ought to know where the fixed police points are—that is, where a constable is always stationed, apart from the policemen on their beats. He ought also to know where to find the fire alarm; also where is the nearest fire brigade station, and the nearest hospital or ambulance station, and chemist.

On seeing an accident, if you cannot help at it you should run and inform the nearest policeman, and ask him how you can help him, whether you can call a doctor, a cab, and so on. If you hear a policeman's whistle sounding, run and offer to help him, it is your duty, as he is a King's servant. If you should happen to see a door or window left open and unguarded at night, it is as well to inform a policeman on that beat, but you should on no account attempt to do detective work by watching people or playing the spy.

If you find a lost child, or lost dog, or any lost property, you should take them at once to the police station.

Sir H. Poland, K.C., had his watch snatched by a pickpocket the other day. The thief darted away down the street; but a small boy jumped on to a bike and followed him, crying, 'Stop thief!' till he was caught—with the watch on him.

Not only can boys help the police, but girls also. Within the last few months I have noticed three cases of girls going to the assistance of constables who were in difficulties with violent men. In each case the girl got the policeman's whistle and blew it for him until assistance arrived. These heroines were Miss Edith Harris at Southampton, Miss Bessie Matthews in Clerkenwell, and Mrs Langley at Brentford.

HINTS TO INSTRUCTORS

MARKSMANSHIP can be taught indoors with the Blanchette Air Gun Tube. Price four guineas with Air Rifle. Targets 10d. per 100.

CROSSBOW.—Scouts can make their own crossbows and learn marksmanship with them.

Get leave to use, or join, a Miniature Rifle Club range.

GAMES

'SHOOT OUT'.—Two patrols compete. Targets: Bottles or bricks set up on end to represent the opposing patrol. Both patrols are drawn up in line at about 20 to 25 yards from the targets. At the word 'fire' they throw stones at the targets. Directly a target falls the umpire directs the corresponding man of the other patrol to sit down—killed. The game goes on, if there are plenty of stones, till the whole of one patrol is killed. Or a certain number of stones can be given to each patrol, or a certain time limit, say one minute.

'FRENCH AND ENGLISH', or 'Tug of War'.—One patrol against another.

THE STORMING OF BADAJOZ.—One patrol (French) mounts on a very strong kitchen-table, or bank, and holds it against all comers. The British attack, and try to gain possession of the fortress by pulling the defenders off. Defenders may have half their number on the ground behind the 'rampart'. If the defenders pull a Briton over the rampart on to the ground behind he is dead. No hitting or kicking allowed.

[Badajoz was a Spanish fortress held by 5,000 French and Spaniards. It was attacked, and stormed, and taken by the British, who lost 3,500 in the assault, on March 17th, 1812.*]

BOOKS TO READ

'The Boys' Book of Bravery', by Power Berry. (C. A. Pearson.)

'The Boys' Book of Battles', by Herbert Cadett. (C. A. Pearson.)

'Rules for Miniature Rifle Clubs'. Secretary National Rifle Association, Bisley, Surrey.

CAMP FIRE YARN.—No. 28

UNITED WE STAND
DIVIDED WE FALL

Our Fleet and Army—Our Union Jack—Our Government—Our King.

HINTS TO INSTRUCTORS

Hoist the flag and salute it every morning when in camp, and on special days get up a show, or sports, or competitions, etc., on such as King's Birthday, Empire Day, May 24th, annually, or on the day of the Patron Saint of your Country: St George, April 23rd; St Patrick, March 17th; St David, March 1st; St Andrew, Nov. 30th.

*Get up tableaux or small pageants by the scouts to illustrate scenes from history of your town, or of Britain, or of Greater Britain.**

These interest the boys and impress the incident upon them, and they educate spectators, and bring in money for your funds.

Take scouts to see meeting of town council and how business is carried out.

If in London, take your boys to the Museum of the Royal United Service Institution, Whitehall, and show them the models of Waterloo and Trafalgar; the gun which we manufactured in Mafeking; the medals of different campaigns; and a hundred other interesting relics.

Take your scouts round and explain each statue in your town.

Hold debates on questions of the day.

OUR NAVY AND ARMY

THE British Navy and Army have made our Empire for us, and if it had not been for their help the Empire would have been broken up by our enemies long ago.

So we must be careful to keep those Services supplied with good men who, like the scouts, must BE PREPARED to give their lives for their country at any time.

There are always members of Parliament who try to make the Navy and Army smaller, so as to save money. They only want to be popular with the voters in England so that they and the party to which they belong may get into power. These men are called 'politicians'. They do not look to the good of the country. Most of them know and care very little about our Colonies. If they had had their way before, we should by this time have been talking French; and if they are allowed to have their way in the future we may as well learn German or Japanese, for we shall be conquered by these.

But fortunately there are other better men in Parliament, who are called 'statesmen'; these are men who look out for the welfare of the country, and do not mind about being popular or not so long as they keep the country safe.

THE BRITISH NAVY.—Every British boy should study the Navy as much as possible, and learn the history of the different ships, and their power and guns, etc. A collection of postcard portraits of all His Majesty's ships is a very interesting one to make.

You should know the badges of rank of the officers, because it is the duty of a scout to salute officers of His Majesty's service.

Badges of rank on the sleeve or shoulder-strap are these.

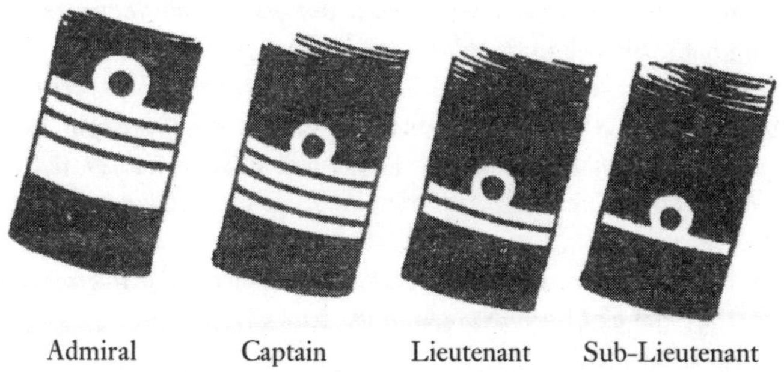

Admiral Captain Lieutenant Sub-Lieutenant

Perhaps you may like to know some facts about the dress of the sailors.

The reason they wear that flap collar on their back is a relic of the time when they wore their hair in pig-tails. The grease used to come off and spoil their jackets, so they wore big linen flaps, which could be easily taken off and washed.

They wear a black silk tie round their neck as a mark of mourning for the death of Nelson at the battle of Trafalgar.

They wear three lines of white braid to commemorate Nelson's naval victories, the Nile, Copenhagen, and Trafalgar.

They wear baggy trousers so that they can easily roll them up above their knees when they want to wade.

Soldiers and sailors tattoo their arms with the idea that when they are killed in battle they can be identified the more easily.

THE BRITISH ARMY.—The Army is made up of—

The Regulars or Active Army, which includes, infantry, cavalry, artillery, engineers, and many other branches of both white and native soldiers.

The Militia at home are to help the Regulars in time of war.

The Militia exist also in most of our Colonies for their own defence.

The Territorial Force is made up of volunteers to protect the British Isles in case of the Active Army being called away for war in other parts.

In the Army, field-marshals and generals (including major-generals and lieutenant-generals) wear cocked hats, with long white cock's feather plumes, and red tunics or black frock-coats. Their swords are curved scimitars, with ivory handles. Colonels wear the uniform of their regiment with crown and star on the shoulder strap, or, in khaki, on the cuff; majors, one crown; captains, three stars; lieutenants, two stars.

You can tell what wars soldiers or sailors have been in by the colours of their medal ribbons. These I will show you later on.

OUR FLAG

SCOUTS will always salute the colours (or standard) of a regiment when they pass. There are generally two such standards, one the 'King's Colour', the other the 'Regimental Colour'.

Men-of-war carry a pennant, *i.e.*, a long thin flag like a whip lash. You may remember that the Dutch fleet under Van Tromp,* after defeating ours, carried a broom at their mastheads to show that they had swept us off the seas. But when we shortly after defeated them we put up a whip at the masthead to show that we had whipped the enemy, and this whip has been carried ever since by men-of-war.

The Royal Navy fly the White Ensign; no one else is allowed to except yachts belonging to the Royal Yacht Squadron. The White Ensign is a white flag with the Red Cross of St George on it and a Union Jack in the corner. It is flown at the stern of the ship, a small Union Jack at the bow.

The mercantile navy flies the Red Ensign; or if the captain of the ship belongs to the Royal Reserve, the ship flies a Blue Ensign.

The Army and Government buildings fly the Union Jack. Private houses and individuals should only fly the Red Ensign.

The Royal Standard, which shows the Lions of England, the Harp of Ireland, and the Lion of Scotland, is only flown when the King is present.

The Union Jack is the national flag of England, and is made up originally of the flag of St George, a red cross on a white ground. In 1606 King James I added to it the banner of Scotland, which was a blue flag with a white St Andrew's Cross diagonal, that is from corner to corner.

In 1801 the Banner of St Patrick of Ireland was added to the flag; St Patrick's Cross was a red diagonal cross on a white ground, so that the flag now means the union of England, Ireland, and Scotland.

But there is a right way and a wrong way of putting it up, which all of you ought to know and understand, because so very frequently one sees it hoisted the wrong way up, which literally means that you are in distress; but people put it that way by mistake or from ignorance. You will notice that the red diagonal arms of the flag have a narrow white band on one side of them and a broad one on the other. Well, the broad one should be to the top of the flag on the side nearest to the flagpost, that is the 'hoist' of the flag, and towards the bottom of the flag in the loose end, or, as it is called, the 'fly' of the flag. (See picture, Part I, page 27.)

It was called a 'Jack', either from 'Jacques', the nickname of King James I, who first started it; or, more probably, from the 'jack' or 'jacket', which the knights used to wear over their armour to show which nation they belonged to. The English knights wore a white Jack with the red cross of St George upon it. This was also their flag.

If the flag is flown upside down it is a signal of distress. If it is half-mast it is a sign of mourning.

On going on board a man-of-war, when you reach the quarter-deck—that is the upper stern deck—always salute the ensign.

In the Navy, flags are hoisted at eight o'clock and saluted. With the Boy Scouts when in camp the same practice will be observed.

Of course you will always rise and salute or take off your hat on hearing the National Anthem played.

The 24th of May, the birthday of the great Queen Victoria, is 'Empire Day', and we all hoist the flag and salute in special honour of the Empire on that occasion.

Remember it is going to be the business of everyone of you to keep the old flag flying, even if you have to bleed for it—just as your forefathers did before you.

We have all got to die some day; a few years more or less of our own lives don't make much matter in the history of the world, but it is a very great matter if by dying a year or two sooner than we should otherwise do from disease we can help to save the flag of our country from going under.

Therefore think it over—BE PREPARED to die for your country if need be; so that when the moment arrives you may charge home with confidence, not caring whether you are going to be killed or not.

If your enemy sees that you are bent on either killing or being killed, the probability is that he won't wait to oblige you.

Don't merely talk, like some gas-bags do, about shedding the last drop of your blood for your country—the difficulty with them, when the time comes, is to get them to shed the FIRST drop of their blood.

The Union Jack stands for something more than only the Union of England, Ireland, and Scotland—it means the Union of Great Britain with all our Colonies across the seas; and also it means closer comradeship with our brothers in those Colonies, and between ourselves at home. We must all be bricks in the wall of that great edifice—the British Empire—and we must be careful that we do not let our differences of opinion on politics or other questions grow so strong as to divide us. We must still stick shoulder to shoulder as Britons if we want to keep our position among the nations; and we must make ourselves the best men in the world for honour and goodness to others so that we may DESERVE to keep that position.

> Unite the Empire; make it stand compact,
> Shoulder to shoulder let its members feel
> The touch of British Brotherhood, and act
> As one great nation—strong and true as steel.*

OUR GOVERNMENT

Of all the different kinds of government in the world, ours is the easiest and fairest for everybody.

Some countries have kings who make their laws for them whether the people like the laws or not; other countries make their own laws, but have not a king or a head who can carry on dealings on equal terms with other foreign countries.

With us the wants of the people are remedied through Parliament. The House of Commons is made up of men chosen by the people to make known their wants and to suggest remedies, and the House of Lords sees whether these are equally good for all and for the future of the country; and what they recommend the King makes into law.

When you grow up you will become voters and have a share in putting members into the House of Commons.

And you will many of you be inclined to belong to Conservative or Liberal or Radical or other parties, whichever your father or friends belong to. I should not if I were you. I should hear what each party has to say. If you listen to one party you will certainly agree that that is the only right one, the rest must all be wrong. But if you go and listen to another you will find that after all that one is quite right, and the first one wrong.

The thing is to listen to them all and don't be persuaded by any particular one, for they all tell fibs; they each want to get into power. And then be a man, make up your mind and decide for yourself which you think is best for the country and future of the Empire—not for some two-penny-halfpenny little local question—and vote for that one so long as it works the right way, namely, for the good of the country.

Many people get led away by some new politician with some new extreme idea. Never believe in one man's idea till it has been well considered from all points of view. Extreme ideas are seldom much good; if you look them up in history you will see almost always they have been tried before somewhere.* The Socialists are right in wishing to get money more evenly distributed so that there would be no millionaires and no paupers, but everyone pretty well off.

But they go the wrong way to work; they want to fight all other people to get themselves up, instead of joining in with everybody in doing a great thing for the whole country by a way which is fair and good for all. They do not read history, which shows that their plans have been tried before, and failed, because they made life a kind of slavery for everybody, and left the country an easy prey to another stronger one.

More thrift rather than change of government will bring money to all. And a strong united Empire, where all are helpful and patriotic will bring us power, peace, and prosperity such as no Socialistic dream could do.

OUR KING

THE word Empire comes from an old Roman word 'Imperium', which means 'well-ordered rule'.

And the title Emperor or ruler of the Empire, comes from the Roman word 'Imperator'. The King signs himself 'R. I', which means 'Rex', or King of England, and 'Imperator' or Emperor of India and the Colonies.

Imperator comes from two Roman words, 'Im' and 'Parere', which together mean 'To prepare for'—that is, to BE PREPARED.* An Emperor is one who has to be prepared to face any difficulty or danger that may threaten the country.

Scouts have in the same way to BE PREPARED to *help* their country in any difficulty or danger; and, therefore, we are all or should be working to back up our King for the good of our country.

GOD SAVE THE KING.

BOOKS TO READ

'The Union Jack and How It Was Made', by F. Wintour. One penny. (St Dunstan's Road, West Kensington, London, W.)

Leaflets at one penny from the Empire Day Association, 83, Lancaster Gate, London, W.

'History of the British Empire', by Arnold-Forster. (Cassell.)

[PART VI]*

NOTES for INSTRUCTORS

SUMMARY

The Empire wants your help.

Bad citizenship, which ruined the Roman Empire, is creeping in among us to-day.

The future of our Empire will much depend on the character of the rising generation. For this too little is at present being done in the way of development.

Peace Scouting is suggested as an attractive means towards developing character and good citizenship.

Can be carried out by young men of all kinds without expense, each training a few boys.

Experiment has already been successful.

Hints to would-be instructors for carrying out the training.

Books to read on the subject.

PLAY THE GAME: DON'T LOOK ON

EVERY Briton who is worth his salt would like to help his country:

Firstly, if he thought it was wanted.

Secondly, if he saw a way by which he could do it.

THE BRITISH EMPIRE WANTS YOUR HELP

OUR great Empire is to-day to the rest of the world very much what the Roman Empire was two thousand years ago. But the Roman Empire, great as it was, fell.

'The same causes which brought about the fall of the great Roman Empire are working to-day in Great Britain.'

These words were lately spoken by one of our best-known democratic politicians,* and they have been confirmed in a recent lecture at Cambridge by Mr Warde Fowler* as also in various pamphlets and writings. That they are true is practically admitted by those who have studied and compared the general conditions of both countries.

FALL OF THE ROMAN EMPIRE WAS DUE TO BAD CITIZENSHIP

THE main cause of the downfall of Rome is similar to that which resulted in the downfall of other great empires, such as the Babylonian, Egyptian, Greek, Spanish, and Dutch, and that cause may be summed up in each case as the decline of good citizenship and the want of energetic patriotism. Each nation, after climbing laboriously to the zenith of its power, seemed then to become exhausted by its effort, and sit down in a state of repose, relapsing into idleness, studiously blind to the fact that other nations were gradually pushing up to destroy it. It is easy to push historical parallels too far, and whether or not these parallels are real or exaggerated, they give us food for reflection. The main point is for us to take the lesson to heart, and see, before it is too late, that our Empire also be not undermined by these defects.

Instruction of Boy Scouts. 'Boyhood of Raleigh', after Sir J. Millais. From such instruction was a great character formed

I am not so pessimistic myself as to think with some people that we are already so far on the downward grade as to be in a hopeless condition. On the contrary, I think that we are only near to the parting of the ways where it becomes incumbent upon everyone of us who has the slightest patriotism in him to earnestly help, in however small a way, to turn the rising generation on the right road for good citizenship.

The aim may seem too big to attain, but most big things are only got by combination of small efforts. A coral island is erected by the work of myriads of sea-insects, the Pyramids of Egypt were the result of co-operation of thousands of workers.

BAD CITIZENSHIP IS BECOMING APPARENT IN THIS COUNTRY TO-DAY

ONE form of bad citizenship among many is evident around us on the part of the people themselves, who, not having been taught to think of the future, or of their country, allow themselves to come under the despotic power of a few professional agitators whose living depends on agitating (whether it is needed or not); and, blinded by the talk of these men, they attack the hand that finds the money, till they force employers to spend fortunes, either in devising machinery that will take their place and not go on strike, or in removing their business to other countries, leaving the agitators fat and happy, and a mass of people unemployed and starving, and unable to provide for the crowds of children they continue improvidently to bring into the world.

FOOTBALL

ONE of the causes of the downfall of Rome was that the people, being fed by the State to the extent of three-quarters of the population, ceased to have any responsibility for themselves or their children, and consequently became a nation of unemployed wasters. They frequented the circuses, where paid performers appeared before them in the arena, much as we see the crowds now flocking to look on at paid players playing football.

Football in itself is a grand game for developing a lad physically and also morally, for he learns to play with good temper and unselfishness, to play in his place and 'play the game', and these are the best of training for any game of life. But it is a vicious game when it draws crowds of lads away from playing the game themselves to be merely onlookers at a few paid performers. I yield to no one in enjoyment of the sight of those splendid specimens of our race, trained to perfection, and playing faultlessly; but my heart sickens at the reverse of the medal—thousands of boys and young men, pale, narrow-chested, hunched-up, miserable specimens, smoking endless cigarettes, numbers of them betting, all of them learning to be hysterical as they groan or cheer in panic unison with their neighbours—the worst sound of all being the hysterical scream of laughter that greets any little trip or fall of a player. One wonders whether this can be the same nation which had gained for itself the reputation of being a stolid, pipe-sucking manhood, unmoved by panic or excitement, and reliable in the tightest of places.

Get the lads away from this—teach them to be manly, to play the game whatever it may be, and not be merely onlookers and loafers.

Indifferent citizenship is, and always has been, the progeny of indifferent government. With it there arises a crop of doctors to suggest remedies: faddists on feeding, faddists on Socialism, faddists like myself on scouting, and so on. Some may be right, some wrong; all mean well. A certain class of Socialist, for instance, has come to the fore lately. As a matter of fact we are all Socialists in that we want to see the abolition of the existing brutal anachronism of war, and of extreme poverty and misery shivering alongside of superabundant wealth, and so on; but we do not quite agree as to how it is to be brought about. Some of us are for pulling down the present social system, but the plans for what is going to be erected in its place are very hazy. We have not all got the patience to see that improvement is in reality gradually being effected before our eyes.

We have a parallel in London just now in the several railway stations, which, having been found to be out of date and inadequate for their increased traffic, are being reconstructed. The Man in the Street has demanded that they should be pulled down at once, and that afterwards something better should be devised and built up. But the management have been wiser; they have recognised the defects of the old, but before pulling down they have seen that it would be fatal to stop traffic during the alterations, and have therefore laid the new foundations outside the old; they have erected the new buildings over the effete ones, and have then pulled these away piecemeal, without interrupting the public convenience, trade, or routine for a moment.

It is easy to pull down; the difficulty is to do so without damage to the country. We ought to begin by building up on a sounder foundation before destroying the old.

OUR FUTURE CITIZENS

THAT foundation seems to me to be in the rising generation. If the whole of our youth were taken in hand and taught good citizenship, we should have a solid foundation on which our nation could stand for a long time to come. But it does not exist at present.

We have at the present time in Great Britain two million boys, of whom one-quarter to one-half a million are under good influences outside their school walls.

(See Sir John Gorst's 'Children of the Nation'* and Dr Macnamara's Report.*)

	2,000,000	boys.
	270,000	under good influence.
Remainder =	1,730,000	independent of such.

The remainder are drifting towards 'hooliganism' or bad citizenship for want of hands to guide them the right way towards being useful.

It is this remainder, nearly two million boys, that we want to tackle and reduce.

They are boys, full of spirit and enthusiasm, approaching the cross-road, where they take the turn, either to good or evil. In spite of the improved school teaching and of the good work of Boys' and Church Lads' Brigades, Y.M.C.A., and kindred associations, a large proportion of them are drifting, owing to their environments, to evil, that is, to becoming 'hooligans' and ultimately 'wasters' for the natural term of their lives; no good to themselves, worse than no good to their country, just from want of a guiding hand or two at the turning point of their career.

Cannot we find these guiding hands amongst us?

PEACE-SCOUTING*

HERE is one suggestion, at any rate, for a remedy by which every young man can help his country. I believe that under the attractive term and practice of 'Scouting', a large number of boys might be taken in hand in a practical way, by every young man, without expense in time or money.

By 'scouting' I do not mean the military work as carried on on active service. The scouting we are considering has nothing to do with this. There is another form, which one might term 'peace-scouting', such as is usual with frontiersmen of our Empire in every corner of the world. The pioneers of civilisation in Central Africa; the ranchmen, cowboys, and trappers of the West; the drovers and bushmen of Australia; the explorers of the Arctic and Asiatic regions; the hunters and prospectors of South Africa; missionaries in all parts of the uncivilised world; and the constabularies of North-West Canada, South Africa, etc., are all 'peace-scouts', men accustomed to live on their own resources, taking their lives in their hands, brave and loyal to their employers, chivalrous and helpful to each other, unselfish and reliable; MEN, in fact, of the best type. These are the peace-scouts of the Empire, and there is no reason why we should not train a large number of boys to follow in their footsteps as regards character and manliness.

A small book* which I published a short time ago on the subject of scouting for soldiers has been so freely taken up by schools and boys' clubs in England* that I am encouraged to think a system organised for the special purpose of teaching boys would be acceptable, and I am still further encouraged in the idea by the fact that a somewhat similar organisation founded by Mr Ernest Thompson Seton in America has had a full and widespread success.

MILITARISM

TWO or three prominent authorities have written deprecating my attempt to 'foster among the boys of Britain a bloodthirsty and war-like spirit'.

I can only fear that either these gentlemen have not read the handbooks very carefully, or that I have expressed myself very badly. The whole intention of the Boy Scouts' training is for peaceful citizenship.

Even if I had advocated training the lads in a military way (which I have not done), I am impenitent enough to see no harm in it. I have not noticed that ex-soldiers are more inclined than other people to commit murders; all that I see in them, as a rule, is that they have been taught self-discipline, to sacrifice themselves, if need be, for others, to obey orders, to be sober, clean, and active, to make the best of things as they find them, to be loyal to themselves and their officers. All of which appear to me to be valuable assets in character for a citizen, whatever may be his grade or trade.

The fact that industrial employers now prefer ex-soldiers in very many of their departments speaks to the peace value of a military training. But when an eminent public man wrote to me that I ought not to teach boys soldiering because, as he puts it, 'he hates war like the devil', I felt bound to reply that had he actually seen anything of war himself, he would, like most soldiers, hate it *worse* than the devil. It is for that very reason that officers almost without exception urge upon their fellow countrymen to be prepared to defend their country. It is not that they wish to make the men bloodthirsty, but it is that they may avert from our own land that worst of all modern anachronisms—the horrors of war, brought on to our own homes, our women and children.

Those who preach shutting our eyes to what is quite patent to all who dare to look out will themselves be guilty of tempting the enemy on, of bringing war upon our country, and of the blood and ruin which will assuredly follow—if there is any truth in history.

With our rising generation brought up as good citizens, sensible of their responsibilities and duties in return for the benefits which they enjoy in a free country, there would be no danger for the State; but without manliness and good citizenship we are bound to fall.

Manliness can only be taught by men, and not by those who are half men, half old women.

HOW TO TEACH SCOUTING

THE first point is to get men to take up the instruction of the boys in the art of peace-scouting. The men I have in my mind as the best qualified and able to do this are schoolmasters, clergymen, members of the Y.M.C.A., Legion of Frontiersmen, officers of Cadet Corps, Boys' and Church Lads' Brigades, Rifle Clubs, country squires, ex-army officers, telegraph-masters, etc. These could carry out the training of a few boys apiece, with very little expense of time or money, by devoting, say, Saturday afternoons and Sundays to the work, which, I can promise them, they will find a pleasure rather than a labour in practice.

My suggestion to them would be for each to select a party of six or eight youths or smart boys, and carefully instruct them in the details of peace-scouting. These boys could then act as assistant instructors or 'patrol leaders' in training each five or six more in the same art in the progressive course of instruction in this handbook.

The instruction is designed for boys of every class.

> To help the lowest from drifting into hooliganism and to give them health, character, and aims.
>
> To teach the middle class how to work well, and to be patriotic first and political second.
>
> To teach the wealthier to be chivalrous and sympathetic with their less-favoured brothers, and ultimately to help in spreading the training.

One wants to bring all classes more in touch with each other, to break down the existing barriers, which are only artifical after all, and to teach them to give and take in the common cause instead of being at snarls of class against class, which is snobbery all round and a danger to the State.

The training is applicable to town or country, indoors as well as out.

Not in Opposition to Existing Organisations for Boys

The scheme is not in any way intended to be in opposition to any existing organisation. On the contrary, we want amalgamation rather than rivalry, and scouting is only intended to be used as an additional attraction by those in charge of boys' organisations of any kind. If scouting is taken up by several it may prove a bond between all. Where such organisations do not already exist it can supply a particularly simple and effective one for catching a number of boys who would otherwise have no hand to guide them.

Experimental Camp*

I have already made a preliminary trial of the scheme with a camp of boys of all sorts* from Eton as well as from the streets, and the results were such as to encourage very great hopes as to the possibilities of the scheme when carried out on a larger scale. A large island was lent for the purpose by the late Mr Charles Van Raalte,* Brownsea Island, near Poole.

Patrol System

The troop of boys was divided up into 'Patrols' of five, the senior boy in each being Patrol Leader. This organisation was the secret of our success. Each patrol leader was given full responsibility for the behaviour of his patrol at all times, in camp and in the field. The patrol was the unit for work or play, and each patrol was camped in a separate spot. The boys were put 'on their honour' to carry out orders. Responsibility and competitive rivalry were thus at once established, and a good standard of development was ensured throughout the troop from day to day. The troop was trained progressively in the subjects of scouting given on pages 9 to 10. Every night one patrol went on duty as night picket—that is, drew rations of flour, meat, vegetables, tea, etc., and went out to some indicated spot to bivouac for the night. Each boy had his greatcoat and blankets, cooking pot and matches. On arrival at the spot, fires were lit and suppers cooked, after which sentries were posted and bivouac formed. The picket was scouted by patrol leaders of other patrols and myself, at some time before eleven p.m., after which the sentries were withdrawn and picket settled down for the night.

Method of Instruction

We found the best way of imparting theoretical instruction was to give it out in short instalments with ample illustrative examples when sitting round the camp fire or otherwise resting, and with demonstrations in the practice hour before breakfast. A formal lecture is apt to bore the boys.

The practice was then carried out in competitions and schemes.

For example, take one detail of the subject, 'Observation'—namely, tracking.

1. At the camp fire overnight we would tell the boys some interesting instance of the value of being able to track.

2. Next morning we would teach them to read tracks by making foot-marks at different places, and showing how to read them and to deduce their meaning.

3. In the afternoon we would have a game, such as 'deer-stalking', in which one boy went off as the 'deer', with half-a-dozen tennis balls in his bag. Twenty minutes later four 'hunters' went off after him, following his tracks, each armed with a tennis

ball. The deer, after going a mile or two, would hide and endeavour to ambush his hunters, and so get them within range; each hunter struck with his tennis ball was counted gored to death; if, on the other hand, the deer was hit by three of their balls he was killed.

This was our principle for teaching most of the items.

Discipline was very satisfactory indeed. A 'court of honour' was instituted to try any offenders against discipline, but it was never needed. In the first place, the boys were put 'on their honour' to do their best: in the second place, the senior boys were made responsible for the behaviour of the boys forming their patrol. And this worked perfectly well.

Results of the Camp Experiment

Since this experimental camp I am more than ever convinced of the possibilities which underlie the scouts' training as an educator for boys of all classes.* Prepared as I was for enthusiastic endeavour on the part of the lads, I was surprised at the effect on their character, which became visible even in the few days we were at work. I have not trusted merely to my own observation, but have had reports from all the parents, bearing out this conclusion, and giving incidentally some very useful hints from the parents' point of view. That the boys enjoyed the training is evident from the letters which I have had from them, and some of them, at any rate, have remembered what they learnt. One of the boys— a working boy—writes: 'The most important thing that a great many boys need to learn is to look at the bright side of things, and to take everything by the smooth handle. I myself found that a great lesson, and I shall never find words enough to thank you for teaching me it. I have already found it a great help even in everyday life.'

AUTHORITIES WHO MIGHT FIND THE SCHEME USEFUL

Lord Mayors and Mayors.—This scheme might suggest some useful forms of instruction for the newly-authorised vacation schools.

Schoolmasters and Teachers.—This scheme may, I hope, supply an additonal means by which to get hold of the more unruly boys and to continue out of hours the practice of the theory which they have learnt in school. Unruly boys are often the best, once you have got the right side of them.* A Commission on our schools has recently shown that there is an excess of book instruction in many of them; possibly if one day a week were devoted to scouting it would greatly benefit both the teachers and the scholars mentally and physically.

CLERGYMEN.—Clergymen would, I think, find in scouting a good means of keeping the wilder spirits among their boys in some kind of order, and also of arousing the loafers among them into some sort of energy and interest in life.

PARENTS.—Parents might be apprehensive that this course would lead their sons to imbibe too much the spirit of adventure and romance, and those whose sons are wage-earners would fear for their getting unsettled and wasting their working hours on a useless fad. But to such I would point out that the course is purposely designed to teach the boys useful knowledge in a form that will attract them, and it can be carried out entirely on Saturday afternoons and Sundays as a counter-attraction to that Sunday loafing which is the ruin of so large a proportion of our young men.

LADIES.—To ladies interested in the care and education of girls, I think this scheme might supply a suggestion for an attractive organisation and valuable training. The experiment of a somewhat similar camp for factory girls has been such an unqualified success as to lead one to hope that scouting camps might with advantage be employed for the rising generation of girls as well as boys.

BOYS' CLUBS AND BRIGADES.—Officers of Boys' Clubs, Boys' Brigades, Church Lads' Brigades, University and Public Schools Missions, Cricket Clubs, and Cadet Corps, but most especially officers of Rifle Clubs, will, I hope, find in this scheme an additional means of attracting recruits and of maintaining their interest in their corps after the first glamour of it has worn off.

LEGION OF FRONTIERSMEN.—The Legion includes many an old scout in its ranks who could at once take up the instruction of a few boys and youths and do really valuable work for the Empire, while reviving for himself many a delightful experience of camp and prairie life.

Ex-Army Officers.—Then there are a number of ex-Army officers, keen and capable, but without occupation, who would here have a great opportunity for the exercise of their special gifts and of their prestige among boys for doing a great national good with very little trouble and expense to themselves.

Country Squires.—Members of county families might do much among their tenants and villagers by making good Englishmen of their lads, somewhat on the old feudal lines, by means of scouting.

Y.M.C.A.—Everyone recognises the keenness and go-a-head manliness of the members of the Y.M.C.A. and Polytechnics in all parts of the kingdom, and I am convinced that if these men could see their way to do a good turn to the rising generation of their countrymen they would take it up with ardour, especially since this kind of work is becoming a part of their policy. It is these gentlemen that I have specially in my eye in suggesting this scheme, as being the men who can, if they wish, get hold of practically the whole of the British boyhood by means of scouting. If every member of the Y.M.C.A. took a friend as his second-in-command and six boys as pupils, each of them being required to bring in another recruit, and then acting as leaders and instructors to further patrols of six, there would at once be the commencement of a great 'snowball' movement for good.

HINTS TO INSTRUCTORS

I do not in these 'Hints' propose to teach my grandmother to suck eggs, and, therefore, I only address them to those who have had no previous practice in teaching boys. They are merely a few notes from my own experience in that line, and tend to explain some of the arrangement of details in the Handbook.

When you are trying to get boys to come under good influence you are as a fisherman wishful to catch fish.

If you bait your hook with the kind of food that you like yourself it is probable that you will not catch many—certainly, not the shy, game kind of fish. You, therefore, use as bait the food that the fish likes.

So with boys, if you try to preach to them what you consider elevating matter you won't catch them. Any obvious 'goody-goody' will scare away the more spirited among them, and those are the ones you want to get hold of. The only way is to hold out something that really attracts and interests them. And I think you will find that scouting does this.

You can afterwards season it with what you want them to have.

To get hold of your boys you must be their friend; but don't be in too great a hurry at first to gain this footing until they have got over their shyness of you. Mr F. D. How, in his 'Book of the Child',* sums up the right course in the following story:

'A man whose daily walk led him down a certain dingy street saw a tiny boy with grimy face and badly-developed limbs playing with a banana-skin in the gutter. The man nodded to him—the boy shrank away in terror. Next day the man nodded again. The boy had decided there was nothing to be afraid of, and spat at the man. Next day the little fellow only stared. The day after he shouted "Hi!" as the man went on. In time the little fellow smiled back at the greeting which he now began to expect. Finally the triumph was complete when the boy—a tiny chap—was waiting at the corner and seized the man's fingers in his dirty little fist. It was a dismal street, but it became one of the very brightest spots in all that man's life.'

'BE PREPARED'

In this book I suggest as subjects to teach your boys such things as Observation of Details and consequent ability to read character and thereby to gain sympathy, the value of patience and cheery good temper, the duty of giving up some of one's time and pleasure for helping one's country and fellow men, and the inner meaning of our motto 'Be Prepared'.

But as you come to teach these things you will very soon find (unless you are a ready-made angel) that you have to acquire them yourself before you can succeed with the boys, and when once this is accomplished the occupation is intensely interesting and improving.

You must 'Be Prepared' yourself for disappointments at first, though you will as often as not find them outweighed by unexpected successes.

You must from the first 'Be Prepared' for the prevailing want of concentration of mind on the part of boys, and if you then frame your teaching accordingly I think you will have very few disappointments. Do not expect them to pay great attention to any one subject for very long until you have educated them to do so. You must meet them half-way and not give them too long a dose of one drink—a short, pleasing sip of one kind and then off to another, gradually lengthening the sips till they become steady draughts.

Thus a formal lecture on the subject which you want to practise very soon palls on them, their thoughts begin to wander and they get bored because they have not learnt the art of switching their mind where they want it to be and *holding it there*.

This making the mind amenable to the will is one of the important inner points in our training.

For this reason it is well to think out beforehand each day what you want to say on your subject and then bring it out a bit at a time as opportunity offers—at the camp fire or in intervals of play and practice, not in one long set address.

The lectures in this book are broken up into sections for this purpose.

Frequent practical demonstrations and practices should be sandwiched in between the sections of the lectures to hold the attention of the boys and to drive home your theory.

CLUBROOM

HALF the battle is to get a room lent for certain nights in the week, or hired as a club for the scouts, even if they only consist of a patrol in a village.

It must be well lit and well ventilated to prevent depression and boredom. Pictures of incidents (not landscapes or old portraits) help to make attraction.

A *bright* fire in winter.

Interesting illustrated books and magazines.

This can generally be got, furniture, games, etc., being given in the first instance by well-wishers.

A coffee-bar, commencing on the smallest lines, will generally succeed, and if carefully managed may develop a regular income for the upkeep of the clubroom.

The scouts themselves must do the cleaning and decorating, and making furniture.

Discipline and good order should be kept inside the room, and neatness insisted on, Patrol leaders being made responsible, Patrols taking it in turn to be responsible for cleanliness and good order of the room for a week at a time.

If a bit of ground, even waste ground or a backyard, is available as club ground so much the better. You want some place where the scouts can make huts, light fires, play basket-ball, make tracks, etc.

Make the boys themselves manage the club affairs, as far as possible, by committees, and putting boys in responsible charge of room, equipment, papers, etc. Sit back yourself and let them make their mistakes at first till they learn sense and responsibility. Committee and annual meetings are very useful for giving self-respect and responsibility to a number of boys.

In America small, self-managed boys' clubs are becoming exceedingly numerous and popular in all towns and villages. And the education authorities help them by allowing them the use of classrooms in the school buildings in the evenings. This might easily be done in England too.

At the same time, when you can get your own clubroom, no matter how small, it gives the boys more a sense of proprietorship and responsibility, especially if they have taken a hand themselves in making the furniture, putting up pictures, etc.

The clubroom must not be made cosy like a lady's boudoir, as the boys must be able to romp in it occasionally, or play handball or 'Bang the Bear', etc. So you want furniture that will pack away into a corner, such as folding wooden chairs, small tables, and a cupboard in which to put away books, games, etc., when the romp comes on.

The ideal club is one of two rooms—one for quiet games, reading and talking; the other for romping, gymnastics, etc.

The boys must of course pay subscription towards rent, lighting, furnishing, etc., and the major expenses must be provided for by means of some joint work by them, such as garden produce, toys, displays or bazaars (as described in 'Scouting Games', below).

One penny weekly, paid strictly in advance, is sufficient as a membership subscription.

A Penny Savings Bank should be started to enable boys to put by money to pay for outings and eventually to start them in the practice of thrift.

A piano is of great help in a club, if you have some one who can play it, to help out with songs, musical drill, war dances, etc.

THE HANDBOOK

THE Handbook is merely intended to offer suggestions, not to tie instructors to one set course.

In such brief space it can only touch sketchily upon subjects whose detail as instructor you must fill in for yourself, according to your own imagination and resourcefulness, to suit your particular local circumstances.

I give with each lecture the titles of books bearing on the subject, to which you can probably get access in your public library, but you will also find every day as you read your newspaper fresh things worth cutting out to use in your lectures. Indeed, if you are ever hard up for a subject, take the leading news items of the past week, and explain them in an interesting way with maps, etc.

I have found the value of this also in dealing with grown-ups in men's clubs, hospitals, etc.

The 'History of England' by H. O. Arnold-Forster* will at all times give you useful subjects in most interesting form. For your own information read 'Duty', by Samuel Smiles.*

I have endeavoured to make the Handbook readable by the boy himself, since a boy should be encouraged to read for himself. The worst of it is that the literature to which as a rule he has access is the cheap and nasty press with little else than crimes and tragedies and big football matches to catch his attention.

He thus becomes educated downwards instead of being elevated by good examples to higher deeds.

The reading of such books as 'Golden Deeds', 'Deeds that Won the Empire',* and so on, are the best of antidotes, especially if impressed by means of modern examples, illustrations and lantern slides, and acting the incidents.

COURSE OF INSTRUCTION

I SUGGEST the following scheme of work, to be altered according to local circumstances.

Give a week to each chapter of the book.

On Saturday evening give a lecture with practical demonstrations and, where possible, *with lantern slides*, on the subject of the following week's instruction.

Among the worst classes in our slums Sunday is, unfortunately, perhaps the most unholy day of the week, but by using it for instruction of the proposed kind I believe that a good proportion of these lads might be won and led to better things than the loafing and vice which are at present incidental to the day.

So, for such lads, I advocate using Sunday morning for teaching the minor practices, and the afternoon for the consequent scouting exercises.

It is true that this suggestion has been criticised in some quarters, but it has, in the end, been generally accepted on the plea that it makes for saving souls, for which work there need be no Sunday closing.

The details thus taught could then be carried out and perfected by the boys individually in their own time during the week, or by occasional parades when possible under their patrol leaders, till the following Saturday afternoon, when you could have a final competition or games on that subject before starting on the next chapter that evening.

This is only a suggestion on the supposition that you and your boys are at other work all the week. If you would thus devote eight Saturday afternoons and Sundays to this work you will have completed a course of instruction which will guide a number of boys for life, and will take them from that present school of loafing which is to be found, to our great disgrace, at the corner of every village street in England on Sunday afternoon.

If funds are then forthcoming amongst the boys, a camp of a week or ten days, or for two or three weekends in the summer, would complete their instruction and put it to a practical test, while serving as a great reward for good preliminary work. And it need not be very expensive if the boys work for it and save up, as suggested in Chapter IV.

As I have before remarked, the training laid down in this book is merely suggestive.

The instructor should use his own knowledge and imagination and enlarge upon it.

There is much useful technical knowledge which he might

incidentally impart to his boys, either himself or by getting friends to come and demonstrate (I don't say 'lecture') on such points as the principles of steam or petrol-engines, or electricity; the work of sailors, soldiers, firemen, police, and so on; pioneer work such as bridging with models, road making, building, etc., also carpentering, modelling, casting, plumbing, gardening, etc.

Excursions from town into country, and seeing farm life, mining, fisheries, etc.; or from country to town and visiting the Zoological Gardens, interesting portions of museums, picture-galleries, armouries, etc., would be valuable and popular.

With a carefully-laid programme of such items the scouts' training can be carried out indefinitely in an interesting way, and on lines that will be of use to them in their future career.

I even advocate taking the boys to a theatre to see something really good, as a very great inducement to them to save the money necessary to pay for their seats. It can be made the first step towards thrift.

METHOD OF INSTRUCTION

THE way to teach a language is not to bore your pupil at first with the dry bones of elementary grammar, but to plunge into fairly deep water with phrases and conversation; the grammar will then quickly follow of itself.

So also with most other subjects of instruction, including scouting. For instance, take tracking. After preparing the boys' minds with a few good tracking yarns and showing a few actual tracks and their meaning, don't wait till they get bored in trying to learn the elementary details, but take them for a real piece of practical tracking. After they have found out for themselves how weak they are at it, give them further 'sips' of the elementary part.

IMAGINATION

BOYS are full of romance, and they love 'make-believe' to a greater extent than they like to show.

All you have to do is to play up to this and to give rein to your imagination to meet their requirements. But you have to treat with all seriousness the many tickling incidents that will arise: the moment you laugh at a situation the boys are quick to feel that it is all a farce, and to lose faith in it forthwith and for ever.

For instance, in instructing a patrol to make the call of its tutelary

SIGNS AND CALLS OF DIFFERENT PATROLS

(A first list of calls was given in Part I, p. 45)

SIGN	NAME	CALL	COLOURS
	PEEWIT	*Whistle—'Peewit'*	GREEN AND WHITE
	WOOD-PIGEON	*Call—'Book-booroo'*	BLUE AND GREY
	CUCKOO	*Call—'Cook-koo'*	GREY
	LION	*Call—'Ee-ugh'*	YELLOW AND RED
	KANGAROO	*Australian—'Coo-ee'*	RED AND GREY

animal, the situation borders on the ridiculous, but if the instructor remains perfectly serious the boys work at it with the idea that it is 'business'—and once accomplished the call becomes a fetish for *esprit de corps* among the members of the patrol.

Bacon* said that play-acting was one of the best means of educating children, and one can quite believe him.

It develops the natural power in them of imitation, and of wit and imagination, all of which help in the development of character; and at the same time lessons of history and morality can be impressed on their minds far better by their assuming the characters and acting the incidents themselves than by any amount of preaching of the same on the part of the teacher.

The recent craze for historical pageants is, in reality, one of the best ideas, educationally, that has come over us of late years. In places where pageants have been held, both old and young have learnt—and learnt for the rest of their lives—something of the history of their forefathers, their town, and their country.

Instructors will similarly find it a genuinely useful practice to make their scouts act scenes from history or of incidents with which they desire to impress them. Such, for instance, as 'Wilson's last Stand', 'The Wreck of the *Birkenhead*', 'The Sentry at Pompeii', and so on.*

For this reason a few suggestions for pageants are given in 'Scouting Games', below.

It is also easy to get up real plays, such as *To Parents and Guardians* (See Messrs Samuel French's List), for which the organisation, rehearsals, and performance are all good, useful practice, especially in the long winter evenings. Begin with a small play first, such as *Box and Cox* or *The Area Belle*.*

When these performances attain some degree of merit they might be used as a means of gaining funds.

RESPONSIBILITY TO JUNIORS

THE great thing in this scheme is to delegate responsibility—mainly through the patrol leaders.

Have, if possible, a good Second in Command to yourself to ensure continuity of instruction should you be unable on occasions to be present yourself, and to relieve you of many minor details of administration.

Give full responsibility and show full confidence in your patrol leaders. Expect a great deal from them, and you will get it.

This is the key to success in scout-training.

Foster the patrol spirit and friendly rivalry between patrols and you will get immediate good results and an improved standard of the whole. Don't try to do everything yourself or the boys will merely look on, and the scheme will flag.

DISCIPLINE

INSIST on discipline and strict obedience; let them run riot only when you give leave for it, which is a good thing to do every now and then.

A nation to be powerful and prosperous must be well disciplined, and you only get discipline in the mass by discipline in the individual. By discipline I mean patient obedience to authority and to other dictates of duty.

This cannot be got by repressive measures, but by educating the boy first in self-discipline and in sacrificing of self and selfish pleasures for the benefit of others. This teaching is largely effected by means of example, and by expecting it of him. There lies our work.

Smiles gives in his book on 'Duty'* Baron Stoeffel's report comparing the discipline of the Germans and the French before the war, 1870–71, in which he foretold the victory of the Germans, on account of their superior discipline; and, in commenting on this, Mr Smiles writes:

'Can it be that we are undergoing the same process in England as in France; that the ever-extending tide of democracy is bearing down the best points of a very vain-glorious people?

'We are a very vain-glorious people.

'We boast of our wealth, our naval and military strength, and our commercial superiority. Yet all these may depart from us in a very few years, and we may remain, like Holland, a rich and yet powerless people. The nation depends on the individuals who compose it; and no nation can ever remain distinguished for morality, duty, adherence to the rules of honour and justice whose citizens, individually and collectively, do not possess the same traits.'

Sir Henry Knyvett,* in 1596, warned Queen Elizabeth that the State which neglects to train and discipline its youth produces not merely rotten soldiers or sailors, but the far greater evil of equally rotten citizens for civil life; or, as he words it, 'For want of true discipline the honour and wealth both of Prince and countrie is desperatlie and frivolouslie ruinated.'

Discipline is not gained by punishing a child for a bad habit, but by substituting a better occupation that will absorb his attention and gradually lead him to forget and abandon the old one.

RELIGION

AN organisation of this kind would fail in its object if it did not bring its members to a knowledge of religion—but the usual fault in such cases is the manner in which this is done. If it were treated more as a matter of everyday life and quite unsectarian, it would not lose its dignity and it would gain a hold. It is often the best not to have religious instruction as a special feature, but to introduce it by 'sips' here and there among other instruction, as I suggest in the chapter on 'Chivalry' and elsewhere in this book.

CONTINENCE*

IN the Handbook I have touched on many important items of a boy's education, but there is scarcely one more important than this, which, under advice, I have relegated from the body of the book to these 'Notes for Instructors'.

The training of the boy would be very incomplete did it not contain some clear and plain-spoken instructions on the subject of continence.

The prudish mystery with which we have come to veil this important question is doing incalculable harm.

The very secrecy with which we withhold all knowledge from the boy prompts him the more readily to take his own line, also secretly, and, therefore, injuriously.

I have never known a boy who was not the better for having the question put to him frankly and openly. It can quite well be done without indelicacy.

You can warn him that 'indulgence' or 'self-abuse' is a temptation more likely to assail him than any other vices, such as drinking, gambling, or smoking, and is more harmful than any of them, since it brings with it weakness of heart and head, and, if persisted in, idiocy and lunacy.

Show him that it is not even a manly vice, but is everywhere looked down upon with contempt; and that it can be overcome by determination and strength of will.

The temptation may arise from physical causes, such as eating rich foods, sleeping on the back in a soft bed with too many blankets on, or from constipation, or it may come from suggestion through pictures, stories, or dirty talk of others.

In any case, knowing their danger, these causes must be avoided, and the temptation met with a mental determination to fight it by substituting other thoughts, by washing in cold water, and by exercising the upper part of the body, with boxing or arm exercises, to draw away the blood, and so on.

The first occasion will be the difficult one, but once this is successfully overcome subsequent attacks will be more easy to deal with.

If the boy still finds difficulty about it he should come and speak quite openly to his officer, who can then advise him what to do.

But for an instructor to let his boys walk on this exceedingly thin ice without giving them a warning word, owing to some prudish sentimentality, would be little short of a crime.

HINTS TO INSTRUCTORS

PRIGGISHNESS or conceit is sure to come to some of your boys as they find themselves good at various games or branches of their work. These must be taken down by the skill and patience of the instructors. Don't get upset by having one or two of these to deal with, but, on the contrary, take it as a sporting adventure, and treat them as interesting subjects. It is far more satisfactory to turn one unruly character the right way than to deal with a dozen milk-and-water cases.

There are also boys who, though with other boys, are not of them. These need special individual study and special treatment, which will avail in almost every case.

Boys of rich parents need the training of a scout quite as much as any poor boy, and should, therefore, be taken in hand by those who are willing to deal with them.

In 'The Boy Problem'* it is shown how in the days of chivalry boys were pages to the esquires in order that they might learn knightly habits, and then they went to one of the young knight's castles to learn knightly ideas. In the same way boys of to-day need contact with chivalrous young men to make them into noble and courtly men.

FORMING CHARACTER

KEEP before your mind in all your teaching that the whole ulterior object of this scheme is to form character in the boys—to make them manly, good citizens.

For the individual it is useful, when describing a situation, to stop narration at the critical point and ask a boy what would be his action under the circumstances, in order to develop quick decision, and so on.

In the games it is of the greatest importance to so arrange that a boy imagines himself running a great danger in carrying out the mission given him. In this way he becomes accustomed to taking risks.

For the mass it is a useful practice frequently to give false alarms to see what they do and to accustom them to face sudden crises. Such alarms, for instance, as having smoke blown into the room and a sudden alarm of fire given, or getting a boy to rush in and report that Johnny Tomkins has fallen from a tree and hurt himself.

Instruction of the individual is the only really successful form of instruction.

In teaching your boy to be alert and energetic, teach him also how to be restful and not to worry.

The physical attitude of the natural man, as one sees it in the savage, is the one to cultivate in the boy in mind as well as body.

The normal attitude of the natural man is a graceful slackness of body, but with eyes and ears alert, able on the instant to spring like a cat from apparent inertness to steel-spring readiness.

Study the individual fads and characteristics of your boys, and, having found them, encourage their development on these directions; then when advising the boys as to their future line of life you will be in a position to direct the square boy to a square hole in the world, and the round boy to a round one. Don't, as many people do, make him aim for some sphere for which he is not really fitted. Aim for making each individual into a useful member of society, and the whole will automatically come on to a high standard.

One great cause of unemployment—in all walks of life in England—is the inability of our men to take up any line other than the one they have first attempted and failed in. We call a sailor the 'handy man' with admiration, because he seems to be the only kind of man among us who can turn his hand to any kind of job. Well, so can anyone if he only has the idea put into his head and tries it for himself. Our aim should be, therefore, to make the boys 'handy men'.

But most of all we want to raise the lowest to a higher place. 'Go for the worst' is the motto of the Salvation Army in its great work. 'Our mission is to the bottom dog' says Colonel Ruston, Mayor of Lincoln.

Mr A. J. Dawson, in his very able articles in the *Evening Standard*, has put the question of the loafer in clear and easy terms.

He points out that the very efficient work of our police in big cities has stopped thieves, but produced a class of criminally-inclined loafers.

'On the Canadian prairie,' he says, 'if a perfectly able-bodied man without means were deliberately to abstain from work for any considerable time he would die and would cease to cumber the earth.' But in London it is different; a man can loaf for months, or years, leaning against a public-house—and they do it by the hundreds. He assigns two reasons for this:

1. Want of discipline in the lives of those who are not absolute criminals.
2. Indiscriminate charity.

We want to save lads from drifting into this class of loafer who swells the ranks of the unemployed. The complaint has recently come from Canada that 'No Englishmen need apply for employment' there. The subsequent Canadian explanation was to the effect that the average type of Englishman who came there was unsuitable, because:

1. He had no idea of discipline.
2. He was generally surly and ready to grumble at difficulties.
3. He could not be relied upon to stick to a job the moment he found it at all distasteful.

These faults are, undoubtedly, very widespread among us, in all classes of society, owing to want of an education like that of the scouts. They are the result of putting self in the first place and ignoring duty or the interests of others; in other words, they mean *bad citizenship*.

CONCLUSION

I FEAR I have stated my hints in very long and formidable array, such as seem to make the instructor's part a very complicated and responsible one, but it is not so when you come to put them into practice. My hints are like the rows of oil-valves on a motor-car, they look complicated, but in reality they are intended to drop their oil automatically and make the wheels run easily.

I merely offer this scheme as one among many for helping in the vital work of developing good citizenship in our rising generation.

Every man of the present generation ought as a matter of duty to take a hand in such work.

This scheme purposes to be one by which any man can do this, since it requires but little time, expense, or knowledge; and it is one which attracts the boys and is at the same time interesting and beneficial to the instructor himself.

If you who read this are a man who has charge of boys in any way, or if you are one who has so far had nothing to do with them but who has a desire to see your country keep her place among the nations for the good of the world, and would take a hand by training half-a-dozen boys and putting them on the right road for good citizenship, you would be doing a great thing for your country, for your younger brothers, and for yourself.

BOOKS ON THE SUBJECT

'Boys of the Street and How to Win Them', by Charles Stelzle. (H. Revell, publisher.)

'The Boy Problem'. A study of boys and how to train them. By W. B. Forbush. (Progress Press, Boston, U.S.A.)

'The Teacher's Problem'. (Perry, Mason, & Co., Boston, Mass.)

'Duty', by Samuel Smiles.

'The Children of the Nation', by Sir John Gorst.

'The Citizen of To-morrow', by Samuel Keeble. (Kelly.)

'The Canker at the Heart', by L. Cope Cornford.

'The Child Slaves of Britain', by M. Sherard.

'The Abandoned Child', by Bramwell Booth.

Pamphlets (at 3d.) on training of children. Secretary, Moral Education Committee, 29, Bloomsbury Square, W.C.

Y.M.C.A. Junior Branch, 13 Russell Square, W.C.

National League of Workers with Boys, Toynbee Hall, London, E.C.

National Institution of Apprenticeship. Secretary, J. Ballin.

SCOUTING GAMES, PRACTICES, AND DISPLAYS

NOTES TO INSTRUCTORS

Instruction in scouting should be given as far as possible through practices, games, and competitions.

Games should be organised mainly as team matches, where the patrol forms the team, and every boy is playing, none merely looking on.

Strict obedience to the rules to be at all times insisted on as instruction in discipline.

The rules given in the book should be altered by instructors where necessary to suit local conditions.

The ideas given here are merely offered as suggestions, upon which it is hoped that instructors will develop further games, competitions, and displays.

Several of the games given here are founded on those in Mr Thompson Seton's 'Birchbark Roll of the Woodcraft Indians', called 'Spearing the Sturgeon' (Whale Hunt), 'Quick Sight' (Spotty-Face), 'Spot the Rabbit', 'Bang the Bear', 'Hostile Spy' (Stop Thief), etc.

A number of non-scouting games are quoted from the book 'Social—to Save'.

SCOUTCRAFT

PRACTICES AND GAMES.—Kim's Game, p. 48; Morgan's Game, p. 49; Scout's War Dance, p. 50; Scout's Rally, p. 41. Teach the scouts to look out trains in Bradshaw's Railway Guide.

'BOOM-A-TATA'.—Kindly supplied by Dr H. Kingston as a good marching rally.

Boom a-ra-ta-ta Boom a-ra-ta-ta
Boom a-ra-ta Chim a-ra-ta Boom- a-ra-ta-ta.
Dāh - ee dāh-ee dāh-ee Boom a-ra-ta-ta
Dah ee dah-ee dah-ee Chim a-ra-ta-ta
Dah - ee dah-ee dah-ee Boom a-ra-ta Chim a-ra-ta
Boom a-ra-ta Chim a-ra-ta Boom a-ra-ta-ta Boom. Boom. Boom.

TRACKING

Practices.—Street Observation, p. 73; Telling Character, p. 74; Scout's Nose, p. 76; Footmarks, pp. 79, 87, 88; Deduction, pp. 94, 95.

Display.—The Diamond Thief, p. 124.

Games.—Observation, pp. 74, 75, 76; Far and Near, p. 76; Spot the Thief, p. 88; Smugglers Over the Border, p. 88.

Alarm 'Stop Thief'.—This is similar to the game of 'Hostile Spy', in the 'Birchbark Roll of the Woodcraft Indians', by Mr Thompson Seton. A red rag is hung up in the camp or room in the morning: the umpire goes round to each scout in turn, while they are at work or play and whispers to him, 'There is a thief in the camp'; but to one he whispers, 'There is a thief in the camp, and you are he—Marble Arch', or some other well-known spot about a mile away. That scout then knows that he must steal the rag at any time within the next three hours, and bolt with it to the Marble Arch. Nobody else knows who is to be the thief, where he will run to, and when he will steal it. Directly anyone notices that the red rag is stolen, he gives the alarm, and all stop what they may be doing at the time, and dart off in pursuit of the thief. The scout who gets the rag or a bit of it wins. If none succeed in doing this, the thief wins. He must carry the rag tied round his neck, and not in his pocket or hidden away.

WOODCRAFT

Games and Practices.—Scout Hunting, Dispatch Running, Deer Stalking, Stalking and Reporting, see pp. 101, 102; Observation of Animals, p. 118; Lion Hunting, p. 118; Plant Race, p. 123; Scout meets Scout, p. 47.

'Track the Assassin'.—The assassin escapes after having stabbed his victim, carrying in his hand the dripping dagger. The remainder, a minute later, start out to track him by the drops of blood (represented by Indian corn or peas) which fall at every third pace. His confederate (the umpire) tells him beforehand where to make for, and if he gets there without being touched by his pursuers, over eight minutes ahead of them, he wins. If they never reach his confederate, neither side wins.

Relay Race.—One patrol pitted against another to see who can get a message sent a long distance in shortest time by means of relays of runners (or cyclists). The patrol is ordered out to send in three successive notes, or tokens (such as sprigs of certain plants), from a point, say, two miles distant or more. The leader in taking his patrol out to the spot drops scouts at convenient distances, who will then act as runners from one post to the next and back. If relays are posted in pairs messages can be passed both ways.

'Spider and Fly'.—A bit of country or section of the town about a mile square is selected as the web, and its boundaries described, and an hour fixed at which operations are to cease.

One patrol (or half-patrol) is the 'spider', which goes out and selects a place to hide itself.

The other patrol (or half-patrol) goes a quarter of an hour later as the 'fly' to look for the 'spider'. They can spread themselves about as they like, but must tell their leader anything that they discover.

An umpire goes with each party.

If within the given time (say about two hours) the fly has not discovered the spider, the spider wins. The spider writes down the names of any of the fly patrol that they may see; similarly the flies write down the names of any spiders that they may see and their exact hiding-place. Marks will be awarded by the umpires for each such report.

The two sides should wear different colours, or be differently dressed (*e.g.*, one side in shirt-sleeves).

'Throwing the Assegai'.—Target, a thin sack, lightly stuffed with straw, or a sheet of cardboard, or canvas stretched on a frame.

Assegais to be made of wands, with weighted ends sharpened, or with iron arrow-heads on them.

Display.—The Diamond Thief. See pp. 124–6.

Play.—*Wild Animal Play*, by Mrs E. Thompson Seton. A musical play, in which boys and girls take parts. Price 6d. (Publishers, Doubleday, Page, & Co., 133 East Sixteenth-street, New York.)

'Animal Artisans', by C. J. Cornish. 6s. (Longmans, Green.)

'Flag Raiding' (from 'Aids to Scouting', 1s. Gale & Polden).

Two or more patrols on each side.

Each side will form an outpost within a given tract of country to protect three flags (or at night three lanterns two feet above ground), planted not less than 200 yards (100 yards at night) from it. The protecting outpost will be posted in concealment either altogether or spread out in pairs not more than 80 yards apart. It will then send out scouts to discover the enemy's position. When these have found out where the outpost is they try and creep round out of sight till they can get to the flags and bring them away to their own line. One scout may not take away more than one flag.

This is the general position of a patrol on such an outpost:—

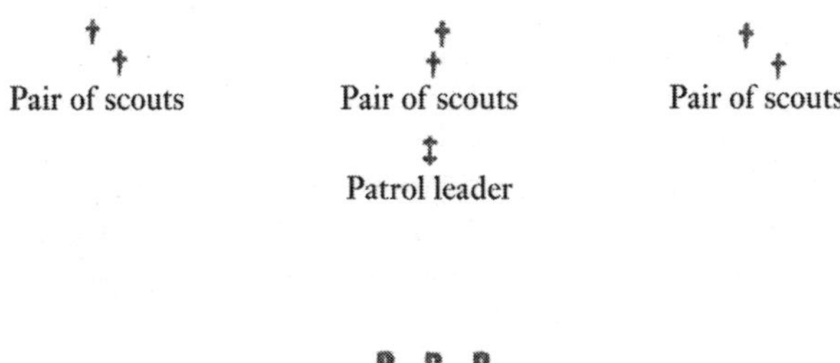

Any scout coming within 50 yards of a stronger party will be put out of action if seen by the enemy; if he can creep by without being seen it is all right.

Scouts posted to watch as outposts cannot move from their ground, but their strength counts as double, and they may send single messengers to their neighbours or to their own scouting party.

An umpire should be with each outpost and with each scouting patrol.

At a given hour operations will cease, and all will assemble at the given spot to hand in their reports. The following marks would be awarded:

For each flag or lamp captured and brought in	5 marks
For each report or sketch of the position of the enemy's outposts ...	Up to 5 marks
For each report of movement of enemy's scouting patrols	2 marks

The side which makes the biggest total wins.

CAMP LIFE

PRACTICES.—Knot-tying, pp. 128–30; hut building, p. 131; bridging, p. 133; self-measurement, p. 134; hurdle-making, p. 136; models, p. 136; handicrafts generally; camp furniture, p. 138; camp fires, p. 139; camp loom, p. 144; cooking, p. 145; making ration bags, p. 148; breadmaking, pp. 147, 148.

'The three B's of life in camp are the ability to cook bannock, beans, and bacon.'

HOW TO MAKE A TENT.—For 'Tee pee' or American Indian tent, see Thompson Seton's 'Birchbark Roll', 25 cents. (Doubleday, Page, & Co., New York.)

For light cyclists' tents, see 'The Camper's Handbook', by J. H. Holding; 'Boy Scout's' tent, with canvas and scouts' stoves. This is made simple and easy by the three pictures showing the different stages.

TO MAKE A LADDER WITH A POLE.—Tie firmly sticks, or tufts of twigs, or straw, across the pole at intervals to form steps.

HOW TO MAKE A SLEIGH.—See 'Camp Life', by Hamilton Gibson. 5s. (Harper.)

GAME.—*Food:* Name not less than twelve different kinds of wild food, such as you would find in Great Britain, supposing there were no supplies available from butchers, bakers, grocers, or greengrocers. N.B.—A pike or a trout are not considered different *kinds* of food for this competition.

FIRE-LIGHTING RACE.—To collect material, lay, and light a fire till the log given by umpire is alight.

BOOKS TO READ

(Additional to those mentioned on pp. 136, 162, etc.)

'The Camper's Handbook', by T. H. Holding. 5s. (Simpkin, Marshall, & Co.)

'The Young Marooners', by F. Goulding. 2s. (Nisbet.) A story of resourcefulness in camp, including raft-building, shoemaking, first aid, etc.

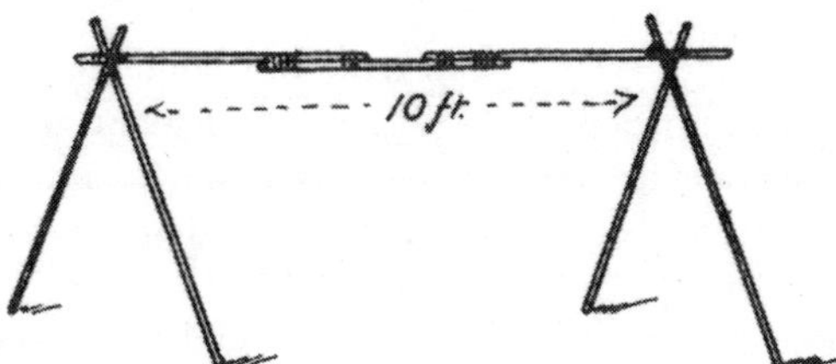

Frame of six scout's staves, and an extra joint to lengthen ridge-pole

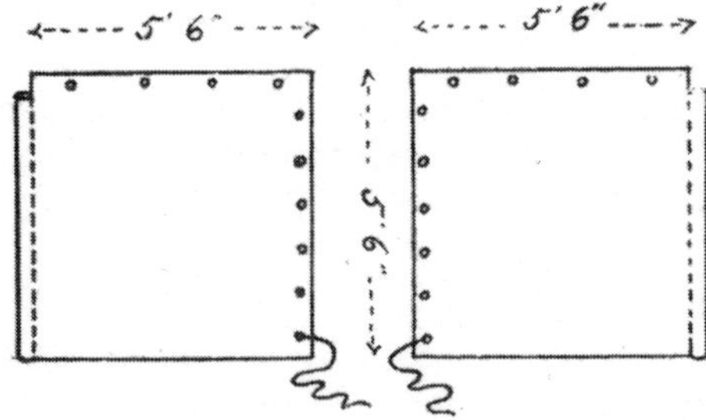

Six squares of canvas, 5 ft. 6 in. square, with eyelets and hemmed tube on one side. Each scout carries one, and can pack his kit in it if necessary, or use it as a cape in rain

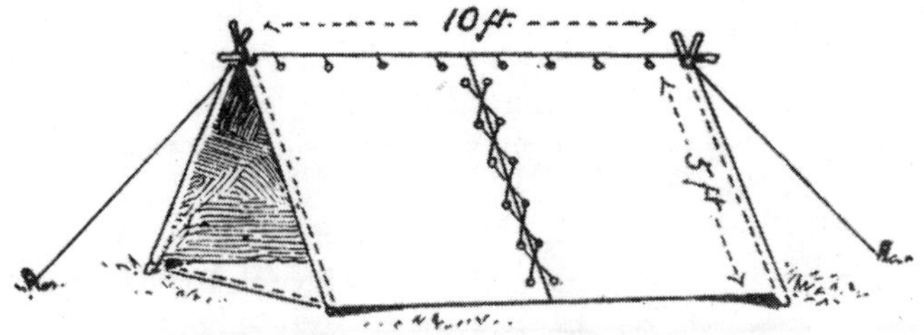

Boy Scout's tent for a patrol. Four canvas squares make the tent. Two make the ground sheet

HOW TO MAKE A TENT

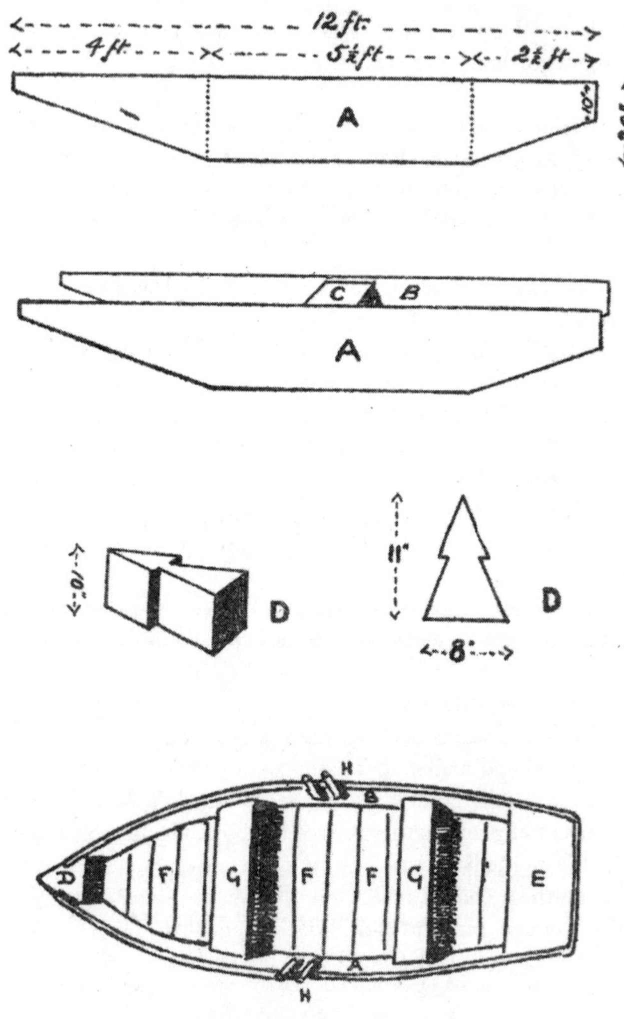

HOW TO MAKE A BOAT

'Carpentering and Cabinetmaking', by W. M. Oakwood. 1s. (C. A. Pearson.)

'Models and How to Make Them', by Cyril Hall. 1s. Including steam-engine, turbine, electric motor, etc.

N.B.—Before making a real article, whether tent, or boat, or other thing, to scale, it is almost always best to make a model on a small scale first—make an inch of model represent a foot of the real thing.

How to Make a Boat, from 'Camp Life', by Hamilton Gibson, 5s. (Harper).

Get two boards, A and B, 12 feet long, 20 inches wide, and ¾ inch thick. Cut them both as in the figure.

Nail a plank (C) between them at the centre to hold them in position, and a second similar plank below it.

Cut solid block of wood (D) to form the stem or bowpiece, and a stern board about 2 feet long, 10 inches deep.

Join the two bow ends of A and B by screwing them into the block D.

Join the two stern ends by screwing them to each end of the stern board, and strengthen by screwing stern seat (E) on to both sides and stern piece.

Turn the boat upside down, and screw on planks F F to form the bottom. Caulk the seams between these by driving in tow by means of a blunt chisel and mallet, and paint them with pitch, if necessary, to make them water-tight. Mark where the seats G G are to come, and nail pieces of plank to the sides of the boat, reaching to a height of one foot from the floor, to act as supports to the seats. Put the seats in resting on these chocks, and screw them to the sides. Screw a pair of strong wooden pins to each side of the boat (H H) to form rowlocks. Knock out plank C, and your boat is ready.

CAMPAIGNING AND PATHFINDING

Practices (see p. 160).—Mountain Climbing, Boat Management, Barometer and Thermometer Reading, Find the North, pp. 166–70; Judging Heights and Distances, pp. 164–6, 170–2, 180; Semaphore and Morse Signalling, pp. 175–7; Drill Signals, pp. 177–9;

Hiding Dispatches, Campaigning Tests, pp. 180–1; Exploration, p. 155.

GAMES.—Night Patrolling, p. 160; Whale Hunt, p. 161; Mountain Scouting, pp. 161–2; Star-gazing, p. 170; Judging Distance, pp. 170–2; Finding North, pp. 166–70; Dispatch Running, pp. 48, 180; Arctic Expedition, p. 46; Siberian Man Hunt, 47.

SCOUTING RACE.—Instructor stations three individuals or groups, each group differently clothed as far as possible, and carrying different articles (such as stick, bundle, paper, etc.) at distances from 300 to 1,200 yards from starting point. If there are other people about, these groups might be told to kneel on one knee, or take some such attitude to distinguish them from passers-by. He makes out a circular course of three points for the competitors to run, say about ¼ mile, with a few jumps if possible.

The competitors start and run to No. 1 point. Here the umpire tells them the compass-direction of the group they have to report on. Each competitor on seeing this group writes a report showing—

1. How many in the group.
2. How clothed or how distinguishable.
3. Position as regards any landmark near them.
4. Distance from his own position.

He then runs to the next point and repeats the same on another group, and so on; and finally he runs with his report to the winning post.

Marks.—Full marks, 5 for each correct and complete description of a group—that is an aggregate of 15 marks for the course. One mark deducted for every ten seconds later than the first boy handing in his report at the winning post. Marks or half marks deducted for mistakes or omissions in reports.

ON TREK.—Make a trek through Central Africa—each scout carrying his kit and food packed in a bundle on his head: walk in single file with scout 200 yards out in front and find the way; he makes scout signs as to the road to follow; make bridge over stream or raft over lake: corduroy or faggots in boggy ground: leave signs and notes for any parties who may follow by day or night.

To teach your scouts, individually, ideas of time and distance, send each out in a different direction on some such order as this. 'Go two miles to North-north-east. Write a report to show exactly where you are (with sketch map if possible, to explain it.) Bring in your report as quickly as possible.'

Then test by ordnance maps or otherwise to see how far he was out of the distance and direction ordered.

Send out scouts in pairs, to compete each pair against the other. Each pair to be started by a different route to gain the same spot, finding the way by map, and to reach the goal without being seen by the others on the way.

This develops map reading, eye for country, concealment, look-out, etc.

For judging time. Send out scouts in different directions, each with a slip of paper, to say how long he is to be away, say seven minutes for one, ten for another, and so on.

Note down his exact time of starting, and take it again on his return. Scouts must be put on their honour not to consult watches or clocks.

N.B.—Many of these games and practices can be carried out in town just as well as in the country.

BOOKS TO READ.—In addition to those mentioned in Chap. V, 'Heroes of Pioneering', by E. Sanderson (Seely & Co.), 'Boys' Book of Exploration' by Tudor Jenks.

ENDURANCE AND HEALTH

PRACTICES.—Making tooth-brushes, p. 191. Measurement, p. 192. Deep breathing, p. 201. Drill, p. 207.

Staff exercises (to music if possible).

'FOLLOW MY LEADER'.—With a large number of boys this can be made a very effective display, and is easy to do—at a jog-trot, and occasional 'knees up', with musical accompaniment. It can also be done at night, each boy carrying a Chinese lantern on top of his staff. If in a building, all lights would, of course, be turned down. A usual fault is that the exercise is kept on too long, till it wearies both audience and performers. Among the most effective figures are the following:

'How to Keep Fit' is a little book, costing 3d., by Surgeon-Captain Waite (Gale & Polden), which tells a man how to look after

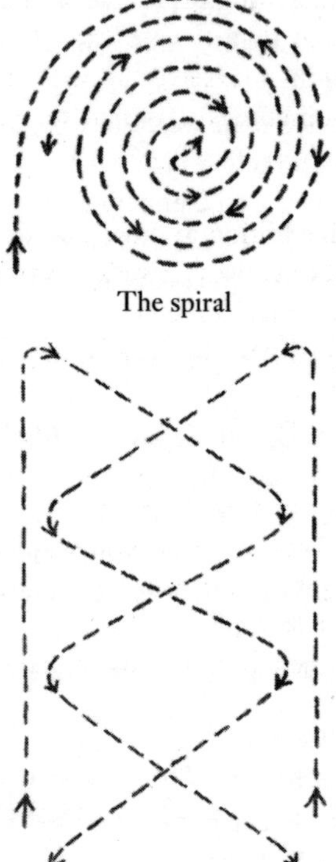

The spiral

Turn at the corners, and double zig-zag

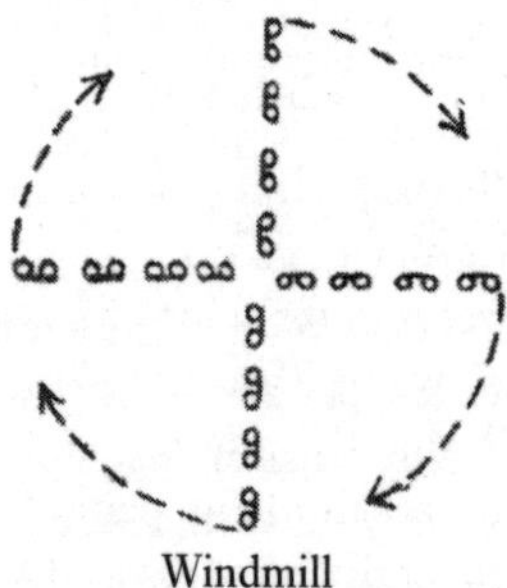

Windmill

FOLLOW MY LEADER

his health, and so avoid getting ill. It is much better to study and act upon advice of this kind than to read the advertisements of patent medicines and then to fill yourselves up with these drugs. They are often harmless, but sometimes very bad for you; very seldom are they any good.

Books to Read in addition to those already suggested:—

'Healthful, Physical Exercises', Swedish system. W. L. Rooper, 2s. 9d. (Newmann, 84, Newman Street.)

'The Fine Art of Ju-Jitsu', by Mrs Roger Watts, with excellent photos. (Heinemann.)

CHIVALRY

Practices.—The knot in the necktie to remind the scout to do a good turn. The money-box to develop thrift and charity.

Archery and quarter-staff play.

Carpentering and other ways of making money, pp. 232–4, 237.

Games.—'Knight Errantry', see p. 221.

'Risking Life', pp. 252–3.

Further displays, etc., will be published in the 'Scout'.

SAVING LIFE AND FIRST AID

Practices.—Dragging insensible man, p. 256; 'scrum', p. 256; rescuing drowning men, pp. 257–8; fire drill; first aid for all injuries, see St John's Handbooks; artificial breathing, pp. 264–5; carrying a patient, pp. 270–1; fire alarm, p. 272.

How to make eye tweezers for removing a piece of grit from eye. Fold a piece of paper in two. With a sharp knife cut it to a point at an angle of 30 deg., and slightly moisten the point. Then bring it straight down over the eyeball of the patient, so that it can nip the obstruction, which it generally removes at the first attempt.

Games.—Dragging Race, see page 272.

Book to read in addition of those mentioned on pp. 272–3. 'R.E.P.' Elliman's Handbook. Apart from its advertising, it contains a very complete *vade mecum* of First Aid and Sick Room Hints and Massage. (Apply to Messrs Elliman, Slough.)

DISPLAYS.—A few ideas for life-saving displays can be taken from programmes of the Boys' Life Brigade, as suggestions. These displays are very popular both with performers and with the audience.

PATRIOTISM

A GOOD map of the Empire is very desirable, as stated on page 273. A globe is of even more value than a map. Paper globes which can fold up or open out like an umbrella can be got, which are inexpensive and most instructive.

PRACTICE: Marksmanship, pp. 284–6.

Flag-flying, p. 290.

Observe Saints' Days. See p. 288.

The visits to museums and armouries (as suggested on p. 288 and elsewhere) are on the lines of what is regularly done in Germany as part of the training of the boys while at school. Classes are taken by the masters to armouries and museums to be taught their National History.

GAMES.—'Shoot Out', p. 287; 'French and English', p. 287; 'Badajoz', p. 287; 'The Empire' card game.

'Navigation', 7s. 6d., Newmann, 84, Newman Street; 'Separate Cruises', 3s. 6d.; 'Contraband', 6s. 6d., Newmann.

DISPLAYS.—Pageants of incidents in local history.

'PLAY THE GAME'.—See p. 336.

'Storming the Kashmir Gate, Delhi'.—See p. 337.

SONGS.—'The Maple Leaf For Ever' (Canada). The song of Australia.

BOOKS TO READ in addition to those already suggested:—

'Heroic Deeds Simply Told'; 'Heroes and Heroines of Everyday

Life as well as those of War', by Ernest Protheroe. 1s. 11d. (Newmann.)

'History of England', by H. O. Arnold-Forster. 3s. 9d. (Cassell.)

'Adventures of Beowulf', by C. L. Thomson. 9d. (Marshall.)

School Atlas, by H. O. Arnold-Forster, 1s. 11. (37, Bedford Street.)

'Through the British Empire in a Few Minutes'. A short address by Sir Howard Vincent. (A. K. Johnstone, 7, Paternoster Square.)

A Bicycle Accident.—Boys returning from camp. A rash cyclist. Misfortune. Injuries attended to and patients carried away to hospital on improvised stretchers.

A Gas Explosion.—Mrs Coddles and family take a walk. They witness a terrible railway accident. Mrs Coddles on her way home meets a friend. Maria is sent on to light the gas-stove and prepare father's tea. Father gets back from work and finds the house full of gas. Ambulance squad to the rescue. 'Fireman's lift' and artificial respiration. Constable A000 arrives on the scene. How not to look for a gas escape. Sad end of a gallant but thoughtless policeman.

Fire Display.—Evening at No. 5 Suburbi Villas. Fire alarm. Inmates aroused. Escape by the chute. Arrival of fire section with jumping sheet. Life-lines and pompier ladders. Rescue of remaining occupants.

Synopsis.—The workmen are engaged in their daily occupation when an explosion occurs, causing a fire inside the building and an exterior wall to collapse, which injures a man who happens to be passing at the time. The uninjured workmen attend to their unfortunate comrades, while others rush off for help and return with the ambulance and fire apparatus. Some of the men are rescued from the burning building by jumping from the tower.

PLAY THE GAME!*

Poem by Henry Newbolt

Scene I: Tableau of boys playing cricket.

RECITATION

There's a breathless hush in the close to-night
  Ten to make and the match to win—
A bumping pitch and a blinding light,
  An hour to play and the last man in.
And it's not for the sake of a ribboned coat
  Or the selfish hope of a season's fame,
But his captain's hand on his shoulder smote.

[*Action: The captain steps up to the batsman, puts his hand on his shoulder, and says to him urgently*—]

'Play up! Play up! And play the game!'

Scene II: Tableau. Soldiers in a hard-fought fight retreating—a young officer among them.

RECITATION

The sand of the desert is sodden red—
  Red with the wreck of the square that broke;
The gatling's jammed and the colonel dead,
  And the regiment blind with dust and smoke.
The river of death has brimmed its banks,
  And England's far and Honour a name,
But the voice of a schoolboy rallies the ranks.

[*Action: The young officer stands forward pointing his sword to the enemy, and the retreating soldiers turn ready to charge with him as he cries*—]

'Play up! Play up! And play the game!'

Scene III: A procession of all kinds of men, old ones at the head, middle-aged in centre, young ones behind—soldiers, sailors, lawyers, workmen, footballers, etc., etc.—Scotch, Irish, English, Colonial—all linked hand in hand.

RECITATION

This is the word that year by year,
   While in her place the school is set,
Every one of her sons must hear,
   And none that hears it dare forget.
This they all with joyful mind
   Bear through life like a torch in flame,
And falling fling to the host behind.

[*Action: The leader flings out a Union Jack, and calls to the rest*—]

'Play up! Play up! And play the game!'

[*One in the centre then calls back to the juniors: 'Play up! Play up! And play the game!' The smallest of the juniors steps forward and cries to the audience*—]

'PLAY UP! PLAY UP! AND PLAY THE GAME!'

THE STORMING OF DELHI

[*Scene, ruined drawbridge at Kashmir Gate. Group of officers and soldiers about to blow in the gate. Description to be read during the picture.*]

LORD ROBERTS, in 'Forty-one Years in India', describes how the Kashmir Gate of Delhi was captured by the British troops during the Mutiny.* Lieutenants Home and Salkeld, with eight sappers and a bugler of the 52nd Regiment, went forward to blow the gate open for the column to get into Delhi.

The enemy were apparently so astounded at the audacity of this proceeding that for a minute or two they offered but slight resistance.

They soon, however, discovered how small the party was and the object for which it had come, and forthwith opened a deadly fire upon the gallant little band from the top of the gateway, from the city wall, and through the open wicket.

The bridge over the ditch in front of the gateway had been destroyed, and it was with some difficulty that the single beam which remained could be crossed. Home with the men carrying the powder bags got over first. As the bags were being attached to the gate, Sergeant Carmichael was killed, and Havildar (native Sergeant) Madhoo wounded. The rest then slipped into the ditch to allow the firing party which had come up under Salkeld to carry out its share of the duty.

While endeavouring to fire the charge Salkeld was shot through the leg and arm, and handed the slow match to Corporal Burgess. Burgess succeeded in his task, but fell mortally wounded as he did so.

As soon as the explosion took place, Bugler Hawthorne sounded the regimental call of the 52nd as a signal to the attacking column to advance. In this way the troops got in through the Kashmir Gate, and Delhi was taken.

Lieutenant Home was unfortunately killed within a few weeks by an accidental explosion of a mine he was firing, otherwise he would have received the V.C.

'THE MAPLE LEAF FOR EVER'

Alexander Muir

In days of yore, from Britain's shore,
 Wolfe, the dauntless hero, came
And planted firm Britannia's flag
 On Canada's fair domain;
Here may it wave, our boast and pride,
 And join in love together,
The Lily, Thistle, Shamrock, Rose entwine
 The Maple Leaf for ever.

 The Maple Leaf, our emblem dear,
  The Maple Leaf for ever,
 God save our King, and Heaven bless
  The Maple Leaf for ever.

At Queenstown Heights and Lundy's Lane,
 Our brave fathers side by side,
For freedom, homes, and loved ones dear,
 Firmly stood and nobly died;
And those dear rights which they maintained
 We swear to yield them never.
Our watchword evermore shall be,
 The Maple Leaf for ever.

Refrain.

Our fair Dominion now extends
  From Cape Race to Nootka Sound,
May peace for ever be our lot,
  And plenteous store abound;
And may those ties of love be ours,
  Which discord cannot sever,
And flourish green o'er Freedom's home,
  The Maple Leaf for ever.
Refrain.

On Merry England's far-famed land
  May kind Heaven sweetly smile;
God bless Old Scotland evermore,
  And Ireland's Emerald Isle;
Then swell the song both loud and long
  Till rocks and forest quiver.
God save our King, and Heaven bless
  The Maple Leaf for ever.
    The Maple Leaf, our emblem dear,
      The Maple Leaf for ever,
    God save our King, and Heaven bless
      The Maple Leaf for ever.

'THE SONG OF AUSTRALIA'

Words by Mrs C. J. Carleton. Music by Herr Carl Linger

There is a land where summer skies
Are gleaming with a thousand dyes,
Blending in witching harmonies;
And grassy knoll and forest height
Are flushing in the rosy light,
And all above is azure bright,
AUSTRALIA.

There is a land where honey flows,
Where laughing corn luxuriant grows,
Land of the myrtle and the rose.
On hill and plain the clust'ring vine

Is gushing out with purple wine,
And cups are quaffed to thee and thine,
AUSTRALIA.

There is a land where treasures shine,
Deep in the dark unfathomed mine,
For worshippers at mammon's shrine;
Where gold lies hid and rubies gleam,
And fabled wealth no more doth seem
The idle fancy of a dream,
AUSTRALIA.

There is a land where homesteads peep,
From sunny plains and woodlands steep,
And love and joy bright vigils keep;
Where the glad voice of childish glee
Is mingling with the melody
Of Nature's hidden minstrelsy,
AUSTRALIA.

There is a land where floating free,
From mountain top to girdling sea,
A proud flag waves exultingly;
And freedom's sons the banner bear,
No shackled slave can breathe the air—
Fairest of Britain's daughters, fair,
AUSTRALIA.

[NOTE.—When sung, repeat at end of third line in each verse as follows: 'harmonies', 'and the rose', 'mammon's shrine', 'vigils keep', 'exultingly'.

GOD BLESS THE PRINCE OF WALES

Among our ancient mountains,
And from our lovely vales,
Oh! let the prayer re-echo,
God Bless the Prince of Wales!
With heart and voice awaken
Those minstrel strains of yore,

Till Britain's name and glory
  Resound from shore to shore.

[*Chorus*] Among our ancient mountains,
  And from our lovely vales,
Oh! let the prayer re-echo,
  God Bless the Prince of Wales

Should hostile bands or danger
  E'er threaten our fair Isle,
May God's strong arm protect us,
  May Heav'n still on us smile.
Above the Throne of England
  May fortune's star long shine!
And round its sacred bulwarks
  The olive branches twine.

Among our ancient mountains, etc.

GOD SAVE THE KING

God save our gracious King,
Long live our noble King,
  God save the King!
Send him victorious,
Happy and glorious,
Long to reign over us,
  God save the King!

Thy choicest gifts in store,
On him be pleas'd to pour,
  Long may he reign.
May he defend our laws,
And ever give us cause,
To sing with heart and voice,
  God save the King!

SAMPLE PROGRAMME OF ATHLETIC SPORTS

Throwing the life line	Open.
Patrol drill (demonstration)	Curlews.
Fire-lighting competition	Wolves *v.* Bulls.

Physical drill or ju jitsu (demonstration)	Ravens.
Dragging insensible men race	Lions *v.* Curlews.
Basket ball (final ties)	Patrols.
Deer-stalking	Wolves.
Spotty face	Bulls.
Shoot out	Ravens *v.* Lions.
Bang the bear	Curlews.
Cockfighting	Wolves *v.* Ravens.
French and English tug of war	Birds *v.* Beasts.
Whale hunt	All patrols.

In place of Challenge Cups it is well to have Challenge Banners. Each scout in the patrol that wins a banner should receive a small copy of the flag to keep as a memento.

NON-SCOUTING GAMES

USEFUL FOR EVENINGS IN THE CLUB OR IN CAMP

NOBODY'S AIRSHIP.—Two patrols sit on two forms facing each other, knees about a foot from those of opposite side. A small air-balloon is thrown in, both sides pat it with their hands to keep it up in the air and try to send it far over the heads of their opponents. If it falls to the ground behind one party that party loses a point. The game is best of five points.

'ARTISTS'.—Players sit round a table, each with paper and pencil. The right-hand one draws a picture, in separate firm strokes, of an ordinary figure or head—putting in his strokes in unusual sequence so that for a long time it is difficult to see what he is drawing. Each player looks over to see what the man on his right is drawing and copies it stroke by stroke. When the right-hand artist has finished his picture, compare all the rest with it.

'TARGET BALL'.—Indoor cricket with a lawn tennis ball, small wooden bat, and a disc or small target for wicket.

'CIRCLE BALL'.—A large circle of players throw lawn tennis ball at one in the centre.

The object of the player in the centre is to remain 'in' as long as possible without being hit; if he catches the ball in his hands it does not count as a hit.

Whoever hits him with the ball takes his place.

The player who remains 'in' longest wins.

COUNTING THE WORDS.—Let someone read out half a page from a book, pronouncing the words with moderate rapidity. As he reads, let the members of the company try to count his words. The persons who comes the nearest to the truth in his estimate is judged the victor. It is astonishing how widely these estimates vary.

ANIMATED PORTRAITS.—Over a door drape a curtain, in the centre of which is hung a frame through which can be thrust the heads of various persons chosen from those present. These heads are to be attired in such a fashion as to represent various well-known characters, such as Christopher Columbus, Queen Victoria, etc. The audience are to be informed that they are at liberty to make frank criticisms on these animated pictures for the purpose of causing a smile. In case the audience is successful in identifying within a certain time, the person who represents the picture must pay a fine.

TO FIT.—Cut a square opening in a pasteboard, which is placed prominently in front of the room. Distribute to the members corks of different sizes. Provide with sharp knives those that are not already provided. Explain that the task before them is to cut the corks so that they will fit the square opening, without measuring the opening, judging entirely by the eye. The one whose cork fits the best wins.

CITY CHAINS.—Place the players in two groups facing each other. Each group must choose a leader, with whom the members of his side communicate in whispers. In the centre is an umpire, who, with his watch, gives each side a quarter of a minute, or less, for their response.

The leader of one side begins by naming a city, such as New York. Within the prescribed time the leader of the opposite side must name a city beginning with the last letter of New York, as Kalamazoo; and so it proceeds, each leader using the wits of all in his group to assist his own.

When a leader fails to respond in time, the opposite leader chooses one player from his opponent's side, and in his turn starts a new chain. The game can be played also with the names of famous persons, but this is harder.

A MEMORY GAME.—In order to play this game successfully, it is necessary that the list of words and sentences given below be in the memory of one of the players, who acts as leader. This leader, turning to his next neighbour remarks, 'One old owl'. He turns to *his* neighbour, and gives the same formula. So it passes around the circle till it comes to the leader again, who repeats it, and adds the formula, 'Two tantalising tame toads'.

So again it goes around, and again, and each time the leader adds a new formula, until the whole is repeated, up to ten. It is safe to say, however, that no society will ever get that far. All who forget part of the formula are dropped from the circle. Here is the whole:

One old owl.
Two tantalising tame toads.
Three tremulous, tremendous, terrible tadpoles.
Four fat, fussy, frivolous, fantastic fellows.
Five flaming, flapping, flamingoes fishing for frogs.
Six silver-tongued, saturnine senators standing stentoriously shouting, 'So-so'.
Seven serene seraphs soaring swiftly sunward, singing, 'Say, sisters'.
Eight elderly, energetic, effusive, erudite, enterprising editors eagerly eating elderberries.
Nine nice, neat, notable, neighbourly, nautical, nodding nabobs nearing northern Normandy.
Ten tall, tattered, tearful, turbulent tramps, talking tumultuously through tin trumpets.

POST.—This game may be played in a large hall, or out of doors on the lawn. It is especially adapted to the juniors, and may be so played as to teach them a great deal of geography. The leader either marks with chalk, or indicates with his fingers, the outlines of some mission country. Let it be India, for example. A rough triangle is fixed, and the places of the prominent mission stations are indicated by marks, sticks, stones, bushes, or trees, and at each of these places one of the players is stationed. One player might stand at Calcutta, one at Bombay, one at Madras, one at Madura, one at Delhi, etc.

The leader then takes upon himself the name of some prominent missionary of India—say Bishop Thoburn; then, declaring that Bishop Thoburn wants to go from Calcutta to Madras, he attempts to reach one of those stations while the two occupants thereof are rapidly changing places. If he succeed in doing this, the player left out has to take his place as Bishop Thoburn, and in this way the game proceeds.

NUMBER GROUPS.—Give each person present a number, printed in large type on a card which is pinned conspicuously on the breast. The numbers range from 10 to 24, and so of course there will be many duplicates. There is a leader, who begins the game by calling in a loud voice some number, such as 180. Immediately the players as rapidly as possible arrange themselves in groups, seeking to form a group the sum of whose numbers will equal 180. As soon as a group has been thus formed it presents itself to the leader, and to each member of this successful group is given a slip of paper.

As soon as one group has thus formed 180 and been rewarded, the half-formed groups are dissolved, since they do not count anything, and the leader calls out a new number. After this has been tried a certain number of times, the person that has received the largest number of slips is adjudged the winner. If you want to make this game very difficult, use higher numbers, and attach them to the backs instead of the fronts, of the members.

THEIR WEIGHT.—This contest will make pleasant material to fill some interval in your socials. Let the committee previously gather six articles, as dissimilar as may be in size, shape, and material, but each weighing a pound. You may take, for instance, a wooden pail, a tin pan, a piece of lead. Call out different members of the company, and request them to arrange these six articles in the order of their weight. Of course, almost every one will think the large article to be the heaviest.

BASKET BALL

THIS is a game something like football, which can be played in a room or limited space. A small football is used, but it is never to be kicked. It is only to be thrown or patted with the hands. Kicking or stopping the ball with the foot or leg is not allowed. The ball may be held in the hands, but not hugged close to the body, nor may it be carried for more than two paces. All holding, dashing, charging, shouldering, tripping, etc., is forbidden; and there is a penalty of a free throw to the opposite side from the fifteen foot mark at the net, which forms the goal. The net is hung up about ten feet above the ground on a post, tree, or wall, so that the ball can be thrown into it. Opposite each goal a path of fifteen feet long and six feet wide, beginning immediately under the basket and leading towards the centre of the ground, is marked out. At the end of this path a circle is drawn of ten feet diameter. When there is a free throw, the thrower stands inside this circle, and no player is allowed within it or within the measured path. Corners, byes, and shies are the same as in Association football; but in ordinary rooms, with side walls, it is not necessary to have 'out' at the sides. The usual number of players is four or five a side, and these can be divided into goalkeeper, back, and three forwards. If there is plenty of room the number of players could be increased. A referee is required, who throws up the ball at the start of each half of the game, and also after each goal. When he throws in, the ball must be allowed to touch the ground before it is played. With four players a side, 7½ minutes each way is sufficient time; with five a side, ten minutes is the usual time. A short interval at half time. The net or basket goal should be about 18 inches diameter at the top and 2 feet deep.

BOOKS TO READ

'School Games', by T. Chesterton. (Educational Supply Association.)

'New Games and Sports', by H. Alexander. (George Philip & Son.)

'Industrial Games', by Mrs Aldrich. (Gale & Polden.)

'Social—to Save'. (Published in New York.)

'Finger Problems: Games with String'. (Plumbe & Richardson, Mansfield.)

SUGGESTION FOR A DISPLAY

By two patrols or more, to demonstrate Scoutcraft, bringing in Drill, Pathfinding, Camping, Pioneering, Life-saving, Hygiene, etc. Can be performed out of doors or in a big arena. Improved by incidental music.

Enter advanced scout, left, finding his way by the map, noticing landmarks, and looking for sign. He crosses the arena and disappears, right, unless it is a wide, outdoor space, when he remains at a distance, squatting, on the look-out.

Enter scouts, left, in patrol formation, followed by second patrol in close formation. Scoutmaster halts them. One scout semaphores to advanced scout. 'We camp here. Keep good look-out.' Patrol leaders drill their patrols at quick, smart drill for about three minutes by whistle or hand signal, etc. (Page 177.)

Camp: Break off and form camp. One patrol makes camp loom (page 144) and weaves a straw mat 4 feet wide 6 feet long, and makes a lean-to frame (page 131) or tent frame, with scout staves, and with the mat form a lean-to shelter.

The other patrol makes a camp grate or kitchen (pages 139–41), and lights fire. It then makes tent frame of staves (page 327), and makes tent with canvas squares (page 327).

One patrol commences cooking, making dough in coat, etc. The scouts of the other give themselves physical exercises, such as body-twisting (pages 202 and 209). Clean teeth with sticks (page 191).

Scout's War Dance: All fall in and carry out Scout's War Dance (page 50), combined with Follow My Leader (page 331). Just towards the end the dance is interrupted by an

Alarm: Shots heard without (right). Alarm signal given by leaders (page 177). Smoke-fire made, alarm signal sent up by one of the patrols, while the other throws down tent and shelter, cuts lashings, and distributes the staves to scouts. One patrol then doubles out in extended formation (right) towards the firing. Sentry staggers in, and falls. One scout attends to him. Second patrol follows the first at a double in close formation. A scout returns from right carrying a wounded one on his shoulder; bandages him. Another scout drags in a wounded one (see pages 256 and 270). Firing ceases; both patrols

Return, cheerful in having driven off the enemy.

One patrol makes stretcher with staves and tent-canvases.

The other tidies camp ground, puts out fire, etc.

Parade and march off. Union Jack in front. Then scoutmaster, followed by one patrol; second patrol carrying one sick man on crossed hands, the other on stretcher.

The whole scene should be frequently and thoroughly rehearsed beforehand.

It must all be carried out as smartly and quickly as possible, without pauses. Everybody doing something, helping the others, never standing idle.

It is well to have a short explanatory story on the programme, so that the public understand what it is all about. Such as this:

THE EXPLORERS

A TROOP of scouts, with an advanced scout finding the way, are exploring a strange country. They halt. A little drill, and then form camp. While food is preparing they gain an appetite by physical exercise and indulgence in a war dance.

The alarm is given and signalled. The camp successfully defended. The wounded cared for, and the expedition continues on its way.

TRUE SCOUTING STORIES

INTERESTING examples of the great value of scouting have, of course, occurred many times. Here are a few—unavoidably omitted from a previous part of 'Scouting for Boys'.*

Captain Stigand in 'Scouting and Reconnaissance in Savage Countries'* gives the following instances of scouts reading important meaning from small signs.

When he was going round outside his camp one morning he noticed fresh spoor of a horse which had been walking. He knew that all his horses only went at a jog-trot, so it must have been a stranger's horse.

So he recognised that a mounted scout of the enemy had been quietly looking at his camp in the night.

Coming to a village in Central Africa from which the inhabitants had fled, he could not tell what tribe it belonged to till he found a crocodile's foot in one of the huts, which showed that the village belonged to the Awisa tribe, as they eat crocodiles, and the neighbouring tribes do not.

A man was seen riding a camel over half a mile away. A native who was watching him said, 'It is a man of slave blood.' 'How can you tell at this distance?' 'Because he is swinging his leg. A true Arab rides with his leg close to the camel's side.'

General Joubert, who was Commander-in-Chief of the Boer Army in the Boer War, 1900, told me (some years before that) that in the previous Boer War, 1881, it was his wife who first noticed the British troops were occupying Majuba Mountain. The Boers were at that time camped near the foot of the mountain, and they generally had a small party of men on the top as a look-out. On this particular day they had intended moving away early in the morning so the usual picquet had not been sent up on to the mountain.

While they were getting ready to start, Mrs Joubert, who evidently had the eyes of a scout, looked up and said, 'Why, there is an Englishman on the top of Majuba!' The Boers said 'No—it must be our own men who have gone up there, after all.' But Mrs Joubert stuck to it and said, 'Look at the way he walks, that is no Boer—it is an Englishman.' And so it was; she was right. An English force had climbed the mountain during the night, but by the stupidity of this man showing himself up on the sky-line their presence was immediately detected by the Boers who, instead of being surprised by them, climbed up the mountain unseen under the steep crags and surprised the British, and drove them off with heavy loss.

An officer lost his field-glasses during some manœuvres on the desert five miles from Cairo and he sent for the native trackers to look for them.

They came and asked to see the tracks of his horse; so the horse was brought out and led about so that they could see his footprints. These they carried in their minds and went out to where the manœuvres had been: there, among the hundreds of hoof marks of the cavalry and artillery, they very soon found those of the officer's horse, and followed them up wherever he had ridden, till they found the field-glasses lying where they had dropped out of their case on the desert.

These trackers are particularly good at spooring camels. To anyone not accustomed to them the footmark of one camel looks very like that of any other camel, but to a trained eye they are all as different as people's faces, and these trackers remember them very much as you would remember the faces of people you had seen.

About a year ago a camel was stolen near Cairo. The police tracker was sent for and shown its spoor. He followed it for a long way until it got into some streets where it was entirely lost among other footmarks. But the other day, a year later, this police tracker suddenly came on the fresh track of this camel; he had remembered its appearance all that time. It had evidently been walking with another camel whose footmark he knew was one which belonged to a well-known camel thief. So without trying to follow the tracks when they got into the city he went with a policeman straight to the man's stable and there found the long-missing camel.

APPENDIX
CONTINENCE

[This excised section, equivalent to Part TS 246–8, and the counterpart of 'Continence', *SfB* 316–17, addressed to instructors, should have appeared in Yarn 18, p. 200 in the present edition. Baden-Powell, who had consulted with his mother about the section's inclusion, reluctantly removed it from *Scouting for Boys* under strong advice from his publisher. See notes to pp. 195 and 316.]

I have told you of the dangers of drink and of smoking which, if indulged in boys, are certain to make you unhealthy in the end and therefore useless as a scout. A good many of you will never feel the want of these so you won't have any difficulty in keeping away from them.

But there is another practice which [is] perhaps more dangerous than either of them and it is one which is sure to tempt every one of you at one time or another. I speak quite openly. People are much too apt to make it such a secret that many boys never hear the truth and suffer in consequence.

You all know what it is to have at times a pleasant feeling in your private parts, and there comes an inclination to work it up with your hand or otherwise. It is especially likely to happen when you see a dirty picture or hear dirty stories and jokes.

Well, lots of fellows from not knowing any better, please themselves in this way until it often becomes a sort of habit with them which they cannot get out of.

Yet I am sure that every sensible boy, if he were told in time of the danger of it, would have the strength not to do it.

So I want to warn you all about it.

The practice is called 'self-abuse'. And the result of self-abuse is always —mind you, *always*—that the boy after a time becomes weak and nervous and shy, he gets headaches and probably palpitation of the heart, and if he still carries it on too far he very often goes out of his mind and becomes an idiot.

A very large number of the lunatics in our asylums have made themselves ill by indulging in this vice although at one time they were sensible cheery boys like any one of you.

The use of your parts is not to play with when you are a boy but to enable you to get children when you are grown up and married. But if you misuse them while young you will not be able to use them when you are a man: they will not work then.

Remember too that several awful diseases come from indulgence—one especially that rots away the inside of men's mouths, their noses, and eyes, etc.

So for all reasons be on the look out against this temptation, it is easier to stop it at first than when it becomes a habit. The next time you feel the desire coming on don't give way to it; resist it. If you have the chance just wash your parts in cold water and cool them down. Wet dreams come from it especially after eating rich food, or too much meat, or from sleeping with too warm a blanket over your body or in too soft a bed or from sleeping on your back. Therefore avoid all these.

Avoid listening to stories or reading or thinking about dirty subjects.

You will soon find that the temptation will not worry you so much. Be strong and don't give way to it.

If at first you find a difficulty about it don't be afraid to go and talk openly to your officer about it and he will tell you what to do.

Restrain yourself while you are young and you will be able to restrain yourself when you grow up. It is at present a disgrace and a danger to England that from want of self-restraint among men and women thousands upon thousands of children are born every year for whom there is no work and no money—and so we get such an enormous crowd of poor people and unemployed. I walked round the other day with some of the unemployed to see if they were really anxious to get work. They were. They tried several places but no hands were wanted. Then one of them made the remark which seemed to me very true. 'There's not enough work to go round. The truth is there's too many of us in this world.'

EXPLANATORY NOTES

ABBREVIATIONS

B.-P.	Baden-Powell, his Scouting nickname
Part MS	the incomplete manuscript of *Scouting for Boys*
Part TS	the incomplete typescript of *Scouting for Boys*
SfB	*Scouting for Boys*
PE	the parts edition (comprising six parts) of *SfB*, the basis of the present edition, first published 15 January 1908
CE	the complete edition of *SfB*, first published 1 May 1908

5 *where these do not exist*: from the beginning B.-P. emphasizes what was to him one of the basic structural principles of Scouting: that it might 'piggyback', or be dovetailed with, other boys' organizations. The enthusiasm of young people for Scouting, however, soon demanded the founding of an independent organization. See pp. 32 and 304–6.

'The Boy Scouts Scheme': a 1907 pamphlet—in fact called *Boy Scouts: Summary of a Scheme*—outlining the basic principles and practices of Scouting which B.-P. sent out to interested parties and potential patrons. Based on an early sketch, 'Boy Patrols', also written in early 1907, the text would be recycled for the promotional lectures he gave around Britain between November 1907 and February 1908. It was more measured in its imperialist tones than a predecessor leaflet, *Boy Scouts: A Suggestion* (which however corresponds to the present *SfB* 295–300).

if it can possibly be avoided: in fundraising, as in other aspects of the organization of Scouting, self-help was laid down as a central tenet. See note to p. 239.

10 *'Pocahontas'*: as with the references to other Scouting games and practices in this sketch for an induction week, the script and instructions for the 'Pocahontas' 'display' are given later on in the text (in this case on p. 51).

on active service: the Part TS reads 'not merely as peace scouts', which is inserted just prior to this phrase. Despite the emphasis throughout the Mafeking Boy Scouts Yarn on military preparedness, this, like the later remarks under the heading 'Scouts' Work', suggests that B.-P. was already at this early stage marking a distinction between military scouting and a Scout Movement designed especially for peacetime.

Mafeking, 1899–1900: there is some controversy as to who authored the exemplary first 'scouting' group, the Mafeking cadet corps. Lord Edward Cecil (see below) was probably its initiator, though some evidence suggests that the corps predated the famous siege of Mafeking (14 October 1899–17 May 1900), one of Britain's few success stories of the first year of the Anglo-Boer War. During the siege the cadet corps was commanded by Lord Edward and Lieutenant Moncrieff. Although B.-P. at times used the giveaway phrase 'my Boy Scouts', and is sometimes given the credit for having organized the boys of Mafeking into a corps, in fact he seems to have shown little interest in the so-called scouts during the siege itself. On p. 283 he again cites the Mafeking story as an example of (self-generated) preparedness, where the besieged town becomes a metaphor for a threatened England. See also pp. 173–4, and Baden-Powell's autobiography. *Lessons from the 'Varsity of Life* (C. Arthur Pearson, 1933), 274.

11 *Lord Edward Cecil, the chief staff officer*: Lord Edward Cecil (1867–1918), a military man and imperial civil servant, became involved in military and diplomatic activities in north-east Africa from the 1890s. After Mafeking he served as the agent-general of the Sudanese government and thereafter in the Egyptian ministry of finance. The Part TS has 'my' chief staff officer. See Hugh and Mirabel Cecil, *Imperial Marriage: An Edwardian War and Peace* (John Murray, 2002).

12 *cadet bicycle orderly*: a strategically loaded intervention. During the final months of the siege of Mafeking, B.-P. had postage stamps issued bearing his likeness in the place of the Queen's head. Once the news leaked out, B.-P.'s effrontery—yet another instance of his delight in practical jokes—rapidly threatened to turn into a scandal and he ever after took pains to disavow the story. See Tim Jeal, *Baden-Powell: Founder of the Boy Scouts* (Yale University Press, 2001), 306.

13 *wherever you may be*: this final short paragraph, again emphasizing the usefulness of Scouts in peacetime, does not appear in the Part TS. See also p. 24 on the national heroism that may be practised by the peace scout.

same kind of abilities: Baden-Powell traces an inventive transnational network of near-synonyms, based on the idea of the scout as a historical constant, the ideal hero of knightly virtues, canny observation, and stout-hearted reliability, ever-present at tight spots in British national and colonial history. This network is again reinforced below, where B.-P. scans a standard pantheon of national heroes, chiefly of exploration, most of them mounted on an imperial pedestal of one sort or another. B.-P.'s choices are strongly suggestive of G. A. Henty's and other *Boy's Own Paper*-style adventure stories for boys, and Victorian illustrated histories for children.

14 *peace scouts*: in order, B.-P.'s paragons of Scouting, some of whom recur on pp. 274–5, are: Richard Cœur de Lion, or the Lion-hearted, Richard I (1157–99), King of England, Duke of Normandy, and Count of Anjou (1189–99), whose knightly successes in the Third Crusade (1189–92) and widely sung military prowess made of him a cynosure of kingship; Sir Walter Raleigh (1554?–1618), English adventurer (especially in Guyana, 1595 and 1616, and against the Irish, 1580), man of letters, and favourite

of Queen Elizabeth I; Sir Francis Drake (*c.*1540–96), talented seaman and renowned navigator, well-known for his circumnavigation of the earth (1577–81), and his starring role in the defeat of the Spanish Armada (1588); Captain John Smith (*c.*1580–1631), adventurer, cartographer, and founder-leader of the first permanent English settlement in North America, at Jamestown, Virginia (1607–9), the man Pocahontas rescued (see note to p. 51); Captain James Cook (1728–79), navigator and explorer involved in three major expeditions across the length and breadth of the Pacific Ocean (1768–71, 1772–5, 1776–9); Lord Robert Clive (1725–74), the first British administrator of Bengal (1755–60, 1765–7), and, as commander of the East India Company's forces, victor over the Mughal army at Plassey (1757); John Hanning Speke (1827–64), sometime collaborator with the explorers Richard Burton and Samuel Baker, and the first European to reach Lake Victoria (1858), which he correctly identified as one of the sources of the Nile (1862); Sir Samuel Baker (1821–93), an explorer with Speke, who later became a governor-general of the Nile equatorial region under the Ottoman Ismail Pasha; David Livingstone (1813–73), Scottish missionary explorer, and leader of three major cartographic expeditions across central Africa (1853–6, 1861–5, 1865–73); Sir John Franklin (1786–1847), the leader of two unsuccessful cartographic expeditions along the northern rim of the North American continent, now Canada, whose final search for the North-West Passage (1845–8) probably reached the midway point between the Atlantic and Pacific oceans; Sir James Ross (1800–62), British naval officer who undertook important magnetic surveys of the Antarctic regions; Frederick Courteney Selous (1851–1917), naturalist, hunter, and traveller in south-central Africa (later Rhodesia) (1871–89), who entered the service of the British South Africa Company in 1890 and helped bring Manicaland under British control; Boyd Alexander (1873–1910), ornithologist, and leader of two British scientific and military campaigns, one to West Africa (1897), and one from West Africa to the Nile (1904–7). Later in *SfB* 'cowboys', too, will be enlisted as peace scouts (p. 191). Notice how B.-P.'s network demonstrates across time an ever greater specificity with respect to Africa, thus coming to point ever more narrowly at the terrain of his own most noteworthy imperial exploits.

in all parts of our Empire: despite the overriding emphasis on manly endeavour, it is worth noting that even in these opening pages of the Scout Movement's inaugural text, B.-P. allows for the potential of girls to become scouts. His standard-bearers of female heroism are: Grace Darling (1815–42), the rescuer, with her father, of survivors of a steamboat disaster (1838); Florence Nightingale (1820–1910), the renowned reformer of hospital nursing; Mary Kingsley (1862–1900), West African traveller, ethnographer, travel writer, and opponent of the Christianization of Africans; Flora Shaw, later Lady Lugard (1852–1929), children's author, gifted columnist, and, from the mid-1890s, Colonial Editor of *The Times*, where she spoke out in favour of imperial federation. (After her marriage to Frederick Lugard, the first British governor of Nigeria, Flora Shaw gave up her journalistic career.) See also p. 162 where Mrs Grace Thompson Seton's book of camping for 'women and girls' is cited.

14 *Sir William Crookes*: chemist and physicist (1832–1919), discoverer of the element thallium, and researcher into the behaviour of the cathode ray.

'*Kim*': Rudyard Kipling's iconic tale *Kim* (1901), the story of the Irish orphan Kimball O'Hara's wanderings through late-nineteenth-century India; his ability to masquerade both as native and European; and his search, together with the Tibetan lama, for a mythical sacred river. On the strength of his faculties of dissimulation, disguise, and deduction Kim is enlisted into the Imperial Secret Service, or Government Intelligence Department. Like the story of John Smith and Pocahontas, Kim's narrative, with its distinctive components of 'Kim's game' and nickname (p. 45) and its rich metaphor of the Great Game of imperial strategy, becomes one of the definitive object-lessons of *SfB*. In later editions Kim's story was shifted forwards in Yarn 1 to precede the account of the Mafeking Boy Scouts. B.-P.'s leaden, sanitized, and highly selective rendition of Kim's tale aside (note that none of the Indian characters are named), it is striking that he wastes no time in erecting, somewhat contradictorily, a literary scaffolding for his book of instruction for robust 'real *men*'. Kipling's work was elsewhere, too, a formative influence on Scouting (as in the creation of the Wolf Cubs in 1916): B.-P. discussed with Kipling as early as 1901 the development of civilian scouting, and referred questions and suggestions to him across the ensuing decades. See pp. 67, 164, and 218. Small single-phrase and sentence additions to the Part TS show B.-P. striving to relate his paraphrase of *Kim* more closely to the business of Scouting. See also Hugh Brogan, *Mowgli's Sons: Kipling and Baden-Powell's Scouts* (Cape, 1987).

18 *The following books*: several of the Camp Fire Yarns end with a list of recommended reading, although many of the titles listed, other than some of the literary texts, are now out of print (as this particular list demonstrates). At times the 'books to read' lists are very obviously incomplete and show signs of having been hastily put together (as on p. 89). If read from a present-day perspective and in the clusters in which they appear, the recommended titles can be regarded as signifiers of bodies of knowledge, or pseudo-knowledge (such as on first-aid, bodily health, and 'the facts of life'), of which B.-P. himself often had little more than an amateur's understanding. See, for example, the book lists on pp. 202 and 211. In the present edition of *Scouting for Boys*, recommended titles will be annotated only where they are particularly significant, as where B.-P. cites a work in the main body of his text, in order to illustrate or develop a point. In this largely literary list it is worth singling out Charlotte Mason's *Parents and Children* (Kegan Paul, Trench, Trübner, and Co., 1897): Mason was an influential liberal educationalist who was not only cited by, but herself cited, B.-P. See also p. 228.

19 *COURSE OF INSTRUCTION*: this is the point at which the Part MS text begins. The page follows its list of contents for Chapter I.

on your honour: the emphasis appears neither in the Part MS nor in the Part TS. Its significance as the fundamental binding spirit of the Scout Promise must have impressed itself upon B.-P. in the course of writing *SfB*. B.-P.'s respect for medieval knighthood was conditioned by the medieval revivalism popular in Victorian society, sparked off by Kenelm Digby's *The Broad Stone of Honour* (1822). See in particular Chapter VII, 'Chivalry of the Knights', and Mark Girouard, *The Return to Camelot: Chivalry and the English Gentleman* (Yale University Press, 1981).

20 '*BE PREPARED*': it followed from the frequent citation of his own experience as exemplary (the Mafeking story, and pp. 156 or 203–4, for example), that B.-P.'s initials (which stood also for 'British Public', as was noted at the time) were so readily called into service as the mnemonic for the Scout Movement's central motto. See also pp. 24, 35, 44, 213, 249, 260, 277, 283, 291, 294, 307–8. (On pp. 35 and 44 the connection is made explicit; on p. 294 a fanciful alternative etymology is given.) The new South African Constabulary, which B.-P. headed up in 1901, took the same motto. B.-P. is fond of folk wisdoms condensed into memorable sayings and mottos: in the chapters on 'Endurance' and 'Chivalry', see pp. 186, 199, 200, 213 (where the scout motto is given knightly provenance), 214–16, and 236. In later editions of *SfB* he was concerned to downplay the egotism embedded in the B.-P. mnenomic.

"savage wild beast"!: this Boer War anecdote, intended as a humorous illustration of B.-P.'s injunction to preserve and value animal life, in fact exposes the contradictions which beset his professed environmentalism. See the sixth Scout Law, p. 45. The hunter in B.-P., the avid pig-sticker of the Northwest Frontier, for whom woodcraft was a more recently acquired skill, found it difficult not to delight in incidents of successful slaughter. (The anecdote was duly removed from later editions.) B.-P.'s contradictoriness on this subject resurfaces on pp. 105–8 and 111–13, which contrast strongly with the objectives of the game of 'Lion Hunting', pp. 118–19. For a further Boer War anecdote, about defensive strategy or spying, see pp. 173–4.

22 *the young Colonial*: as on p. 13, 'Colonials' are consistently the contemporary heroes of the piece: survivors, champions at roughing it, the superior type of 'real *men*'. The notion tallied with B.-P.'s idea, as expressed in a speech to the army prior to writing *SfB*, that the 'great overseas states of our Commonwealth' offered 'golden opportunities' for self-improvement to men of true British blood, as long as they were prepared to work like colonials (Jeal, *Baden-Powell*, 418–19). Scouting for B.-P. in many ways equated with working as a frontiersman of the Empire, expanding and consolidating British spheres of influence. See pp. 153, 217–18, 274, 300. See also Robert H. Macdonald, *Sons of the*

Empire: The Frontier and the Boy Scout Movement, 1890–1918 (University of Toronto Press, 1993).

22 *'tenderfoot'*: the first instance of one of the commonplaces of Scouting terminology, a *soi-disant* Native American transliteration for greenhorn, which probably reached B.-P. via Victorian tales of the American Wild West, Bill Hamilton (see note to p. 153), or Ernest Thompson Seton (see note to p. 36). See also, for example, pp. 25, 66, 139, 148, 154, 162.

to be a man: as on p. 13, the emphasis is on Scouting as manliness training.

scouts of Britain: joining the illustrious company of British heroes enumerated on p. 14, medieval knights, too, are invoked as ideal types of Scouts. See also pp. 155, 212–14.

Japs: taking into account B.-P.'s respect for Japan's martial culture, a culture founded, as he saw it, on discipline and honour, his use of this term does not have quite the same derogatory connotations as the word does post-1941. He was writing of course in the immediate aftermath of the 1905 Japanese victory over the Russians, the triumph of an island-people over a far more powerful foe. Even so, though the abbreviated word enhances the conversational quality of B.-P.'s form of address, it is worth asking whether he would have referred to a European people in quite the same way. See also pp. 188–9, 196, 216 and the notes to pp. 25, 44, and 188. In *Boy Scouts Beyond the Seas* (1913), as in elided sections of the Part MS (some of which were retrieved for the CE, p. 200), B.-P. again celebrates the heroism and chivalry of the Japanese, embodied in their practice of martial self-slaughter or *hari-kiri* (see p. 226). See also his *Yarns for Boy Scouts* (1909).

23 *British nation*: an important change from the Part MS and Part TS is that 'England' has, by and large, been replaced in the final text with references to Britain, to match the text's lessons in *British* patriotism (see, for example, pp. 26–8). Despite the status which he continued to attribute to St George, the patron saint of England, B.-P. consolidated these changes in later editions.

24 *escaping from fire*: instead of this phrase, the Part MS has: 'how to hold a carpet to catch people jumping out of burning buildings'. B.-P. assiduously modified both drafts and later editions of the text where he had (such was his reliance on common knowledge and very basic medical lore) unwittingly recommended unsafe practices.

25 *weaken him*: the first euphemistic reference to the distracting and dangerous effects of night-time stimulation, particularly masturbation. It is interesting that B.-P. recommends, unabashed, his own far-from-conventional practice, as a married man, of sleeping alone, on a verandah, out of doors. The practice had saved him from the debilitating headaches that he experienced in the first stressful months of married cohabitation with his wife Olave.

ju-jitsu exercises: forms of unarmed self-defence and physical training developed by the Japanese samurai. The samurai comprised feudal warrior clans who were dominant in Japan from the twelfth century until 1879 when the modernizing Meiji regime curtailed their powers. In the early twentieth century karate and judo grew out of ju-jitsu. See also notes to pp. 188 and 299.

good rub-down: in both Part MS 15 and Part TS 29 this paragraph begins: 'A regular daily rear is of utmost importance, as also at least a good rub down daily . . .' B.-P.'s explicit reference to boys' bowel movements so early on in the text was probably deemed inappropriate by his image-aware publisher, C. Arthur Pearson. A 'rough towel' was a piece of equipment deemed essential for all boys attending the first scout camp at Brownsea Island.

through the nose: B.-P.'s concern about the 'daily rear' is equalled only by his obsession with the openness of the orifice of the nose. See p. 188, as well as pp. 76 and 159.

26 *Edward VII*: the playboy king, and eldest son of Queen Victoria (1841–1910; reigned 1901–10).

28 *the great Roman empire*: towards the end of *SfB*, in Part VI addressed to Instructors, B.-P. expands feverishly on this well-known and doom-laden analogy. See pp. 277–8, 294, and 295–7.

A brutal murder: B.-P's yarn is based on a 1791 murder at Pele Raw, near Elsdon in Northumbria. His use of the archaic word 'stob', signifying the gibbet post, suggests that he may have derived the murder story either from a literary source or from oral tradition. Compared to the Part MS version, the final text adds two or three realistic details, such as concerning the fate of the accomplices, as well as the final paragraph about Winter's brother's name-change, which reflects the born-actor B.-P.'s belief that one can become what one appears to be. A note to Part TS 4 (verso) suggests that B.-P. may at one stage have considered using the Elsdon story as the opening Yarn.

32 *Secretary of State for War*: Viscount Richard Haldane, the lawyer and statesman, served in this capacity in Henry Campbell-Bannerman's Liberal government (1905–12), presiding over army reform, and the creation of a Territorial Army, at a time when such developments were deeply unpopular amongst Liberals. B.-P. held several constructive conversations with Haldane in 1907 when planning *SfB*. Haldane's mother, the woman here referred to, was Mary Burdon Sanderson. See Jeal, *Baden-Powell*, 372–3.

other work or play: this repeats the claim made also in the Foreword for Instructors, and again on pp. 304–6, that scouting should be complementary to other boys' organizations, in towns where these existed. B.-P. is developing an idea he had previously outlined in his 1907 report on the Brownsea Camp, 'Boy Scouts' (Part MS 6–13), and in the promotional leaflet *Boy Scouts: Summary of a Scheme* (1907).

34 *helping others*: the second half of this sentence constitutes another

addition to the final text, accentuating B.-P.'s dual focus on scouts of war and of peacetime.

35 *B. P., my initials*: added in red ink, not in B.-P.'s hand, to the Part TS. See note to p. 20.

36 *fighting tribes in South Africa*: although he tends elsewhere to represent Africans as bloodthirsty savages or corrupted reprobates, as in his book on Prempeh, *The Downfall of Prempeh: A Diary of Life with the Native Levy in Ashanti 1895–6* (Methuen, 1896), or on the Ndebele Rebellion, *The Matabele Campaign, 1896* (Methuen, 1897), B.-P., like other colonial writers such as H. Rider Haggard or John Buchan, professed respect for the militaristic and ceremony-loving Zulus he had met on campaign in Natal (see *The Matabele Campaign*, 24, 64; Jeal, *Baden-Powell*, 133–4), just as he did for Native Americans or the 'Red Indians' of his boyhood reading. He cites so-called 'Zulu' initiation rituals, for example, as models for the upbringing of British boys as scouts (p. 152); borrows without proper acknowledgement a Zulu praise song for the Scout's War Chorus (p. 40), and suggests a 'Red Indian' war dance by way of accompaniment (pp. 50–1). See also pp. 44, 61, 99, 132. The native runners and message-carriers of the Mafeking siege he also respected as scouts, as on p. 174. See the Introduction to this edition, pp. xxxiv and xxxvii–xxxviii.

'The Wolf': according to *The Matabele Campaign*, 233, B.-P. overheard some Ndebele fighters calling him 'Impeesa', or *impisi*, seemingly as part of a warlike threat. The word in fact means hyena, spy, or creature that skulks by night: wolves are not native to Africa. It is a revealing instance of his self-invention that B.-P. chose 'Wolf', and elsewhere 'Wolf that never sleeps', as a more dignified translation, in line with the romantic descriptors of Rider Haggard's Allan Quatermain, or his own friend Frederick Burnham (called by Africans 'He who sees in the dark'). It was Ernest Thompson Seton who informed B.-P. that the North American Indians considered the grey wolf the ideal scout amongst the animals because it observed everything, yet remained unobserved. The Ndebele fighters may well, however, have been praising B.-P.'s skill and stealth as a scout by calling him a hyena, rather than, or in addition to, insulting him (personal communication, 27 January 2003). See Jeal, *Baden-Powell*, 177; Neville Jones (Mhlagazanhlansi), *My Friend Kumalo* (Rhodesian Publishing Co., 1944), 52; Michael Rosenthal, *The Character Factory* (Collins, 1986), 36.

Mr Thompson Seton: the Canadian Ernest Thompson Seton (1860–1946) was, in the early 1900s, the founder of the Woodcraft League (1902), and later helped introduce Scouting to North America. While working as a Government naturalist in Manitoba Seton published a number of self-illustrated, finely observed books on wildlife and woodcraft, including *Lives of the Hunted* (1901) and *Two Little Savages: A Book of American Woodcraft for Boys* (Doubleday, Page and Co., 1903), from which B.-P. later quotes. It was Seton's belief that the charged, unruly emotions of young male adolescents could be constructively channeled into woodcraft, ritual-based activity, and group work. B.-P. first met Ernest

Thompson Seton in 1906 and read his *The Birch-Bark Roll of the Woodcraft Indians* (Curtis Publishing Company, 1903; first published in the *Ladies' Home Journal* in 1902) at the time that he was planning *SfB*. Seton's ideas certainly were fundamental to the early development of Scouting. Although Seton worked closely with B.-P. for a number of years, he soon became convinced that the Founder was appropriating if not stealing his ideas. B.-P. remained affably nonplussed at these charges of plagiarism, but Seton was to hold a grievance against him until the end of his days. The number of occasions on which Seton is cited in *SfB* give the reader a fairly shrewd sense of his profound influence at least upon the text's making. See pp. 87, 161–2, 300, 321–2, and 326 and the notes to pp. 87 and 118.

38 *nothing slavish about it*: there is concern to demonstrate that the salute, far from implying the existence of internal hierarchies (which are, however, the basis of Scout organization as described in these pages), instead signifies a yeoman-like fraternity and mutual respect between Scouts.

40 *The Scout's Chorus*: one of B.-P.'s conspicuous borrowings from the Zulu military culture he admired. In place of his inelegant spelling and attentuated form of the song, a Zulu-speaking informant offers the following alternative: 'Uyingonyama—gonyama! | Yebo! Ungcono kunalokho; uyimvubu!' (private communication, 6 May 2002). See also *Lessons from the 'Varsity of Life*, 99.

41 *PATROL SIGNS*: called 'SECRET SIGNS' in Part MS 32. Although a case could be made for shoulder knots relating to patrol signs, the short paragraph, 'A white . . . games', probably constitutes a misplaced insertion, in that it does not occur in the corresponding Part MS 32 or Part TS 43. It relates more closely to the 'Scout's Uniform' section above.

42 *'Wolves'*: in this section 'Wolves' and 'Ravens' have replaced the less robust 'Curlews' in Part MS 32.

44 *their ancient codes*: B.-P. includes non-Western peoples amongst those who count law-respecting scouts in their number.

THE SCOUT LAW: inspired by the laws and pledges of Ernest Thompson Seton's Woodcraft Indians, and of the League of Boy Friends (both founded in 1902), B.-P. made sure to cast his laws in the affirmative, avoiding Old Testament-like prohibitions. This, accompanied by an avoidance of military drill, is often regarded as one of the aspects of Scouting that has ensured its worldwide popularity across the twentieth century. In the 1911 edition the Scout Law was turned into a decalogue with the addition of a tenth law which captured Baden-Powell's preoccupation with moral purity: 'A scout is pure in thought, word, and deed.'

45 *'Little friend of all the world'*: a parallelism exists with the title B.-P. was presently to assume: 'Chief Scout of the World'.

46 *never*: the Part MS and Part TS read 'don't'.

48 *KIM'S GAME*: in Part MS 59–61 (Part TS 79–82) this appears under

'Games in Observation' (see *SfB* 75 ff.), and is followed by a long description of the game in Kipling's *Kim* itself.

50 *SCOUT'S WAR DANCE*: see note to p. 36.

51 *THE CAPTURE OF JOHN SMITH*: although B.-P.'s seventeenth-century 'Red Indians' have foresightedly formed themselves into scouting patrols, the ideological burdens of the dramatization of the legendary December 1607 capture of John Smith (see note to p. 14), and his rescue via the intercession of Chief Powhattan's daughter Pocahontas, are undisguised. The 'Sioux' (in fact Pamunkey) scouts are impressionable and easily cowed while John Smith, calling upon St George, is given ample opportunity to demonstrate his superior English mettle and moral fibre. His 'final' speech, before what is anticipated as certain death, merges Britain's imperial creed with the Scout Law (p. 58). Linda Colley, *Captives: Britain, Empire and the World, 1600–1850* (Cape, 2002), 401, and Peter Hulme, *Colonial Encounters* (Routledge, 1986), 137–56, both speculate that Smith's mock-execution and rescue may in fact have served as a ceremony of rebirth into the Algonquin tribe, or of alliance between themselves and the whites. B.-P.'s marvellously hybrid play (the 'Indians', for example, break into the Zulu 'Ingonyama' chorus) draws on his early reading of travel and adventure tales by George Catlin and others involving 'Indians'. It also gives hectic expression to his identification with an English national hero to whom he laid (unsubstantiated) claim as an ancestor. This is made explicit in an edited section of the Part MS, which weaves a highly subjective narrative of John Smith's early career as a scourge of the Turks (see note to p. 275). The somewhat paradoxical 'Never Say Die' motto recurs on pp. 186 and 226. See also pp. 175, 201, 215, 227.

56 *KING*: the juxtaposition of two speeches by the 'King' may be an error or oversight.

PRINCESS POCAHONTAS: according to the myth, Pocahontas (*c.*1595–1617), daughter of the Tidewater Algonquins' leader Powhattan, acted as a mediator in negotiations between the Virginian colonists and the Native Americans (1607, 1609). Married to the colonist John Rolfe in 1613, she died of smallpox on a visit to England in 1617. See p. 275.

64 *HINTS TO INSTRUCTORS*: this corresponds to the 'Hints' section immediately below (on p. 64), and does not appear as part of the 'Woodcraft' section on p. 97.

65 *Mrs Smithson*: given that close observation and 'character reading' are conventionally identified as feminine skills, B.-P.'s first example of reading 'sign' is suggestively taken from a female informant, though it involves male native trackers. 'Mrs Smithson' was the wife of Walter Charles Smithson, who was, like B.-P., an officer in the 13th Hussars during the 1880s when they were stationed in India.

67 *Camorra*: a nineteenth-century Neapolitan secret society. The embryonic form of the Mafia, the society was officially suppressed in 1911.

Houdini: Harry Houdini (1874–1926, original name Erik Weisz), the world-famous American illusionist and escape artiste. In ways resembling B.-P.'s advocacy, Houdini trained his son in his craft by following the methods of Kim's game. On Captain Cook, see note to p. 14.

tell from their boots: the phrase is inserted into the Part MS 41–2 sentence by caret, as is 'foreign looking boots' on the previous page. B.-P.'s intense interest in the eloquent 'meaning' of footware, suggests that he may fetishize feet as much as he does noses (see pp. 69–70). He is also of course fascinated by the telltale signs of 'genteel poverty'. He might have agreed with the class-aware Mrs Isabella Beeton's observation in 1859: the 'footgear of a lady, is one of the few things left [given new clothing manufactures] to mark her station, and requires special care'. See *Mrs Beeton's Book of Household Management* (Oxford World's Classics, 2000), p. xxvii. See also pp. 68, 77, 79, and 240. On p. 207 B.-P. gives advice on Scouts' feet and footwear.

68 *suspicious of him*: a back-reference to the Elsdon Murder story, pp. 28–32. See also p. 72.

69 *Mr Nat Goodwin*: an American actor who B.-P. met at 'one of Beerbohm Tree's jolly supper parties'. The same anecdote is narrated in *Lessons from the 'Varsity of Life*, 46.

70 *in a bad way*: a very similar incident, again involving a 'lady's' reduced or lowly circumstances betrayed by her boots, is recounted on p. 240.

that boot: at this point in Part MS 42, B.-P. has pasted a clipping from an *Illustrated Paper* article by a Valentina Steer recommending observation as a pleasant and useful pastime.

'Sherlock Holmes': the first of several references to this paragon of detective work. Arthur Conan Doyle (1859–1930), who served as a medical doctor in Bloemfontein during the first year of the Anglo-Boer War (1899–1900), published his Sherlock Holmes stories from 1887. Like Holmes's many admirers, including Dr Watson, B.-P. is impressed at how the detective is able to make the most dazzling deductions from tiny details and neglected bits of evidence, that is, from observation of an urban kind. In the story 'Silver Blaze', in *The Memoirs of Sherlock Holmes* (1894), Holmes characteristically describes detective work as 'our duty to see what inferences may be drawn, and which are the special points upon which the whole mystery turns.' The careless reader B.-P. has miscast the encounter in question, perhaps misremembered it, from a conversation between Holmes and his brother Mycroft in the story 'The Greek Interpreter' (also in *The Memoirs of Sherlock Holmes*), in which they *together* identify the circumstances of a passing N.-C.O. in *full* mourning dress from the *Royal Artillery* not the Royal Marines. See pp. 71, 93–4, and 95–6.

71 *'The Resident Patient'*: this story, from *The Memoirs of Sherlock Holmes*, becomes at the end of Chapter II the basis of an exercise in observation. The italics here are probably unintentional as the paragraph is not

addressed to instructors (the italics do not occur in the Part MS). See also pp. 95–6, and the note to p. 94.

72 *Captain D'Artagnan*: the fourth musketeer in the 1844 novel by Alexandre Dumas (*père*). The reference to further discussion anticipates the lengthy extract cut or torn from the novel which appears as Part MS 75–6 (corresponding to *SfB* 89–91). Like other of B.-P.'s cut-and-paste citations, it was not, however, included in the final PE. A residue remains in the D'Artagnan game recommended on p. 96.

importance: at this point in Part MS 49–50, B.-P. includes the 1896–7 Matabele Rebellion incident (from *The Matabele Campaign*) in which he himself is shown successfully 'reading sign'. This now appears on pp. 89–91.

'*The Pathfinder*': one of five tales in the *Leatherstocking* saga (1840) by James Fenimore Cooper (1789–1857), the author who was an important literary source for the myth of the American frontier. In Part MS 51, opening with the words, 'Here is the story', B.-P. begins by summarizing the incident which is sketchily described here, but rounds off with the instruction to his typist to transfer the rest of the narrative direct from the pages he has torn from the novel's chapter V. See also Part TS 64–70. B.-P., however, deletes from Fenimore Cooper's narrative the death of the noble Iroquois who makes the observation in question.

73 *those asleep*: in Part MS 51–2 (Part TS 70–3) a second long extract (or literal 'tear-out'), a 'description of night sounds' from *The Pathfinder*, follows, as well as two further pages by B.-P. on night scouting, also omitted from the final text, and including a long quotation attributed to President Theodore Roosevelt (see p. 153) concerning hunting *wapiti* stag by scent. Compare note to p. 189.

Dr Gross: the English translation of Dr Hans Gross, *System der Kriminalistik*, the standard (and highly graphic) textbook on police detection. See p. 96.

'*Aids to Scouting*': the first reference to B.-P.'s 1899 handbook for 'N.-C.O.'s and Men', which will later form the core of the paragraphs on tracking. See pp. 83 ff.

HINTS TO INSTRUCTORS: this section should, strictly speaking, be italicized. It appears in the appropriate red ink in the Part MS, B.-P.'s colour coding for instructors' guidelines. See also examples on pp. 242 ff. and 287.

74 *etc., etc.*: a near repetition of a paragraph on p. 67.

77 *GENERAL DODGE*: General Robert Irvine Dodge, of the American government forces involved in wresting the West from the Native Americans in the mid-nineteenth century. See his *Our Wild Indians: Thirty-Three Years Personal Experience* (1882; Corner House, 1978).

78 *Burnham*: Major Frederick Russell Burnham, an American scout B.-P. met in south-central Africa (what in 1898 became Rhodesia), who worked as a guide for the British South Africa Company in the campaign

against the Ndebele in 1893, and acted as chief of scouts to the commander of the imperial relief force in the 1896 campaign. His nickname for B.-P. was 'Sherlock Holmes'. Burnham had gained military experience with the North American government forces during the Apache Wars, and had learned from their Native American scouts. From Burnham B.-P. acquired the term *woodcraft* as signifying observation and survival in the wild. See *The Matabele Campaign*, 51, 70–1. Burnham's so-called courageous escape from the Wilson ambush was held in some suspicion in later years. See Frederick Russell Burnham, *Scouting on Two Continents* (1926; Wolf Publishing Co., 1994).

finding the line: see *The Matabele Campaign*, 88. A Scout troop has since carved on one of the stones in the rocky Matopos hills a marker to the effect that this was where B.-P. was first inspired to found Scouting as a system of training (Terence Ranger, personal communication, 30 November 2002).

83 *Native trackers . . . continually improving*: a direct (and largely unmodified) quotation from *Aids to Scouting for N.-C.O.s and Men* (Gale and Polden, 1899), 53–5. B.-P. first quotes from the handbook, though more briefly, as part of the paragraph on pp. 78–9, 'Hunters when they are looking about . . . do much the same as regards their enemies.'

84 *last man to be suspected*: Part MS 63–4 goes on to offer two more stories of tracking 'in Soudan and Egypt from personal observation' (in the spring of 1907), which B.-P. has shifted to the end of Part VI of the PE (p. 348), as additional, or filler, information.

Mr Deakin: the Australian politician and man of letters Alfred Deakin (1856–1919), active in the 1890s Federation Movement. He was Prime Minister of Australia in 1903–4, 1905–8, and 1909–10. He reported regularly, though anonymously, on Australian subjects for the London *Morning Post* throughout his time in the Federal Parliament. Deakin was, like Baden-Powell, a multi-talented man, who wrote verse, literary criticism, and reports on agriculture. The Deakin anecdote is written on Savoy Hotel notepaper turned upside down. It is followed in Part MS 67–8 by a short, awkward narrative concerning the theft of a vase by a 'gentleman', Mr Anstruther, who is discovered by a bootblack boy, but pardoned by his gentleman-host in the interests of class solidarity. This sensitive element no doubt warranted its excision from the final text.

Scinde: Sind, the south-eastern region of contemporary Pakistan.

87 *In tracking where the spoor . . . to his resting place*: the second lengthy, practically direct quotation from B.-P.'s own *Aids to Scouting*, 56–8. (Part MS 70 consists of an instruction to Mr Cavan the typist to 'Quote pp. 58–59–60 "Aids to Scouting",' and to add two annexed sheets of notepaper, possibly that from the Savoy, Part MS 66: see second note to p. 84). The quotation here differs mainly in the addition of the detail of looking at tracks *against* the sun on p. 86, and in its paragraph breaks.

'Tracking Irons': Part MS 71 has ' "Deerfoot Irons" ', an invention of

Ernest Thompson Seton's and named by him. The name change disguises the awkwardness of the borrowing from Seton, amongst so many others, as the 'N.B.' also registers.

89 *'Forest and Stream'*: the American woodcraft magazine, a publication current from the 1890s, in which Ernest Thompson Seton published.

90 *letter by letter*: the analogy between deciphering 'sign' and conventional reading is first developed in B.-P.'s *The Matabele Campaign*, 98–9, and transferred from its pages almost word-for-word. The analogy, and the exemplary scouting incident which follows involving B.-P. and a 'native' reading the evidence of fallen leaves during the Ndebele Rebellion, also appears in *Aids to Scouting*, 61–4. Significantly, in his first account of the reading leaves incident, in *The Matabele Campaign*, 100, unlike in the following two renditions, B.-P. gives the 'native' (Jan Grootboom, an expert Fingo scout from the Cape) the credit for having detected the telltale leaves and read their origin. Grootboom, 'a white man—if in a black skin', is acknowledged as an important influence in *Lessons from the 'Varsity of Life*, 138–41, where he is described as saving B.-P.'s life by scouting an ambush.

[Show on map]: the map's inclusion (another borrowing from B.-P.'s own published work, a 1907 book of sketches) is more or less gratuitous, becoming meaningful chiefly if the Founder's biography is regarded as a source of lessons in Scouting.

wide grassy plain: this tracking experience in the Matopos in present-day Zimbabwe is taken almost unchanged from *The Matabele Campaign*, 100 ff. Instead of this incident (which occurs at an earlier point: see second note to p. 72), Part MS 76 (Part TS 108–12) contains an extract torn from Dumas's *Louise de la Vallière*, chapter 1. D'Artagnan, in response to Louis XIV's praise for his skill in observation, explains, with many references to 'reading sign', his reasons for thinking that a secret duel has recently taken place. B.-P. scores out in the original the sentences referring to the fact that the King is writing poetry just prior to his interview with the musketeer.

92 *Tighe Hopkins*: a writer of historical fiction (1856–1919).

'World's Work': a periodical current between 1901 and 1932.

93 *Dr Bell*: Dr Joseph Bell, Arthur Conan Doyle's teacher at medical school in Edinburgh, upon whose methods and mannerisms, as B.-P. notes, he modelled the detective Sherlock Holmes.

94 *Sherlock Holmes*: prior to these 'Hints', as part of the section on deduction, Part MS 77–84 draws on examples of Holmesian analysis from, amongst others, 'The Resident Patient', and 'The Stockbroker's Clerk', in *The Memoirs of Sherlock Holmes* (1894). See p. 71. Conan Doyle's *The Adventures of Sherlock Holmes* was published in 1891.

96 *D'Artagnan elucidated*: see note to p. 72 and third note to p. 90.

98 *escape being noticed*: hereafter follow several quotations from *Aids to*

Scouting, section iv, 'Keeping yourself hidden and dodging the enemy': 'In choosing your background . . . red earth or rocks, and so on' corresponds to *Aids to Scouting*, 42–3; 'In making use of hills . . . sky-line' to p. 46; 'It is quite a lesson . . . higher ground' to pp. 47–8, and also p. 37; and, 'By squatting low . . . fling my arms around him' is taken from p. 49. The last-mentioned incident was recounted for the first time in Baden-Powell's narrative of his Asante campaign, *The Downfall of Prempeh*, 120–1, and was captured in his cover illustration for the book. See also p. 324.

100 *a wolf if seen*: as part of its discussion of camouflage, Part MS 92–3 here includes pasted-in cuttings or tearings from Fenimore Cooper's *The Deerslayer* (1841) and *The Pathfinder* (1840) depicting an instance of hiding while on the run, and a Native American disguise in the form of a bush. These were no doubt simply removed at the proof stage to avoid charges of excessive borrowing.

103 *'Beasts of the Field'*: the moose-calling incident is from the North American naturalist William Long's *Beasts of the Field* (Ginn and Co./The Athenaeum Press, 1901), 193–7. B.-P. edits the incident considerably, in particular the complicated getaway sequence, omitting also to mention that the use of the call as decoy forms a crucial part of moose *hunting*.

105 *My brother*: his youngest brother, Baden Baden-Powell.

'With Flashlight and Rifle in Africa': Carl Schilling, *With Flashlight and Rifle, a Record of Hunting Adventures and of Studies in Wild Life in Equatorial East Africa*, 2 vols., trans. Frederic Whyte (Hutchinson and Co., 1906). B.-P.'s anti-hunting message notwithstanding, Schilling's two-volume text is all about the hunt and the kill, and ends with a list itemizing his collection of dead animal trophies (a convention at the time —Frederick Selous's *A Hunter's Wanderings in Africa* has a similar inventory). The photograph in question is the second in vol. 2 (facing p. 378) and shows a lion springing onto a *donkey*.

baby: the pets formed part of the household at 'Bloater Park', the regimental bungalow home B.-P. and his close army friend Boy McLaren set up at Muttra in India in the early 1880s. The boar was the pet 'pig called Algernon' (Jeal, *Baden-Powell*, 70); the panther the men named Squirks (*Lessons from the 'Varsity of Life*, 103).

109 *'Mammals of Great Britain and Ireland'*: John Guille Millais, *The Mammals of Great Britain and Ireland* (1904–6). Note that B.-P.'s infantilizing pseudo-etymology subtly marginalizes biological mothering. From Part MS 113–14 it is unclear which paragraphs exactly of 'The Hedgehog and the Viper' story are quoted from the Millais text. Significantly, B.-P. begins the section on wild animals (Part MS 111) by coming perilously close to categorizing plants as animals for the reason that they both provide food in the jungle. These remarks were later deleted.

110 *'The School of the Woods'*: William Long, *The School of the Woods* (Ginn and Co. The Athenaeum Press, 1902), 3–4. Long's description of otter training is distinguished from B.P.'s by its literary embellishment,

including the use of Native American names as proper names for the animals. Long's otters are also significantly far more diffident than B.-P.'s. As the Founder would quote from Sir Percy Fitzpatrick in the CE: 'Boys is like pups—you've got to help them some, but not too much and not too soon. They've got to learn themselves. I reckon if a man's never made a mistake he's never had a good lesson.'

110 *Long writes*: Long, *The School of the Woods*, 11–12. *SfB* adds the paragraph break and modifies the punctuation of the last sentence.

111 *Mark Twain*: the pen-name of the American writer Samuel Langhorne Clemens (1835–1910), who described his Mississippi Valley frontier upbringing in a number of different books, including *Life on the Mississippi* (1883).

115 *grin a smile*: as in *The Downfall of Prempeh*, 164–5, keeping cheerful in adversity is an article of faith for B.-P.

118 *LION HUNTING*: the game, which depends on the use of tracking irons, is based on the ideas of Ernest Thompson Seton. See note to p. 87. Other games silently appropriated from Seton, usually with a name-change to disguise the borrowing, are: 'A Whale Hunt' (p. 161: Seton's 'Spearing the Great Sturgeon'); 'Find the North' (p. 173: Seton's 'Pole Star'); 'Dispatch Running' (pp. 180–1: Seton's 'Man Hunt'); 'Old Spotty-face' and 'Quick Sight' (pp. 192–3: Seton's 'Spot the Rabbit' and 'Quick Sight'). See also p. 321, and notes to pp. 151 and 161.

119 *Sir Percy Fitzpatrick*: *Jock of the Bushveld* (1907), a South African classic. Once again B.-P. pads his reading list with literary texts, adding also Rudyard Kipling's *The Jungle Book* (1894).

120 *bad luck*: see also p. 146.

the leaf on the tree: that is, with the appearance of the leaf on the appropriate tree.

the nails in them: this sentence is an accidental insert, slotted into the text along with the accompanying pictures (see Part MS 133; Part TS 170–2). The subsequent sentence therefore—'And then get to know . . .'—refers back to the previous paragraph on tree observation.

128 *the West Coast of Africa*: in *The Downfall of Prempeh* (1896), from which the sketch on page 130 is taken, B.-P. makes much of his raising of a successful native scouting levy, probably as compensation for his disappointment at the Asantehene Prempeh's avoidance of military engagement. See also pp. 133 and 142.

129 *string or rope, etc.*: the knot diagrams which follow are based on those in the draft of B.-P.'s 1907 Brownsea Camp letter to parents.

136 *'roughing it' in camp*: the phrase may allude to Mark Twain, *Roughing It* (1872) (though this would have been pre-empted as a title by Susannah Moodie's Canadian *Roughing It* (1852)).

little dodges: B.-P. first used this word to denote scouting schemes and stratagems in his handbook of instruction in army scouting, *Reconnais-*

sance and Scouting: A Practical Course of Instruction, in Twenty Plain Lessons, for Officers, Non-commissioned Officers, and Men (William Clowes and Son, 1884), p. viii. In the following chapters on camping and campaigning (up to p. 172), *SfB* makes several further references to *Reconnaissance and Scouting*. The first was the instruction concerning the usefulness of self-measurement (see p. 134, and *Reconnaissance and Scouting*, appendix C). See p. 164 and the note to p. 170.

140 *sitting right at home*: Ernest Thompson Seton, *Two Little Savages*, 124. In the Seton text the boy reciting this is self-consciously quoting an adult. *Two Little Savages* concerns two young boys at the brink of adolescence who achieve self-discipline through the practice of woodcraft. B.-P. noticeably omits to mention the author's name.

142 *as I have pointed out*: in fact the text makes references to flies at a *later* point, on p. 150.

151 *'Bang the Bear'*: see Ernest Thompson Seton's *The Birch-Bark Roll of the Woodcraft Indians*, 42–3. Given the influence of Seton's ideas the omission of this important reference text from the recommended reading further down the page, is again noteworthy. So, too, in the original PE, is the inversion of Thompson Seton's name, and the use of an incorrect book title (the word 'Roll' was omitted both here and on p. 161). See note to p. 118.

152 *The native boys . . . to look after himself*: B.-P. is describing initiation practices (also carried out in groups) more typically associated with the Xhosa, and other southern African peoples, than with the Zulu.

153 *Bill Hamilton*: a Rocky Mountain trapper, interpreter for, and scourge of Native American tribes in the West (1822–1908). His memoir, *My Sixty Years on the Plains, Trapping, Trading and Indian Fighting* (n.d.) is laden with advice on bush survival.

Mr Roosevelt: Theodore Roosevelt (1858–1919), twenty-sixth President of the United States of America, 1901–9, and Honorary Vice-President of the Boy Scouts of America from 1910. Roosevelt was, as B.-P. observes, a stern advocate of character-building exercise and bodily training, based on his own programme of self-development. He led the 'Rough Riders' or First US Volunteer Cavalry in Cuba in the 1898 Spanish-American War. See p. 284, as well as Roosevelt, *The Strenuous Life* (1900).

156 *two of my brothers*: see *Lessons from the 'Varsity of Life*, 26–7.

161 *'Birchbark Roll of the Woodcraft Indians'*: from Ernest Thompson Seton's book, p. 43, where the game is called 'Spearing the Great Sturgeon'. See note to p. 118.

162 *Mrs Ernest Thompson Seton*: Grace Gallatin Thompson Seton, *A Woman Tenderfoot* (David Nutt, 1901), teaches women with great enjoyment to be 'vulgarly robust'. See p. 324.

169 *'Ingolubu'*: B.-P. badly mangled or mistook the Zulu term for Orion, *iMpambano*.

170 *A X*: the exercises in estimating distance across a river and finding height, and the accompanying diagrams, are taken from *Reconnaissance and Scouting*, 13–15, and 19–20. The compass drawing on p. 166, too, is based on that in *Reconnaissance and Scouting*, 23 (plate VI). See second note to p. 136.

172 *Mr G. L. Boundy*: an adult Scout and informant of Baden-Powell's, possibly a former frontiersman or imperial soldier. See also p. 238.

175 *Captain John Smith*: see notes to pp. 51 and 275.

Lieutenant Boyd Alexander: 7th Battalion Rifle Brigade captain, and leader of two British scientific and military expeditions to West Africa (1897, 1904–7), the second of which is described in the two-volume *From the Niger to the Nile* (1907). See note to p. 14.

176 *Boer War*: the incident of message interception is drawn from B.-P.'s involvement in military action against the Boers in the Rustenburg area of South Africa following the Mafeking siege (July–August 1900).

177 *'Esperanto'*: a synthetic language for universal communication, invented *c.*1887 by the Polish physician L. L. Zamenhof. See also p. 238.

186 *F. C. Selous*: the account of Frederick Selous's demonstration of endurance is a summary of his book *Travel and Adventure in South-East Africa* (Rowland Ward and Co., 1893), 221–6, 229, and 230–3, pages which are pasted into Part MS 141–8 with B.-P.'s elisions of the more humdrum material and annotations pointing out examples of right action. Selous wrote up his travels in several articles (1883) and books, also including *A Hunter's Wanderings in Africa* (Richard Bentley and Son, 1881). He was a model for the hero Allan Quatermain in H. Rider Haggard's *King Solomon's Mines* (1885). See also note to p. 14.

188 *Regular daily 'rear'*: see third note to p. 25, and pp. 144, 188, 196, and 204, on the importance of a 'daily rear' for keeping the blood in good order. Two or so of B.-P.'s several references to this (to him) crucial bodily function were edited from the Part TS.

Japs: the following paragraphs form B.-P.'s longest expression of praise for the disciplined and cleanly Japanese: 'They are the best example that we can copy.' See also note to p. 22.

189 *Mr Catlin*: George Catlin, author of *Letters and Notes on the Manners, Customs and Condition of the North-American Indians* (1841), as well as of the cranky book in question, *Shut Your Mouth* (N. Trübner and Co., 1869), which seeks to impart the 'savage' wisdom that the open or 'black' mouth prevalent among 'civilized' peoples not only causes snoring (a give-away in the bush), but induces ill-health, and is itself a symptom of illness. See pp. 25–6.

195 *Avoid Self-Abuse*: the section of explicit and strenuous advice designated by this subheading (Part TS 246–8), which was to appear just before 'Early Rising' (p. 200), B.-P. was persuaded 'under advice' from both his publisher and his printer to cut down, and to 'relegate' in an edited form

to the Notes for Instructors towards the end of the book (pp. 316–17). The reference in this summary was retained, however, as was the reference to Sylvanus Stall's book at the end of the yarn (p. 203, and see p. 183), as B.-P. had thought that Pearson would include at an appropriate point a note to the effect that a 'separate paper' on continence would be disseminated to all interested boys 'on request'. Pearson evidently resisted this. In this edition the excised section appears *in full* as the Appendix. So important was it to B.-P. to warn boys against the 'unmanly' vice that he was prompted in these paragraphs on continence to speak with significantly less prudish reserve than was customary at the time. He also develops the association between self-abuse and national deterioration (see also pp. 184–5).

David Livingstone: see note to p. 14.

Dryden: 'Cymon and Iphigenia' by John Dryden (1631–1700), based on a tale from Boccaccio about the power of 'Desire' to 'amend' human character, appeared in *Fables, Ancient and Modern* (1699). Once again B.-P.'s citation is careless as the quoted lines appear not in this poem but in 'To my honoured kinsman John Driden' (1700). Perhaps he found the lines in a book of aphorisms and mistook the poem title. He abandons Dryden's seventeenth-century capitalizations.

197 *Sir William Broadbent*: royal physician and clinical teacher (1835–1907), a leading authority on heart disease and researcher into hemiplegia.

Professor Sims Woodhead: Sir German Sims Woodhead (1855–1921), an internationally renowned pathologist and author of an 1898 book on the prevention of infectious diseases.

198 *Eustace Miles*: an amateur racquets champion, and editor and author of several books on physical fitness, including *Let's Play the Game, or the Anglo-Saxon Sportsmanlike Spirit* (Guilbert Pitman, 1904). See p. 195.

Professor Osler: Sir William Osler (1849–1919), the Canadian-born Regius Professor of Medicine at Oxford (from 1904).

200 *Emperor Charlemagne*: the first Holy Roman Emperor, recognized as the founder of modern Europe (742–814).

203 *Sylvanus Stall*: the American DD Sylvanus Stall's *What the Young Boy Ought to Know* (Vir Publishing Co., 1897), a handbook of Christian moralizing in the United States 'Self and Sex' series, sets out to equip boys with enough knowledge of human reproduction to be able to withstand 'pernicious habits', where hands are used for 'degraded means'. As with B.-P. on pp. 316–17, however, the aim to be explicit collapses under the demands of social decorum. Fears of physical and national decline—hollow chests, inferior reproductive secretions—dominate instead. B.-P. shares with Stall, or derives from him, injunctions against too many bedcovers and tobacco, as well as recommendations about regular bowel movements. If boys become addicted to self-abuse, Stall writes, it may be necessary to place them in a straitjacket to save them from physical self-destruction. Compare the Appendix and see first note to p. 195.

203 *Some years ago*: the accompanying illustration (p. 204) originally appeared in Part V as a filler.

205 *Eustace Miles*: see note to p. 198.

212 *'In days of old, when knights were bold'*: B.-P.'s a-historical picture of the medieval knight and his men as the patrol leader and scout patrol of old allows him to accomplish some important ideological work: to make a special plea for the cavalry, in which he had served; to build the lineage of the legendary King Arthur into his retrospective history of Scouting; and, also, in so doing, to attach Scouting to a heroic myth of Englishness, for which St George is the well-known symbol. In the Preface to the definitive 1922 edition B.-P. recommends that Scouts read *SfB* on 23 April each year, St George's Day. It is relevant to mention, however, that St George is also the patron saint of chivalry (Paul Moynihan, personal communication, 19 March 2003).

215 *JOHN SMITH*: see pp. 175, 227–8, and the notes to pp. 14, 51, 275. John Smith did not in fact fight in 'every part of the world'.

KING RICHARD I: see note to p. 14.

'The Talisman', by Sir Walter Scott: set at the time of the Crusades, the 1825 novel by the Scottish writer (1771–1832) tells the story of a poor but valiant Scottish knight who is found to be Prince David of Scotland.

218 *'The White Company'*: an 1891 romance by Arthur Conan Doyle, based on the exploits of a fourteenth-century company of English mercenaries.

221 *See Part VI*: B.-P. may have intended this play to appear in the final section of Part VI, 'Scouting Games, Practices and Displays', to accompany 'Play the Game' and 'The Storming of Delhi'.

222 *Browning*: the lines from Robert Browning (1812–89) form the penultimate stanza of the 'Epilogue' to *Asolando: Fancies and Facts* (1889), the last poem of Browning's last collection famously published on the day of his death. The reflective 'Epilogue' became one of the most quoted of Browning's poems, and was said to be a mainstay of British soldiers during the Anglo-Boer War, when Baden-Powell must have encountered it. As before B.-P. supplies his own punctuation, in particular the dash in the final line. See William Clyde Devane, *A Browning Handbook* (Appleton-Century-Crofts, 1955), 552–3.

Lycurgus: the legendary lawgiver of soldierly Sparta (*c.* ninth century BC), credited with having supplied the city-state with its system of education. See Plutarch's *Lives*.

223 *Major MacLaren*: the inclusion of the name of Kenneth (or 'Boy') McLaren, B.-P.'s chief, if not only, close male friend (from the 1880s till about 1910), can be read as the signature of his affection towards him. B.-P. does, however, misspell his surname. Boy McLaren who, like B.-P., enjoyed polo, hog-hunting, and amateur dramatics, was the person in his life with whom he was probably most ideally matched. McLaren helped him organize the first scout camp at Brownsea Island in 1907 and was the

first manager of the Boy Scouts until his surprise resignation in March 1908.

224 *Birkenhead*: a transport ship sunk off Cape Town, South Africa, in 1852. A commonplace in nationalist tales of British pluck and self-discipline, the incident is cited in, amongst other texts, Charlotte Yonge's *A Book of Golden Deeds* (Macmillan and Co., 1864), and Samuel Smiles's work.

225 *Gibraltar*: annexed to Spain in 1501, the Rock of Gibraltar was captured by the British in 1704 during the War of the Spanish Succession, and formally ceded to Britain under the Treaty of Utrecht (1713). Spain, however, made several attempts to retake it, most notably in the protracted siege, 1779–83, to which B.-P. refers. Gibraltar became a British Crown Colony in 1830, although Spain has several times since questioned its status.

226 *It is very like bathing . . . header into the water*: a favourite B.-P. metaphor for preparedness. See p. 12.

227 *J. M. Barrie*: Scottish playwright and novelist (1860–1937), author of B.-P.'s favourite play, *Peter Pan* (1904). See Introduction.

230 . . . *dwell in peace for ever*: this popular Victorian analogy, reputedly addressed by the pagan chieftain Edwin to Bishop Paulinus, is taken from Bede's *Ecclesiastical History* (731). In *King Solomon's Mines* H. Rider Haggard places the same story in the mouth of the Zulu Umbopa.

231 *One writer says*: where B.-P. quotes directly from a text, even if inaccurately, he will usually cite the author's name. The lack of attribution on these pages suggests B.-P. is drawing mainly from popular collections.

232 *J. Astor*: John Jacob Astor, the German-born rag-to-riches millionaire (1763–1848), who immigrated penniless to New York in 1784, and was by 1812 the richest man in the United States.

234 *Cuba*: in the Spanish-American War (1898), fought over the independence of Cuba, the United States sided with the Cuban liberals.

235 *McKinley*: William McKinley (1843–1901), twenty-fifth President of the United States (1896–1901), succeeded by Roosevelt following his assassination.

239 *S. Smiles*: with books like the hugely influential, widely quoted *Self-Help* (1859), *Thrift* (1875), and *Duty* (1880) (see pp. 228, 310, 315), the Victorian man-of-all-trades Samuel Smiles (1812–1904) applied principles of laissez-faire and bourgeois individualism to social reform. The Smiles virtues of industry, thrift, and self-help—'men are their own best helpers'—are fundamental to the moral economy of *SfB*. Significantly, where *Self-Help* was the English-language bestseller, after the Bible, in the second half of the nineteenth century, *SfB* won this place in the twentieth century. (Given B.-P.'s praise for Japan, it is significant that Smiles's texts were largely responsible for introducing European culture to that country.)

Sobriety . . . Notes to Instructors: in PE, the following sections (to the end of Part IV) were inserted at the start of Part V.

239 *He tells the story*: in the Part MS several of the following examples appear earlier in the text (42 ff.), along with the 'details of people' in Chapter II, on Tracking.

240 *Dr Gross*: see second note to p. 73.

242 *Gordon*: Charles George Gordon (1833–85) distinguished himself for his daredevil courage in the Crimea and China (1854–6, 1860), and later served as the Governor of Equatoria in the Sudan (1873–80). Following an attempt to evacuate the Egyptian garrisons from Khartoum, 'Chinese' Gordon was besieged for much of 1884, and was killed following the Mahdi's attack on the town on 26 January 1885, the British forces having failed to relieve him. From Thomas Pakenham's account in *The Scramble for Africa* (Weidenfeld and Nicolson, 1991), it would seem highly *un*likely that Gordon could have 'got away . . . had he liked'. See Henry Newbolt's 'Vitaï Lampada', quoted on pp. 336–7, an iconic imperialist poem which makes chilling reference to the battle to relieve Gordon.

dizzy climax: from Charles Stelzle's *Boys of the Street and How to Win Them* (Fleming H. Revell Co., 1904), 61—an instructional memoir based on Christian principles from this founder of urban boys' clubs. '[W]ork in a boys' club', writes Stelzle, 'should have for its supreme purpose the building up of character'. See also p. 320.

243 *the gift of sleep*: R. L. Stevenson's morning prayer is from the posthumously published *Prayers Written at Vailima* (Chatto, 1905).

Mr John Burns: the socialist and later Radical Liberal (1858–1943), entered Parliament in 1892, and served in Henry Campbell-Bannerman's Liberal Cabinet (1905–14).

244 *Battle of Fontenoy*: battle (11 May 1745) between the French and the Austro-Hungarians during the Austrian War of Succession, which led to the French conquest of Flanders.

250 *. . . eternal disgrace*: a repetition of the incident first reported on p. 25.

253 *shoot-escape*: probably 'chute-escape'. See p. 335, but also p. 272.

254 *Jews*: note that, according to B.-P. in this description, Jews, like the working class elsewhere, are unreliable in a situation of panic. See also p. 66.

257 *Mr Holbein*: Montague A. Holbein, the channel swimmer and author of *Swimming* (C. Arthur Pearson, 1903). See p. 263.

259 *Hon. George Wyndham*: see second note to p. 295.

261 *Sir Thomas Fowell Buxton*: Liberal politician and social reformer (1837–1915), interested in colonial welfare, the Church Missionary society, and the Missions to Seamen.

268 *I was once travelling . . . into conversation*: the meeting took place on a trip to North Africa in 1893, and is described in more detail in the highly fictionalized *My Adventures as a Spy* (C. Arthur Pearson, 1915), 97–100.

273 *Arnold-Forster*: see note to p. 310.

274 *Many of you scouts . . . prosperous countries*: the Ruskinian idea that

England's worthiest men should go out to found and help build up colonies 'as far and fast as they are able'. See Elleke Boehmer, *Empire Writing* (Oxford World's Classics, 1998), 16–20.

275 *Captain John Smith*: puts in yet another appearance. In a long section edited from the final text (Part MS 153 verso; Part TS 259–62), B.-P. describes Smith's bravery in fighting with the Austrians against the Turks or 'Mahomedans', and openly describes him as an ancestor (a fantastical claim he continued to uphold until 1930). After Smith killed three Turks in single combat, B.-P. writes, Emperor Sigismund 'gave him as coat of arms Three Turks heads [*sic*] which some of my family wear to this day'. The incident is repeated in *Lessons from the 'Varsity of Life*, 51–3, in which B.-P. describes his efforts to model Smith's bust in clay, using his own head as a template. B.-P. omits to mention in either text that Smith was captured while fighting against the Ottomans, and sold as a slave in Constantinople. On Drake and Raleigh, see note to p. 14. Sir John Hawkins (1532–95) was a legendary British naval commander (and slave trader) and a harrier of the Spanish American coasts in the 1560s. Sir Martin Frobisher (*c.*1535–94) was a British navigator (of the North-West Passage in the 1570s) and a commander against the Spanish Armada.

278 *Play up . . . play the game!*: the entire Henry Newbolt poem, 'Vitaï Lampada' (The Lamp of Life, 1897), with its well-known refrain 'Play up! Play up! and play the game!' closely identifying public school games and the ethos of self-sacrifice motivating imperial battles, is quoted on pp. 336–7 as the script for a dramatized recitation. See also pp. 281, 295, 297; Boehmer, *Empire Writing*, 287–8, 457; and J. A. Mangan, *The Games Ethic and Imperialism: Aspects of the Diffusion of an Ideal* (Frank Cass, 1998), 44.

Colonial songs: see B.-P.'s own selection of songs, pp. 338–41. Part VI, addressed mainly to Instructors, is on several levels an adumbration and expansion of this chapter, 'Patriotism', addressed to boys.

Fitchett: B.-P.'s approach to history bears strong comparison with the Revd W. H. Fitchett's canonical and imperialist *Deeds that Won the Empire: Historic Battle Scenes* (Smith, Elder & Co., 1897). War, Fitchett comments, has noble features 'by which the Empire in a sterner time than ours, was won, and by which, in even these ease-loving days, it must be maintained' (pp. v–vi); 'The tales here told [of Trafalgar, Waterloo, etc.] are written, not to glorify war, but to nourish patriotism' (p. v). See p. 310.

279 *DISPLAY*: B.-P.'s vengeful, unpleasant pageant is derived like the recitation on pp. 336–7 from a poem by Henry Newbolt, in this case 'A Ballad of John Nicholson', collected in *Poems: New and Old* (John Murray, 1912), 61. The display, which encapsulates the vindictive humiliation inflicted on Indian troops by the British at the end of the 1857 Mutiny, directly flouts the emphasis elsewhere on international co-operation and

peace. It was removed from all future editions of *SfB*. John Nicholson (1821–57), a fanatical commander in the Indian Army, saw action in the Afghan War of 1841–2, and was instrumental in securing Kashmir for British India (1846–8, 1849). As the Administrator of the Punjab (from 1851) he was known for his ability to enforce law and order with absolute severity. He commanded the Punjab movable column during the Indian Revolt or Mutiny (as in this incident, where it was passing through 'Jullundur'), and played an important part in the attack on Delhi, in which he lost his life. See Christopher Hibbert, *The Great Mutiny: India 1857* (Penguin, 1978); Lord Roberts, *Forty-One Years in India*, vol. 1 (Richard Bentley and Son, 1897), 136; Lionel J. Trotter, *The Life of John Nicholson* (John Murray, 1904), 228–30. Compared with Roberts's account, B.-P. significantly exaggerates Nicholson's scorn and Singh's cringing inferiority.

284 *When Mafeking . . . when needed*: these paragraphs on boys' preparedness to defend their country are taken from a published 'note [B.-P.] wrote to a Boys Newspaper [probably *The Boys' Brigade Gazette*, June 1906] about 2 years ago', which was 'taken up by schools and cricket clubs' (Part MS 161). That this embedded section represents the remnant of an earlier text, one of the first seeds of what became *SfB*, may explain the somewhat jarring emphasis on the ability to shoot well.

Roosevelt: see second note to p. 153. In Part MS 164 the quotation appears as a cut-out of a printed page. In the first line B.-P. changes Roosevelt's 'soldier' to 'scout'.

Lord Roberts: Lord Frederick Roberts of Kandahar, familiarly called 'Bobs' (1832–1914), British Field Marshal who served in the Indian Mutiny and the Second Afghan War (1878–80); Commander-in-Chief in India (1885–93), Ireland (1895–9), and South Africa (1900–1); as Commander-in-Chief in Britain (until 1905) he was a strong advocate of military conscription.

287 *March 17th, 1812*: that is, during the Peninsular War.

288 *Greater Britain*: that is, the 'Empire across the seas', 'the Union of Great Britain with all our Colonies across the seas' (p. 292), and in particular the brotherhood or 'family' of 'white' colonies of Anglo-Saxon origin, or (after the First World War) Dominions (Canada, Australia, New Zealand). See Rudyard Kipling's 'A Song of the English' (1893) and 'A Parting of the Columns' (a Boer War poem); Boehmer, *Empire Writing*, 72–9, 112–13, 493–4.

290 *Van Tromp*: Admiral Maarten Tromp (not Van Tromp, 1598–1653), was the commander of the Dutch navy in several massive sea-battles against the English concerning trade routes and colonial privileges. He lost his life in a final crushing reverse off Scheveningen, the Netherlands.

292 *Unite the Empire . . . true as steel*: probably another extract from Henry Newbolt. See notes to pp. 278 and 279.

293 . . . *somewhere*: at this point Part MS 173 (Part TS 281) continues: 'I

should have liked to be a Socialist at one time to get money more evenly distributed so that there would be no millionaires and no paupers, but everyone pretty well off. When I looked it up in History it proved to be a very old story and one which won't work. It needs such tremendous discipline that it would be something like slavery to everybody.' These sentiments relate to the young Baden-Powell's egalitarian 'Laws for me when I am old', a short desideratum believed to have been written when he was eight. In the 3rd edn. of *SfB* and subsequently B.-P. omitted the potentially compromising references to socialism. See also Rosenthal, *The Character Factory*, 183–4.

294 *Imperator . . . that is, to Be Prepared*: a somewhat fanciful exercise in etymology. 'Imperator' signifies 'he who rules' and B.-P.'s 'parere' should read 'parare'.

295 *[Part VI]*: charged with imperialist angst, B.-P. experienced great trouble in writing this final, short Part VI addressed to Instructors, which recapitulates and enlarges on some of his main points regarding the importance of patriotism raised in Part V. The Part TS contains two incomplete drafts, lengthier, more frantic and paranoid than his statements here—and there were in all probability others. The original intention was to use his reflections on empire as the introduction to the entire PE, but the tone of his remarks, and his difficulty in ordering them, aborted the plan. The fact that Part VI lacks a contents page reflects the haste with which it was at the last put together. B.-P.'s two 1907 pamphlets, *Boy Scouts: A Suggestion*, and *Boy Scouts: Summary of a Scheme* (see second note to p. 5), sketch many of the ideas laid out here, in particular the conviction that the empire can be maintained by encouraging good citizenship in boys. His report on the Brownsea Camp of 1907 is also produced virtually in full (see notes to pp. 302 and 304). The analogy between the Roman and British Empires, and its portents for the future of the British imperium, was a commonplace of colonial discourse at this time.

our best-known democratic politicians: in Part MS 175: 'a prominent member of the Radical Party'. The politician was George Wyndham, the Tory Chief Secretary in Ireland, 1902–5. See p. 259.

Mr Warde Fowler: William Warde Fowler (1847–1921), a classical historian and author of, amongst other studies, *Julius Caesar and the Foundation of the Roman Imperial System* (1896).

299 *Sir John Gorst's 'Children of the Nation'*: Sir John Eldon Gorst (1835–1916), a British lawyer and Conservative politician of democratic sympathies with a background in New Zealand politics (MP 1866–8, 1874–1904). He became a member of Randolph Churchill's Fourth Party, the Liberal or 'Radical' wing of the Conservative Party (see second note to p. 295). From the 1890s he developed an interest in social reform, and the education and welfare of children, as expressed in *The Children of the Nation: How their Health and Vigour should be Promoted by the State* (Methuen, 1906), dedicated to the Labour Members of the House of

Commons. Arguing on the basis of figures showing a serious deterioration in the social conditions of children, he urged that the child's health and training were central to the national interest. He, too, spoke in favour of 'Jiu-jitsu', a system which 'has come to us from our new Eastern allies the Japanese' (pp. 207–9), as well as of the Swedish drill system. See p. 320.

299 *Dr Macnamara's Report*: Thomas James Macnamara (1861–1931), a Liberal reformer and editor of the *Schoolmaster*, who, citing Gorst, published on poor conditions in schools. B.-P.'s figures concerning boys under, and not under, good influence, are based on two facts outlined in Part TS 313. According to the findings of a committee chaired by Macnamara (and confirmed by Gorst) there were in Britain 1½ million 'unemployed lads'; at the same time the Boys' Brigades, Church Lads' Brigades, Cadet Corps, and other boys' organizations were providing 'good training in citizenship' for up to half a million boys. B.-P.'s calculations therefore numbered the boys of the nation at 2 million altogether.

PEACE-SCOUTING: a recapitulation of 'Scout's Work' (pp. 13–14), where Colonials are first described as real men and true role models for Scouts.

300 *A small book*: *Aids to Scouting*, 1*s*. (Gale and Polders, 1899) (B.-P.'s own note).

schools and boys' clubs in England: that is, including the Boys' Brigade, Church Lads' Brigade, and the Boys' Empire League. See p. 301.

302 *EXPERIMENTAL CAMP*: these pages (to p. 304) are roughly based on 'Boy Scouts', B.-P.'s 1907 report on the first scout camp at Brownsea Island, Poole (Part MS 6–13), which he called 'an experimental test of various points in my proposed scheme of instruction'.

sorts: B.-P. revised the Part MS 'classes' to 'sorts' as the class profile of the Brownsea group was not as diverse—extending 'from Eton' to 'St Giles'—as he had at first claimed (Part MS 7). Eleven were from public schools; nine were from Boys' Brigades in Bournemouth and Poole.

Mr Charles Van Raalte: van (not Van) Raalte was a London stockbroker and owner of Brownsea Island in Poole Harbour, where the first experimental Scout camp was held in August 1907.

304 *boys of all classes*: the 1907 Brownsea report goes into more detail about 'the interesting experiment of putting boys of all classes to live and work together', while also emphasizing that this 'fortuitous experiment . . . does not necessarily come into my scheme'.

305 *the right side of them*: in Part TS 289 B.-P. now goes on to quote A. K. Orage in the *Planet* on how the unruly boy has the potential to become tomorrow's leader.

307 *'Book of the Child'*: F. D. How, *The Book of the Child: An Attempt to Set Down What is in the Mind of Children* (Sir Isaac Pitman and Sons, 1907), a disturbingly precious manual about the observation of children, and how to make friends with them, justified by the self-confessedly childless

author in the name of increasing the profile of the child in public life. As ever, the quotation (from the last page of the penultimate chapter, 'Wayside Children') is not quite accurate: 'little fellow' should read 'boy', and 'man's life' 'man's walk through life'.

310 *H. O. Arnold-Forster*: Hugh Oakley Arnold-Forster (1855–1909), author and Unionist politician, grandson of Thomas Arnold. Arnold-Forster produced, for Cassells publishing firm, illustrated educational handbooks propagating patriotism through the study of geography and history, as in his *History of England for Children* (1897). He was a strong supporter of imperial federation. See pp. 294, 335.

Samuel Smiles: see note to p. 239.

'Deeds that Won the Empire': see third note to p. 278. The other text B.-P. makes reference to is Charlotte Yonge's not dissimilar *A Book of Golden Deeds*.

313 *Bacon*: Francis Bacon (1561–1626), the courtier, philosopher, and man of letters. Concerning his thoughts on how work might be leavened with play, see *The Advancement of Learning* (1605), and the essay, 'Of Studies' (1625).

314 . . . *and so on*: the 'scenes from history' refer, respectively, to Burnham's daring escape in Matabeleland (see p. 87), and to two canonical instances of exemplary loyalty and obedience popular in books like Yonge's *Golden Deeds*, described in more detail on pp. 224–5. See third note to p. 278.

Box and Cox or The Area Belle: popular choices for Victorian amateur theatricals, such as those in which B.-P. himself often participated during his time in India. He played in *Cox and Box* (note the reversed title), 'the immortal operetta by Burnand and Sullivan', on twenty-six occasions across his life (*Lessons from the 'Varsity of Life*, 33). *The Area Belle* is a farce by William Brough.

315 *'Duty'*: see note to p. 239.

Sir Henry Knyvett: an Elizabethan soldier noted for his courage (d. 1598). *The Defence of the Realm* (1596; Tudor and Stuart Library, 1906) advocates compulsory military training for men.

316 *CONTINENCE*: see note to p. 195, and compare the Appendix. Notice B.-P.'s concern that in order to deal openly with this most secret and insidious of vices, it is important to overcome conventional social reticence. It was with B.-P.'s conviction in mind that the decision was made to reproduce the excised section addressed to boys, complimentary to these paragraphs for instructors, as the Appendix to this edition.

317 *'The Boy Problem'*: a book by W. R. Forbush. See p. 320.

336 *PLAY THE GAME!*: while the preceding sections of 'Scouting Games, Practices and Displays' can be regarded as a recapitulation of, and even as a kind of index to, *SfB*, the songs, games, and suggestions for displays which follow are undisguisedly fillers, bulking out the truncated Part VI, which B.-P. found so difficult to write. B.-P. had himself once participated

in a dramatized recitation of 'Play the Game!', as he called the often-quoted poem by Henry Newbolt (1862–1938). 'Vitaï Lampada' memorializes a British Army defeat by the Mahdi in 1885—a failed attempt to relieve General Gordon at Khartoum. As is characteristic, B.-P. changes not only the 'Vitaï Lampada' title but the punctuation throughout the three stanzas; and the river of death's masculine gender is neutralized to 'its'. See notes to pp. 242 and 278, and compare B.-P.'s *Scouting Games* (C. Arthur Pearson, 1910).

337 *Lord Roberts . . . the Mutiny*: see note to p. 279; on Lord Roberts, see third note to p. 284.

348 *unavoidably omitted from a previous part of 'Scouting for Boys'*: probably due to word restrictions on individual numbers of the PE, which were intended to be of more or less equal length. The stories from Captain Stigand (see next note) and Mrs Piet Joubert are described in Part MS 85–7 (CE 78–9). The horsetracking incident outside Cairo, followed by the tale of the 'long-missing camel', is narrated in Part MS 64 (CE 79), equivalent to p. 80 of the present edition.

349 *'Scouting and Reconnaissance in Savage Countries'*: Captain (not Major) Chauncy Hugh Stigand, *Scouting and Reconnaissance in Savage Countries* (Hugh Rees, 1907), a book about taking bearings and reading 'spoor', written in the spirit of B.-P.'s *Aids to Scouting*, was recommended on p. 89. The narrated incidents are taken from Stigand, *Scouting and Reconnaissance*, 103–4. For the slave-spotting anecdote, however, B.-P. characteristically adds the reported speech.

INDEX